"A MAGNIFICENT FIGHT"

"A" The Battle for Wake Island

MAGNIFICENT

FIGHT"

ROBERT J. CRESSMAN

NAVAL INSTITUTE PRESS   ANNAPOLIS, MARYLAND

© 1995
by the United States Naval Institute
Annapolis, Maryland

LIBRARY OF CONGRESS CATALOGING-IN-PUBLICATION DATA

Cressman, Robert J.
  A magnificent fight : the battle for Wake Island / Robert J.
Cressman.
       p.   cm.
  Includes bibliographical references and index.
  ISBN 1-55750-140-8
  1. Wake Island, Battle of, 1941.   I. Title.
D767.99.W3C74   1994
940.54'26—dc20   94-32013
                                                  CIP

Printed in the United States of America on acid-free paper ∞

9 8 7 6 5 4 3 2
First printing

To the Defenders of Wake Island

CONTENTS

PREFACE

The first battle for Wake Island occurred not on the triangular atoll itself but in the United States Congress, which at times appeared to be very reluctant to provide money for that advanced base in the mid-Pacific. Fiscal austerity, however, ultimately gave way to a desperate race against time to fortify the atoll while diplomatic relations between the United States and Japan deteriorated.

The second, more famous battle—the one around which this work centers—occurred between 8 and 23 December 1941, in the aftermath of one of the most devastating defeats in American military history, the Japanese air raid on Pearl Harbor. Soon after Vice Admiral Nagumo Chuichi's carrier-based planes attacked the U.S. Pacific Fleet at Pearl, on the other side of the International Date Line, Japanese land-based bombers pounded Wake Island. Over the next two weeks, Wake was bombed almost daily either by land-based medium bombers or flying boats.

Wake's determined defenders held out and in so doing provided a badly needed lift to American morale, a ray of hope in the midst of dark clouds of despair. Wake proved such a tough nut to crack (its seacoast batteries and aggressively handled Wildcat fighters drove off one landing attempt) that Admiral Yamamoto Isoroku, commander in chief of the Combined Fleet, had to order the First Air Fleet, whose planes had ravaged Admiral Husband E. Kimmel's battle line, to detach forces to soften it up for a second try.

In 1994, when the concept of "jointness" seems to dominate the thinking of the modern American military in the aftermath of Desert Shield/Desert Storm, it is an interesting parallel to note that Wake's defense force in 1941 reflected a true multiservice effort born of desperate improvisation: an understrength marine defense battalion detachment and a composite aviation unit equipped with a dwindling number of fighter planes, augmented by sailors and volunteer civilians. An army signal corps radio unit was the garrison's only contact with the outside world. The defense was commanded and coordinated by a naval aviator.

Much that has been written suggests that the defense of Wake was a magnificent improvisation born on 8 December 1941 (west longitude date), in the tradition of Americans spontaneously uniting to face a common adversary. War planners, however, contemplated such an improvisation—and planned for it—as early as the summer of 1941, long before the first bombs fell.

"*A Magnificent Fight*" is the first Western study of Wake's defense to rely on extensive Japanese materials—many never before used by or unavailable to historians—to document the oft-neglected enemy perspective, identifying the enemy order of battle and the roles each unit played. This book also details the activities of those brave American civilians who volunteered to serve alongside the marines—and thus share the same privations—and those who carried out vital support duties.

ACKNOWLEDGMENTS

Many people assisted in the preparation of this book. Unfortunately, a mere recitation of names reflects neither the contribution of each person nor the indebtedness I feel.

I thank my friends and colleagues at the Naval Historical Center, including John C. Reilly, Jr., Raymond A. Mann, and James L. Mooney of the Ships' Histories Branch; John E. Vajda and Tonya T. Montgomery of the Navy Department Library; Edward J. Marolda, Gary E. Weir (who had to listen to Wake Island tales in the carpool), Robert J. Schneller, Richard A. Russell, and Curtis A. Utz of the Contemporary History Branch; Edwin C. Finney, Jr., of the Curator Branch; Roy Grossnick and Steven D. Hill of the Aviation History Branch; and especially Bernard F. Cavalcante's magnificent research staff in the Operational Archives: Kathleen M. Lloyd, Richard M. Walker, John L. Hodges, Ariana A. Jacob, and Regina T. Akers.

At the Marine Corps Historical Center, I thank Brigadier General Edwin H. Simmons, USMC (Ret.), Richard A. Long, Robert E. Struder, Catherine A. Kerns, Steve Hill, Danny J. Crawford, Robert V. Aquilina, Anne Ferrante, Benis M. Frank, Evelyn A. Englander, and Amy Cantin, as well as those formerly associated with the Center, Joyce E. Bonnett, Lance Corporal Tom Clarkston, Gunnery Sergeant Bill Judge, J. Michael Miller, and the late Regina Strother.

Former Wake Islanders who proved most helpful include Brigadier Generals Woodrow M. Kessler and John F. Kinney, Colonel Arthur A. Poindexter and Major Robert O. Arthur, Sergeant Major Robert E. Winslow, Master Sergeant Walter A. Bowsher, Gunnery Sergeant Walter T. Kennedy, Lieutenant Commander George H. Henshaw, Clifford E. Hotchkiss, and Charles R. Loveland. Brigadier General Robert E. Galer and Colonel Milo G. Haines provided recollections of life in VMF-211 in 1941. I extend special thanks to family members of Wake Islanders, especially Henry Elrod Ramsey, nephew of the late Captain Henry T. Elrod; Mrs. Virginia Putnam (who allowed me use of her husband's papers); Mrs. Hilda Hesson; Mrs. Marylee Fish; and George Halstead, whose late brother's letters from Wake, arriving when I was recovering at home from a heart attack, inspired me to press on and tell the Wake Island story as it had not been told before.

Also of great assistance were Major John Elliott, USMC (Ret.); Technical Sergeant Barry Spink, USAF, of the Air Force Historical Research Agency, Maxwell Field, Alabama; R. E. G. Davies of the Aeronautics Branch of the National Air and Space Museum, Washington, D.C.; Ann Whyte of Pan American Airways; Barry Zerby and Richard von Doenhoff at the National Archives in Washington, D.C.; Kathleen O'Connor at the National Archives Pacific-Sierra region facility in San Bruno, California; Margaret Goostray of the Boston University Library; David W. Lucabaugh, a tireless researcher in the subject of naval aviation and the one who first provided me with material on the Wake Island Wildcats; Stan Cohen, who shared the information he had gathered on the civilian contractors; the late Captain Roger Pineau, USNR (Ret.), who proved very helpful concerning the Imperial Japanese Navy; and John DeVirgilio, who provided me with anecdotes concerning Japanese carrier operations against Wake. Invaluable for helping me to acquire material in Japan were Captain Chiyaha Masataka and Kageyama Kōichirō. D. Y. Louie provided superb assistance in translating some of the Japanese documents.

Special friends, who are owed much gratitude for their contributions, which ranged from translations of Japanese documents to detailed critiques of the narrative at various stages in its life, include J. Michael Wenger, James C. Sawruk, John B. Lundstrom, Charles R. Haberlein, Jr., and Jeffrey G. Barlow.

I also owe a large debt of gratitude to my parents, Lieutenant Commander and Mrs. Wilmer H. Cressman, who not only provided a loving and nurturing home but who supported my academic pursuits for so long, giving me the pleasure and privilege of working under the late Gordon W. Prange at the University of Maryland, who instilled within me a love of researching and writing U.S. naval history.

And last, but certainly not least, I thank my family: my long-suffering wife, Linda, daughter, Christine, and son, Bobby, for their unusual patience with me when mine ran thin and for putting up with me during the lengthy process of research, writing, and rewriting.

SPECIAL NOTES

All times and dates in this book, unless otherwise specified (such as for Pearl Harbor and Washington, D.C.), are for the zone in which Wake and the Marshall Islands lie.

Japanese names are rendered with the surname first, the given name second.

Allied code names for Japanese aircraft were not adopted until November 1942, and because they are anachronistic, they have been omitted from the text.

SPECIAL JAPANESE TERMS USED IN TEXT

Buntaichō	Division officer (command echelon)
Chūtai	Unit of six to nine planes
Chūtaichō	*Chūtai* commander
Hikōtaichō	Air group officer (command echelon)
Kanbaku	Abbreviation for *Kanjō bakugekiki* (carrier [dive] bomber)
Kankō	Abbreviation for *Kanjō kōgekiki* (carrier [torpedo] attack plane)
Kansen	Abbreviation for *Kanjō sentoki* (carrier fighter)
Kidō Butai	Carrier striking force (literally, mobile force)
Kōkūtai	Land-based naval air group
Rikkō	Abbreviation for *Rikujō kōgekiki* (land attack plane; medium bomber)
Shōtai	Unit of two to four planes
Shōtaichō	*Shōtai* commander

JAPANESE NAVAL AIRCRAFT REFERRED TO IN TEXT

(Post-November 1942 Code Names in Brackets)

Aichi D3A1 Type 99 carrier bomber	[VAL]
Aichi E13A1 Type 00 reconnaissance seaplane	[JAKE]

Kawanishi E7K2 Type 94 reconnaissance seaplane   [ALF]
Kawanishi H6K4 Type 97 flying boat   [MAVIS]
Mitsubishi A5M4 Type 96 carrier fighter   [CLAUDE]
Mitsubishi A6M2 Type 00 carrier fighter   [ZERO or ZEKE]
Mitsubishi F1M2 Type 00 observation seaplane   [PETE]
Mitsubishi G3M2 Type 96 land attack plane   [NELL]
Mitsubishi G4M1 Type 1 land attack plane   [BETTY]
Nakajima B5N2 Type 97 carrier attack plane   [KATE]
Nakajima E8N1 Type 95 reconnaissance seaplane   [DAVE]

"A MAGNIFICENT FIGHT"

"A LAND RESERVED
TO THOSE WHO FLY"

"A horseshoe of bright turquoise, framed in flashing white, stands sharply out against the indigo blue of encircling ocean. Wake Island! . . . Barely a mile long, less than half a mile wide, Peale Islet . . . is an exciting spot. From the cool veranda of your hotel you look across the beautiful lagoon whose lovely colors change constantly before your eyes. Beyond, the fascinating crest of the surf beats high as it dashes itself on the barrier reefs . . . Wake Island, so newly added to the world's travel map, is already becoming a favorite vacation spot for travel-wise voyageurs. A beautiful, unspoiled land a world away from the hustle and bustle of modern life. . . . A land reserved to those who fly, where every comfort and convenience, excellent food and expert attention are as much a part of your stay as the breath-taking sunsets, the soft thundering of the sea and its magnificent thirty-foot surf. Not soon can one forget these rainbow waters, soft deep sands, the friendly sun, the cool sweet trade winds blown from across the broadest sea."[1]

An affluent world traveler of 1940 might have eagerly anticipated the adventure of a transpacific aerial voyage in a well-appointed Pan American Airways *Clipper* and a stay at the modern and comfortable hotel there, but Wake Island had not always been regarded so romantically. Lacking potable water and inhabited only by hump-backed Polynesian brown rats, hermit crabs, and seabirds, Wake before the transpacific aviation era offered practically nothing more exotic to a prospective visitor except perhaps a scenic sunset.

Westerners most probably first saw the island that would become known as Wake when Alvaro de Mendaña, the twenty-five-year-old nephew of the governor of Peru, Lope Garcia de Castro, happened across the "low and uninhabited island" on 2 October 1568 while en route back to Peru from the Solomon Islands. Desperately low on water and provisions, Mendaña overruled his pilots, who saw the reefs and feared that they were too near land, and ordered his ship, the *Capitana*, taken close inshore. Seeing no signs of human habitation, however, only "sandy places covered with bushes," Mendaña wrote off San Francisco (the name he gave it because he discovered it on the eve of the feast of St. Francis) as "useless" and grimly sailed on.

A little over two centuries later, a Briton, Captain Samuel Wake of the schooner *Prince William Henry*, modestly named the place for himself when he came across it in 1796, but he essentially agreed with Mendaña's assessment and apparently made no effort to claim it for his sovereign. Indicative of the state of map-making and navigation of the those times, characterized by "long voyages and the habit of exchanging even hearsay data," the island not only bore other names—Wake's Island, Wakers, Weeks, Wreck, Halcyon, Helsion, and Wilson, among others—but also was placed on maps in locations at various spots in the general vicinity.

One American whaling ship reported sighting "Wake's Island" when the *Almira* spoke three other whalers off the atoll on 24 April 1826. The U.S. Navy's first visit occurred fourteen years later, when Lieutenant Charles Wilkes, in the sloop of war *Vincennes*, reached the atoll on 20 December 1840 and conducted a brief survey of the low, triangular coral formation. Over the next half-century, "Wake's Island" served only as the backdrop for dramatic shipwrecks such as that of the bark *Libelle* on 4 March 1866 and the tea clipper *Dashing Wave* on 31 August 1871.

Ironically, though it had been Spaniards who had been the first Westerners to see Wake Island, it took a war with Spain to interest the United States in annexing it. Following Commodore George Dewey's victory over a Spanish naval squadron in Manila Bay in May 1898, American expansionists pressed for the country to acquire bases to support projected operations in the Philippines. Consequently, on Independence Day 1898, the U.S. Army transport *Thomas* hove to off Wake en route to the Philippines, and General Francis V. Greene raised a fourteen-inch flag "tied to a dead limb." By such unpretentious beginnings, however, Greene did what neither Mendaña nor Wake had done for their respective rulers—he claimed the place for his country. Acquiring Wake, along with the Hawaiian Islands and the Spanish possessions of Guam and the Philippines, meant that America no longer could isolate itself geographically, protected by an oceanic barrier. Subsequently, in keeping with growing interest in an American transpacific cable route, Secretary of the Navy John D. Long sent the *Bennington* (Gunboat No. 4) to the atoll, where on 17 January 1899, Commander Edward D. Taussig, the warship's captain, took possession of Wake for the United States.

Although Midway was ultimately chosen as the point through which the cable would pass, when the United States became concerned with Japanese aims in the Pacific, American naval strategists conceived plans

Wake Island, 30 March 1939. The small Pan American Airways settlement on Peale (top, center) is barely visible in this picture. Wilkes lies at upper left, separated from Wake (foreground) by a narrow channel. Note extensive vegetation on all three islets, that on Wake being deemed "very thick, almost impenetrable." (USMC)

to cover contingencies. Those who formulated strategy were aware that Wake occupied a place on the map, yet they dismissed its usefulness. In 1911, for example, war planners noted only that the Japanese (who had been assigned the color code ORANGE) might establish an outpost there. Three years later, they recorded Wake's proximity to the American fleet's hypothetical line of advance to the Philippines.

In 1921, however, the celebrated naval writer Hector C. Bywater rescued the place from obscurity—at least in the public eye (the navy, of course, knew Wake existed)—and accorded it great importance when he discussed a hypothetical Pacific campaign in his book *Sea-Power in the Pacific: A Study of the American-Japanese Naval Problem.* "The conversion of Wake Island into a well-defended fuelling station," he declared, would help the United States consolidate a "vital line of communication" between Hawaii, Guam, and Manila. An advanced base at Wake could allow the U.S. Fleet to operate off the Japanese homeland or reach as far as Guam, but the island had limited anchorage facilities and lay only a hundred miles north of a possible submarine rendezvous in the Japanese mandates.[2]

Fortifying or developing Wake, however, had to remain in the realm of speculation, for Article XIX of the Washington Treaty of 6 February

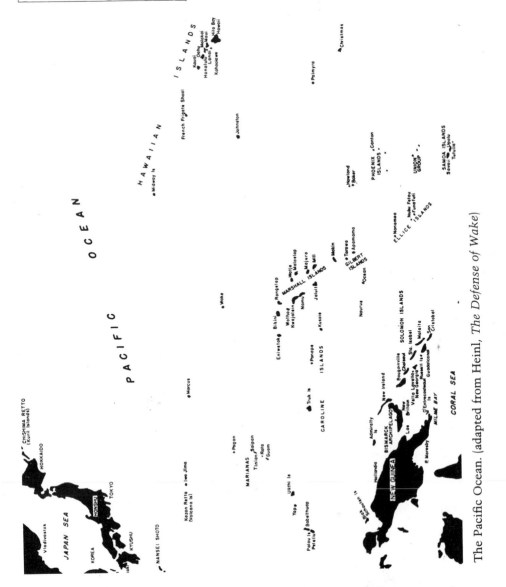

TABLE OF DISTANCES FROM WAKE IN NAUTICAL MILES	
Manila	2626
Guam	1302
Midway	1034
Honolulu	2004
Pokaakku Atoll	304
Kwajalein Atoll	660
Roi	620
Majuro	840
Wotje	600
Jaluit	814
Marcus	760
Saipan	1260
Truk	1120

The Pacific Ocean. (adapted from Heinl, *The Defense of Wake*)

1922 prohibited the United States from fortifying its possessions west of the 180th meridian (encompassing Guam and Wake). Despite that prohibition, Bywater's description of Wake's potential (as well as the navy's interest in Pacific war planning over the years) had prompted not only intellectual curiosity on the U.S. Navy's part but practical investigation.

Typical of the short visits to Wake by U.S. Navy ships in the 1920s and 1930s was that of the submarine tender *Beaver* (AS-5), which reached the atoll on 19 June 1922 during an eastward voyage from the Asiatic station. "Wake is of interest by reason of its extreme isolation; over 300 miles from the nearest land, and that only another atoll," Lieutenant Commander Sherwood Picking, the tender's captain, observed later, "but especially because of its location on the route between Hawaii and our Asiatic Stations." Although Wake lay "almost directly on the course between Honolulu and Guam," ships rarely visited let alone sighted it. Lying so low and close to that course, Wake would present a navigational hazard "were it not for the almost constantly prevailing fair weather." The *Beaver*'s landing party found several shacks long since abandoned by Japanese poachers, as well as some sake jugs and a broken-down still. They also noted the sand and coral boulders, the dense scrub, the "innumerable" birds (who "showed no fear and . . . were so tame that they could be handled"), the large rats, and a few lizards. Having read in the sailing directions that the lagoon was "well stocked with fish," the tender's men found this to be so, and with "a few rifle shots and some lively grabbing" managed to net "a considerable number" of "excellent" specimens. The party then collected samples of coral, sponges, and shells before returning to the ship.[3]

Picking subsequently reported that use of Wake "as a base for surface vessels" was "out of the question." Destroyers or submarines could heave to to enable members of the crew to go ashore for recreation, he speculated, but the place would be useful as a fueling base only "for the sake of the slight lee it affords." "It is as a base for aircraft that Wake . . . would be of use," Picking posited. "A large area of the lagoon is clear of dangers to a depth of five feet and over, and its smooth water offers excellent opportunities for refueling, repairing and resting the crew." He went on to note that although natural obstacles would make landing supplies difficult, "twenty men equipped with tools and dynamite could in a week open the channel to the lagoon" and permit launches to enter. "Such a party could subsist itself indefinitely," he declared expansively, "especially as supplies could be landed from transports which pass at least once a month. If the long-heralded trans-Pacific flight ever takes place," Picking suggested, Wake "should certainly be occupied and used as an intermediate resting and fueling port."[4] War planners at that time, however, did not accord it that status in their schemes.

To follow up the *Beaver*'s visit to Wake, a scientific expedition—the brainchild of Herbert E. Gregory of Yale University, the director of the Bernice Pauahi Bishop Museum in Honolulu—transported in the minesweeper *Tanager* (AM-5), explored the atoll between 27 July and 5 August 1923, carrying out survey work and natural history studies. Wake Island was deemed to be three separate islets, and the two smaller ones were named Wilkes and Peale, respectively honoring Lieutenant Wilkes and Titian Peale, the latter the naturalist for the Wilkes Expedition that had called there in 1840.

On 13 November 1934, following a brief visit by the transport *Chaumont* (AP-5) the previous year, Admiral William H. Standley, the Chief of Naval Operations (CNO), directed the ammunition ship *Nitro* (AE-2) to survey Wake. A little over a month later, on 29 December 1934, President Franklin D. Roosevelt, by executive order, placed Wake under the jurisdiction of the Navy Department.

The *Nitro* reached Wake on the morning of 8 March 1935 and sent ashore a party of nine officers and forty-three enlisted men under Lieutenant Commander John L. Reynolds, the ammunition ship's executive officer. The work of carrying out an airplane field investigation as part of the survey fell to Lieutenant Jesse G. Johnson of the Pearl Harbor–based Patrol Squadron (VP) 1F, who was temporarily attached to the ship. Johnson made a survey flight before returning to the ship a little after noon. Operations were completed by the next afternoon, and the *Nitro* sailed for Pearl Harbor, arriving on the fifteenth. The next day, Rear Admiral Harry E. Yarnell, the commandant of the Fourteenth Naval District (ComFourteen)—in whose bailiwick Wake lay—called on Commander Henry T. Markland, the ship's commanding officer, who showed him the fruits of the *Nitro*'s two-day labor.[5]

Lieutenant Johnson posited that seaplane operations could be carried out within a six-square-mile area, that the island contained no water and limited plant life, and that the steep beaches rendered the atoll vulnerable to deep-draft enemy ships. Because Wake's highest elevation was only about twenty feet, however, an enemy would have great difficulty observing any activity on the island from an offshore vantage point.[6]

At that juncture, naval and commercial aviation joined hands in a significant, yet clandestine, partnership. On 12 March 1935, soon after Lieutenant Johnson and the *Nitro* had wrapped up their work, Secretary of the Navy Claude A. Swanson gave Pan American Airways (PanAir) permission to construct a facility at Wake from which its *Clippers* could operate on the projected mail and passenger service to the Orient. A little over two weeks later, a PanAir expedition left the west coast of the United States to start the necessary work.

The freighter *North Haven*, loaded with enough equipment to build "two complete villages, [and] five air bases," sailed through the Golden Gate on 27 March 1935, steaming first to Honolulu, where, on 7 April, Lieutenant Willis E. Cleaves, who, like Johnson, was attached to VP-1F, joined the expedition. Stopping first at Midway (12 April to 1 May) and then rendezvousing with the transport *Henderson* (AP-1) en route, the *North Haven* reached Wake on 5 May. Finding a suitable place to anchor, however, took a week. Dropping her "hook" off the south beach of Wilkes, just east of the place marked as a "boat landing" on the charts, the *North Haven* began disembarking the forty-four airline technicians and the seventy-four-man construction force and getting the materials ashore across the steep, sloping, rocky beach swept continuously by the surging surf. The *North Haven* sailed for Guam on 29 May, and two days later a Japanese passenger liner passed close by but did not respond to signals. The *North Haven* returned to Wake on the morning of 3 July but lingered only until the afternoon of the following day, when she sailed for Midway, en route to Honolulu, where Lieutenant Cleaves disembarked on 18 July.

Those who arrived at Wake in the spring of 1935 to begin the development of an airport there found an atoll lying midway between Hawaii and Guam and consisting of three islets, Wilkes, Wake, and Peale, that nearly surrounded a lagoon opening to the northwest, its apex pointing to the southeast. Situated in the Pacific at latitude 19 degrees, 18 minutes north, and longitude 166 degrees, 35 minutes east, four and one-half miles long and two and a quarter miles wide, Wake had a total land area of about three square miles. A practically submerged barrier reef of rough, solid coral, ranging from twenty-five to thirteen hundred yards beyond the shoreline and narrowest along the southwestern side of Wilkes and Wake, surrounded the group, pounded constantly by a roaring, booming surf whose waves normally reached only two to three feet but sometimes reached heights of fifteen. The only natural break in the reef—to permit boats to pass through from the open sea to the beach or to sheltered waters to land troops, equipment, and supplies—occurred near the channel between Wilkes and Wake.

Located on the same latitude as Hawaii, Wake generally enjoyed the same "agreeably monotonous" strong northeasterly trade winds, warm sunny days, and cool nights common to that territory. Humidity, however, was high, rainfall averaged about forty inches a year, and visitors to the atoll between July and November could expect typhoons during the nearly coincidental stormy and rainy seasons.

Along the southwestern side of Wilkes and Wake, the beach sloped gently from the sea to a line of vegetation, except at one place adjacent to the boat landing near Wilkes Channel, where it rose steeply. In contrast, the beaches on the northern and northeastern sides of the atoll rose sharply from sea level to a height of ten feet. An area devoid of undergrowth and brush then extended inland, varying from fifty to two hundred feet wide. Almost without exception, Wake's seaward beaches were flat at low water, extending some twenty-five feet back from the water's edge, covered with boulders—some weighing several thousand pounds and rounded smooth by the action of the ocean—and coral rock. The size and location of the boulders bore mute testimony to the fury of the sea that had moved them.

The average elevation on Wake was almost twelve feet, the highest elevation on Wilkes twenty-one feet, on Wake twenty-one, and on Peale eighteen. Just beyond the reef, the bottom dropped sharply, the sides of the ancient volcano (of which the atoll is only the tip) virtually perpendicular, rising in coral splendor from the two-thousand-fathom depths. At one point, where a shelf projected from the steep slope, a ship's anchor could be dropped onto it, though the ship was in deep water. As one sailor would later remark, you could spit from your bridge into the surf.

Dense dark green shrubs, some growing closely together to a height of seven to ten feet and practically impenetrable in places, covered the interior of each islet—no coconut palms waved languidly in the trade winds. Thick brush, together with some umbrella and hardwood trees, covered the higher elevations (a maximum of twenty-one feet above sea level) of each islet. Some scrub trees, larger than the variety found on Midway, had trunks up to a foot in diameter but were of soft wood; another variety of tree that produced small dark green leaves and white flowers had a harder, more substantial wood.

Under Frank McKenzie, PanAir's airport maintenance engineer (a "good, capable [man]," Lieutenant Cleaves noted, "who overcame obstacles ingeniously"), the construction crew surmounted numerous problems, starting with the discovery that Peale, rather than Wake, would be "ideal" for the location of the airport. Only after building a freight dock on Wilkes and hacking their way through the tangled brush on that islet to enable them to construct a narrow-gauge railroad across it from "steel strips and wheels meant for another purpose" could the *North Haven*'s crew, the construction workers, and the airline technicians unload the cargo.[7] They lightered it ashore to the freight dock and then took it across Wilkes on the railway to the shore of the lagoon, at which point it was loaded onto another lighter and towed across to Peale. In five months, the workmen exhausted the five tons of dynamite allocated for clearing the myriad coral heads in the emerald-green lagoon.

PanAir Settlement, 5 March 1940. The Y-shaped hotel at upper left would not only host notables such as publisher Henry Luce and his wife, Clare Boothe Luce, author Ernest Hemingway, Soviet diplomat Maxim Litvinov, and Japanese envoy Kurusu Saburo but also navy pilots ferrying Catalina flying boats and Army Air Force pilots ferrying B-17s; Wake proper lies across the lagoon at top. "Pagoda" at far right lies at the landward end of the pier that extended out into the lagoon. (NA, 80-G-411112)

Because the wells dug on Wake yielded only brackish water and the distillation plant brought out in the *North Haven* proved inadequate, McKenzie's engineers designed and built a catchment system to collect and store rainwater. Wake's unproductive soil, meanwhile, led to hydroponic gardening.

The work crews installed seaplane landing pontoons initially developed for PanAir's Caribbean installations, which allowed a seaplane or flying boat to taxi to a dock that had "permanent fuel and fresh water connections, electrical contacts for power poles and lights for night operation" connected to the shore. The pontoons could double as a work platform, permitting an engine change if required. PanAir had pioneered night landing techniques for commercial seaplanes, and it equipped Wake to carry out nocturnal as well as daytime flight operations. Lieutenant Cleaves's subsequent report of what he had observed at the end of July 1935 not only detailed the particulars of PanAir's ambitious building program but noted the feasibility of establishing a landplane field on either Peale or Wake. The latter was the site ultimately chosen for such development.[8]

Between July and October 1935, U.S. Navy war planners mapped out a thrust into the Japanese-controlled Marshall Islands; flying boats based at Wake were to play a major role in covering that advance. Although Wake seemed finally to have secured a role in the navy's plans, at that point it was only a theoretical one: no naval facilities existed there.

In the meantime, PanAir employed a specially equipped Sikorsky S-42 flying boat to carry out aerial surveys of its projected avenue to Asia. Its investigators completed work on the Midway-Wake route in August 1935 and on the Wake-Guam route in October. Subsequently, between 22 November and 5 December 1935, the four-engined, high-winged flying boat, the Martin M-130 *China Clipper*, pioneered PanAir's transpacific air mail-carrying service to Manila and back in a 16,420-mile round trip.[9]

The widening political and diplomatic gulf between the United States and Japan over their respective policies concerning the Far East and western Pacific, however, as well as the increasing reach of air power, accentuated the military—not just commercial—importance of Wake to the United States. The imperial ambitions of Japan caused the U.S. Navy to scrutinize anew the role the little atoll would play in a potential Pacific campaign, lying as it did 2,004 miles from Honolulu, 2,772 from Manila, 1,034 from Midway, but only 597 from Roi in the Marshalls.

Within six months of Lieutenant Cleaves's report, Rear Admiral William S. Pye, director of war plans, was suggesting to the CNO that although the Washington Treaty forbade military development of Pacific atolls such as Wake, it said nothing about the navy's encouraging private "commercial development." On 12 December 1935, Pye, who was thought to possess one of the navy's finest tactical minds, suggested reexamining the place of Wake and Midway in a future Pacific campaign in light of PanAir's "recent pioneer work." He urged that PanAir's efforts be guided "to meet naval requirements, and, if not within the limitations of current development, assisted by Government funds in the same manner as would any other harbor projects undertaken to aid commerce." Pye urged notifying PanAir "confidentially as to the items [required by the navy] so that their [PanAir's] own development . . . may be guided from the beginning." He thought it was unnecessary to develop Wake and Midway as full-fledged naval bases. If the channel and anchorages were modified, Wake and Midway could be useful as auxiliary seaplane bases or as limited bases from which submarines and "light forces" could operate. By extending the navy's reconnaissance line from the Hawaiian area, Pye posited, Wake (and Midway) could be valuable to war plans. "Their possession in a Pacific campaign," he observed, "must be denied [the enemy] from the very beginning," lest an enemy base submarines and seaplanes of its own there. Pye accorded Midway priority, but Wake, too, needed to be "controlled by our own forces." "We must," he declared, "get there first."[10]

The acting CNO, Rear Admiral Joseph K. Taussig (whose father had annexed the atoll for the United States in 1899) agreed with Pye. He believed, though, that until they learned the outcome of the arms limitation talks in London, "it seems that there is nothing we can do except to support everything actually needed for the successful operation of the commercial planes which are using these islands."[11]

Japan's abrogation of the treaties she had signed, however, and her imperialistic stance in China (threatening to shut the Open Door), coupled with her suspected development of the Marshalls, spurred naval interest in Wake and other Pacific bases. Subsequently, with Japan's undeclared war against China not quite a year old, Congress, on 17 May 1938, directed Secretary of the Navy Swanson to appoint an investigating board to look into possible naval base sites on the coasts of the United States, its territories, and possessions. Acting Secretary of the Navy Charles Edison accordingly appointed that committee and placed it under Rear Admiral Arthur J. Hepburn, a former commander in chief of the U.S. Fleet and then commandant of the Twelfth Naval District.

The Hepburn Board's report, submitted shortly before Christmas of 1938 and published on 3 January 1939, ranked Wake next in strategic importance to Midway, which the panel viewed as "second only to Pearl Harbor in the mid-Pacific." The board recommended that facilities be constructed there at the earliest possible time, to permit the operation of one patrol plane squadron, and that a pier be built and a channel and a turning basin be dredged out of the lagoon to accommodate a tanker or a large seaplane tender. With these improvements, the board believed, Wake would be "admirably suited" to operate tender-based aircraft. The "immediate continuous operation of patrol planes from Wake," the board declared, "would be vital at the outbreak of war in the Pacific."[12] To that end, the navy needed to stockpile an adequate supply of fuel and to build and maintain an air base there.

The defense of such an advanced base, however, would fall to the marines, to whom such missions had been formally entrusted shortly after the turn of the century. In the autumn of 1938, paralleling the work of the Hepburn Board, Major General Thomas Holcomb, the Commandant of the Marine Corps, ordered an inspection of Wake to determine the necessary requirements. He enjoined those to whom he entrusted the task to note carefully fields of fire, possible gun positions, and the number of men required to man the works.

Hearings in the House of Representatives Naval Affairs Committee ensued. On 25 January 1939, the first day of those congressional deliberations, the CNO, Admiral William D. Leahy, declared the immediate expansion of the navy's shore establishment—including within its scope installations at Guam, Midway, and Wake, among other places—to be "sound and conservative requirements for peacetime operations, and for measures of preparedness upon which to base wartime expansion." Although most of Leahy's testimony concerned Guam, the CNO did emphasize Wake's importance in the chain of bases sought in the Pacific.[13]

The following day, Admiral Hepburn appeared before the committee to answer questions, and the next, Rear Admiral Arthur B. Cook, chief of the bureau of Aeronautics (BuAer), did likewise, reiterating the Hepburn Board's suggestions for Wake and explaining to the assembled congressmen the navy's plans for the atoll. The money asked for, Cook explained, would allow Wake to be used as a base for patrol planes—there would be no permanent facilities (plans called at one point for only a four-man caretaker force)—that could gather information on any enemy's movements toward the Hawaiian Islands. Another navy witness who testified on the projects sought for Pacific island bases was Rear Admiral Ben Moreell, the chief of the Bureau of Yards and Docks. Before the

Colonel Harry K. Pickett, seen here ca. 1940, accepted his commission in 1913 and served in France during World War I. Pickett surveyed Wake in 1939. His predictions of how Japanese forces could attack the atoll proved perceptive. (Harry K. Pickett Biographical File, MCHC Reference Section)

hearings concluded on the authorization to allow the navy to construct certain public works and only a little over a month after the publication of the Hepburn Board's findings, on 16 February 1939 Admiral Leahy announced plans for organizing four defense battalions to garrison Wake, Midway, Unalaska, and Guantanamo.

Recommendations about Wake's significance notwithstanding, the right circumstances were needed to compel Congress to recognize the importance the navy placed on it. President Roosevelt approved the legislation that included it among the urgent projects for fiscal year 1940 on 25 April 1939, and Congress parceled out $2 million of the total $65 million appropriation package for Wake, but the tardy submission of the supplemental estimates for the regular naval appropriation bill prompted the Appropriations Committee of the House of Representatives, which claimed it needed more time to scrutinize the details, to disallow the expenditure of funds for Wake, along with those for Midway, Johnston, and Palmyra. Although the House reinstated the latter three island development items, it omitted Wake from the bill the president ultimately signed on 25 May 1939. Although it had authorized the money, Congress did not appropriate it.

In the interim, the work of finding firms to build the bases soon began to move ahead at the behest of energetic Rear Admiral Moreell, who "already had plans for prying a Wake appropriation out of the next Congress." The Naval Air Base Construction Board began meeting to "decide upon the exact form of the contract, to study the qualifications of contractors offering their services, and recommend candidates from among them" and submitted its initial findings to Moreell on 4 May 1939. Those contemplating the building of Pacific bases knew that the work would require "builders with resourcefulness and imagination sufficient to the task, and with the courage to abandon all precedent and stake their reputations on sheer pioneering." Moreell and his Yards and Docks staff emphasized the most important priority: "*We must get the work done.*" They set out to find the right companies to do just that.[14]

Meanwhile, the projected survey of Wake to determine what defenses the atoll would require in the event that Congress eventually provided the necessary funds proceeded. Concurring with the Hepburn Board's assessment of Wake's strategic importance, Colonel Harry K. Pickett—who, assisted by Captain Alfred R. Pefley, had conducted the survey—noted its possible use as an advanced base for reconnaissance forces in the early stage of a naval campaign in the Pacific, as a base for land-based air in any operations aimed at seizing the Marshalls, as another link in the line of communication westward, and as valuable in itself to deny Japanese possession. The marines believed that Japan coveted

Wake to eliminate it as a threat to the Mandates (and add it to its own chain of outposts in the process) and as a base for a naval campaign to the eastward.

Pickett believed that the United States and Japan would contend for Wake. Not only could Japan hurl carrier-based air strikes against the atoll, but her possession of such islands as Marcus, Eniwetok, and Wotje afforded her the opportunity to launch land-based air raids as well. An American base at Wake could expect "attacks varying in effort from capture or destruction to that of a harassing nature" unless U.S. forces drove the Japanese from the area. Nor did Pickett underestimate the Japanese ability to carry out such attacks because Japan's military—as demonstrated convincingly in China—possessed "aircraft, bomb-sights, and munitions comparable to our own." Pickett credited the Japanese with being "too intelligent and aggressive to be deceived very long as to the real strength of [Wake's] defenses" and advocated providing strong antiaircraft defenses to defeat "frequent and heavy attacks." Pickett even predicted that "the enemy's desire for air superiority would make our aircraft and aircraft installations his first objective."

Pickett observed that Wake had no beaches to permit boats to come in from the open sea, ground in shallow water, and disembark troops and equipment. After visiting the atoll in May 1939, when the seas were calm, Pickett opined that any landing force "would encounter considerable difficulty in landing . . . a unit as small as a rifle company even under the most favorable weather and sea conditions," but small groups of enemy troops might succeed in getting ashore to threaten the atoll's garrison. Except in very calm weather, the sea and the reef constituted an excellent natural barrier to any landings attempted from the weather (north) side of the atoll. Pickett thought that it would be "dangerous if not entirely impossible to land a motor boat with men and combat equipment under any conditions of the weather and sea on any point on Wake" except near the point of land slightly to the westward of Wilkes Channel. Except for small raiding parties, Pickett deemed it "unlikely that any considerable force could land" there.

Despite the natural difficulties that would be encountered in putting men and equipment on shore, Pickett predicted that Japan would "greatly desire the control of Wake." If undefended, Wake would be quickly occupied by Japan at the outset of hostilities; if defended, it would be subjected to an attack "of a determined nature . . . with a view to capturing it or destroying its installations." Because Japanese bases lay within seven hundred miles of the atoll, Pickett acknowledged the feasibility of a coordinated air and surface attack, plus a landing operation. Although he predicted that an adversary would not use capital ships in the endeavor, he believed that it would involve "cruisers, destroyers, and submarines, in conjunction with aircraft and landing forces." Even should Wake be defended, it might be possible only to drive off an enemy or hold him off for a certain period of time: a determined enemy could take Wake. Nevertheless, Pickett and his assistant duly noted prospective five-inch gun positions—marking the sites by driving angle-iron spikes into the ground and surrounding them with little piles of stones. They estimated that between 510 and 725 men would be required to man the defenses.

Constructing a base at Wake that would require those defenses, though, had to wait for appropriations, and over a year went by before Congress made the necessary money available. On 22 June, the Bureau of Yards and Docks advisory board recommended five suitable companies for consideration. By mid-July, Moreell and his staff had narrowed the field to three: Turner Construction of New York, which had built the War and Navy Department buildings—the "temporary" structures that sprawled along Constitution Avenue in Washington, D.C.; Raymond Concrete Pile, also of New York, "veterans in heavy foundation work" and a firm that "could handle heavy construction work anywhere"; and Hawaiian Dredging of Honolulu, which "had been clearing Pacific harbors for thirty-five years." The consortium would be known as Contractors, Pacific, Naval Air Bases (CPNAB); the navy awarded the Hawaiian-Raymond-Turner group the contract on 5 August. These companies "knew how to build in the United States or at the ends of the earth."[15]

The signing of contract NOy-3550 came not a moment too soon. Although the Wake installations had been cut from the 1940 expenditures, the commencement of hostilities in Europe in September 1939 and the resounding success of Hitler's armed might in the spring of 1940 prompted Congress to reconsider the navy's request to fortify the atoll.

Until military facilities could be built there, though, only temporary operations involving flying boats could take place. Consolidated PBYs from VP-21, which took off on 21 September 1939 bound for the Philippines to carry out neutrality patrols, proceeding via the PanAir route, stopped briefly at Wake on their way west. The seaplane tender *Wright* (AV-1) steamed to the atoll in early March 1940, carrying out aerological flights with one of her planes and then tending six PBYs from VP-22 that arrived on 6 March and departed two days later. During that time, the *Wright* maintained a temporary base on shore at the PanAir facility.

On 16 May 1940, President Roosevelt asked Congress for national defense funds totaling $1,182,000,000. Six days later, on 22 May, Congressman Carl Vinson convened the House Committee on Naval Affairs to take up the matter of constructing or acquiring naval aircraft, the construction of "certain public works," and "for other purposes."[16] Among the public works taken up—again—was Wake Island.

Admiral Harold R. Stark, who had relieved Admiral Leahy as CNO in August 1939, testified about Wake's importance. When Illinois congressman Ralph E. Church questioned spending $5 million "way out in Wake Island" instead of east of the Rocky Mountains on reserve fields at Glenview and Detroit, Stark countered, "If I did not think that money spent on Wake Island defended the people behind the mountains of these United States I would not back it."[17]

While the legislative wheels in Congress ground on, the second ferry flight of PBYs to the Philippines unfolded and VP-26 (Lieutenant Commander Arthur N. Perkins) flew fourteen newly overhauled PBYs out to the islands via the PanAir route, departing Pearl Harbor on 4 June 1940. The destroyers *Patterson* (DD-392), *Tucker* (DD-374), *Jarvis* (DD-393), and *Shaw* (DD-373) plane-guarded the Midway-to-Wake leg while the heavy cruisers *Pensacola* (CA-25) and *Salt Lake City* (CA-24) did likewise between Wake and Guam. The *Wright* provided two temporary gassing stations for the PBYs at Wake, supplementing PanAir's. The enlisted men berthed in their planes or in a building ashore that accommodated thirty-nine, while the officers lived at the PanAir hotel. The airline provided meals (with fifteen-cent beer—a nickel cheaper than on Midway) for all hands. Subsequently, Rear Admiral Aubrey W. Fitch, commander of Patrol Wing (PatWing) 2, noted that the facilities at Wake had not been improved much since the previous autumn. Gasoline on hand there proved sufficient, but getting people and equipment into the lagoon still constituted a "major problem." He urged that the "proposed small boat channel into the lagoon be completed as soon as possible." He also praised PanAir's "advice, experience, and facilities," which materially aided in the flight's success.[18]

The First Supplemental Appropriation Act for 1941, approved on 1 July 1940, allocated funds to build a naval air station at Wake. Two more construction firms—Morrison-Knudson Company of Boise, Idaho, and J. H. Pomeroy and Company of San Francisco—were added to the CPNAB consortium. On the same day that Congress okayed the money to build at Wake a pier, a channel, and a turning basin to accommodate a tender or tanker and complete facilities to house one patrol plane squadron, a twenty-man survey party departed Pearl Harbor, bound for the atoll to conduct a preliminary reconnaissance, under the officer who was to serve as the island's resident officer in charge of construction projects, thirty-five-year-old Lieutenant (j.g.) Harold W. Butzine, Civil Engineer Corps (CEC), USNR. The party arrived on 9 July 1940 and soon constructed a camp of wood-floored tents that the men christened Coral Gables.

On 11 September 1940, Acting Secretary of the Navy Lewis Compton ordered Rear Admiral John W. Greenslade to survey the navy's shore establishment. One of the bases for which the requirements would be considered was Wake Island. The imminent addition of Wake to the list of bases needed to be supplied from Pearl Harbor, however, prompted concern on the part of Rear Admiral Claude C. Bloch, ComFourteen, the flag officer under whose auspices the construction would proceed.

"We are going to be pretty well up against it for transportation to the outlying islands this winter," he wrote to the CNO on 1 October, "to Wake alone we estimate 300,000 tons," with almost that much earmarked for Midway. "In addition," he continued, "at Midway we have our garrison which must be fed and rotated, to say nothing of the large civilian work forces and the requirements for their rotation once every six months." He planned to carry out that work with the cargo ship *Sirius* (AK-15), the transport *William Ward Burrows* (AP-6), and "occasionally" the "odd ship from the forces afloat here." Estimating that those ships could just about take care of Midway, Johnston, and Palmyra, Bloch opined that "it would be necessary to get another ship to do the Wake Island business" because a round-trip out to that atoll and back would consume "a little over a month." He suggested using the fleet tug *Navajo* (AT-63) to tow loaded two-thousand-ton barges out to Wake "and take them inside [the lagoon] at once for unloading."[19]

On 10 October, a little over a week after ComFourteen's letter to the CNO, however, hurricane-force winds lashed Wake shortly after the departure of the survey party, considerably damaging the PanAir installations and demolishing Coral Gables. That storm, however, proved only an ominous foretaste of things to come, for on 19 October a typhoon practically completed the destruction of the PanAir airport begun nine days earlier. The wind pushed buildings off their foundations, felled a steel light beacon tower, defoliated trees and bushes, and ripped the roof off one wing and the lobby section of the PanAir hotel. Wind velocities were clocked at one hundred knots before the tempest took the roof off the main office building and rendered any further readings impossible. Despite the damage to the facilities, PBY flying boats again staged through to the Philippines in December, supported by the *Wright*.

Transforming paper plans to coral and concrete and steel, however, was not an easy process, as PanAir's people knew well. "Coral reefs grow naturally," Commander Ross A. Dierdorff, the modest, jovial commanding officer of the *William Ward Burrows* reflected, "but air bases do not." The task of starting the construction of the naval air station on Wake fell to an eighty-man pioneer party under the dynamic forty-year-old Nathan Daniel ("Dan") Teters. No one could have asked for a better superintendent for the job. Once an engineer for the reclamation

Rear Admiral Claude C.
Bloch, Commandant,
Fourteenth Naval District,
with Secretary of the Navy
Frank Knox (right) at Pearl
Harbor, September 1940.
(NHC, NH 57377, cropped)

The transport *William Ward Burrows* (AP-6) (formerly the motorship
Santa Rita) at the Pearl Harbor Navy Yard, 25 November 1940, a month
before her voyage to Wake with the pioneer party of Contractors, Pacific
Naval Air Bases. (NA, RG-19 Bureau of Ships)

service and then an independent contractor, Teters had ended up with Morrison-Knudson and had become "one of the best on-the-job executives" that general contracting firm had. When the CPNAB concept had arisen, Teters, who had arrived at Honolulu on 15 July 1940, had eagerly sought the Wake Island job because he had dreamed of "going on to conquer the Far East with bulldozer and shovel." Eager to succeed, he believed that the job at Wake would prove "the making of his future."[20]

His men embarked in the *William Ward Burrows* at Honolulu—"some laden with leis, some with hang-overs, and some with both"—before Christmas of 1940. Crammed into every available space on board the "Weary Willie" were "trucks, tractors, road scrapers and road rollers, cement and cement mixers, lighting plants, air compressors, stoves, refrigerators, boilers, distilling plants, steel, lumber, dynamite, gasoline, lubricating oil, beans, bacon, popcorn, cigarettes, chewing gum, and candy—everything needed to set up a self-sustaining community for eighty men and to pave the way for hundreds more and thousands of tons of building materials." Nested in the steel-hulled experimental open cargo lighter *YCK-1* that lay secured across hatch number two was the thirty-five-foot motor sampan *Hopei*. The "Willie B" sailed on 26 December 1940, with the fifty-five-foot diesel tug *Pioneer* and a forty-by one-hundred-foot barge *Wake No. 1* in tow.[21]

Though twice delayed en route when the barge came adrift, the *William Ward Burrows* reached her destination on 9 January 1941. Sailors and contractors caught a glimpse of the atoll through intermittent rain squalls. As Commander Dierdorff, who held the Navy Cross for his participation in saving the badly damaged *Shaw* (Destroyer No. 68) in World War I, and whose "expert seamanship and cheerful nature" would endear him to the CPNAB men his ship transported to Wake, later recounted, the first sight of Wake and its "low-lying shoreline with its forbidding and unbroken fringe of white surf" could scarcely have reassured Dan Teters and his workers.

When the weather permitted a first reconnaissance the following day, Dierdorff discovered the landing site to be a sorry sight indeed, the devastation wreaked by the typhoon of 19 October 1940 still very much in evidence. The PanAir cove proved too small to handle the large volume of traffic that planners called for in the future construction program, so work commenced immediately to widen and deepen it. The CPNAB men ran lighters as close to shore as possible; using air compressors mounted on the lighters, they then ran hose lines to jackhammer operators who worked in the shoulder-deep water that turned milky when they disturbed the coral bottom. Finally, the first barge could be brought within ten feet of the shore, with a ramp bridging the remaining distance. A light tractor led the procession, followed by the

Admiral Husband E. Kimmel, ca.
spring 1941. (NHC, NH 57100,
cropped)

Photographed on 25 May 1941 from a PBY flying over the waters off Heel
Point (foreground, center), Wake lies in foreground, connected by a
causeway with Peale. Visible is the sprawling contractors' camp with its
barracklike workers' living quarters, nearby supply dumps, and aggregate
plant; PanAir settlement is visible on Peale as the cluster of white-roofed
buildings, beyond which is the site of the future naval air station. Seven
PBYs from VP-23 lie moored along the shore. Wilkes is on the opposite
side of the lagoon. In the foreground are the superintending contractors'
and guest cottages. (NA, 80-G-411160)

heavier bulldozers, whose operators soon filled in the gap between barge and shore, permitting the eighty-ton Caterpillar crane (used subsequently to unload the heavier items of cargo) to creep to dry land. Other workmen then anchored the barge offshore and ran cables from it to winches and "deadmen" on Wake; the tug *Pioneer* and motor launches could then tow in the cargo-laden lighters.

The *William Ward Burrows* lay to off Wake's south shore and, over the next two weeks, discharged cargo and disembarked the rough-and-ready veterans of Boulder, Bonneville, and Grand Coulee who had worked together before on similar projects. PanAir kindly placed a "small, asthmatic tractor" at the disposal of the contractors, as well as a fifteen-ton cargo lighter. The CPNAB men immediately built a temporary tent camp into which half of the contractors' men moved on 14 January 1941. Forty additional men arrived on the morning of 1 February in the *Chaumont* when she stopped there en route to the Asiatic station; joined there by the light cruiser *Concord* (CL-10), the transport quit Wake at noon the same day, bound for Guam.[22]

On 1 February 1941 (Pearl Harbor date), less than a month after the CPNAB pioneer party had arrived at Wake, Admiral Husband E. Kimmel relieved Admiral James O. Richardson as Commander in Chief, United States Fleet (CinCUS). Kimmel had proved an able administrator firmly grounded in strategy and tactics. Vigorous, detail-conscious, and dedicated, the gray-haired, blue-eyed Kimmel was energetic and resourceful, honest, indefatigable, and an excellent seaman. His Naval Academy classmates had found him to be "intensely in earnest about everything," and one borrowed a line from Tourgenieff to describe his bearing: "He had the air of his own statue erected by national subscription."[23] On 3 February, under Navy Department General Order No. 143, Kimmel became Commander in Chief, Pacific Fleet (CinCPac).

While Kimmel acclimated himself to his new post, work at Wake—eight hours a day, six days a week—proceeded to enlarge the tent camp to house 121 men. Within two weeks, about the same time (14 February) that President Roosevelt declared Wake a "national defense area," a road—nicknamed Wilshire Boulevard for the famed thoroughfare in Los Angeles—extended from one tip of the atoll to the other. Within a month, the permanent camp stood nearly 85 percent complete, and the entire force moved in. By mid-March 1941, workmen had excavated fifteen hundred feet of channel so larger barges could be unloaded. By the end of March, the permanent 259-man-capacity permanent camp was completed, as was a guest house and a superintendent's quarters, and a second, 1,000-man-capacity facility had been started. With the completion of the first permanent camp, the pace of work quickened to ten-hour days, seven days a week. For part of that time, the CPNAB crews worked two shifts per day.

Wake, however, though only one of the CPNAB projects under way as the year 1941 began, still boasted not even a rudimentary military presence for its protection; other outlying islands in the Fourteenth Naval District, such as Midway, Johnston, and Palmyra, did. Indicative of the concern shared by Pacific marines about the problem of the defenses at the outlying bases (even before Wake had any), Colonel Pickett, then commanding officer of the Marine Barracks at Pearl Harbor, wrote on 25 February that supplying and relieving the detachments at the outposts "will be no small problem . . . particularly since the Depot of Supplies is at San Francisco." Pickett, who possessed a wide knowledge both of the territory and of artillery, also recognized the stresses of isolated deployments and thought it "most desirable not to keep men and officers too long on these [outpost] islands." Although there would be a "tremendous lot of work in setting up the armament" in the beginning, "the routine will be rather dull" once the batteries were emplaced. Even if the units were "somewhat mixed" as a consequence, he urged that marines taken off one island not be sent back to the same place. The change would boost morale.[24]

Rear Admiral Bloch continued to worry about how Wake would be sustained, a concern that mirrored Colonel Pickett's about the distance between the Depot of Supplies and the outlying islands. To maintain Wake, ComFourteen wrote to the CNO on 2 April, required a "continuous stream" of cargo vessels, which were in short supply. Stark responded that Wake was "extremely important to mid-Pacific operations" and urged Bloch to develop the island "with vigor."[25]

Within three weeks of Bloch's anxious missive to Stark, Kimmel was echoing Colonel Pickett's 1939 appreciation of Wake's strategic importance as well as previous ones. CinCPac, too, felt that the triangular atoll lying less than seven hundred miles from the Marshalls could serve as a vital advance base from which U.S. Navy patrol planes could observe the Mandates or cover the fleet's advance toward the ORANGE Saipan-Honshu line. He also knew that if it were in ORANGE hands, enemy patrol planes operating from there could warn of any surprise moves made by the U.S Fleet toward the Mandates.

Denying Wake to the Japanese if the Americans did not hold it, Kimmel believed, would prove difficult. Writing to Admiral Stark on 18 April 1941, CinCPac also acknowledged that wresting the atoll from the Japanese if they were to seize it early in a war would "require operations of some magnitude." He surmised that since the Japanese Fourth Fleet contained amphibious forces, "it appears not unlikely that one of the initial operations of the Japanese may be directed against

Wake." Although Kimmel's appreciation of Wake's strategic value was not novel, his belief that a defended advance base there might induce the Japanese to expose their ships in an area that would afford the U.S. Fleet an "opportunity to get at naval forces with naval forces" in the central or eastern—rather than the western—Pacific was a new idea.[26]

Kimmel considered it essential that nothing arrest the work then in progress because enemy action could seriously interrupt or even halt it. To ensure that construction of the necessary facilities continued unhindered, Kimmel recommended that "units of a marine defense battalion be progressively established on Wake as facilities there permit."[27]

The weapon Kimmel sought to employ, the defense battalion, seemed like "nothing but a Marine Corps version of coast artillery, adapted to rapid oversea movement and equally rapid occupation of a strategic point for defensive purposes." Nearly 750 officers and men manned batteries equipped with 5-inch/.51-caliber navy guns modified for shore emplacement, 3-inch/.50-caliber army-pattern antiaircraft guns with the newest directors, searchlights and sound locators, and forty-eight each of .50- and .30-caliber machine guns for antiaircraft and beach defense. "All hands retain[ed] their rifles [the dependable bolt-action M-1903 Springfields]," to enable "the battalion [to] provide its own infantry-support." Needing "relatively little tactical mobility" and taken out to its base via navy transport, the defense battalion required little transportation other than what was "necessary to install weapons." "In defense of a base," one marine observed, "the enemy comes to you."[28]

Those who served in the defense battalions, however, knew there were no cut-and-dried solutions to the difficult problems of protecting bases on small outlying atolls such as Wake, which involved emplacing appropriate weapons to deal with a multiphased enemy assault. Knowing of the problems, however, was one thing; being able to surmount them was another. On 18 April, Kimmel wrote that if CPNAB met their estimates, sufficient water and provision storage at Wake would exist for construction forces, as well as for a full defense battalion, by 1 June. Until the building schedule could be adjusted to provide barracks, however, any marines sent to Wake would have to make do living under canvas. Kimmel suggested that as soon as transportation could be arranged—augmented if necessary by warships—elements of the First Defense Battalion, along with the four five-inch guns and eight mobile three-inch guns earmarked for Johnston and Palmyra, then awaiting shipment at Pearl, be sent to Wake instead to allow timely completion of its defenses.[29] Pacific war planners thought Johnston's proximity to Oahu made it less likely to be attacked at the outset of hostilities.[30]

The First Defense Battalion—the unit Kimmel contemplated sending elements of to the atoll—had begun life as the redesignated Second

Battalion, Fifteenth Marines, at the Marine Corps Base, San Diego, in November 1939 and moved to Pearl in February 1941. Elements of the battalion were then sent to Johnston and Palmyra. Ultimately, Kimmel envisioned increasing the Wake detachment—the last to be deployed from the parent battalion—to full strength (facilities, transportation, and circumstances permitting) and modifying the construction program to encompass defensive installations.

On 7 May, Rear Admiral Bloch wrote to the CNO with more worries about the pace at which the work at Wake was proceeding. Because the harbor there was not slated to be ready for another two years and the longest recorded time for unloading a vessel there was ten days, he feared that an enemy would enjoy a "submarine picnic" off the atoll. Back in Washington, Captain Harry W. Hill, in the War Plans Division, later downplayed Bloch's apprehension over the submarine menace as "exaggerated and misleading." War would probably curtail the construction work, but Hill thought the logistics problem "negligible." Putting ashore 125 tons of supplies a month (excluding ammunition) for a five-hundred-man defense battalion, he calculated confidently, came out to "the equivalent of about 9 trips of a 50' motor launch."[31]

Less than a month after Kimmel had written Stark concerning Wake, on 14 May 1941, Secretary of the Navy Frank Knox "approved and promulgated" the Greenslade Board's report, which recommended that Wake be developed to provide "interim repairs to local forces," an anchorage for tenders and "light forces," a base for six submarines, complete facilities to operate twelve patrol planes, emergency aviation facilities for two marine squadrons (thirty-six planes), storage for three months' worth of supplies and fuel, accommodations for one defense battalion, and a twenty-bed dispensary.[32]

As May ended, the War Plans Division continued to contemplate the problem of Wake in deliberations perhaps propelled to the forefront by the recent Greenslade Board. Captain Charles J. Moore sounded a cautionary note in a memorandum to the chief of the division (Rear Admiral Richmond K. Turner) on 24 May 1941. Moore mentioned that maintaining lines of communication with a defense battalion at Wake, even if construction programs there were suspended at ComFourteen's discretion, might become "burdensome" and "a diversion from other offensive operations." Noting that CinCPac had anticipated an early attack on Wake at the start of a war with Japan, "with the reduced forces available and the nature of the early operations required of the Pacific Fleet [at that juncture]," Moore believed that "the prospects of meeting an enemy naval force at Wake under advantageous conditions . . . [were] . . . not favorable." Defending Wake might seriously handicap the fleet's early wartime operations. Although he urged that Wake be developed "as rapidly as possible," Moore recomended that in the event of war "good strategy" dictated occupying and defending Makin and abandoning Wake.[33]

While those in Washington contemplated Wake's place in the event of war, the difficulty of maintaining the outlying bases continued to weigh heavily on the CinCPac's mind at Pearl Harbor. Kimmel declared that "our potential enemy [Japan] is far away and hard to get at." Because Japan possessed "no exposed *vital* interests within reach of Pearl Harbor," its defenses in the Marshalls required "landing operations, supported by sea forces," to breach or capture them. Such required a preponderance of "light force and carrier strength" which, thanks to the recent transfer of ships—including the carrier *Yorktown* (CV-5)—to the Atlantic Fleet, he did not then have. The Japanese, he went on, were loath "to expose their main fleet until . . . forced to do so by our obtaining a position close enough to threaten their vital interests [such as in fortifying an advance base at Wake]."[34]

"In the Pacific," Kimmel continued, echoing ComFourteen's concerns of early April, "with enemy vital interests so far away, and no bases of our own within striking distance," the logistics problem was "acute." Perceiving that the "real battleground" would lie in the western Pacific, he knew that his fleet possessed insufficient auxiliaries to support operations there. He urgently needed transports and cargo ships.[35]

Captain Hill, in a memorandum to Rear Admiral Turner two days later (28 May), acknowledged the importance the CNO had attached to Wake and Stark's urging vigorous prosecution of the program there. Hill declared that the navy was "definitely committed to push the work." By the same token, "we are, therefore, definitely committed to the defense of that project, at the earliest time that it may be of value to ourselves or to the enemy. That time," Hill concluded, "appears to be now." The time had come to send marines to Wake.[36]

"AN UNINVITING LOW-LYING ATOLL"

Even while the decision was being made to send marines to Wake, a growing shortage of building materials beginning in May 1941 began to retard the pace of construction of the facilities they were to defend. As part of the effort to bring the project up to speed, the cargo ship *Regulus* (AK-14) made two round-trips to the atoll, on the second towing the tug *Justine Foss* from Midway. The addition of the *Justine Foss* on 23 May promised to expedite cargo handling at Wake because she could join the *Pioneer* in towing loaded barges through the swift-running Wilkes Channel. Another cargo vessel, the *Sirius*, disembarked ninety additional workmen at Wake between 1 and 6 June.

On the same day that the *Sirius* departed, 6 June, the fleet oiler *Kanawha* (AO-1) reached Wake with the 326-foot-long dredge *Columbia* in tow. The dredge had been acquired by CPNAB for the navy from the port of Portland, Oregon, in March 1941 and had left for Hawaiian waters in tow of the oceangoing tug *Seminole* (AT-65) on 26 April. Those in charge of the Wake project expected much of the *Columbia*, which was given a trial run on 30 June. It was to be used to widen the existing channel between Wake and Wilkes to three hundred feet and increase its depth to thirty, dredge a channel across the reefs to the north of Wilkes and a thirty-foot-deep turning basin in the lagoon proper, and extend a small channel from the turning basin to Peale. The work primarily would be "easy suction dredging on [a] sand bottom" except where the reef was involved, and the Bureau of Yards and Docks speculated that if the *Columbia* performed as advertised, the thousand-foot turning basin would be completed by September 1941, the cut through the reef at the tip of Wilkes (the shipping channel suggested by those who visited Wake from the *Chaumont* in 1934) by February 1942, and the entire channel by June 1942.[1]

Up to that point (summer 1941), other than the occasional wife of a PanAir employee, Wake had no permanent female residents. Dan Teters's superiors, however, perhaps as an incentive, had allowed him the privilege and pleasure of having his wife, Florence, join him there.

In time, "permanent" residents and visitors alike, passing through on board the Clippers, came to regard her as the "Queen of Wake Island." All appreciated her effervescent personality.

As efforts progressed slowly but steadily toward establishing the Wake base facilities, Kimmel promulgated the Pacific Fleet's operating war plan (WPPac-46) in support of the CNO's "Rainbow Five" (WPL-46) scheme on 21 July. Early in a Pacific campaign, initial U.S. Fleet operations would be aimed at the Marshalls, to divert Japanese strength from the Malay Barrier. Patrol planes were to be advanced to Wake, Midway, and Johnston, whence they were to reconnoiter Taongi and Bikar atolls in the Marshalls and provide the commander of Task Force 2 (Commander Aircraft, Battle Force) with intelligence gleaned in the course of those flights. Those who formulated WPPac-46 knew that tenders could not base at Wake but that in an emergency PanAir facilities could be commandeered or used "by special arrangement." To help safeguard Wake, submarines were to patrol off the atoll.[2]

The plan also discussed four potential avenues of action by the Japanese "in the area subject to [American] patrol plane search." Japanese submarines could raid and reconnoiter Oahu, the outlying islands, and lines of communication between them; Japanese surface ships might try to sever American lines of communication; Japanese surface ships and planes could raid Wake, as well as Midway, Johnston, Palmyra, and Canton. The last avenue of action, the plan noted, was "possibly [a Japanese] carrier raid against Oahu."

Kimmel had completed his preparations for hostilities just in time, for on 24 July, Japanese forces began occupying the southern portion of French Indochina, a step that prompted President Roosevelt, by executive order, to freeze Japanese assets in the United States and to bar Japanese shipping from the Panama Canal; the British and Dutch abrogated their commercial treaties with Japan. Soon afterward, Roosevelt issued an executive order incorporating the Philippine army into United States service, and the War Department appointed Major General (later Lieutenant General) Douglas MacArthur as commander of the joint American-Filipino force in the Philippines. MacArthur, recalled from duty with the Philippine Commonwealth, promptly began a strenuous program of training and equipping his force, animated by a fervent belief in the defensibility of the archipelago, an American protectorate until 1946.

Encouraged by favorable reports of the performance of Boeing B-17 Flying Fortress heavy bombers in the Royal Air Force and seeing that production schedules made it possible, for the first time, to send large amounts of modern matériel to the Philippines, the War Department abandoned its defeatist notion that the islands would fall swiftly to the Japanese. Doubtless infected by General MacArthur's "contagious optimism," the War Department hoped that reinforcing the Philippines could perhaps deter Japanese aggression. The B-17s would be flown across the Pacific via the PanAir route.

During the last three weeks of July 1941, however, while Wake's importance waxed as the army's efforts to reinforce the Philippines gained momentum, construction efforts began to wane. No new building materials reached the atoll. Lieutenant Butzine reported to his superiors that July had been the least productive month per man since work had begun on Wake's projects. Except for wolmanized wood, which the contractors were not yet ready to use, all the lumber had been used up—even the scrap boards were used as forms for concrete footings. The lack of steel erection bolts prevented work on superstructures from commencing, and the nonarrival of material compelled Dan Teters to put riggers and cargo handlers to work "painting, repairing equipment, and [doing] odd jobs."

The shortage of essential materials that continued well into August, however, proved to be only one reason for the paucity of progress. The *Columbia*, for which such high hopes had been held, had clawed out only thirty thousand cubic yards before its cutter engine exploded on 11 July, shutting it down until the last day of the month. In August, however, CPNAB bulldozers, power shovels, carryalls, and other grading and excavating equipment began work on the landplane runways.

Although the requirements for the base had grown "like Topsy" by the start of the summer, the marine presence to protect it still existed only on paper. While work on the base facilities was at low ebb and that on the airfield just beginning, the progressive establishment of the marine garrison on the atoll began. At 0740 on 8 August, the *Regulus*, alongside Pier 31A at Honolulu, began embarking the 6 officers and 173 enlisted men and sailors from the First Defense Battalion.

Commanding the detachment was Major Lewis A. Hohn, a quiet and genial forty-three-year-old Ohioan, on temporary duty from the Sixth Defense Battalion, where he had commanded the three-inch antiaircraft group and the headquarters and service battery. The sinewy, small-statured Hohn, who had earlier in his career twice won the prestigious Wimbledon Cup for marksmanship, had served in Nicaragua and China and had graduated from the U.S. Army's Coast Artillery School at Fort Monroe, Virginia. Hohn, who was keenly interested in the profession of arms and had shown proven administrative ability and unremitting industry, had proved himself a natural "shooter" who deeply believed in the importance of accurate fire; some marines had nicknamed him "peepsight."[3]

His executive officer, Captain Wesley M. Platt from South Carolina,

Captain Lewis A. Hohn at Shanghai, China, in 1937, serving with the Fourth Marines. His prowess as a marksman is plainly shown by the medals he wears. (NA, USMC Photo 521006, cropped)

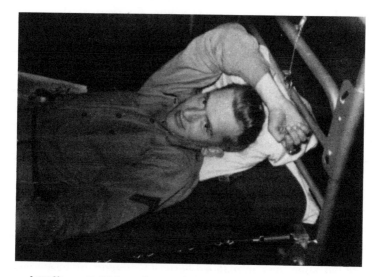

Corporal William C. Halstead, seen here relaxing in his bunk at Pearl Harbor before he shipped out to Wake in the summer of 1941, wrote perceptive letters home to his family describing the enlisted man's perspective of the feverish buildup of defenses at Wake. (George Halstead)

An M3 three-inch antiaircraft gun on an M2A2 mobile mount with outriggers partially extended, like those that equipped the antiaircraft batteries at Wake Island. (Charles A. Holmes Collection, MCHC Personal Papers)

ably complemented the detachment commander. A graduate of Clemson College, where he had been active in boxing and football, the small but husky Platt had served in China with the Second Marine Brigade, and, like Major Hohn, had witnessed a portion of the battle for Shanghai in late 1937. Regarded by his peers as "quiet, serious, conscientious, generous, and helpful," he led by personal example. Consequently, marines from enlisted men to officers who served under or with the twenty-seven-year-old Platt invariably found that his personality and demeanor prompted all with whom he came in contact to respect and even revere him.[4]

First Lieutenant John B. Heles, detailed as the detachment's five-inch artillery officer, had received his second lieutenant's commission in 1937. After instruction at the Basic School at the Philadelphia Navy Yard, he served on shore at the Marine Barracks at the Norfolk Navy Yard. After a tour at sea commanding the marine detachment in the gunboat *Erie* (PG-50), Heles attended the Base Defense Weapons Class at Marine Corps School, Quantico, Virginia. Assigned then to the Second Defense Battalion, he commanded Battery C (five-inch), headquartered at the Marine Corps Base, San Diego, before being deployed to Hawaii.

First Lieutenant Cyril E. Emrich had been assigned as the detachment's three-inch antiaircraft officer. A June 1938 graduate of the Naval Academy (the only Annapolis man in the group of officers initially sent

A 5-inch/51 caliber gun of Battery A, First Defense Battalion, at Marine Corps Base, San Diego, 21 October 1940. Private Edward F. Eaton, striking a Napoleon-like hand-in-shirt pose beside the gun, serves as a human yardstick to give a viewer an idea of the weapon's size. (Charles A. Holmes Collection, MCHC Personal Papers)

to Wake), the popular, personable Emrich had been a standout athlete there, lettering in football, basketball, and track. His speed had earned him the nickname "Cyclone" (or "Cy" for short). Emrich had excelled on the drill field as well, where his "military attitude and crisp commands" had helped him to emerge as a recognized leader among his classmates; his men regarded him as one of the best officers in the Corps. Like John Heles, he had received instruction at the Basic School at Philadelphia, then served in the Barracks Detachment at Marine Barracks, Quantico, before being transferred to the Fleet Marine Force at San Diego and then assigned to Battery D of the First Defense Battalion.

Second Lieutenant Arthur A. Poindexter, USMCR, the detachment's machine-gun officer and the only Marine Corps Reserve officer in the initial group, had enlisted in the reserves in June 1938. He was honorably discharged and then accepted his second lieutenant's commission in November 1939. Poindexter, a twenty-four-year-old midwesterner, served at Quantico and at the Marine Corps Base, San Diego, before being deployed to Hawaii in February 1941.

Lieutenant Commander Arthur H. Pierson, MC, USN, whose fine sense of humor would keep spirits up and whose career had included duty ashore at receiving stations and naval districts, as well as at sea in the light cruiser *Memphis* (CL-13), boarded the *Regulus* to take up his duty at Wake as the detachment's medical officer. Assisting Pierson in setting up a dispensary to serve the marines were three pharmacist's mates drawn, as he had been, from the headquarters and service battery of the First Defense Battalion.

Following the embarkation of the last man, the *Regulus* sailed for Wake with the equipment-laden *PanAir Barge (PAB) No. 3* in tow at 0915 on 8 August. The eight-to-ten-knot passage proved long and monotonous. The officers' accommodations in the *Regulus*'s "officer's country" seemed adequate, but the enlisted men's were not.[5] For the latter, the passage proved no pleasure cruise because their accommodations consisted of makeshift bunks and cots in the 'tween-decks portion of number four hold. Workmen at the Pearl Harbor Navy Yard had added head facilities in the ship's former armory compartment, but only two showers and wash basins for the passengers made shaving and bathing difficult. The removal of hatch boards and tarpaulins, together with an awning spread over the hold, provided a modicum of comfort.

Sighting the PanAir beacon a few minutes after midnight on the eighteenth, the *Regulus* transferred her tows at 0625 on the nineteenth and lay to, awaiting the arrival of a lighter so that she could discharge passengers and cargo. She disembarked the marines to the *Justine Foss* and the *Pioneer* and lightered ashore their equipment within three days, sailing for Honolulu within an hour after disembarking the last man on 22 August.

That day, flaxen-haired Corporal William C. "Whitey" Halstead, two months shy of his twenty-first birthday, wrote to his mother and father from his new duty station:

I guess I'd better write & let you know where I'm at. I've moved 2,100 miles further west to help build a new base in the Pacific. From what I hear I guess I'll spend the next 18 months going here, there & someplace else with not more than three or four months at any one place. If I have to stay out in this part of the world, I hope I spend it traveling around. . . .

We've been working 18 to 22 hours a day getting the ship and two water-tight seagoing barges unloaded. It sure was a 'tub.' . . . It took us 11 days to sail 2,100 miles, towing one watertight barge.

Things have sure come to a pretty pass around here. It's gotten so a corporal isn't a non-commissioned officer except officially. All he is is an overpaid private. They've put all corporals to work out here & we're supposed to work harder than the privates to set a good example.

Soon thereafter, the marines built their own camp (designated as Camp 1) of pyramidal six-man tents near a temporary wooden headquarters and a two-hundred-man-capacity mess hall/galley on the land once occupied by the contractors' temporary dwellings. Support plants included cold storage, water distillation, and power, in addition to storage tanks of fresh and salt water. Once encamped, Hohn's marines soon began the arduous task of hewing out the initial five-inch and three-inch positions from the coral and brush with little more than picks and shovels or the occasional borrowed civilian bulldozer, grappling squarely with the acknowledged problem confronting a defense battalion with regard to its main battery—its five-inch guns.

Unlike the army M3 three-inch guns on M2A2 mobile "spider" mounts (the four outrigger arms deployed like a spider's legs) shipped to Wake, the five-inchers required fixed positions. Although "never designed to be more than slightly portable at best" ("the guns were not mobile," one defense battalion officer later remembered, "unless you consider a house to be mobile"), the five-inch guns offered the advantages of "fire-power, muzzle-velocity, standardization within the Naval Service, and supply." Preparing the emplacements for those naval rifles, however, would prove particularly difficult because the massive timbers upon which they were to be mounted required the services of an articulated Le Tourneau crane; both guns and timbers "act[ed] as physical brakes upon a defense battalion, not only in sheer weight and mass [each five-inch/51 assembly weighed between 22,400 and 23,300 pounds] but in the relative awkwardness with which they must be handled . . . by the most expert and practical personnel."[6] And the men who did this work had to subsist on an allowance of fifty-two cents per day for emergency canned rations—"hardly sufficient for a hard-working man"—with little fresh produce and no capacity to bake their own bread. Second Lieutenant Poindexter, the mess officer, recorded many a complaint about the frequency of canned tongue. Fortunately, the excellent deep-sea fishing off Wake enabled the anglers among the little garrison to add variety (sharks) to their otherwise monotonous fare, while the enlisted marines and sailors could quaff Lucky Lager beer after a day's toil—a luxury not enjoyed by the contractors although the canned beverage left a taste similar to formaldehyde in one's mouth.

For "periodic relief and replacements" for the men on the lonely atolls, Kimmel asked for another defense battalion.[7] Officials in Washington appreciated CinCPac's situation but apparently felt that they had done all they could, given the prevailing manpower levels. On 21 August, Rear Admiral Turner, director of war plans, who had been asked to comment on Kimmel's latest request, observed to the CNO: "We are doing the best we can about getting more marines for the Pacific, but the difficulty of enlisting and training them is great. We are planning on four more . . . battalions for the Pacific, but it will by many months before they can be gotten ready. We have already made available a . . . battalion for periodic relief of the outlying garrisons."[8]

On 26 August, Kimmel informed Stark that the five-inch guns were being emplaced and when that work was completed the marines then on the atoll could man four three-inch guns (of the twelve there), two (of six) five-inch, eight (of eighteen) .50-caliber machine guns, eight (of thirty) .30-caliber, and three (of six) searchlights. Kimmel posited that in an emergency many civilians, including a "considerable number of ex-service men," would augment the marines' efforts. Furthermore, he promised to provide Wake "speedy reinforcement . . . when required."[9]

The next day, Rear Admiral Bloch wrote to Major Hohn; in the confidential letter that Bloch enjoined Hohn to keep to himself, the admiral charged the major with the defense of the island, acknowledging that he had a "very difficult job in getting your place built according to plans" while at the same time "carrying on your own activities" without interfering with the construction work. He urged Hohn to work closely with Lieutenant Butzine and to devote his principal effort to completing Wake's facilities as quickly as possible. "There should be no friction in any way," ComFourteen reminded him, "nor should construction personnel be called off their jobs except when it is absolutely necessary." If there were delays, Hohn was to inform ComFourteen why they had occurred and how long it would be until progress could be resumed.[10]

Although Hohn's marines were "actually the military defenders of the place," the admiral observed that "in every case they will be found to be inadequate in numbers . . . [because] they have so many jobs to do in connection with the defense." Bloch posited that among the civilian workmen at Wake, "unquestionably" a great many had seen some military service. "If we should be so unfortunate as to become involved in hostilities and your island is attacked," the admiral went on, "it will call for the combined efforts of everybody to beat off the attack." Reflecting the thoughts that Kimmel had expressed to the CNO the day before, ComFourteen suggested that Hohn sound out the contractors about organizing volunteers who "once or twice a week" would be willing "to take a one-half hour's drill in serving the various guns . . . and in performing other duties in connection with [the] defense" so that in an emergency "each and every civilian would know where he is to go and what he is to do and . . . what his duties are and how to perform them."[11]

"Great discretion will be required," Bloch continued, to begin such training and to perfect and continue it. Hohn would need to obtain the "goodwill and voluntary cooperation" of all concerned. "The drills must not be irksome," the admiral advised, "and the men . . . kept in a pepped up frame of mind by jokes and their willing cooperation rather than being scared into it by fear of an outside enemy." Bloch enjoined Hohn not to say or do anything that would make the civilians get the "jitters" or feel that "something is about to happen." ComFourteen thought that nothing was about to, but he reiterated his belief that "with such a large number of men each and every one of them should have some job, know what it is, and how to do it." He expressed "great confidence" in Hohn's ability to perform the task at hand and hoped that the marine could get the civilian workmen involved in such instruction "quietly and without any undue notice . . . without causing the men to believe that they are in danger." Creating anxiety, the admiral warned, "would be unfortunate as it would cause undue publicity, probably causing a lot of the chicken-hearted to quit working."[12]

As Kimmel had noted, the contractors' civilians would soon be taking steps to "augment" the marines' efforts. A notice appeared on the bulletin board outside the library in Camp 2 soliciting volunteers for weapons training. The first meeting with the marines attracted some 150 to 165 men. Eager contractors signed up for training with .30-caliber machine guns and rifles. They attended classes on Wednesday afternoons and on weekends, the first of which was held on the baseball diamond at Camp 2. Later, machine-gun instruction was provided in emplacements near Camp 1; the civilians learned how to strip the gun on a ground sheet, change the barrel, belt and feed ammunition, clear a jam, and fire the weapon.

The addition of a submarine base to the complex of facilities at Wake prompted proposals on how best to carry out the work. Among the ideas put forth to expedite construction was to excavate a channel *through* Wilkes instead of at its tip. The conclusion that the *Columbia* could not cut through the iron-hard coral reef seems to have been reached both on Oahu and on Wake, when George Youmans, vice-president of Morrison-Knudson and a member of the CPNAB operating committee (OpCom), finally prevailed upon the navy to scrap the idea of trying to conquer the reef with the *Columbia.* Youmans, who was said to be blessed with a "fine balance of judgment and the capacity for taking infinite pains," had the job of overseeing the Wake project from OpCom headquarters in Honolulu.[13]

Meanwhile, Vice Admiral Inoue Shigeyoshi, a blunt-spoken flag officer considered a progressive thinker and a politico-military affairs expert, was appointed to command the Japanese navy's Fourth Fleet, or South Seas Force. Although not an aviator, Inoue understood air power—particularly naval air power—and had served as chief of the Department of Naval Aeronautics in the Navy Ministry.[14]

Inoue had vociferously condemned the strategy that centered around the all-out fleet battle and urged consideration of the use of naval aircraft and submarines instead. Believing that the U.S. Navy would deploy its submarines and planes to try to sever Japan's lines of communication and supply, Inoue wanted Japan to accord priority to securing its sea routes, not preparing for a Jutland or another Tsushima. Thinking that no potential American adversary would ever be so "very ignorant and reckless" to engage in a decisive battle fleet encounter (ironically, very much like the type of engagement that Admiral Kimmel was hoping to precipitate over Wake), Inoue declared that the "struggle over island bases will be the primary mode of operations in the war between the United States and Japan." Furthermore, he believed "that the future of the Empire depends on the success or failure of [island warfare], the importance of which is equal to that of the decisive battles between fleets of capital ships in the old days."[15]

Inoue recommended assembling "operational forces capable of capturing enemy island bases" to extend the range of Japanese land-based naval air, spearheaded by an invasion fleet that consisted predominantly of older warships no longer maintained in first-line status. "At the present time," he wrote early in 1941, "when no decisive fleet encounter is likely . . . we should plan and construct forces designed for seizing bases from the outset." He equated "the capture and use of enemy air bases" with the "destruction of enemy battleships in former times."[16]

Some within the Japanese navy apparently felt that Inoue's appointment to the Fourth Fleet had resulted from his outspoken criticism of the big-navy plans of the "War Faction" (to get him out of Tokyo), but a case could be made that perhaps it was because he championed the concept of island warfare. Although he, like his good friend Admiral Yamamoto Isoroku, commander in chief of the Combined Fleet, had opposed war with the United States, Inoue loyally set himself to the task that lay before him. His views on how the war in the Pacific should be fought virtually assured that when given the Fourth Fleet in August 1941 he would devote his full energies toward wresting island possessions—such as Wake—from the Americans. The problem confronting Inoue, though, largely paralleled that which faced Admirals Kimmel and Bloch—getting the material, ships, and men, in timely fashion, to do the job, with one important exception: the Americans regarded the outlying bases as important, whereas the Japanese accorded them second place.

Although shortages of building materials slowed the growth of Wake's facilities during the summer, ships such as the *Regulus* and the *William Ward Burrows* continued to shuttle workmen and supplies between Honolulu and the base. Three times the *Seminole* towed PanAir barges out to Wake from Honolulu; the use of the fleet tug in that role was Rear Admiral Bloch's idea the previous autumn.[17] When equipment and supplies arrived, CPNAB men unloaded the ships, lightered the matériel into the beach, and got it ashore, providing the necessary heavy lift support to help the marines, who had to interrupt their work only long enough to handle the matériel consigned specifically to them.[18]

As if Hohn's leathernecks did not have enough to do, the army's lack of ground crew compelled the marines to service the initial transpacific ferry flight of army air force Boeing B-17D Flying Fortresses. Pausing at Hickam Field until the contractors put the finishing touches on Wake's main east-west airstrip, the nine B-17s from the Fourteenth Bombardment Squadron (Provisional) under Major Emmett C. "Rosy" O'Donnell, Jr., had departed Hamilton Field, just north of San Francisco, on 28 August 1941, beginning a journey that would take them via Hickam, Midway, Wake, Rabaul, and Port Moresby to Clark Field, near Manila, the only airfield in the Philippines then ready to operate them.[19] For their part in the trail-blazing flight, each army air force officer and enlisted man who flew received the Distinguished Flying Cross.

As arduous as those additional duties had been for Major Hohn's leathernecks—*they* received no decoration for their vital supporting role in the pioneering flight—the successful staging of the nine B-17s emphasized the atoll's importance. Writing to Admiral Stark on 12

Boeing B-17D Flying Fortress heavy bombers at Hamilton Field, California, before the October 1941 ferry flight across the Pacific via Wake. (John H. Hamilton)

September, Kimmel observed presciently that though Wake was "by no means 'impregnable,' its present defensive strength is considerable and will require the exposure of quite a force to capture it. It is even possible," he continued, "that should its capture be an early objective of Japan, such an effort might be supported by a substantial portion of their Combined Fleet, which would create for us, a golden opportunity *if we have the strength to meet it.*"[20]

Maintaining the fleet at a level capable of meeting Japanese aggression was one thing, but what of the atoll's "present defensive strength" to which Kimmel referred? The number of marines in the Fourteenth Naval District as a whole concerned Headquarters Marine Corps, but the size of Wake's garrison, in place by mid-September, mirrored the general "shortage of Marines everywhere." Headquarters felt that the Fourteenth Naval District possessed "more than a reasonable proportion of those [marines] available for the many jobs [they were] being called upon to perform."[21] They would simply have to make do.

The weather, however, often hampered the work schedule. Writing on 10 September, well into the rainy season, Corporal Halstead described it to his mother and father as "swell . . . for ducks. We have a shower or two every day, but this is the third day of steady rain. I haven't even seen the sun once in three days." When the rain let up, the sun radiated warmth like a giant coal in the sky over the blinding white coral and sparkling ocean. "You think its's hot there [in Michigan]. You should be out here in the middle of the Pacific." "Boy, have I got the blisters on my hands & fingers," he recounted to his parents on 19 September, "not to mention various & sundry cuts from sandbag strings and coral. We've been filling sandbags all over the place."

Other matters concerned him the following day. Having received another letter from home, he responded promptly and faithfully on the twentieth and related two complaints that were apparently topics of conversation among his shipmates and that reflect some of the annoyances of daily life at an advance base. "Are we ever burned up out here," he wrote. "Back at Pearl Harbor we paid $2.50 a month, flat rate, for our laundry and that included starching and pressing. Out here these civilians have the nerve to charge us $3 a month for washing our clothes in salt water, no starch, no pressing & plenty of rips, tears, & lost buttons, and plenty of shrinkage, just so they can draw from two-hundred to two-hundred & fifty bucks a month. How's that," he added sardonically, "for robbing the 'defenders of democracy.'" He also noted that "some of the fellows have been complaining of having their letters home lost in the mail or having them opened & resealed before they get home." If that were to happen to his correspondence, he asked his parents to let him know. "It [the censorship of outgoing mail from Wake] isn't being done officially or we would have been told about it."[22]

The "civilians" Corporal Halstead complained of lived comparatively well. One contractor would write: "The camp was neat and clean . . . in each of our [eighty-man] barracks . . . were two screened porches, running water, water coolers, electric lights, showers and inside lavatories. . . . When the lunch bell rang we swarmed to the mess hall [one-thousand-man capacity] and were served a bountiful meal, many varieties of food and plenty of it, well prepared."[23] Support facilities included a cold and dry storage plant, a power plant and a water distilling plant, and water storage tanks that held rain and saltwater. A sixteen-bed hospital served the contractors' medical needs. In addition, there was a laundry, a machine and blacksmith shop, a warehouse, a carpenter shop, a plumbing and electrical shop, and an aggregate and mixing plant. Tank farms accommodated the required fuel and diesel oil and gasoline.

The CPNAB workmen also enjoyed movies six nights a week if they chose, and they frequently populated the recreation building; a camp paper (the *Wake Wig-Wag*) was published—and read—regularly, and its coverage of international dispatches lessened the isolation of life at Wake. Some of the men formed clubs, some of which were branches of national organizations such as the American Legion and the Veterans of Foreign Wars. By October 1941 the library circulated more than one hundred books per day, not keeping up with the seemingly insatiable demand for nonfiction books, but the magazines, though well received, were often as much as two years out of date. Recreational pastimes included swimming, fishing, and shell hunting, but the tennis courts stood little used, promoting the resident officer in charge of construction to inaugurate tournaments to stimulate interest. There was also that American staple: baseball. The marines followed similar leisure pursuits when time permitted.

The sailors who transported those workmen to and from Wake, however, occasionally saw evidence that despite the wages and comparative creature comforts, a man might "crack" as the result of the isolated life. The *Regulus*, for example, embarked contractor Thomas P. Howell, who had been diagnosed as a "mental case," at 0840 on 1 October 1941, shortly before she sailed. A little over two hours later, at 1049, the *Regulus* sounded "man overboard" shortly after someone saw Howell leap into the ocean and lowered her motor whaleboat inside of three minutes. Howell spurned the life ring thrown in his direction, though, and swam away from it, choosing to drown.

While work proceeded on Wake's defenses and facilities, the latter built by crews of men who had worked together on the mainland and who had the advantage of using plans already proved successful in the construction of Midway's facilities, Admiral Kimmel urgently believed that the time had come to assess the development of his outlying bases. Those aspects that concern Wake are noteworthy. The resulting study, completed in early October 1941, which in many important respects echoed Pickett and Pefley's, posited that Wake would probably be raided first "in such force as to permit, in the event of quick and easy success, the capture and garrisoning of the Island." Those who studied the matter believed that such a force would comprise four cruisers, one carrier with forty-eight planes, six destroyers, and one thousand troops, supported by a logistics ship from the Marshalls, but did not expect capital ships to be involved.[24]

For defense, the study recommended assignment to Wake of a battalion of 1,374 men (including corpsmen; 1,095 men provided that men from the air base and civilians could augment the marines) to man six 5-inch guns, sixteen 3-inch antiaircraft guns, sixty .50-caliber machine guns, forty-eight .30-caliber machine guns, and four mobile 37- or 75-millimeter antiboat guns. Four SCR-268 radars were to be installed and one SCR-270B. For marine aviation, the study recommended that 477 men (80 officers and 397 enlisted) be assigned to Wake to operate thirty-six fighters, fifteen scout/dive bombers, and four utility planes. Running a full-fledged naval air station required an aggregate strength of 665 men; a submarine base, 5 officers and 100 enlisted men.

Efforts to induce civilian volunteers to step forward for military training could yield, in the estimation of those who worked on the CinCPac study, at least 500 men. Kimmel's staff based that estimate on comments made by an officer at Midway who had had daily contact with CPNAB workmen, knowledge that many of the civilians had seen military service, and "the results expected when the instinct [for] self-preservation asserts itself." An officer at Wake, the study asserted, had "stated that he believed [CPNAB] employees would aid [in the] defense but recommended that no open expression of the intention to use them [be made] at that time because it would bring a realization of the 'hot spot' in which they were and might cause some to leave the island, thereby delaying progress."[25]

Concerning the organization of the defense of each outlying base, the study posited that it was essentially an "all-hands" operation—aviation ground crew, men assigned to the air station, "and civilians where present"—not one confined to the marines. CinCPac's staff posited that the base commander—recommended to be a senior captain in Wake's case—be responsible for organizing the base defense force. "Subordinate commanders" (such as marine detachment commanders) would "act as

tactical and technical advisors in matters affecting their own forces."
Owing to the deficient numbers of marines to perform strictly defensive functions, a "mobile reserve . . . and service troops (ammunition
and food carriers, litter bearers, truck drivers, etc.)" could be drawn
from "aviation . . . base, and civilian personnel," and though certain
weapons (such as five-inch guns) required "highly trained crews," ammunition handlers required "no special and continuous training" to
serve and operate a weapon efficiently. The study further recommended that PanAir be required to place its gasoline stowage underground.[26]

    CinCPac contemplated relieving the First Defense Battalion with
the Sixth on Wake, where, at the time of the study there were twelve
mobile three-inch guns. Ultimately, those entrusted with such matters
planned to transfer four of those mobile mounts to Hawaii to equip the
projected Eighth Defense Battalion and install eight fixed three-inch
guns to augment the eight mobile mounts already emplaced by Major
Hohn's marines that summer and autumn. Kimmel earmarked the First
Defense Battalion to garrison Johnston and Palmyra.[27]

    Providing more marines for the defense and workers to build the
facilities occupied the Pacific Fleet's workhorse transports and cargo
ships into the autumn. On 10 October 1941, the *William Ward Burrows*
arrived at Wake after having departed Honolulu on 29 September and
proceeding via Johnston Island. Heavy weather, however, compelled
the transport to heave to, unable to disembark her marine or civilian
passengers or discharge cargo for two days.

    Thus it was not until 12 October 1941, that short, wiry, soft-spoken
thirty-seven-year-old Major James P. S. Devereux, from the headquarters
and service battery of the First Defense Battalion, came ashore and
relieved Major Hohn as commanding officer of the detachment and the
senior naval officer on the atoll.[28] Wake's marines would soon find that
the dignified-looking little major differed noticeably from his affable,
genial predecessor. Jim Devereux insisted on "all the niceties of military
etiquette." Behind his back, his men swore that their new detachment
commander's first three initials, J. P. S., had scatological implications:
"Just Plain Shit."[29]

    Born in Cuba, the son of an army officer, and educated in the United
States and in Switzerland, the taciturn Devereux had enlisted in the
Marine Corps in 1923. After he had attained commissioned rank, he
had seen service in a succession of home posts and stations at Norfolk,
Philadelphia, Washington, D.C., and Quantico, among other places;
abroad on expeditionary service in Cuba and Nicaragua and in China,
in the mounted "Horse Marines" in Peking; in the Hawaiian Islands in

Captain James P. S. Devereux, before his promotion to major on 5 April 1940. (Charles A. Holmes Collection, MCHC Personal Papers)

a study of antiaircraft defenses for outlying bases; and in the mounting of the five-inch gun batteries at Johnston and Palmyra.

Other passengers who disembarked that day were Aerologist First Class Walter J. Cook, who was to establish the aerological office for the new naval air station, and Machinist's Mate Second Class Harold R. Williams. The latter petty officer, detached from Patrol Wing Two, had been ordered to Wake for work in the maintenance of small boats. Their arrival brought the number of sailors attached to the Wake Detachment, First Defense Battalion, to thirteen.

On 14 October, the day that the *William Ward Burrows* sailed for Honolulu with Major Hohn on board, Lieutenant Commander Elmer B. Greey, CEC, USNR, relieved Lieutenant Butzine to become resident officer in charge of construction at Wake. The sandy-haired forty-two-year-old Greey, a 1920 Princeton graduate, had been third vice-president of Matthews Construction Company before entering the naval service in April 1941. He had arrived at Pearl Harbor in May, and, in the words of one contemporary, "clearly loved engineering" as much as an aviator loved flying.[30]

Indicative of the scope and pace of the work at Wake, two additional CEC officers, assigned administratively, like Greey, to the Public Works Division of the Pearl Harbor Navy Yard, assisted the resident officer in charge in overseeing the base-building work. One was the thirty-one-year-old son of Rear Admiral Samuel M. Robinson, the chief of the Bureau of Ships, Lieutenant (j.g.) James B. Robinson, whose most recent service had been at the Pearl Harbor Navy Yard. The other was twenty-nine-year-old Ensign Belmont M. Williams, whose most recent civil engineering work had been with the Grade Crossing Bureau of the New York State Department of Public Works.

Among the problems that confronted Lieutenant Commander Greey was the disappointing performance of the *Columbia*. Less than a month before his departure, Greey's predecessor, Lieutenant Butzine, in recounting the *Columbia*'s woes since its arrival, did not seem sanguine about its being able to do its job—in fact, he had written that "the outlook for the future of the dredge . . . is worse than its past." It had lost eight days of work during August (seven to leaking boiler tubes and one to an approaching typhoon) and then had broken down again in September. Constant repairs, Butzine believed, might enable the *Columbia* to work 40 to 50 percent of the time, but putting it into good working condition would require a "major overhaul." CPNAB flew an expert out to Wake in October to survey it and make recommendations, but Butzine stated regretfully that the *Columbia* was not rugged enough. He recommended a "thorough study of the best and quickest way of improving the situation."[31] The *Columbia* had accomplished only some of the dredging and deepening of the channel and some of the dredging of the planned turning basin and of a small construction channel across the lagoon; the amount of time it had spent under repairs, however, caused its crew to grumble about the lack of overtime and bonuses.

Shipping men and increasing amounts of matériel to Wake continued into the autumn. On 15 October, the seaplane tender *Curtiss* (AV-4) sailed from Pearl Harbor with a cargo of gasoline, lubrication oil, and bombs; passengers included three marines and ninety-two civilians. The same day, Tokyo time, as the big auxiliary set course toward Wake, a singular political event occurred in Japan that cast an ominous shadow across the Pacific basin and represented the culmination of a battle that had been going on for several years over who would chart Japan's course in its international relations. The cabinet of Prince Konoye Fumimaro resigned, replaced by one headed by General Tojo Hideki.

Admiral Stark informed Admiral Kimmel that the fall of the Konoye cabinet created a grave situation because the reins of government and the destiny of the island empire had passed firmly into the hands of militarists. Stark correctly perceived that Tojo's regime would probably be strongly nationalistic and anti-American. On 17 October, against the backdrop of those events, Rear Admiral Bloch, commenting on Kimmel's study of defenses and installations at outlying Pacific bases, wrote that in the event of war he believed that the Japanese would raid Wake only to destroy forces and facilities and not capture or garrison it.[32]

In Washington the same day, the subject of raids on Wake concerned General George C. Marshall, the army's chief of staff. The atoll was "a vital link in [the reinforcement of the Philippines]," and if the Japanese put it out of commission, that artery to Asia could be severed. The general feared that Japanese surface raiders might attack his Philippine-bound B-17s on the ground. Troubled, Marshall telephoned Stark on 17 October, anxious for reassurance that the way via Wake was secure. He wanted the navy to make "some sort of reconnaissance" to help him feel at ease with that leg of the transpacific route.

Stark could not allay the general's fears. He dismissed such a raid as improbable but allowed that "a carefully planned raid on any of these Island carriers [such as Wake] . . . might be difficult to detect." Nevertheless, Stark informed Marshall that the navy was "on guard to the best of our ability." Stark's advice to the army's chief of staff, the CNO confided in a postscript to a letter to Kimmel dated 17 October, was "not to worry."[33]

That same day, reflecting Marshall's anxiety over Wake, Stark sent a dispatch to Kimmel: "Because of the great importance of continuing to reinforce the Philippines with long-range army bombers you are requested to take all practical precautions for the safety of the airfields at Wake and Midway."[34]

Still seeking to allay the fears of the uneasy chief of staff, in a memorandum later that day Stark assured Marshall that the navy would take special precautions to safeguard Wake and Midway and acknowledged the importance of the continued delivery of B-17s to the Philippines via the two bases. Although Midway's defenses were complete, he acknowledged that those on Wake were not. Nor did Wake's garrison have enough men to serve the guns then emplaced there. That crews for those weapons existed in Hawaii must have seemed small consolation to the anxious army officers. Stark also telephoned Brigadier General Leonard T. Gerow, chief of the army's War Plans Division, and told him the gist of what he had told the chief of staff orally and in writing.[35]

The disturbing international situation prompted continued and determined preparations for hostilities in the Pacific. Kimmel ordered Rear

Admiral Bloch to put the outlying islands on alert, and Rear Admiral Thomas Withers, Commander, Submarines, Scouting Force (ComSub-ScoFor), to employ Pacific Fleet submarines on simulated war patrols. Kimmel directed Withers to have six boats readied to depart for Japanese home waters on short notice. In accordance with WPPac-46, Withers sent the *Narwhal* (ss-168) (Lieutenant Commander Charles W. Wilkins in command) and the *Dolphin* (ss-169) (Lieutenant Commander Gordon B. Rainer), two of the oldest fleet boats in the force, to Wake. Both sailed from Pearl on 17 October to inaugurate patrols within a fifteen-mile radius of the atoll, enjoined to report any contacts and be prepared to "take offensive action only if attacked" or if CinCPac ordered them to do so.[36]

In response to Kimmel's directive, Rear Admiral Bloch, whom CinC-Pac had included as an information addressee to his orders to Withers, sent a message that day to the naval air stations at Midway, Johnston, and Palmyra, as well as to the marine detachment at Wake: "In view international situation assume alert status."[37]

Upon receiving that dispatch, Major Devereux immediately summoned Dan Teters to a meeting in the latter's office in Camp 2. Up to that point, as Teters later admitted candidly, despite the "considerable war talk" that had gone around, "there had been so many false rumors and unsubstantiated reports that we . . . were pretty well lulled into a [false] sense of security." Others attending included Lieutenant Commander Greey and the visiting George Youmans from the CPNAB OpCom headquarters.

Devereux informed the little group of the alert he had just received. Teters later recalled that "a general discussion followed concerning immediate activities and also procedure[s] in the event of attack." In keeping with the study on the defense of outlying bases, the group agreed that in the event of war "the civilian laborers would mine the airfield, take over all transportation, feed the entire population, and take over all other work" to free the marines for "purely military duties." Should the island be attacked, the volunteers who had been trained by the marines would attach themselves to the defense force. Despite the "alert status" that Bloch had ordered Devereux to observe, however, ComFourteen seemed unwilling to direct the CPNAB people to do anything other than fulfill their contractual obligations to erect only base facilities, not defenses.

While the marines went on the alert and the CPNAB men continued building an airfield and beginning the submarine base that had been added to Wake's list of projects that same month, the *Curtiss* reached Wake on 21 October, as did the *Seminole*, which had sailed from Honolulu on 7 October with twenty-two CPNAB passengers and towing the barges *PAB No. 2* and *PAB No. 9*. It had been a rough passage for the sturdy tug because about an hour and a half past sunset on 15 October, the tow wire had carried away, leaving the barges adrift and necessitating the *Seminole*'s maneuvering as necessary to keep her errant charges in sight. She recovered the barges the following morning, but they came adrift again on the afternoon of the eighteenth. A "huge sea" breaking over the stern of the tug hurled three men against bitts and hatch coamings, injuring them. The surging water likewise prevented a party of the *Seminole*'s seamen from renewing the port side of the towing bridle on the nineteenth.

On the morning after the *Curtiss*'s arrival, Major Devereux and Lieutenant Commander Greey went out to the ship to confer with Commander Samuel P. Ginder, the tender's captain, only to be marooned there by the worsening weather as the *Curtiss* alternately drifted or steamed on courses set to await favorable weather to unload cargo or disembark passengers. The *Seminole* loitered off Wake's south coast, too, waiting to disembark the contractors she had on board and transfer the two barges to the *Pioneer* and the *Justine Foss*. The tug *Storm King*, one of three such craft chartered to service the outlying bases, arrived on the scene around the same time with two additional cargo-laden barges.

The pace of the development of Wake, Johnston, and Palmyra, meanwhile, pleased ComFourteen. Noting the increases in those garrisons, Rear Admiral Bloch wrote to the CNO on 23 October (more prophetically than he could know with respect to Wake): "Anyone who wants these places now will have quite a tussle to get them."[38]

On the twenty-sixth, the *Narwhal* and the *Dolphin* arrived off Wake's south coast, and their captains called for a conference on board the *Curtiss* "to arrange for cooperation between [the] forces present." The rough seas compelled the two submarines to "proceed close inshore to find sufficient lee" to allow the *Curtiss* to lower a boat, but once on board, Lieutenant Commanders Wilkins and Rainer informed Devereux and Ginder of their mission and the operations they were to conduct. Then they went over recognition signals and formulated a communication plan. Before they left the tender (each bearing five gallons of ice cream for their respective crews, a gift from Commander Ginder), Wilkins and Rainer requested Devereux to inform any patrol planes in the vicinity of their "prescence and location" and to inform them of any subsequent conferences the marine might deem necessary. They also requested Ginder to pass along what they had discussed with the captains of the destroyers *Jarvis* (DD-393) and *Blue* (DD-387), "due to arrive the next day."[39]

Stormy conditions delayed the mission assigned to the stores issue ship *Castor* (AKS-1), which arrived with the *Jarvis* and *Blue*, as scheduled, on the twenty-seventh. The *Castor* had sailed from Pearl on 18 October, the two destroyers providing her antisubmarine screen and the three-ship task unit under Commander Samuel B. Brewer in the *Jarvis*. The stores issue ship brought out Major George H. Potter, a big, plain-spoken Montanan and graduate of the Naval Academy Class of 1927, slated to become Devereux's executive officer and the detachment's five-inch battery officer, and an additional 8 officers (slated to serve as battery commanders) and 194 enlisted men.

Also arriving at Wake on the twenty-seventh was the westbound *China Clipper*, with Major General Lewis H. Brereton, on his way to take command of MacArthur's fledgling Far East Air Force, and Rear Admiral Francis W. Rockwell, slated to assume command of the Sixteenth Naval District, among the passengers. Hard on the heels of the *Clipper*'s arrival, twenty-six B-17s began descending to land at the airstrip.

The arrival of the B-17Ds from the Nineteenth Bombardment Group under Lieutenant Colonel Eugene Eubank caused yet another interruption for Wake's marines. Crowded conditions at the field resulted in Private Robert E. Winslow accidentally backing a truck into the wing of one of the Flying Fortresses (for which "carelessness" he was "chastised severely") and damaging an aileron.[40] Fortunately, PanAir and CPNAB came to the rescue and effected repairs. While Wake's crushed, graded coral and shell airstrip proved adequate for twenty-five planes (although the tie-down rings were not spaced properly to accommodate the B-17s), the single available fifteen-hundred-gallon gasoline truck, once emptied, required two hours to refill—by hand. The army generously left six portable gasoline-powered pumps at Wake to service future flights.

The bad weather that had prevented the *China Clipper* from taking off prompted General Brereton to do some local sightseeing and chat with Rear Admiral Rockwell about the worsening international situation. Brereton marveled at the skill of the CPNAB people as they brought the barges in and noted that the weather had finally improved enough to allow the landing of the marines from the *Castor* on the thirtieth. The *Curtiss* disembarked her passengers in her fifty-foot motor launches at the same time.

The leathernecks who disembarked from the auxiliary, however, brought the strength of the Wake Detachment to only 15 officers and 373 enlisted men, much less than specified in the standard table of organization for a full battalion. Ideally, such a unit consisted of 900 marines manning a headquarters battery, three five-inch seacoast and

The surf pounding on the south shore of Wake, 1 November 1941. Note protruding coral heads. (Heinl, *The Defense of Wake*)

three three-inch antiaircraft batteries, a sound locator and searchlight battery, a .50-caliber antiaircraft battery, and a .30-caliber beach defense battery.[41]

One of the newly arrived officers, First Lieutenant Woodrow M. Kessler, described Wake as "an uninviting low-lying atoll," with a water tower that seemed to be "the most significant evidence of human habitation." He peered at the shoreline "trying to identify objects of comforting familiarity" but saw nothing except "sand, rocks, low bushes, the breaking surf, and sea birds." Viewing Wake from the *Castor*'s deck "was much like seeing an oasis in the desert," he later wrote, "but much less inviting when you knew what was actually there." It reminded him of a "replacement troop of cavalry after having travelled across plains and desert of the Southwest to finally come upon the isolated fort set up in Apache country."

Kessler and his fellow battery commanders soon found conditions as primitive as those at any fort on the frontier. Upon his first inspection of his assigned position on Toki Point, on the tip of Peale, Kessler found the two 5-inch/.51-caliber guns "bolted to a criss-cross of huge timbers . . . buried in the coral sand." An "unfinished circular wall of sandbags about two feet high"—a protective feature that neither Battery A, on Wake, nor Battery L, on Wilkes, had—surrounded the guns. The Ford fire-control director had been placed in position but had no protection; there were no ammunition magazines.

Having learned before he had left Pearl that his future battery did not possess one, he had managed to acquire a twenty-foot Model 1911 coincidence range finder that he had to emplace some thirty feet from the director. Telephone wires had been buried only three inches beneath

The mouth of Wilkes Channel (left) and a portion of Wake (right), as seen from the bridge of the seaplane tender *Curtiss* (AV-4), 1 November 1941. Note buoyed gasoline hose in foreground and tanks of the fuel dump at right. (Heinl, *The Defense of Wake*)

Another view from the *Curtiss*'s bridge, 1 November 1941, showing Camp 1 visible just above the seaplane tender's bow, clearly illustrates one enduring first impression of Wake as an "uninviting low-lying atoll." (Heinl, *The Defense of Wake*)

the sand, and wires had been laid atop the ground from the director to the nearby Battery D. Looking at the position for the first time, Kessler sensed a "lack of elbow room" on Toki Point because of the cheek-by-jowl position of the two batteries, which made them a concentrated target. He further noted that the brush on Wake was conspicuous by its absence on that part of Peale, making it difficult, if not impossible, to use natural camouflage.

While the marines who had arrived in the *Castor* acclimated themselves to their new surroundings, the weather improved enough to permit the delayed *China Clipper* to get aloft. Headwinds and a typhoon in her path, however, compelled her precipitate return to Wake. That evening, the eastbound *Clipper* arrived, with twenty-two passengers on board, overburdening the accommodations. The crowding was no respector of rank: General Brereton slept little, sharing a room with Rear Admiral Rockwell and Brereton's chief of staff, Colonel Francis M. Brady; the latter snored so loud that the general "knocked a water pitcher off the table throwing a pillow" at him.[42]

Eventually, the weather cleared enough so both *Clippers* could resume their respective aerial voyages. Her mission completed, the *Seminole* departed Wake on the morning of the thirty-first, the *Storm King* around midday and the *Castor*, along with the *Jarvis* and the *Blue*, shortly before midnight. On board the cargo ship was First Lieutenant Heles, the first of the original complement of junior officers of the Wake unit to be detached. For the *Curtiss*, however, more work remained; on 1 November she pumped 210,000 gallons of hundred-octane gasoline to fuel tanks ashore. Three Dutch Catalinas landed in the lagoon that day, en route to the Netherlands East Indies.

Back at Pearl Harbor, Rear Admiral Bloch received orders from Secretary of the Navy Knox on 31 October to initiate the immediate evacuation of dependents from the outlying bases. The PanAir wives had been flown out earlier, and Florence Teters had to leave her husband; she boarded the next eastbound *Clipper* and departed Wake on 1 November.

The movement of the B-17s through Wake had revealed that the navy's handling of messages sometimes caused a twenty-four-hour delay and PanAir's people seemed unable to operate the homing beacon to satisfy the army. Colonel Clay I. Hoppaugh, the communications officer for the Hawaiian Air Force, felt that Wake constituted the most critical link in the communication chain between Hickam and Manila. The officer charged with reorganizing the radio traffic of the Philippines-bound bombers, Captain Henry S. Wilson, Signal Corps (Army Air Force) felt that Wake's importance required upgrading its radio facilities. Consequently, the army earmarked for Wake a long-range SCR-197 radio installation and loaded it on board the *William Ward Burrows*, which sailed on 1 November from Honolulu with the men detailed to place it in operation also on board. Although developed to air corps specifications for a big, powerful mobile radio that could be transported by plane or truck, that service had found the SCR-197 cumbersome and unsatisfactory, complaining of its poor mobility, an underpowered truck, and an overcrowded trailer.

Up to that point, the Wake Detachment had been free of breaches of discipline. On 3 November, however, Private First Class James O. King disobeyed the order of a noncommissioned officer; the court remitted his reduction to the next inferior grade if he could "maintain a record satisfactory to his CO [commanding officer] for the next three months."[43]

Three days after the *William Ward Burrows* began her voyage to Wake, on 4 November, the venerable fleet tug *Sonoma* (AT-12) embarked seventeen sailor passengers, one of whom, Seaman Second Class Floyd A. Dixon, held orders to report to the naval air station (NAS) at Wake as an aerographer striker. The following day, with PanAir barge *PAB No. 10* in tow, the *Sonoma* sailed for Wake; she was to pick up *PAB No. 6* at Midway en route.

While work proceeded on the facilities and the marines toiled on the gun positions, troubles with the *Columbia* continued, too. A heart ailment, perhaps induced by stress, had compelled W. A. Hanscom, the dredge superintendent, to leave Wake on 7 November to return to the United States for treatment. Less than a week later, the discontented crew alleged that promised bonuses had not been paid them, although the work the *Columbia* was to perform was far behind schedule.

By early November, international tensions hung over the Pacific like a threatening cloud; the United States and Japan deadlocked over their respective policies. In an attempt to sever the diplomatic Gordian knot, General Tojo, on two days' notice, dispatched Kurusu Saburo, who as ambassador to Germany had signed the Tri-Partite Pact with the Germans and Italians, as a special envoy to assist Ambassador Nomura Kichasaburo in Washington. Because of the urgency of the mission, the dapper Kurusu and his secretary, Yuki Shiroji, of the American Bureau of the Foreign Office, boarded the *Hong Kong Clipper* (which had been held for them) at Hong Kong and flew to Manila. There they caught the eastbound *China Clipper* and left the Philippine capital on 8 November.

Kurusu, who had served as Japanese consul in Chicago (1913–19), where he had met and married an American woman, Alice Little, harbored no illusions over the seriousness of the situation. On the eve of his departure from Japan he confided to his son Ryo that he might "not be able to come back" and enjoined Ryo to "look after the family." He knew he had difficult problems to solve, and undoubtedly they occupied his mind as he alighted from the *China Clipper* at Wake on 9 November, to be met by Major Devereux. The cold formality of their initial meeting warmed once they sat down in the lobby of the PanAir hotel. After they had ordered drinks—the Japanese envoy insisted "on paying for every round"—Kurusu "began to thaw," and the marine found ample evidence of his guest's "carefully acquired American slang and a good imitation of the airs of what Anglo-Saxons call 'a good fellow.'"

Expressing a preference for scotch and soda, to which he had become accustomed while serving in Manila (1919–22), Kurusu spoke "perfect English" as they chatted for nearly an hour, skirting "the one topic that must have been uppermost in both our minds." "Once he agreed with me," Devereux later recorded, "that if people could travel more and so come to know each other in their home countries, 'perhaps these things [international tensions] would not come up.'" Kurusu, who twice mentioned that he had married an American woman, stated at one point: "I am just going to Washington to see what I can do. I hope I can straighten out affairs and avoid trouble."[44] When they parted company, Devereux sensed that Kurusu, who left Wake on 10 November, sincerely hoped to avoid war between the United States and Japan.[45]

The day after the Japanese envoy's departure, the *William Ward Burrows* reached the atoll and unloaded, among other cargo, the SCR-197 equipment. She also disembarked Second Lieutenant Robert T. Hosken, Signal Corps, of the 324th Signal Company (Aviation) and Sergeants James B. Rex and Harry W. Burpee of the 407th Signal Company (Aviation), Staff Sergeant Clifford E. Hotchkiss and Sergeant Carl W. Dilkes of the Headquarters Squadron of the Eighteenth Bombardment Group, and Sergeant Ernest G. Rogers, Jr., and Private First Class Paul F. Fultrup of the Air Corps Detachment, Communications, the men assigned to place the system in operation.

Another passenger who left the transport that day was Lieutenant (j.g.) Gustave Mason Kahn, MC, USNR, slated to relieve Lieutenant Commander Pierson—who embarked in the "Weary Willie" on the thirteenth to return to Oahu—as the detachment's medical officer. Kahn, born in Galveston, Texas, had been appointed assistant surgeon, with the rank of lieutenant (j.g.), USNR, in August 1936. He had attended Purdue and Vanderbilt universities and earned his medical degree from the University of Texas Medical College. In February 1941, he had been assigned to the First Defense Battalion. "A dermatologist in civilian practice," then First Lieutenant Kessler recalled of Kahn, the newly arrived medico "spent hours studying an old anatomy book . . . drawing and redrawing the illustrations so as to fix the details in his mind." He also shared an interest in listening to records with Captain Platt; both enjoyed, among other things, Gilbert and Sullivan's *Mikado*.[46]

Perhaps engendered by the pace at which work was proceeding on Wake, eight days after Private First Class King had had a run-in with a noncom, Private First Class Earl M. Broyles, Jr., USMCR, went beyond verbal disobedience and struck a noncommissioned officer "in the execution of his duties" on 11 November. Broyles was sentenced to lose $15 per month for the next six months.[47]

Their gear was ashore within two hours of their arrival on the eleventh, and the U.S. Army Detachment, Wake Island, moved its equipment to the airfield: the K-19C trailer (the operating position) adjacent to the parking mat and the K-18C truck (transmitter unit) about a thousand feet east of the trailer.[48] Although their first attempt to raise Hickam Field failed on the day they arrived, Hosken and his men established communication with Oahu the following day. By the time they had done so, CinCPac had begun the process of furnishing Wake with an aviation component to its defenses, little knowing that the Japanese navy was taking steps to add the atoll to its own defensive perimeter. Among the tasks assigned Vice Admiral Inoue's Fourth Fleet in early November was the capture of Wake Island early the following month. Admiral Kimmel's actions had come not a moment too soon. Only time would tell whether they were too late.

"LIKE THE FATTED CALF"

Wake's exposed and isolated position among the outlying bases, as well as the probability that it would be an early Japanese objective in the event of a Pacific war, compelled Admiral Kimmel to urge the swift completion of its defenses. Less than a fortnight after the arrival of the *Castor* and the same day the *William Ward Burrows* arrived at Wake, on 10 November 1941 (Pearl Harbor date), Kimmel informed Commander Aircraft, Battle Force (ComAirBatFor) (Vice Admiral William F. Halsey, Jr.) and Commander Patrol Wing (ComPatWing) 2 (Rear Admiral Patrick N. L. Bellinger) that he wanted twelve patrol planes and either twelve marine scout bombers or marine fighters based at Wake. He also wanted twelve additional patrol planes (to augment the twelve already based there) and either eighteen marine scout bombers or marine fighters at Midway. To minimize the logistical demands on the air stations, CinCPac required that the planes be flown in (the landplanes delivered by carrier) and that they operate once there "without attendant transportation of material or personnel by ship."

These units were to operate independently for six weeks, then the planes or flight crews would be rotated out or additional men brought in by ship. "Tools, spares, and equipment for minor repairs, adjustments, and checks" would be transported along with the minimum number of men necessary to operate the planes, assuming the full availability of sailors and marines "already present for non-technical manpower assistance."

Deeming the supply of machine-gun ammunition at Wake sufficient, Kimmel directed that 150 of the hundred-pound bombs there be earmarked for use by marine planes. The patrol plane crews would live at Camp 2, but the marines would have to make do "adjacent to the landplane runways" in a tent camp built by marines—again interrupting the erection of defensive works. He directed ComPatWing 2 to transport men and matériel by seaplane tender and ComFourteen to make bombs available at the two stations, to provide for stowing them near the landplane runways there, and to ensure that CPNAB made accommodations available. He also charged the latter with arranging the bulk subsistence and potable water requirements of the advanced detachments, for expanding stowage of aviation gasoline at Wake, for estimating the gas and oil requirements, for providing lumber for the required tent camps, and for seeing that NAS and marine defense units made men available for the construction of camps and, after the planes arrived, for providing ground support for aircraft operations.

Resupplying the outlying islands, however, a task that had haunted Bloch from the beginning, prompted him to complain to Admiral Stark on 14 November that the recent increases there had "overtaxed our ability" to do so. If he could not get another ship, he declared, he would have to decrease the number of civilian workmen because he knew that Kimmel would not want to reduce his garrisons. Bloch thought that Wake's projects were progressing well, but he, like Admiral Kimmel, evidently believed that Washington would provide the Pacific commanders with ample warning of imminent hostilities with Japan—or could buy time. "Wake Island is making splendid progress," Bloch declared to Stark on 14 November, "and if you can hold off unpleasantness until after April or May [1942] I believe that we will have enough harbor completed to get a thirty-foot [draft] ship into a projected anchorage."[1]

As if underscoring the tempo at which Wake's garrison was toiling to ready the defenses to meet the expectations of those above them in the chain of command, on 14 November 1941, Bill Halstead wrote to his brother Ray, who had just enlisted in the Marine Corps, "We're working like Hell out here."[2]

On 15 November, Second Lieutenant Hosken's army communicators took over the link to Port Moresby from the navy radio station at Wake (NCL) and borrowed a generator from the marines to provide power for a complete radio station. A few days later, after erecting lance poles between the truck and the trailer, the requisite power, keying, and interphone lines overhead between those two points, and requisitioning a small stock of gasoline and oil for the equipment, Hosken's men established communication with the army radio station at Midway (EY3).

Back at Pearl on 17 November, Commander Winfield Scott Cunningham, who only a week before had been detached from the *Wright*, reported back on board the ship that had been his home since late May of the previous year, with orders assigning him the task of officer in charge of naval activities, Wake Island. Originally ordered to command NAS Johnston Island, Cunningham had been assigned Wake instead just two days before.

A quiet but energetic member of the Naval Academy Class of 1921, "Spiv" Cunningham had flown fighters and flying boats and had been

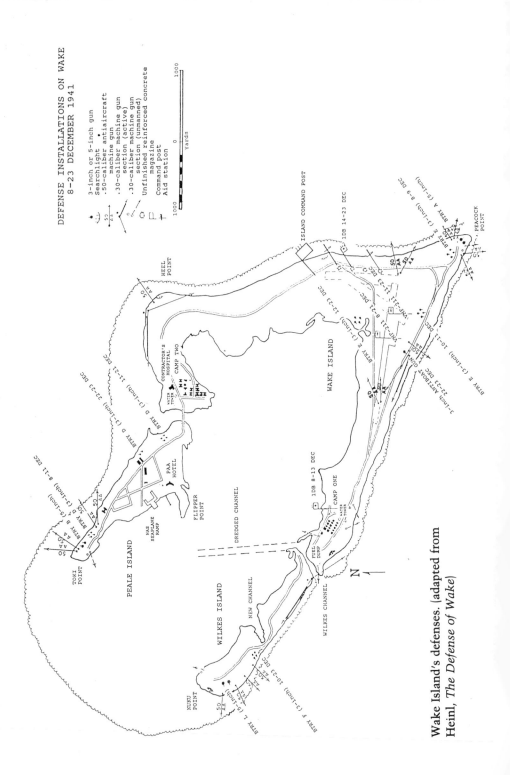

Wake Island's defenses. (adapted from Heinl, *The Defense of Wake*)

Captain Winfield S. Cunningham, in a post–World War II view. (NHC, NH 102629)

schooled in strategy and tactics. His contemporaries regarded him as energetic, unswervingly loyal, quick-witted, and coolheaded, with exceptional moral courage. Those who served under his command found him to be quiet and somewhat reserved, never harsh or assertive, a man who kept to himself but who always had a trace of a smile on his lips.[3] His long and varied experience in aviation duty had left him well-fitted for the independent administrative duty entrusted to him at Wake. Cunningham had been to the island twice before, during the *Wright's* support of PBY ferry flights to the Philippines in June and December 1940. His being sent to Wake reflected the policy adopted for Midway, Johnston, and Palmyra, where the NAS commanding officer would be senior to all other unit commanders on the island.[4]

Other embarking passengers included two junior officers from the PatWing 2 communications pool, Ensigns George H. ("Buck") Henshaw and Bernard J. ("Ben") Lauff, USNR, who had volunteered for duty setting up communications for the new NAS Wake. Heretofore, the task of encoding and decoding messages had been handled by the marine officers—another disruption of their work setting up the atoll's defenses.

When Henshaw informed his adopted uncle, Rear Admiral William L. Calhoun, commander, Base Force, on board the auxiliary *Argonne* (AG-31), where he and Ben Lauff were going, a look of dismay crossed Calhoun's countenance as he said, "I hope you two guys look good in a kimono."[5]

The following day, twenty-six sailors, who were to handle flying boat operations at the atoll, trooped on board the *Wright*, as did Ensign James J. Davis, SC, USNR, age twenty-five, who held a bachelor of science degree in chemical engineering from the Georgia School of Technology. Commissioned ensign in the Supply Corps on 15 August 1938, Davis had served as disbursing officer for Destroyer Division 1 and later as fuel and outgoing stores officer at NAS Pearl Harbor before being ordered to Wake.

While the Wake-bound sailors were getting settled on board the *Wright*, providing Wake with a marine air component was the difficult first order of business for the new commanding officer of Marine Aircraft Group (MAG) 21, Lieutenant Colonel Claude A. ("Sheriff") Larkin, who had relieved Lieutenant Colonel Lewie G. Merritt at Ewa Mooring Mast Field that very morning. His first letter—"short and full of grief"—to Brigadier General Ross E. Rowell, commander of the Second Marine Aircraft Wing at San Diego, recounted the shortages the imminent movement, "which," he wrote, "is most confidential and which I can not write you" would cause his new command.

"We are putting 108 enlisted men aboard [*sic*] a Navy ship in the morning," Larkin wrote on 18 November. "Within a day or so, we will embark thirty VSB planes and eighteen VF type planes for an operation which will require a minimum of six weeks and may go up as high as six months. When these planes are embarked, they will be flown by officer pilots and a crew chief for each airplane including the VFs. As you can see, this takes forty-eight officers away from the group and an additional forty-eight men." After recounting the various moves of pilots within the group, he continued, "You can see I am stripped of officers and must have replacements for the ones we have lost and a few additional in order to carry on as required by the Commander-in-Chief and Commander Aircraft, Battle Force." He requested that Rowell send the fighting squadron then at San Diego, VMF-221, out to Oahu as soon as Vice-Admiral Halsey could provide transportation.

The following day, 19 November, the fleet submarines *Triton* (SS-201) (Lieutenant Commander Willis A. Lent) and *Tambor* (SS-198) (Lieutenant Commander John W. Murphy, Jr.) departed Pearl to relieve the *Narwhal* and *Dolphin*. That same morning, the move that Sheriff Larkin had lamented began to unfold as 107 enlisted marines and 2 navy corpsmen, drawn from Headquarters and Service Squadron (HQ&SS) 21, Marine

Fighting Squadron (VMF) 211, and Marine Scout-Bombing Squadrons (VMSB) 231 and 232, received orders to embark, along with their equipment, in the *Wright* for what they were only told was "advanced base exercises." Larkin tapped Second Lieutenant Robert "J" Conderman, from VMF-211, to command one of the advanced base detachments, Second Lieutenant Loren D. Everton, from VMSB-232, the other. It had not been decided which units would be sent to which bases so each detachment would be a composite of men and matériel from three squadrons.

The youthful, red-haired, freckled, Conderman—whom Cunningham thought looked "scarcely more than a boy"—had been born in New York and had graduated from the University of North Carolina with a bachelor's degree in commerce in 1939.[6] Commissioned a second lieutenant in the USMCR upon graduation, he commenced aviation training at Pensacola on 28 December 1939, was awarded his wings on 4 September 1940, and was assigned to duty with the Second Marine Aircraft Wing soon thereafter.

Also embarking on board the *Wright* on the nineteenth was affable thirty-five-year-old Major Walter L. J. Bayler, who had been pulled from the MAG-21 staff with orders to establish a base radio station for air-ground communications at Wake. Bayler, a member of the Naval Academy Class of 1927 and a classmate of the Wake Detachment's executive officer, Major Potter, was MAG-21's adjutant and radio officer. He had received postgraduate training at the Naval Academy and a master of science degree from Harvard University in 1933. "Jolly . . . kind and congenial toward all—ready to lend a helping hand to anyone in need of it," an academy classmate had once written, "he [Bayler] is one whom all would like to have as a shipmate and friend."[7] Once Bayler had set up Wake's installation, he was to set up a similar station at Midway.

The *Wright* sailed on 20 November. In addition to the navy and marine aviation people on board, there were two officers—First Lieutenant Bryghte D. ("Dan") Godbold and Second Lieutenant Robert W. Greeley, USMCR—and five enlisted men earmarked for duty with the defense battalion, as well as four CPNAB contractors, one of whom, Joseph T. McDonald, was to assume the post of recreation director. That same day, when the *Wright* was en route to her destination, Rear Admiral Bloch announced the formal establishment of NAS, Wake Island.[8]

In the meantime, the *Sonoma*, having often used her main trysail and staysail as she plodded westward, observed the glow of the lights on Wake late on 23 November. She stood in the next morning and, aided by most unseasonal weather, transferred her tows to the *Pioneer* and *Justine Foss*. She moored at 0843 and disembarked Seaman Second Class

Second Lieutenant Robert "J"
Conderman, USMCR, ca. September
1941. (Mrs. Virginia Putnam)

Major Walter L. J. Bayler, ca. 1942. (USMC)

Dixon at 0915. On the day the *Sonoma* fueled for her return voyage, 25 November (Wake date), the *Triton* and the *Tambor* arrived on station. The next day, the *Justine Foss* brought out two barges, *PAB No. 2* and *PAB No. 4*, and the *Sonoma* took them in tow; shortly after sunset, the navy tug sailed for Honolulu.

On the twenty-sixth, two B-17s arrived from Midway with a complete field lighting system because the one called for in the navy's contract would have had only 70 percent of the preparatory work done on it by the end of November and no work at all on the actual site. One of the Flying Fortresses brought Captain Wilson to take charge of the army communications detachment on Wake. Over the ensuing days, although they did not get to know him very well, some of his men found him outspoken, overbearing, humorless, hotheaded, and easily irritated.

Back on Oahu, Admiral Kimmel received two dispatches from Admiral Stark on 26 November. In the first, the CNO urged Kimmel to consider the army's offer to make infantry available to reinforce the outlying islands—if CinCPac so desired—although no antiaircraft units could be provided. In the second, Stark informed CinCPac that to keep the Second Marine Aircraft Wing's planes available for expeditionary use, the War Department had assented to a request from the Office of the Chief of Naval Operations (OpNav) that the army station twenty-five pursuit planes at Midway and the same number at Wake—provided that Kimmel considered it "feasible and desirable." Kimmel would need to provide an aircraft carrier to transport the planes, however, and the men and matériel required to support them would have to be taken out by either the carrier or other ships. The War Department understood that the men would have to be quartered in tents and that the navy would have to supply water and subsistence as well as transport other gear. Stark enjoined Kimmel, however, that the stationing of army pursuits at Wake (and Midway) must not interfere with the planned movement of army bombers to the Philippines. If the international situation required it, army bombers might be sent to the outlying bases to support navy operations. Stark asked if the bombs then at those stations could be carried by army aircraft.[9]

Because the deployment of pursuit planes significantly reduced the army's aerial umbrella available to protect Oahu, during the discussions with his staff about the War Department's offer Kimmel asked Captain Charles H. McMorris, his war plans officer, when he thought there would be an air attack upon Pearl. "Soc" McMorris answered unequivocally: "Never."[10] Kimmel himself had come to regard such a possibility as "remote."[11]

As Stark had directed, Kimmel conferred with Lieutenant General Walter C. Short, commanding general of the Hawaiian Department.

Kimmel asked what he could expect of army fighters based at Wake, and when told by Brigadier General Frederick L. Martin, the commander of the Hawaiian Air Force, that they were not allowed "to go more than fifteen miles offshore," the admiral replied that in that case, "they are no damn good to me." Short pointed out that if army troops were placed on the outlying islands, he would have to command them. "Over my dead body," Kimmel shot back, "the Army should exercise no command over Navy bases." "Mind you, I don't want those islands," Short replied, "I think they are better manned by Marines. But if I must put planes and troops on them then I must command them."[12] Kimmel, however, was not about to take up the War Department on its offer of pursuits and troops.

The next day, 27 November 1941, reflecting the serious international situation, the CNO—privy to information gleaned from intercepted and translated Japanese diplomatic message traffic—sent a priority dispatch to Admiral Kimmel and Admiral Thomas C. Hart, commander in chief of the Asiatic Fleet:

> This dispatch is to be considered a war warning X Negotiations with Japan looking toward stabilization of conditions in the Pacific have ceased and an aggressive move by Japan is expected within the next few days
>
> The number and equipment of Japanese troops and the organization of naval task forces indicates an amphibious expedition against either the Philippines Thai or Kra Peninsula or possibly Borneo
>
> Execute an appropriate defensive deployment preparatory to carrying out the tasks assigned in WPL-46 X Inform district and army authorities X A similar warning is being sent by War Department.[13]

As part of the "appropriate defensive deployment" that was to prepare the fleet to sally forth and carry out its war plan, Kimmel decided to leave Wake and Midway in the hands of the marines. Defense battalions, "organized, equipped, and trained for work of this particular character," were already established, "habited to the mode of life, and experienced in fitting their activities to accord with the various other naval activities" in the outlying bases. "It is no reflection upon the army to say," Kimmel reflected, "that their units would require considerable time to acquire the proficiency in this specialized work that the marines already have."[14]

As Kimmel later explained to the CNO, army fighters, though superior to the navy's and plentiful enough to allow for the basing of one squadron at each atoll, possessed no "offensive capabilities against hostile surface craft or submarines" and lacked navigational equipment. Additionally, army pilots lacked experience in flying over water and, consequently, were, in Kimmel's opinion (reflecting his recent conversation with Brigadier General Martin), "much averse to flying more than fifteen miles from land." Evacuating army planes flown into Wake would prove "virtually impossible" in an emergency because they were not equipped with arresting gear and could not be recovered by a carrier.[15] Consequently, Kimmel designated the *Enterprise* (cv-6) to ferry twelve of VMF-211's Grumman F4F-3 Wildcats to Wake and the *Lexington* (cv-2) to take eighteen Vought SB2U-3 Vindicators of VMSB-231 to Midway.[16]

That same day, Lieutenant Colonel Larkin told Major Paul A. Putnam, commanding officer of VMF-211, of an upcoming secret mission that was to be disguised as a training exercise. Putnam had relieved Major Charles L. Fike in command of 211 at Ewa just ten days before. As Fike's executive officer, the "calm, quiet, and determined" Putnam, whose personality contrasted markedly with that of his predecessor, had proved conspicuously able in carrying out his duties and handling men. Awarded his wings at Pensacola in May 1929—but, ironically, "not recommended for combat duty"—he had flown almost every type of marine plane from a Ford Trimotor to a Loening amphibian and from a Grumman F3F-2 to an F4F-3. He had distinguished himself in Nicaragua in 1931.[17]

Larkin instructed him to report to Captain George D. Murray, the *Enterprise*'s commanding officer, and confided to him that his ultimate destination was Wake. Putnam hurried over to Pearl and strode on board the carrier as she lay alongside Ten-Ten Dock but soon discovered that he was to report not to Murray but to Vice Admiral Halsey. When the two of them were alone in the flag officer's cabin, Halsey told the balding, soft-spoken marine of his upcoming errand. Curiosity seized Putnam. "What will be my mission," he asked, "to whom shall I report?"

"Putnam," the bushy-browed admiral growled, "I can't answer those questions. Your only orders are to go to Wake, and your only instructions are to do what seems appropriate when you get there." Cryptically, Halsey added that Putnam and his men could be "recalled . . . as suddenly and secretly" as they were being sent out. The admiral told Putnam to tell his pilots only that they were going to sea for two days. He was not to divulge 211's ultimate destination to anyone but his executive officer.

Soon thereafter, after having confided only in his executive officer, Captain Henry T. Elrod, Putnam told his pilots that "they were going to fly over to Maui for the night." They did not suspect that it was anything other than a routine "hop" until he emphasized that in the event of starter trouble they were to leave their plane at Ford Island and hitch a ride out to the *Enterprise* in a Douglas TBD-1 Devastator from Torpedo Squadron Six that would be standing by for such a contingency.

Despite the need for secrecy, that afternoon on board the *Enterprise*, scuttlebutt not only apparently indicated that she would be taking marines to sea the next day but where they were headed. "There was a lot of credence being given to the idea that mebbe [*sic*] we take the Marines to Wake," speculated Lieutenant (j.g.) Wilmer E. "Swede" Rawie of Fighting Squadron (VF) 6 in his diary, "[It] should be a nice ride."

On the same day that Paul Putnam learned of his mission, the *Wright* moored off Wilkes Channel. First Lieutenant Godbold and Second Lieutenant Greeley disembarked to take up their duties ashore, and Ensign Robert C. Walish, who had been employed for three years by the Dahlman Construction Company of Milwaukee on heavy construction projects and had served a tour at NAS Pensacola, soon joined Wake's burgeoning public works department.

Commander Cunningham went ashore soon thereafter, along with Ensign Davis and the three junior officers assigned to the Wake Base Detachment, Ensigns Henshaw, Lauff, and Chester W. Olcott. Major Bayler and Second Lieutenant Everton then disembarked, to begin establishing the communications and advance base facilities; by the end of the day on the twenty-eighth, all of the sailors and marines had gone ashore, too.

Cunningham, who had met Jim Devereux briefly at a picnic on Oahu

Major Paul A. Putnam, ca. September 1941. (Mrs. Virginia Putnam)

the previous summer, subsequently relieved him as senior naval officer on Wake. "Reassured . . . by the clear indications that Devereaux . . . was a good officer to have in my command," Cunningham thought Devereux "quiet in manner and conscientious in his application to duty."[18]

While the necessary preparatory work moved ahead at Wake, the movement of the planes the base was to support began. Outwardly, Halsey's sortie on the morning of 28 November (29 November, Wake date)—duly reported by the Japanese spies operating out of their consulate in Honolulu—appeared to be (and was, as specified in the quarterly operations schedule) the beginning of regularly scheduled training. Three battleships—the *Arizona* (BB-39), *Nevada* (BB-36), and *Oklahoma* (BB-37)—sailed with the *Enterprise* and attendant screening heavy cruisers and destroyers. The *William Ward Burrows* departed Oahu, *PAB No. 7* in tow, that same day, bound for Wake. Thirty-two marines, fifty-six sailors, and fifty-five civilians made up the passenger list as the transport once more turned in the direction of that familiar triangular atoll.

"Fully expect[ing] that the trip with these Marines was leading us into the lion's mouth," Halsey detached the battleships and a screen of destroyers, and his force became Task Force 8. Once at sea, with Halsey's approval, Captain Murray issued "Battle Order No. 1" declaring that Task Force 8 was operating under war conditions.[19]

As Oahu faded astern, the *Enterprise* recovered her air group—minus one Wildcat that had had starter trouble—but brought on board only eleven of VMF-211's Wildcats. A malfunctioning starter had grounded Second Lieutenant Frank J. Holden's F4F-3 at Ford Island, compelling him (like Ensign Eric Allen, the VF-6 pilot whose engine refused to start) to ride out to the ship in a Devastator.[20] Onlookers noted that the light gray color scheme of the marines' Wildcats that taxied out of the arresting gear and up the blue-stained flight deck, directed by the yellow-jerseyed plane handlers, contrasted markedly with the *Enterprise*'s planes, most of which had worn "war paint" (nonspecular blue-gray upper surfaces and light gray undersurfaces) for some time. To enable 211 to carry out its mission fully equipped, Halsey quickly "sold" one F4F-3 (BuNo 3988) from VF-6 to give Putnam the twelve he needed.

Despite the scuttlebutt, the only people who knew—officially —where they were going before the *Enterprise* task force had sailed, or before the first Wildcat had taken off from Ford Island, were Halsey, his chief of staff, Captain Miles R. Browning, VMF-211's commanding officer, Major Putnam, and his executive officer, Captain Elrod. If there was danger, "Talmage" Elrod was a good man to have on one's side. Born in Georgia in 1905, Elrod had attended the University of Georgia and Yale University, apparently uncertain as to whether to pursue a career as an architect or as a physician. He enlisted in the Marine Corps in 1927 and received his commission in 1931. Regarded by contemporaries as a colorful, hard-drinking maverick, close to the enlisted men in the unit, and a daredevil, hell-for-leather pilot, he had once angered the landing signal officer of the *Saratoga* (CV-3) during carrier qualifications in the spring of 1939 when he ignored a wave-off and came on board anyway. "In case of combat," though, then Captain Milo G. Haines, one of 211's pilots in the rear echelon left at Ewa, recalled "I'd rather be with him than against him."[21]

Putnam and Elrod may have known where they were headed (Putnam even packed fishing tackle and his .22-caliber rifle), but the other pilots, as Swede Rawie observed, appeared to have been caught "rather flat [footed]—they thought it would be an overnite stay." "Flat footed" or not, twenty-two-year-old Staff Sergeant Robert O. Arthur, one of 211's two enlisted pilots, was excited at the prospect of going to Wake. For the voyage, the marines shared quarters with their navy shipmates; Putnam, for example, roomed with Lieutenant Wilmer E. Gallaher, Scouting Squadron 6's executive officer. Young Staff Sergeant Arthur, though, slept in the more spartan surroundings of a paint locker.[22]

That same day, at Wake, Commander Campbell Keene came ashore from the *Wright* to command the Wake Base Detachment. The "big, bald, good-natured" Keene had attended Phillips Exeter Academy and Bowdoin College before enrolling in the Naval Reserve in November 1917. He received his commission five days before the armistice in 1918 and served ashore and afloat in duty that ranged from air stations to commanding aviation units in cruisers before becoming the *Wright*'s air officer in May 1940. Enlisted men regarded him affectionately as a "Hell-for-leather old cuss with a lot of punch."[23] "He cared about his men," Buck Henshaw later wrote, "and as a result his men cared for him."[24] Under Keene were the three officers and thirty enlisted men assigned to the recently established NAS Wake. Before his departure from Pearl, he had been told by Rear Admiral Bellinger "to prepare the island for patrol plane operations and to operate patrol planes when they arrived."[25]

The *Wright* continued to embark passengers during the day, including Technical Sergeant Burpee, his communication duties completed, four marines, thirty-three civilian contractors, and First Lieutenant Cy Emrich, his tour of duty at Wake finished. Later that afternoon, after Major Bayler and Second Lieutenant Everton received word of VMF-211's imminent arrival, they readjusted men and equipment to "better fulfill the needs of a fighting squadron." Everton reembarked in the *Wright* soon thereafter.[26]

The next morning, Second Lieutenant Conderman came ashore to join Major Bayler and command the advance base detachment. Second Lieutenant Hosken, his task done at Wake, embarked in the *Wright* at 0915, the last passenger to do so; the tender soon set course for Midway. That same day, the army detachment moved its transmitting equipment to a new location about five hundred feet behind the parking mat so the CPNAB men could continue working on the cross runway.

In the meantime, Major Bayler and Technical Sergeants Vincent W. Bailey and Harmen DeHann (the latter, at forty-one, the oldest marine in the advance base outfit at Wake) and Corporal Carroll E. Trego, USMCR, three enlisted radio operators from HQ&SS-21, set up the air-ground network. The leathernecks establishing the facilities and providing technical assistance for a twelve-plane fighting squadron included Second Lieutenant Conderman and thirteen enlisted men from VMF-211, a navy hospital corpsman from HQ&SS-21, fourteen enlisted men from VMSB-231 (a squadron normally equipped with Vought SB2U-3s), and sixteen from VMSB-232 (Douglas SBD-2s).

Notwithstanding the rumors about the task force's ultimate destination, no one on board Halsey's ships knew where they were going until the admiral made it official on 29 November. "We learned today that we are taking the marines to Wake to support the Patrol Group there," Ensign James G. Daniels III, of VF-6, wrote in his diary that night, "sure glad I can stay aboard [sic] this bucket."

Back at Pearl on 30 November, the war warning apparently prompted heightened concern for the safety of the outlying bases. Captain McMorris outlined "steps to be taken in case of [an] American-Japanese war within the next twenty-four hours." McMorris advocated allowing Task Force 8 to carry out its mission of delivering VMF-211 to Wake, after which Halsey was to cover Wake until joined by Task Force 3 (one heavy cruiser, with the commander of the Scouting Force, embarked). The battleships of Task Force 2 (that Halsey had detached), along with their accompanying destroyers, would return to Pearl. He then suggested that a modified raiding and reconnaissance plan be put into effect; cruiser operations west of Nanpo Shoto were canceled and any reconnaissance delayed until Task Force 2 and Task Force 3 could join up off Wake. Other measures concerning that atoll that McMorris enjoined CinCPac to contemplate included not modifying the *Wright*'s steaming toward Midway, directing the *William Ward Burrows* to continue on to Wake (Halsey was to detach two destroyers to screen her), and not withdrawing any civilian workmen from the outlying bases inasmuch as plans had been made to incorporate them into the defense organization. CinCPac's war plans officer decided that the *Regulus* should continue on to Midway (along with other ships then en route to Christmas and Canton islands) and escort the *Saratoga*, slated to leave the west coast the first week of December, to Pearl Harbor.[27]

While Kimmel and those who advised him considered options for Wake in the event of hostilities, within a few days' time a sailor came ashore at the atoll—although not voluntarily. Overnight occupants of Wake's small naval dispensary had been few and far between. Torpedoman Second Class Charles E. Daniel from the *Dolphin* had been transferred ashore for observation on 6 November but had returned to his ship two days later. The *Triton*'s crew had been healthy, with the exception of many colds. On the evening of 30 November, however, thirty-three-year-old Chief Electrician's Mate Harold R. Thompson, suffering from a high fever, had been placed on the sick list. His fever persisted for two days so at 0625 on 2 December, the *Triton* sent him ashore for medical attention, "diagnosis undetermined." He thus became the second temporary resident patient in Lieutenant (j.g.) Kahn's dispensary, joining Corporal Clarence G. Cooper, Jr., who had been injured on the morning of 22 November when a tractor had backed into him, inflicting a three-inch gash in his left knee, during the excavation of a searchlight position on Kuku Point.[28]

Meanwhile, on board the *Enterprise*, VF-6's pilots soon learned that none of the marines, who had turned in the last of their stubby Grumman F3F-2 biplanes on 10 October, had more than fifteen to twenty hours' flight time in the F4F-3. The marines had practiced little bombing or gunnery in their new mounts, which lacked homing gear and armor plate. Only one had self-sealing gasoline tanks. On top of that, for most of 211's pilots who came on board on 28 November, it was their first carrier landing in that type.[29] In response to Putnam's request that Fighting Six teach his pilots how to fly Wildcats, one VF-6 flier lamented wryly: "Wish *we* knew." Furthermore, VF-6's scribe felt that although the marines were good, "a dozen of them seems kind of light to take on the whole Jap air force." But despite their small numbers, Paul Putnam seemed confident that his men would give a good account of themselves.[30]

He knew, however, that though 211 was "excellently trained and well qualified for war duty in a general sense," it had only recently been equipped with an airplane "radically different from the type in which training had been conducted [Grumman F3F-2 biplanes]" out of Ewa—a type received "too recently to permit familiarization in tactical flying and gunnery." Reflecting in later years, he would bluntly assess the squadron's handling of planes, timing of maneuvers, and gunnery in late November and early December 1941, following its transition to the Wildcat, as "pitifully poor."

Nevertheless, the *Enterprise*'s air department pitched in to ready 211's Grummans as the carrier steamed westward. During one evening meal in the wardroom, Lieutenant Richard H. Best, Bombing Squadron 6's executive officer, overheard someone from VF-6 remark: "You would think that he [Putnam] is going to fight the war alone" because he seemed to be "scrounging all of the portable gear (small enough to be stored on board his planes) that he could from Fighting six to improve his spares."[31]

Covered by patrol planes flying from Midway and Johnston, as well as by the *Enterprise*'s own aircraft, Task Force 8 advanced steadily westward. On 30 November, while VF-6's Ensign John C. Kelley, A-V(N), a onetime Pensacola classmate of Frank Holden's, schooled VMF-211's pilots in gunnery and recognition silhouettes of Japanese planes (mostly fixed-gear or biplane types, one VF-6 pilot scoffed), painters from the ship's air department camouflaged the upper surfaces of 211's F4F-3s "war color," blue-gray, the same color scheme the *Enterprise*'s planes had worn for several weeks. Painters numbered the Wildcats 211-F-1 to 211-F-12 in black block characters.

Back at Pearl, PBY-3s from VP-22, under Lieutenant Commander Frank O'Bierne, started for Wake, where they would commence their patrols in support of Halsey's advance. They would arrive at the atoll late on the afternoon of 2 December.

Admiral Kimmel, meanwhile, worried. On 1 December, he had learned that the Japanese navy had changed its call signs. Fragmentary information gleaned from radio intelligence indicated that its carriers were in home waters, but no one knew for sure. Not only did the whereabouts of the Japanese carriers concern CinCPac, but so did the sustenance of Wake, the jewel in his outlying base crown.

"We cannot expect to supply Wake quickly and expeditiously," he wrote plaintively to Admiral Stark on 2 December, "until we have a space to put a ship alongside for loading and unloading." ComFourteen had been and continued to exert "every effort" toward having such facilities constructed, but none existed in December 1941. It was common knowledge that ships sometimes had to wait as long as four weeks for good weather to start unloading, and it was not unusual for discharging cargo, once begun, to take as long as a week to complete. "This, in the face of any opposition," Kimmel declared, "presents an impossible situation."[32] Facilities cried out for improvement, particularly those for the storage of fuel oil, aviation gasoline, food, and ammunition. The 1,146 contractors laboring there were essential if the work was to be completed as expeditiously as possible—Rear Admiral Bloch estimated that the ship channel would be completed in May 1942. The only way Kimmel could increase the number of marines at Wake was to decrease the number of contractors—and the press to finish building the bases there made that impossible.

By December 1941, even if the rest of the garrison necessary to man all of Wake's batteries existed on Oahu, as Kimmel candidly admitted, Wake did not have the facilities to support more people than were already there. Among these problems confronting Commander Greey and the contractors were delays in the delivery of pipe that would enable them to complete the sewer and water systems simultaneously with the barracks for the marines and sailors on Peale. Greey knew that the speedy completion of those buildings (the navy facility was 75 percent completed, the marine only 50 at the end of November) would enable the leathernecks to vacate Camp 1 and move into permanent quarters.

Kimmel reminded Stark that six five-inch and twelve three-inch guns had been emplaced there, "well knowing that we did not have sufficient Marine personnel to man them." But "good progress" had been made in organizing CPNAB workers to help man Wake's defenses. If tensions with Japan eased, Kimmel hoped that the marine fighters then on their way could be withdrawn, thus decreasing the strain on the facilities.[33]

In a dispatch to Stark, also on 2 December, Kimmel opposed interjecting army forces into the defense of the outlying bases, positing that "the current setup . . . is in accordance with long and well considered plans that should not now be changed." CinCPac intended to maintain the marine defense battalions already at Wake, as well as at Midway, Johnston, and Palmyra, and to continue basing marine planes at Wake and Midway "as circumstances require."[34]

That same day (3 December on Wake), Commander Cunningham completed his initial appraisal of the atoll's defenses in a progress and readiness report to Rear Admiral Bloch. Though satisfied with the number of navy officers and enlisted men under his command, he lamented the woefully understrength defense battalion. He urged that it be "brought up to full strength" to "properly prepare and man all required stations" and that the number of men assigned to the air station be increased to free the marines from the extra duty occasioned by the understrength aviation detachment. While allowing that he had not yet "sized up" the "assembly of outfit and stores," Cunningham noted the inadequate storage facilities. He expected that time would remedy the situation. The lack of medical facilities also concerned Cunningham. He considered the existing ones "inadequate." "Any increase in the number of cases," he declared, "would be difficult to handle as to [the] lack of space and equipment at the Marine camp." The sixteen-bed contractors' hospital in Camp 2, he observed, was "constantly filled."[35]

The *China Clipper* arrived from Guam at 1630 the same day. Cunningham met the ship upon her arrival, for among the disembarking

Aerial mosaic of Wake taken at 0900, 3 December 1941, from a Catalina of Patrol Wing 2—the last prewar view of the atoll in American hands. (NA, 80-G-411053)

passengers was Soviet diplomat Maxim Litvinov, en route to take up his post in Washington as Soviet ambassador, accompanied by his wife, Ivy, and secretary, Anastasia Petrova. Cunningham welcomed the war-weary travelers, informing the envoy that "we would do what we could to make his brief stay a pleasant one."

The commander of Wake's naval activities observed little of Litvinov's "keen intelligence . . . double-edged wit . . . lack of social graces" and fluent spoken English "irremediably tainted by years of association with London's East End slums," however, for the ambassador, perhaps suffering the effects of the arduous trip, turned down the offered hospitality "politely but briefly" before he fell into "glum silence." The British-born Madame Litvinov told Cunningham that she and her husband had had a long and tiresome journey. She politely asked a few questions about Wake, he later recalled, and "we chatted about the weather, and at the hotel I left them." When they parted company, Cunningham noted that the portly envoy, wearing a "plain and some-what rumpled business suit," forced a "perfunctory smile." Litvinov, out of communication with his government during the arduous trip that had taken him from the provisional capital in Kuibyshev to Iran and Singapore, had good reason to be glum and silent because his country was hard-pressed by Hitler's legions. "There was clearly little we . . . could do to make [him] comfortable," Cunningham reflected thought-fully, "and even less to ease his preoccupation with world conditions." Madame Litvinov went to the movies that night, escorted by Second

Lieutenant Poindexter, but said little during the course of the evening's entertainment. The *China Clipper* took off the next day for Midway.

On board the *Enterprise*, steaming resolutely toward Wake, Paul Putnam took pencil and paper in hand on 3 December and brought Sheriff Larkin up to date on 211's activities and reflected on the previous days' events. Halsey, he wrote, had spared nothing to see that the marines got off with twelve planes in as fine a condition as possible. "All hands . . . have continuously vied with each other to see who could do the most for me. I feel a bit like the fatted calf being groomed for whatever it is that happens to fatted calves." He also noted Halsey's determination "to maintain secrecy regarding the position and activity of this Force," reflected in the continuous inner air patrol during the day and a full squadron search to the front and flanks each morning and evening. "Armed to the teeth," he wrote, they had orders "to attack any Japanese vessel or aircraft on sight in order to prevent the discovery of this Force." After reflecting on his vague orders to do what was "appropriate" upon his arrival, Putnam asked jokingly: "What's the price on starting a war these days?"[36]

At 0530 on 4 December, the *Enterprise* launched the day's first combat air patrol, followed by an antisubmarine patrol and a scouting flight. As the air operations unfolded, 211's pilots climbed into their cockpits, Second Lieutenant John F. Kinney carrying a bon voyage present from Swede Rawie of VF-6—a bottle of scotch.[37] Shortly after 0700, when a VP-22 Consolidated PBY Catalina from the squadron that arrived at Wake on 2 December began orbiting the formation, VMF-211's Wildcats roared down the *Enterprise*'s Douglas fir flight deck and wobbled aloft. They circled the carrier after she had completed flight operations, while her scout bombers proceeded ahead. The *Enterprise* then signaled the PBY to escort the marines to Wake, and at 0730 the Wildcats and the Catalina set out. Later that day, the pilot of one of the searching planes from the *Enterprise* sighted what looked like three unidentified ships in formation, but it proved to be the Oahu-bound *Sonoma* with the two PanAir barges in tow astern.

Halsey's schedule called for his force to reach Pearl on the afternoon of 6 December to keep up the appearance of a usual training evolution that saw the ships return to port for the weekend. On board the carrier that night, a VF-6 diarist expressed relief that the marines had gotten away without incident and reached their destination safely. "And now," he wrote, "let's get the hell out of here before they decide to leave us. All hands agreed that this is no place for a plane with no armor plate and no self-sealing gas tanks."[38]

Their destination lay ahead of Putnam's twelve Wildcats. On 4 December, the *Wake Wig-Wag*, reporting world news gleaned from the regular news broadcasts from San Francisco, Los Angeles, and Shanghai, China, said the United States and Japan were at an impasse over the situation in the Far East. The *Wig-Wag* noted that Assistant Secretary of the Navy Ralph Bard, speaking in Norfolk, Virginia, had declared that the navy did not underestimate Japan's power in the Pacific and was "thoroughly prepared to face the fact that in the event of trouble in the Pacific that trouble will not be a minor one." In a more bellicose tone, Congressman Andrew Jackson May, the Kentucky Democrat who chaired the powerful House Military Affairs Committee, suggested to newsmen that President Roosevelt tell the Japanese to renounce their imperial aspirations "or we will blow them out of the air and off the water."

Such thoughts probably meant little to those on Wake. In the days since his arrival, Commander Cunningham had familiarized himself, as best he could, with the defenses and was energetically occupied with the administrative business of naval activities on Wake; Major Devereux continued to drive his marines hard. By the end of November, all of the preparation work for NAS Wake had been completed and the off-site work for most of the buildings was nearly done. Only the seaplane ramp on Peale had been finished, but the garage and fire station were 85 percent completed. The submarine base, a comparatively recent addition to the program, however, existed largely on paper; of the twenty-seven projects, ranging from piers, a quay wall, and berthing facilities, to fuel and diesel oil storage and roads, walks, and distribution systems, preparatory work had been done only on twelve. No actual construction had begun.

Once they taxied their planes to a stop and climbed out of their cockpits and set foot on the ground at their new advance base, VMF-211's ten officer and two enlisted pilots found Wake to be far less "advanced" than they had anticipated. The five-thousand-foot east-west crushed coral runway looked long enough, but it was wide enough for only one plane to take off at a time—thus prolonging the time needed for the squadron to get aloft. A tie-down area easily accommodated the twelve F4Fs, but the ground around it was so rough that moving planes over it, even by hand, might cause serious damage. Fueling at the field could be done from tank trucks, but those vehicles had to be filled by hand from fifty-five-gallon drums. The necessary support, Putnam soon found, was also not what he had anticipated: the exigencies of war meant that his squadron had to operate new planes without proper instruction manuals, maintained by aircraft or engine mechanics more familiar with Douglas SBD-2s and Vought SB2U-3s than Grumman F4F-3s.

The new arrivals spent most of the first day sorting out supplies and transporting tents to the new field to prepare their accommodations by the only means available—a pickup and a two-ton truck. Meanwhile, Putnam conferred with Cunningham, Keene, and Devereux on setting up the air patrols and agreed to have four F4Fs aloft on patrol while four stood by at the downwind end of the strip. The remaining four would be at the field for upkeep.

Cunningham and Keene then met with Lieutenant Commander Greey and Dan Teters and decided to employ the contractors' force to build the necessary revetments for planes and men. That same day (4 December), unbeknownst to the men on Wake, Lieutenant Ando Nobuo reconnoitered the atoll in a Mitsubishi G4M1 Type 1 land attack plane (*rikkō*) from Roi, in the Marshalls.[39]

On Friday, 5 December—the day Major Devereux wrote optimistically to his wife that they were "ready for anything"—the PBYs that had covered Task Force 8's advance departed the atoll, and the civilian tug *Arthur Foss* (Captain Oscar Ralsteadt, master), with two barges in tow, arrived. Indicative of the still primitive nature of NAS Wake, Rear Admiral Bellinger soon observed that VP-22's twelve PBY-3s returned to Pearl "in relatively poor material condition because of its extended operations at advance bases [Wake and Midway] with inadequate facilities for repair and upkeep."[40] VMF-211's men, meanwhile, removed all the excess gear—spark plugs, starter cartridge shells, and hard tail wheels—brought in on board the Wildcats.

Cunningham had directed Putnam to conduct a 360-degree search around the island with a radius of not less than fifty miles. Dawn and dusk flights of four planes commenced on 5 December, combining search with rudimentary navigation and instrument training, to allow the pilots to "find out something more about the airplanes than just to pick them up and set them down again." Time permitted few opportunities for tactical familiarization flights.

That morning, Putnam, backed up by a written request from Vice Admiral Halsey, had asked Cunningham to have CPNAB begin construction immediately on revetments similar to those that had been built at Ewa to protect his planes. VMF-211's commanding officer had emphasized speedy construction rather than "neatly finished work," but upon visiting the field that afternoon, he discovered a conscientious young civil engineer "laboriously setting out stakes with a transit and three rodmen." An hour of "frantic rushing around and some very strong language" soon resulted in the replacement of the young engineer and his rodmen "with a couple of Swedes and bulldozers" that soon began the necessary preparatory work for the revetments.

Keeping the F4Fs safe when running up engines or taxiing proved a concern because loose coral on the oiled tie-down mat constituted such a danger to propellers that a warming-up platform had to be constructed.

That same day, Captain Herbert C. Freuler, VMF-211's gunnery and ordnance officer, a thirty-three-year-old Californian who looked more like a professor than a warrior, discovered that the one-hundred-pound bombs on the island would not fit the wing racks of the F4Fs (the suspension lugs were ninety degrees out of line with the hooks on the Wildcats' wing racks) and decided to try to adapt the bands of the water-filled practice bombs to the live ordnance.

The next morning (6 December), the *Triton* surfaced off the south shore and lay to at 0625; Lieutenant Commander Pilly Lent then came ashore at the request of Commander Cunningham and Major Devereux to discuss the general situation, as well as the fighter patrols that would operate from the island. They planned periscope detection drills for VMF-211 and the test-firing of the five-inch guns at Peacock Point. Cunningham informed Lent that no patrol planes were due to operate from the atoll for at least a week. The two men also arranged for the hospitalized Chief Electrician's Mate Thompson, who, it turned out, had suffered from appendicitis, to be put on board the next available transport—most likely the *William Ward Burrows*, then en route to Wake—bound for Pearl. Lent returned to his boat soon after 0900, and the *Triton* resumed her patrol. That same day, at the airfield, five of VMF-211's pilots (including one to stand watch in the operations tent) stood on the alert all day, subsisting on meals brought down from Camp 1 by truck. The *Arthur Foss* sailed for Oahu, towing two empty barges, at 1730.

At Pearl Harbor, at noon on 5 December (0930, 6 December, at Wake), the continuing deterioration of relations between the United States and Japan prompted Captain McMorris to recommend courses of action to be adopted should war break out within the next forty-eight hours. Among them, McMorris suggested delaying the fleet's raiding and reconnaissance efforts until Task Force 2 and Task Force 3 joined up. He also proposed that two oilers be sent to rendezvous with Task Force 3 (then en route to Johnston Island) at a designated point east of Wake. McMorris also recommended that Task Force 8 (then bound for Pearl) return to Pearl, fuel, and sail with the rest of Task Force 2 (less the battleships) to join Task Force 3. The *Lexington* (which, along with her screen, had gotten under way at 0728 that very morning) would fly off VMSB-231 to Midway and then head for Wake. The *William Ward Burrows* would continue on to Wake but delay her arrival until the tenth; the *Lexington* task force (instead of the *Enterprise*'s) would detach two destroyers to cover her. In addition to advising against changing the movements of ships bound for Midway, Christmas, and Canton, McMorris once more counseled against withdrawing "any civilian workmen from [the] outlying islands."[41]

One of the ships in McMorris's scenario, the *William Ward Burrows*, had been plodding due west with *PAB No. 7* riding easily astern. Late during the first watch on 4 December, however, in response to a request for assistance from the Honolulu-bound *Sonoma*, which had reported an ailing man on board, the transport abruptly reversed course. The *William Ward Burrows* doubled back during the mid- and morning watches on the fifth, intercepted the tug shortly after the forenoon watch began, and brought on board Fireman Third Class W. Karnas, USNR. Once she had embarked the sick sailor, she resumed her voyage toward Wake; soon thereafter, Lieutenant Commander Roy F. Cantrell (MC), her medical officer, diagnosed Karnas's ailment and performed an appendectomy.

On Wake, the general quarters drill during which the marines manned their battle stations had proceeded so well that day (Saturday, 6 December), that the hard-driving Jim Devereux granted his men a holiday on the seventh. Dan Teters likewise gave his people a breather from their nearly ceaseless toil. For the men of VMF-211, however, Sunday, 7 December, was anything but a day of rest as they began pumping gasoline from fifty-five-gallon drums to the just-completed twenty-five-thousand gallon tanks set up on cradles near the runway and into the tank trucks for immediate use. By the end of the day, some six hundred drums of aviation fuel, as well as drummed lubrication oil, sat near those aboveground tanks. Work crews began dispersing other gasoline and oil drums to remote locations on the island.[42]

In the brief time they had been on Wake, Conderman and his advance party, assisted by defense battalion marines, had dispersed the radio station, squadron office, engineering and ordnance shops, and heads as widely as possible in the open area south of the runway that extended from east to west. Work began on the seventh to install electricity in the tents.

That day's flight operations, however, did not go smoothly. Second Lieutenant Kinney, after having trouble starting 211-F-6, discovered that water had contaminated the gasoline. Further investigation showed that oil preservative in the magnetos had worked its way out and had fouled the points of the spark plugs. Such were the headaches encountered in the field by men working against time to hone the fighting effectiveness of their unit.

The men spent their leisure time on Sunday, 7 December 1941, according to their personal tastes. Husky Ensign Buck Henshaw bested Commander Cunningham at tennis. First Lieutenants Clarence A. ("Barney") Barninger, Jr. (Naval Academy Class of 1937), and William W. ("Wally") Lewis (Virginia Military Institute Class of 1937) of the First Defense Battalion, took their sailboat, the *Whitecap*, out into the lagoon, where a contrary gust of wind capsized her.[43] Barninger's Naval Academy classmate and friend First Lieutenant Kessler and Second Lieutenant John A. McAlister rowed a flat-bottomed boat out to explore the reef northwest of Kuku Point and then washed down a picnic lunch of canned sardines and crackers with warm beer.

John Kinney took advantage of his free time that afternoon to ride over to Peale and watch the arrival of the *Philippine Clipper*—sister ship of the *China Clipper* that had passed through just a few days before. "The gossip the passengers brought and the news we heard on the radio," Devereux later wrote, "were neither better nor worse than they had been."

Reflecting the tension in the Far East, Thomas E. Barnett, the *Clipper*'s first engineer, informed Kinney that PanAir was "evacuating all women of their employ from Manila." Kinney, who held a bachelor of science degree in electrical engineering from Washington State College, had worked for PanAir as a mechanic after graduation and was working toward his Federal Aviation Administration mechanic's license before he entered the USMCR in May 1938. Out of curiosity, he inspected a change he had made on board the Martin in 1937 and proudly found his workmanship "still as good as new."

Among those who disembarked from the *Clipper* was Herman P. Hevenor, an auditor from the Bureau of the Budget, whose report the previous summer concerning the protection of the supply of bauxite in British Guiana had proved particularly interesting and beneficial to the navy. Hevenor, flown out to Midway in a naval plane on 3 December, had gone over the books for the construction programs there before catching the *Philippine Clipper* on the sixth for Wake. He soon found that 65 percent of the facilities called for had been completed by the first week of December and noted that the "saturated salt air . . . readily [attacked] the steel frame and steel sash structures as well as equipment, including automotive vehicles." It was not unusual to see "only a remnant of a fender left." The damage was caused by the combination of coral sand and rainwater, "the destructive effect aggravated by an alkaline action which corrodes the running gear of trucks and mobile equipment."[44] That was one of the two major difficulties (the other being the repeated breakdowns of the *Columbia*) encountered by CPNAB at Wake.

At the airfield that day, Captain Elrod was on duty, as was Captain Frank C. Tharin, the only Naval Academy graduate (Class of 1934) in VMF-211, who had been pulled from the MAG-21 staff to bring the squadron up to a full complement of officer pilots for the "advanced base exercise." Tharin, who possessed "a merry laugh and a wealth of good humor," had attended the Basic School at Philadelphia before going to sea in the marine detachment of the heavy cruiser *Northampton*

(CA-26). "Happy-go-lucky . . . with a streak of seriousness . . . generous to a fault . . . a fit shipmate on any voyage to anywhere," he had won his wings on 30 July 1937.[45]

Second Lieutenant Carl R. Davidson, age twenty-four, who hailed from the tiny town of Canistota in southeastern South Dakota, had duty, too. A June 1938 graduate of the University of South Dakota, he had been appointed aviation cadet, USMCR, on 20 December 1939 and had commenced his training eight days later. Awarded his wings on 7 September 1940, he was assigned soon thereafter to the Second Marine Aircraft Wing at San Diego—his second choice for duty.[46]

The resourceful Captain Freuler took up an F4F; slung under each wing was a hundred-pound bomb that had been modified with bands taken off practice bombs. He dropped two bombs with the "Wake Model Bands" without incident. That night, John Kinney wrote optimistically in his diary, "Tomorrow we will start our first gunnery with the F4F-3—The sleeves are ready."[47]

In Camp 1 that evening, First Lieutenant Kessler sorted through his mail. He read of his staid New England father's purchase of a Dodge convertible and his wife's account of "late news of the Marine Corps Birthday Ball" festivities at Pearl. As he wrote his return letters, he cast loving, tender glances at his helpmate's portrait, "painted in color on ivory," that sat on his desk.[48]

Unbeknownst to the sailors and marines of the Pacific Fleet, throughout the latter part of 1941 Imperial Japanese Navy pilots and aircrewmen were undergoing intensive training, while a diligent intelligence-gathering operation on Oahu reported the movements of Kimmel's ships in and out of Pearl. The focus of these endeavors was to be a daring air strike, hurled like a thunderbolt against the Pacific Fleet as it lay in its Oahu base, when the political relationship between the United States and Japan had deteriorated to a point that the latter felt was beyond return. Simultaneously, the Japanese war machine would be set in motion against American, British, and Dutch possessions in the Far East and Pacific. While plans for those operations were put into motion, the First Air Fleet, formed around six aircraft carriers, shaped an undetected course across the northern Pacific, bound for Pearl. Submarines deployed in support skulked past Wake, submerged to avoid detection by the patrol planes believed to be based there.[49]

Admiral Kimmel had acknowledged as late as mid-October that Japan might precede a declaration of war with a surprise attack on the fleet at Pearl. Because priority was given to the Atlantic theater, the reinforcement of the Philippines, and the army's willingness to transfer significant numbers of pursuit planes to the outlying bases, however, he came to discount that possibility.[50] Few but the most prescient believed that the Japanese would strike simultaneously at a multitude of places with forces appropriate to the task. If hostilities broke out, Pacific Fleet war planners felt, Wake, which Kimmel knew to be vulnerable but had attempted to make as secure as possible, was much more likely to be attacked than Pearl.[51] Could the carefully woven tapestry of Kimmel's war plan, fashioned with desperate intensity in the late autumn of 1941, withstand the calculated thrust of a carefully forged and honed samurai blade that hung like a Damoclean sword over the Pacific?

"I'LL SEE THAT YOU GET A MEDAL AS BIG AS A PIE"

Shortly before 0800 on Sunday, 7 December 1941, planes from six Japanese aircraft carriers descended upon naval and military installations on Oahu in a surprise attack that burst "like a thunderclap out of a clear sky."[1] In contrast to the carnage on Oahu, Monday, 8 December 1941, dawned serene and tranquil, a regular workday at Wake. At 0655, after taxiing out across the turquoise lagoon, the silver *Philippine Clipper* took off for Guam. A short time later, First Lieutenants Barninger and Lewis stepped outside their tent in Camp 1, bound for breakfast, when they saw Captain Wilson half-running, half-walking, carrying something toward Major Devereux's tent.

Only moments before, Wilson had awoken, knowing a flight of planes—perhaps the two Dutch PBY-5 Catalina flying boats then at Midway, bound for the Netherlands East Indies—was due that day.[2] As he always did, he telephoned the sergeant on duty. On 8 December, a perplexed Sergeant Rex answered Wilson's call, "Captain, I don't believe what I am hearing." After he told Rex to "place the earphones against the telephone transmitter," Wilson heard a Morse message in clear; "SOS SOS Japs attacking Oahu X This is the real thing X No mistake."[3]

Wilson recognized Lieutenant Colonel Hoppaugh's "fist" (the "rhythm and manner" that characterized the sender) and knew at once that the alarm was genuine. After telling Rex to try to obtain "all details possible," he bolted to inform Devereux.[4] Rex meanwhile tried vainly to contact Hickam and Midway but was able to inform Port Moresby that war had begun. Awakened from slumber in the transmitter truck, Staff Sergeant Hotchkiss greeted the news of the attack on Pearl Harbor with disbelief.

After he had received the word of war from Captain Wilson, who hurried to the mess hall for a quick cup of coffee before he continued on toward the airfield, Devereux summoned Field Music First Class Alvin J. Waronker to sound the "call to arms." Inside the mess hall in Camp 1, where First Lieutenant Kessler sat enjoying a stack of six thick hotcakes, "the notes of the bugle call were blurred, but there was no mistaking a frantic appeal vibrating through the open doorway." Having already devoured two-thirds of his flapjacks, Kessler gulped down the rest on the way to the door. Devereux soon assembled his officers and told them "that the Japanese had attacked Oahu, and that we could expect the same thing in a very short time."[5]

Almost simultaneously, Commander Cunningham learned of what had happened at Pearl as he was leaving the contractors' mess hall in Camp 2 with several other officers, following a breakfast of bacon and eggs. A messenger from the communications office reported breathlessly that an operator at Pearl had told of an attack, repeatedly emphasizing the words "this is no drill." Cunningham ordered the marines to battle stations.

Lieutenant Commander Greey called Dan Teters and told him of the bombing of Pearl and that a state of war existed. Teters hastened to his office and contacted both Cunningham and Greey; they agreed that the civilians would proceed with their scheduled work, Cunningham deeming their dispersal throughout the atoll sufficient to minimize the danger. Teters then contacted Devereux to discuss where the marine-trained civilian workmen would go; Devereux asked that they be turned over to his command.

Cunningham then contacted John B. Cooke, PanAir's airport manager, and requested that he recall the *Philippine Clipper*. Cooke promptly sent the prearranged code telling of the outbreak of hostilities—"Case 7, Condition A"—to the airborne aircraft. The island commander then set off in his pickup truck for the airfield.

Soon marines were embarking in trucks at Camp 1 and moving out with a smoothness and precision that belied the fact that they had done it only once before—on Saturday, the sixth. Neither the *Triton* nor the *Tambor*, though, lurking submerged offshore and temporarily incommunicado, knew of developments on Oahu.

The Wake-bound *William Ward Burrows* learned of the attack on Pearl Harbor three hours into the morning watch on the eighth. At 0710, Commander Dierdorff mustered all hands, including the passengers, and told them the news. Some of the CPNAB men, many of whom had had some military service, immediately volunteered to serve on board in any capacity. Less than an hour later, the *William Ward Burrows*, having crossed the 180th meridian during the first dog watch on 7 December, began zigzagging, still headed toward her original destination.[6]

At Wake, Marine Gunner Harold C. Borth, with Sergeant James W. Hall as his assistant, climbed to the top of the water tower in Camp 1, the highest point on the atoll, which both the *Triton* and the *Tambor* had found to be an excellent landmark, and manned the observation post there.[7]

Although CinCPac had recommended that one SCR-270B radar be installed on Wake for the detection of aircraft, the small number of sets available in the Pacific (there were only two at the time his study on outlying bases had been completed in October) militated against the vulnerable atoll's getting its required equipment. Because Wake possessed no radar and the roaring surf drowned out most noise, its rudimentary early warning capability rested solely on the keen eyesight of its lookouts.

Devereux informed Cunningham after the latter had reached Camp 1 that he would soon be vacating his office amid the well-ordered rows of pyramidal tents and establishing a command post in the scrub east of it. The island commander then informed the marine that he was retaining his own headquarters—at least for the time being—in his office in Camp 2. Cunningham then drove back to the contractors' cantonment.

The commencement of hostilities saw Wake's marines dispersed throughout the atoll, connected with Devereaux's command post in the brush east of Camp 1 by the J-line, the main communication artery set up by Technical Sergeant Randolph M. June and the detachment's communications men. Unfortunately, the employment of the only two mechanical trench diggers at Wake in the construction of the utilities on Peale had meant that the J-line was not placed underground, where it would have been less vulnerable. One BD-72 switchboard, installed at the detachment command post, served all units. It was the best that could be done for the shorthanded detachment, and the simplicity of the system released needed men to repair and replace damaged portions of lines—a comparatively easy matter owing to the short distances between posts served by the main line. The five- and three-inch batteries used sound-powered phones for interbattery communications.[8]

Second Lieutenant Robert M. Hanna, USMCR, the detachment's .50-caliber machine-gun officer, established his command post in VMF-211's communications tent at the airfield and reported that his station was manned and ready at 0800. Under his command were the .50-caliber machine-gun positions that studded the shoreline around the edge of the atoll.

Second Lieutenant Poindexter, the detachment's .30-caliber machine-gun officer, whom Devereux had placed in command of the Mobile Reserve and all military and civilians around Camp 1, established his command post in the area where the Mobile Reserve was to assemble. Some sixty sandbagged open pits—numbered by pairs—extended along the fifteen- to eighteen-mile coastline from Kuku Point to Toki Point. Unfortunately, because of the paucity of people and guns, only six (three sections of two) could be manned continuously. Permanently sited to cover perceived critical areas were Section 12 under Corporal Christian Oelberg, Jr. (the mouth of the channel between Wilkes and Peale and the south beach of Wilkes); Section 17 under Corporal Ralph J. Holewinski (the south beach of Wake south of the airfield); and Section 24 under Corporal James G. McWiggins (Heel Point, a portion of the northern beaches of Peale and Wake and the causeway linking the two islets). Civilian clerks, laborers, and civil engineers who had been instructed in use of the guns augmented the marine crews. Poindexter would ultimately disperse the remaining .30-calibers to places where marines stationed near them could man them in an emergency. Two trucks were furnished to the Mobile Reserve.

Marine Gunner John Hamas, the detachment's munitions officer, proceeded immediately to the storeroom in Camp 1 and unpacked Browning automatic rifles, Springfield '03s, and ammunition, issuing them to some of the civilians who had volunteered for combat duty with the leathernecks. Some of the younger marines had come to regard Hamas, a serious, sometimes quixotic man, as "something of a father figure . . . a great burly Santa Claus without the beard." A veteran of service in the Austro-Hungarian army during World War I and decorated for heroism on the Italian and Russian fronts, he also held a Navy Cross—the United States naval service's highest award for valor, which he earned in Nicaragua in April 1932, when his Guardia patrol had taken a Sandinista stronghold from a larger force of bandits under Augusto Sandino himself. After issuing the weapons under his charge, Hamas and a working party began distributing seventy-five cases of hand grenades."[9]

The dawn patrol had landed by the time Major Bayler's radiomen picked up word of an attack on Pearl.[10] Putnam immediately sent a runner to direct Captain Elrod to disperse the planes and men and keep all aircraft ready for flight, while work began on dugout shelters for the planes. The news of the attack on Hickam had sparked lively discussions at the airfield concerning its authenticity, but when confirmation arrived, Putnam immediately placed VMF-211 on a war footing.

Captain Freuler supervised the removal of the supporting bands from the water-fillable practice bombs and their installation on the hundred-pound bombs on Wake. He also dispersed the supply of starter cartridges and supervised the belting of additional machine-gun ammunition. Armorers hung a hundred-pounder under each wing of the eight Wildcats not scheduled for the midday patrol. Staff Sergeant Arthur continued his work with the homing devices.

Soon thereafter, Captain Elrod (flying 211-F-9) and Second Lieutenant Davidson (211-F-10) in one section, Second Lieutenant Kinney (211-F-11) and Technical Sergeant (NAP) William J. Hamilton (211-F-12) in the other, took off, with orders to remain in the immediate vicin-

Marine Gunner John
Hamas, on duty at
Shanghai, China, during
the 1930s. (John Hamas
Biographical File, MCHC
Reference Section)

Second Lieutenant John
F. Kinney, ca. September
1941, who became VMF-
211's engineer officer on
8 December. (Mrs.
Virginia Putnam)

ity of the island. Rightly thinking that any inbound Japanese planes would come from the Marshalls, Kinney took his section to the south-southwest at thirteen thousand feet; Elrod took his to the north. With only plotting boards as their navigational equipment, the pilots had to stay relatively close to Wake because if they were forced down at sea, they could not expect to be rescued.

Meanwhile, PanAir's Captain John H. Hamilton had received the "Case 7, Condition A" message and had brought the *Philippine Clipper* back to Wake. Hans W. Whitney, a CPNAB laborer, standing atop the skeletal steel framework of the 30 percent completed bachelor officers' quarters on Peale, remarked to a fellow workman: "There must be a bad storm between here and Guam, the *Clipper* is coming back." "Haven't you heard the news?" his foreman replied, incredulously. "The Japs are boming Pearl Harbor, right now." After hearing his co-worker relate the feared damage, Whitney responded confidently, "Let them come. The Marines will show them a thing or two."[11]

After dumping three thousand pounds of fuel to get down to landing weight, the *Philippine Clipper* alighted in the lagoon at 0714. Cunningham immediately requested the stocky, bullnecked pilot, whom he knew from his days at the Naval Reserve Air Base at Oakland and who, along with his first officer, William W. Moss, Jr., held Naval Reserve commissions as naval aviators, to carry out a scouting flight. The *Clipper* was unloaded—its cargo included tires for the American Volunteer Group in China—and refueled with sufficient gasoline for both a patrol flight and a flight to Midway, in addition to the standard reserve. Commander Cunningham laid out a plan and gave the *Clipper* a two-plane escort. Hamilton then called Putnam by telephone and concluded the arrangements for the *Clipper* to take off at 1300.

In the meantime, soon after receiving word of hostilities, Battery B's First Lieutenant Kessler and his men had loaded trucks with equipment and small arms ammunition and moved out. Kessler, a drop or two of syrup still glistening on his chin, had been the last man on board the last truck, and as it passed Devereux, he saluted the little major. On the way to Toki Point, Battery B's trucks passed a barracks under construction on Peale, workmen on scaffolds busily painting the building white. As they rode by, some of the marines shouted, "Don't you know there's a war on?" At 0710, soon after they arrived at Toki Point, Kessler began distributing gear and had a sentry post established. Thirty rounds went into rudimentary ready-use boxes near the guns. At 0800, he reported Battery B ready for action, ammunition up, and Condition II set.

General quarters called Captain Godbold's Battery D to their stations southeast of Battery B at 0700, and those marines moved out to their position by truck, reporting "manned and ready" within a half hour.

The lack of men, however, prevented Godbold from operating more than three guns. Within another hour and a half, each had fifty rounds ready for firing. At 1000, Godbold received orders to keep one gun, the director, the height finder—the only one at Wake for the three three-inch batteries—and the power plant manned at all times. After making those arrangements, Godbold put the remainder of his men to work improving the position. Fifteen minutes later, the crew of gun 4 left with a tractor and a trailer to fill sandbags near the bridge between Peale and Wake. At 1140, a truck pulled up abreast gun 4, at Toki Point, with the noon meal.

Over at the airfield, Sergeant Rex had suggested to Captain Wilson that the SCR-197 be moved into the brush southwest of the parking mat along a low ridge south of the airstrip. Wilson agreed, and he and his men—even those who had had the duty the night before—moved the transmitter and receiver some distance from the airfield and camouflaged it. At 1149, they reestablished contact with Hickam.

While the atoll's defenders prepared for war, Japanese planes droned toward them. Four years before, during the "China Incident," Japanese navy land-based bombers had flown missions of unprecedented length, their crews excelling in overwater navigation.[12] Those who wanted Wake's defenses reduced from the air entrusted that task to the Chitose *Kōkūtai* (Captain Ohashi Fujiro), a unit of the Twenty-fourth Air Flotilla under Rear Admiral Goto Eiji. Consequently, between 0710 and 0720 on 8 December, thirty-four Mitsubishi G3M2 Type 96 land attack planes (*rikkō*) of the Chitose *Kōkūtai*—all that were available at that base—took off from Roi; shackled beneath the bellies of the G3M2s were 13 250-kilogram and 321 60-kilogram bombs. Lieutenant Commander Matsuda Hideo, the group's *hikōtaichō*, rode in the command seat of the aircraft of the first *chūtai* leader (Lieutenant Watanabe Kazuo). Lieutenant Kotani Shigeru led the second *chūtai*, Lieutenant Nakai Kazuo the third, and Lieutenant Yamagata Shigeo the fourth.[13]

With nothing along their route to guide them, wrote Tsuji Norio, a war correspondent riding in one of the *rikkō*s, "only the wide, vast expanse of the boundless sea, no matter how far we went," extended below them. Even a miscalculation in the course of as little as 5 percent could result in Matsuda's bombers missing their objective. Shortly before noon, however, their navigation having been excellent, the men in the Chitose *Kōkūtai*'s G3M2s spotted Wake thirteen thousand feet below through the "heavy, spreading clouds." Correspondent Tsuji saw what looked like Wildcat fighters in the distance—"a worthy foe!"—and worried. Rain squalls cloaked their approach, however, and as the thundering surf drowned out the noise of their engines, Matsuda's *rikkō*s dropped down to fifteen hundred feet. Marine lookouts spotted the twin-engine,

A formation of Mitsubishi G3M2 Type 96 land attack planes (later code-named "Nell") in formation, ca. 1942. Bombers of this type, from the Chitose *Kōkūtai*, were frequent visitors to Wake's airspace in December 1941. (NA, 80-G-179013)

twin-tail bombers a few hundred yards off the atoll's south shore, emerging from a dense bank of stratocumulus clouds, and sounded the alarm. At Battery E, First Lieutenant Lewis telephoned Major Devereux's command post to inform him of the incoming planes. Then, with swift and terrible suddenness, the falling bombs began to explode and do their bloody work.

First Lieutenant Kessler's marines had "knocked off for lunch" shortly before noon, and the talk gravitated toward "what had happened at Pearl Harbor and what steps the United States would take to put the Japs in their place." Suddenly, the sound of multiple explosions drew their attention to the airfield. "Full realization of what was happening did not come readily," Kessler later recounted, "yet it was but seconds before we knew that the war had finally come to us."

Earlier that morning, Paul Putnam had been confronted by a difficult decision. Although he had been rushing work on the six revetments being built along the seaward side of the runway, he knew none would be ready before 1400. He also knew that moving the eight F4Fs any further from where they sat already dispersed entailed the risk of damage and the danger of obstructing the runway. Any damage could mean the loss of a plane because Wake had virtually no spare parts. Consequently, Putnam decided to delay further dispersal of planes and matériel until suitable places existed to protect them. Thus, as high noon neared, 211-F-1, 211-F-2, 211-F-6, and 211-F-4 sat on the oiled tie-down mat; 211-F-5 and 211-F-3 to the west of the mat; 211-F-7 near the flight and radio tents; and 211-F-8 near the rough ground to the east of the mat.

No foxholes had been dug near the field, but the rough ground nearby afforded natural cover to those who reached it. Except for those working near the airplanes and on the parking area, Putnam trusted that his men would be able to reach shelter if an attack came. Moving gasoline, bombs, and ammunition, installing electrical lines and generators, and relocating radio facilities kept all hands busy.

Staff Sergeant Arthur lay in the cramped confines of the belly of 211-F-1, which sat parked on the northwest corner of the oiled tie-down mat, installing a homing device. Hearing someone outside say, "Here comes the Army," Arthur squeezed himself out of the access hatch from the Wildcat's interior, took one look, and loudly uttered an expletive. After the shouted warnings, he and the rest of 211's men had no more than one minute to find cover as the *rikkōs* swept in, ruthlessly machine-gunning and bombing whatever lay beneath them in their path. "We strafed the soldiers," Tsuji wrote later, "as we determined to let not even one escape."

Second Lieutenant Conderman and First Lieutenant George A. Graves were in the ready tent, going over final instructions concerning their escort of the *Philippine Clipper*. When the alarm sounded, both men, in flight gear, sprinted for their planes. Graves, the squadron's energetic and capable engineering officer only since 17 November, reached 211-F-7, the Wildcat nearest the operations tent, but a direct hit demolished it in a ball of flame as he was climbing into the cockpit, killing him instantly. Three enlisted men—Technical Sergeant Jack "V" Allen and Sergeants Henry D. Nanninga and Clyde D. Wilsford—died fiery deaths as well. Conderman, shot through the neck and legs, fell before a bomb hit his waiting Wildcat and demolished it. Pinned beneath the wreckage, he called to Corporal Robert E. L. Page to come over and help him, but when the mortally wounded pilot heard another man calling out, he told Page to help the other man.

Strafing cut down Second Lieutenant Holden, the squadron's assis-tant matériel officer, as he raced for cover. Holden, aged twenty-three, the junior pilot on Wake, had been awarded his wings on 10 January

1941 and had reached the Hawaiian area in April.[14] The squadron's assistant flight officer, twenty-two-year-old Second Lieutenant Henry G. Webb, fell with bullet wounds in the abdomen and shrapnel wounds in his face and left foot. "Spider" Webb, awarded his wings on 16 May 1940, had been deployed to the Hawaiian area in January 1941. Fighters had been his second choice for duty.

Over near Wilkes Channel, the strafing killed Electrician's Mate Second Class Thomas P. Kilcoyne and Seaman Second Class Richard W. Jacobs of the Wake Base Detachment; civilian John E. Hall, a potwasher who had volunteered to serve with Cunningham's garrison, died as well. Also among the first of the navy casualties was Coxswain George J. Wolney, a member of the small boat crew at Wake attached to the defense battalion, who, struck by several bullets as he exited a panel truck near the airfield, fell "like a sack of grain." Bomb fragments wounded Boatswain's Mate Second Class Kirby Ludwick, Jr., the petty officer in charge of Wake's small boat unit, and Seaman First Class James B. Darden, a member of the same boat detail.[15]

Marine Gunner Hamas, who still had fifty cases of hand grenades in his truck, having just delivered twenty-five to Kuku Point, saw the red sun insignia on the planes and ordered the vehicle stopped and told his men to head for cover. Marines at Battery B fired their rifles at the *rikkōs* as they flew low overhead.

Confident that his airborne planes would be able to provide sufficient warning of an incoming raid, Commander Cunningham was working in his office at Camp 2 when he heard the crump of explosions begin around 1155. Fearing that the noise was from a local accident, he leaped up from his chair and joined the men in the adjoining large drafting room as they crowded toward the door. Bullets tearing through the roof compelled both the curious contractors and the island commander to scramble for safety. One man nearby sought shelter under a desk; Cunningham did so, too.

Elsewhere in the contractors' camp, a loud explosion rattled the casemate windows, prompting John R. Burroughs, one of CPNAB's construction engineers, to think that work crews had placed some "particularly heavy charges" in the lagoon to blast coral heads. He joined the exodus from the building, however, when he and the others heard the roar of engines and the staccato sound of machine-gun fire.

Near the laundry building in Camp 2, John N. Valov, a CPNAB laundry helper, had heard that Pearl had been bombed but thought the newly arrived aircraft were American. "The Japs," he thought, initially uncomprehending what was happening, "wouldn't dare to start a war." When the bullets started spattering the ground nearby, though, he quickly scampered to cover behind a mound of coral.[16]

Battery D's guns 1 and 2 opened up ineffectively on the attackers, firing a total of forty rounds, hindered by low visibility and the altitude at which the Mitsubishis flew. Although no bombs fell near the battery, concussion from their own gunfire caved in the sandbags ringing the guns. On Peacock Point, Battery E had been standing ready to fire within fifteen minutes. Like Godbold, Lewis had only enough marines to man three of his four guns. Lewis had manned two of the three-inchers, along with the M-4 director, while the rest of his men busily completed sandbag emplacements. After telephoning Devereux's command post when he saw the falling bombs, Lewis estimated the altitude and ordered his gunners to open fire. The height at which the attackers came, however, rendered Battery E's fire ineffective, too.

Neither Dan Godbold nor his range officer, Second Lieutenant Bob Greeley, had observed any hits on the attackers, but marine antiaircraft fire had holed eight Type 96s and killed Seaman Second Class Iwai, a crewman on board the *rikkō* commanded by Warrant Officer Okabe Kazuo, the number one plane in Lieutenant Yamagata's fourth *chūtai*. The returning Japanese claimed to have set fire to all aircraft on the ground and reported sighting only three airborne American planes.

After conferring with Cunningham, PanAir's Captain Hamilton was on his way back to the *Philippine Clipper* in a car, along with John Cooke. As the bombs began to fall, their chauffeur, a Chinese known as "Tommy," observed with perhaps unintended irony: "We haven't a Chinaman's chance!" Hamilton, Cooke, and Tommy jumped out of the car and threw themselves into an unfinished foundation hole just as a bomb landed some twenty feet away and exploded, showering them with sand. Hamilton, commenting that that spot was "too hot for him," rose and sprinted for the cover afforded by a nearby concrete culvert. Strafing bombers prompted Cooke—who would soon see his house blasted to rubble by a direct hit (it lay only some two hundred feet from the hotel)—and the chauffeur to stay put.[17]

William Moss, Hamilton's first officer, in the PanAir hotel when the attack began, heard the bomb explosions and rushed outside to see Matsuda's bombers, having finished their runs on the airfield, circling left for a run on Peale. To Moss, their formation flying "was very good—as if on parade." He ran for cover, and as the Type 96s released their bombs, he threw himself flat on the sand.

Captain Wilson, caught on Peale by the bombing, winced as a bomb fragment tore into his right leg above the knee. Near the airfield, shrapnel riddled the transmitting trailer, one piece striking Sergeant Rex in the back, while two bullets holed the trailer "and a thick safe (borrowed from the Marines), went on through the receiving position, but failed to wreck the set."[18] Bomb fragments and strafers' bullets destroyed all spare parts for the field lighting system and badly damaged the marines' radio installation, which lay only one hundred feet from the former position of the SCR-197.

Captain Hamilton observed that the Japanese seemed to be familiar with the topography and building projects under way on Peale because they paid particular attention to the PanAir facilities and little "if any" to the construction at the NAS site. He did allow, though, that the G3M2s "thoroughly ground-strafed" the entire area. The explosions of the bombs on Peale brought the war "close enough to become more personal" to the marines on Toki Point.[19]

In about seven minutes, the Japanese totally wrecked the PanAir station while the employees found cover wherever they could: one dove into the water and hid under a raft; another burrowed into the sand; still another crawled into a length of dredging pipe. Bombing and strafing set fire to the hotel from whose verandas travelers had once savored breathtaking tropical sunsets. Other bombs had destroyed the stockroom, fuel tanks, and many other buildings that had once stood near the well-tended magnolia-lined paths and demolished the radio transmitter. All told, five of PanAir's sixty-six-man staff lay dead, and Flight Steward Charles P. Relyea and the *Philippine Clipper*'s first radio officer, Donovan V. McKay, had been wounded.

Almost miraculously, the twenty-six-ton *Philippine Clipper*, empty of both passengers and cargo but fully fueled, rode easily at her moorings. A bomb had splashed one hundred feet ahead of her, and bullets had holed her in twenty-three places, but none had hit her large fuel tanks. Seeing the *Clipper* intact, chief mechanic Jack Eagan sprinted down the dock, boarded the flying boat, and began preparing her for flight.

Although Cunningham had apparently assented, in theory, to Hamilton's proposed evacuation of the passengers and staff on board the *Clipper*, its precipitate departure in the aftermath of the Japanese raid surprised him. Willing hands had stripped the Martin 130 of all superfluous equipment (and ejected two Guamanians who attempted to stow away in the tail of the plane) and, soon thereafter, the five passengers (Herman Hevenor of the Bureau of the Budget for some reason not among them) and the twenty-six Caucasian PanAir employees joined the eight-man crew on board the *Philippine Clipper*. After two anxious tries, Hamilton finally coaxed the fully loaded ship off the turquoise waters of the lagoon at 1330 and flew toward Midway.[20] Among the passengers was Frank McKenzie, escaping from the base he had helped design and build a little over six years before.

Before his departure, John Cooke had told Jesus A. Garcia, the spokesman for PanAir's stranded Guamanians, to take his people to Camp 2 and report to Dan Teters. Cooke claimed that the arrangement had already been made between Cunningham (which the commander later denied) and Teters. Garcia obediently led his remaining countrymen (five had died in the bombing of the hotel) over to Camp 2 and reported to the general superintendent to take their places alongside the CPNAB men.[21] August Ramquist, a Caucasian and a carpenter on PanAir's staff, on his own initiative, had aided the Chamorros who had been hurt that morning. Driving the atoll's only ambulance, he sacrificed his only opportunity to escape.

Once the Japanese had gone, Cunningham sprinted to his pickup truck and sped off toward the airfield. The ominous clouds of smoke rolling skyward did not prepare him for the sight of "desolation and destruction" that awaited him. As he later reported, "aid to the wounded was the first order of business" in the aftermath of the attack. His initial dispatch to ComFourteen noted that the attack had destroyed seven marine planes, that there had been numerous casualties among the aviation people, and that the Japanese had set fire to gasoline storage tanks at the PanAir facility and at the airfield.

Although a bomb fragment had nicked his left shoulder, a dazed Major Putnam, who considered the initial Japanese raid "tactically well conceived and skillfully executed," immediately took over the terrible task of seeing to the many injured at the field. His dedication to duty set the tone for the many instances of selfless heroism that occurred in 211's camp.

Master Technical Sergeant Andrew J. Paskiewicz, a knowledgeable and highly respected senior noncom whose right leg had been shattered by bomb fragments and bullets, fashioned a makeshift crutch and hobbled about, aiding the wounded and dying. Staff Sergeant Arthur, a bomb fragment embedded in his left wrist, turned to rescue hurt men from burning camp areas. He persisted in that task and refused evacuation until others had received attention first. Sergeant Howard D. Comin, six days short of his twenty-sixth birthday and unable to sit comfortably because of the nature of his wounds, helped evacuate men more seriously wounded than himself before he reported for treatment. After his wounds were treated, Technical Sergeant Earl R. Hannum left the hospital to return to the squadron to assume the duties of leading line chief.[22] The attack had left five pilots and ten enlisted men from VMF-211 wounded and eighteen dead. Most of the latter had formed the core of its mechanics. Fortunately, among those who survived the aerial onslaught was Private First Class Dale K. Taylor, VMF-211's only armorer at Wake.

The squadron's tents were shot up, and virtually no supplies—tools, spark plugs, tires, and what sparse spare parts there were—escaped destruction. Fortunately, though both twenty-five-thousand-gallon gasoline storage tanks lay demolished and ablaze, the vital airstrip remained untouched.

As Lieutenant Commander Matsuda's *rikkōs* departed after having sown death and destruction over the atoll so precisely as to suggest a checkerboard pattern, correspondent Tsuji noted that some of the aircrew he could see, thankful for the "aid of Providence," grinned widely. As he recounted later, "Everyone waggled his wings to signify 'Banzai.'" The Japanese had reason to exult; their ordnance had done its work well. The marines assessed the enemy's work with grudging professional admiration: the fragmentation and fuse action was "excellent," the bombs having left craters only six to eight inches deep in the coral sand. There had been no "duds." Fuel drums and equipment near the exploding bombs had been damaged by flying shrapnel within a foot from the ground.

After the last of the bombers disappeared and the columns of smoke rolled into the sky behind them, Gunner Hamas recalled his men from the bush and set out to resume delivery of hand grenades. As he neared the airfield, he stopped to help wounded men board a truck that had escaped destruction. He then continued toward his original destination and ultimately returned to Camp 1, where more civilians had reported for duty.

Meanwhile, Kinney and Hamilton had climbed through the squalls to thirteen thousand feet and patrolled out sixty miles to the southeast of Wake, above the high overcast. Nearing the atoll around noon, they were letting down through broken clouds when Kinney spotted two formations of twin-tail, twin-engine planes at about fifteen hundred feet, three miles out. Wake was not in view, and he had not yet received verification that war had broken out, but after he came around a cloud formation he saw oily black smoke corkscrewing upward from the blazing gasoline tanks at the airfield. Perceiving at once "what was up," Kinney charged his guns and fired a test burst. He and his wingman caught a brief glimpse of Matsuda's bombers as they retired westward through the overcast and pursued them, though they could not get within shooting range before the enemy eluded them in the clouds. Neither Elrod nor Davidson—the latter, after landing, performed particularly "heroic work" in helping the wounded and dying—had seen the enemy. Kinney and Hamilton remained aloft until after 1230, when they landed to find a scene of destruction that defied description.[23] The enlisted pilot thought the island was "in a state of confusion."[24]

Less than two hours after the Chitose *Kōkūtai* had scattered its bombs with such deadly precision a message came from ComFourteen telling Wake to "execute unrestricted submarine and air warfare against Japan." The only unit that might possibly comply with that order, however, VMF-211, had been very badly battered. Paul Putnam decided that keeping the remaining planes operational was central to 211's reorganization. Graves, his engineering officer, was dead. Consequently, Putnam appointed Kinney, who had just turned twenty-seven years old a little over a month before and who had been the squadron's matériel officer and assistant engineering officer, to take his place. The former PanAir mechanic, one contemporary in VMF-211 would recall, was a "multi-talented" man who seemed to possess "unlimited energy."[25] "We have four planes left," Putnam told him, "if you can keep them flying I'll see that you get a medal as big as a pie." "Okay, sir," Kinney responded, "if it is delivered in San Francisco."

Putnam established VMF-211's command post in the woods near the operations area while his men dug foxholes in the brush; all men who remained on duty stayed at the field. Ordering pistols, Thompson submachine guns, gas masks, and steel helmets issued and machine-gun posts established near each end of the runway and near the command post, Putnam organized two ground combat groups, one under Captain Freuler, the other under Captain Tharin, to be stationed at each end of the field to go into action as infantry in the event of a Japanese landing if the squadron's planes were rendered ineffective. He also planned for the groups to be employed as a mobile reserve for the defense battalion.

In the meantime, the ground crews dispersed the flyable planes into revetments, a task not without risk. During the afternoon, Frank Tharin, who had received a superficial shrapnel wound that morning that pained him when he sat down, accidentally taxied 211-F-9 into an oil drum and ruined its propeller, temporarily reducing the number of flyable planes to three.

Captains Elrod and Tharin later supervised the efforts to construct protective works and mine the landing strip with large charges of dynamite placed about 150 feet apart, 3 feet below the surface of the runway, connected to three electric generators that had escaped destruction. Two of the generators were placed at each end of the airstrip; a third went into a position opposite the middle of the field.

Meanwhile, Dan Teters's "catskinners" bulldozed portions of the cleared land bordering the northern and western sides of the airstrip so that any enemy planes that attempted to land there would come to grief on rough, furrowed ground. Outside of flying hours, Caterpillar tractors and bulldozers would be parked to obstruct the field. Men packed the YCK-1 with dynamite and moored it between Wake and Wilkes; if a landing threatened, the charges would be exploded and the lighter sunk to block the swift-running channel.

Of the Grummans that had been caught on the ground, 211-F-8 had been parked to the east of the oiled tie-down mat. Kinney noted that bullets had pierced both wings, the stabilizer, fuselage, elevators, hood, fuse box, radio cables, reserve gas tank, and left flap. Most of VMF-211's tools had been destroyed so he borrowed some from PanAir, while CPNAB provided sheet metal, self-tapping screws, lacquer, paint, and thinner. Through diligent labor, 211-F-8 was ready to fly the next morning, although the plane had only one usable gas tank—the main one—and its sliding hood lacked some glass.

On the afternoon of the eighth, at Battery D, Godbold's men repaired their caved-in emplacements, improved the director position, and received gas masks, hand grenades, and .30- and .45-caliber ammunition. Still later that afternoon, eighteen civilians reported for duty and a contractor drove a station wagon over for the battery to use as a utility vehicle. Godbold ordered Sergeant Walter A. Bowsher, Jr., to take charge of sixteen of the CPNAB volunteers, fourteen to serve the previously idle gun 3 and the remaining two to go to the director crew as lookouts. Under Bowsher's capable leadership, instrumentmen Harold F. Clift, Arthur W. Griffith, and George S. Laubach; material clerks Eldon F. Hargis and Marshall K. Talbot; chainmen Burdette Harvey, Darwin L. Meiners, William I. Murdock, and Chester M. Ratekin; sheet metal foreman Don W. Ludington; chief of work parties Elzo ("Doc") Robnett; telephone operator Earl R. Row; riveter Floyd H. Turner; and carpenter Amos J. White would soon be serving gun 3 "in a manner comparable to the Marine-manned guns."[26]

Gunner Hamas and his men, meanwhile, dispersed ammunition from the quartermaster shed into caches of about twenty to twenty-five boxes each, west of Camp 1, near Wilkes Channel, and camouflaged them with coral sand. Next, they dispersed hundreds of boxes of .50- and .30-caliber ammunition among the bushes that lined the road leading to the airfield. Before nightfall, Hamas delivered .50-caliber ammunition and metal links to Captain Freuler and furnished him with the keys to the bomb and ammunition magazines.

The Wake Detachment's storeroom held a ninety-day supply of provisions; the CPNAB storage had six months' worth. Canned food and dry commissary stores were cached in proximity to all activities throughout the atoll, as well as in the shelters that had been constructed and at command posts. Water had been distributed in three thousand five-gallon cans. A further three hundred thousand gallons of fresh water were in storage tanks, steamed-out fuel drums, and five-gallon cans stored on board a lighter in the lagoon.

About twenty-five civilians, equipped with trucks, responded to Wally Lewis's request for assistance in improving Battery E's position. He then had his men run a telephone line to Battery D's height finder so that he could obtain altitudes for the incoming enemy bombers from

Sergeant Robert S. Box, the skillful and efficient noncommissioned officer in charge of the height finder section who transmitted the necessary data to the two antiaircraft batteries.

Among the other civilians who sought to serve was Donald W. Butler, a CPNAB machinery designer, who had availed himself of the marine training. After reporting to Camp 1, he was assigned to a .30-caliber machine-gun crew across the road from the water tower observation post; he was soon digging foxholes, stringing telephone line, and belting ammunition.

John Valov had hopped on a truck bound for Camp 1. When he reached his destination, Second Lieutenant Poindexter was looking over the volunteers. Apparently remembering Valov from the weapons training he had participated in, Poindexter said: "Valov, stand over there." His name "being an odd one to remember," it surprised him when he was thus singled out. Another man stepped forward and told Poindexter that although he did not know anything about machine guns he would do anything he was told to do.[27]

Harry L. McDonald, the contractors' soda fountain manager, had helped fight the fires that consumed the PanAir hotel that morning. That afternoon, he reported to Camp 1 and, along with Leo L. Nonn, a canteen clerk, sought out Poindexter and asked to be assigned a battle station. Sent over to Wilkes, McDonald reported to Sergeant Raymond L. Coulson, who assigned him to .50-caliber machine gun 11, under Private First Class Erwin "D" Pistole, on that islet's south beach.[28] Among the other civilians who stepped forward for service was Robert G. Hardy, a forty-five-year-old laborer; he had served in the U.S. Army in World War I and had fought in the Argonne and at St. Mihiel. Another veteran was Harold E. Lochridge, a forty-three-year-old chief file clerk, who had also seen combat in France.

Commander Keene, meanwhile, having concluded that no seaplanes would be basing at Wake any time soon, reassigned his men (for whom no weapons existed). Retaining Ensign Olcott as his aide, Keene sent Ensigns Henshaw and Lauff to Cunningham's staff, where they would perform "excellent service in straightening out the previously confused codes and ciphers and in coding and decoding" message traffic. Lauff, Patrol Wing 2's radio officer, proved to be an expert at internal combustion engines and would "[do] much toward keeping needed [boat] transportation operating." Keene sent Boatswain's Mate First Class James E. Barnes and twelve enlisted men to join the defense battalion to drive trucks, serve in galley details, and stand security watches. He assigned the rest to "various miscellaneous duties."[29] Barnes and his bluejackets reported to Poindexter in Camp 1 and were immediately assigned to lookout duties atop the water tower. In between those rotating watches,

Poindexter and his marines instructed the sailors in the use of .30-caliber machine guns and grenades.

The Wake Base Detachment commander also sent Aviation Machinist's Mate First Class James F. Hesson and Seamen Second Class Norris H. Troney and Theodore D. Franklin to VMF-211. Told that Hesson had specialized in instruments, Kinney and Technical Sergeant Hamilton soon found the light-brown-haired Pennsylvanian, who had served in the air corps before joining the navy and who had just turned thirty-five years of age, to be good at any task he was given.

VMF-211 also benefited from the services of thirteen eager and competent civilians, six of whom Major Bayler regarded as "excellent engine mechanics," while six had experience with machine guns and automatic weapons and joined Private First Class Taylor, 211's armorer, in caring for the squadron's machine guns and bombs. Square-jawed Harry H. Yeager and Clinton L. "Doc" Stevenson were among those who shared their mechanical skills, as did welders Fred S. Gibbons and his son George. The thirteenth civilian, John P. "Pete" Sorenson, the contractors' structural steel superintendent, volunteered to drive a truck and, because he had some mechanical aptitude, to serve as general handyman. "These men," Bayler remembered, "behaved admirably, worked willingly, and . . . expressed their desire to be of use to their country in some manner or form."

Over at the contractors' camp, as he shouldered his bedroll and approached the main thoroughfare, John Burroughs, who was among the civilian workers who had volunteered to serve with the marines, saw two large trucks and a pickup driving across the bridge that connected Peale with Wake. Stepping aside to let the vehicles pass down the road that led to the contractors' hospital, he saw an unforgettable sight: the truck's bed "covered with wounded, dying, and dead men, sprawled on rumpled, bloody quilts"—the casualties from the bombing of the facilities on Peale. At least twenty-five civilian workmen had been killed.

For the remainder of the day and into the night, in the CPNAB hospital in Camp 2, Lieutenant (j.g.) Kahn and the contractors' physician, Dr. Lawton E. Shank, a thirty-four-year-old Hoosier, who possessed not only high professional skill but a calm and cheerful personality, tried to save as many wounded as possible. Kahn, aided by his corpsmen, and Shank by the civilian medical staff—dentist James A. Cunha and dental nurse William O. Smith; nurses Ned Daly, Paul E. Dettra, and Henry Gottlieb; and surgical nurses Henry M. Dreyer, Samuel R. Kerr, and John K. Pace—did their best, but some men were beyond help, and four from VMF-211 died that night: Second Lieutenant Conderman, Sergeant Maurice R. Stockton (the youngest marine in the aviation detachment that had come out in the *Wright,* two weeks shy of his twentieth birthday), Corporal David E. Woodruff, and Private First Class James E. McBride.

After the attack on the airfield, Second Lieutenant Hanna moved his command post near the army radio trailer that lay along the south beach road and reestablished contact with the scattered elements of his unit at 1700. His men reported possible hits on several *rikkōs* but did not believe that they had inflicted any significant damage.

That afternoon, at Peacock Point, Barney Barninger's men completed their foxholes—overhead cover, sandbags, and chunks of coral would come later. At dusk, evidently sensing that the atoll might be in for a long siege and thinking they might not be in camp again for some time, Barninger sent some of his men back to Camp 1 to obtain extra toilet gear and clothing. In the gathering darkness, he set his security watches and rotated beach patrols and observers. Those men not on watch slept fitfully in their foxholes. Godbold took advantage of the lull to send a work party back to Camp 1 to gather bedding for his men.

Meanwhile, the *Tambor* offshore to the north and the *Triton* to the south did not know about the bombing of Pearl Harbor or of Wake. Up to that point, both had been encountering "uniformly unfavorable" sea conditions that had prevailed since shortly after their arrival on station. Strong trade winds varied from the northeast and the east, and long, heavy ground swells made running at periscope death impracticable at low speed. Consequently, the *Triton* and the *Tambor* had had to run at deep submergence except for frequent short periods of periscope observations.

On 8 December, the *Triton* noted "two large columns of whitish smoke" at about 1245. She closed the island "for a better view" and noted an additional column of black smoke at 1400. An hour later, two miles offshore, Pilly Lent saw what looked like dredges in operation. Although he assumed the smoke was from fires on Wake, he had not heard one word about it on the periscope antenna. The *Triton* came to periscope depth again at 1550 and remained there until 1625 for the planned exercise with 211's planes, but, inexplicably, none showed up. Still unaware of the attack on Wake, the *Triton* surfaced at 1735 and began charging her batteries at 1800. At about that time, her radiomen picked up a news broadcast that told of raids on Pearl Harbor, Midway, and Manila. Lent and his crew learned the reason for the smoke columns over Wake at 1810, when a signal light blinked word that the island had been bombed about noon by what appeared to be twenty-five Japanese twin-engine bombers. There had been many casualties and planes destroyed. Hostilities with Japan had commenced. The *Triton* was advised to stay clear of gun range.

The *Tambor* had last observed the atoll at 0700 that morning; she picked up a radio broadcast ten and a half hours later that provided Spuds Murphy and his men with the first word of hostilities but did not mention Wake. The *Tambor* was roughly forty miles east-northeast of the atoll, and Murphy ordered a course change to allow the *Tambor* to regain her patrol station, while his radiomen deciphered messages that painted a "hazy, general picture of the situation." In one dispatch "CinCPac advised Wake and the patrolling submarines that a renewed attack on Wake by air and surface craft was probable during [the] daylight [hours] of Dec[ember] 8–9." Murphy later said that "was the first indication I had that Wake had been attacked."

That night, Cunningham sent a dispatch to ComFourteen reporting that Wake had lost eight planes on the ground. The landing field, however, was still usable, and ample gasoline remained. Twenty-five men had been killed and thirty injured. No one knew whether there would be more raids or whether the casualties would mount.

The ninth of December dawned with a clear sky overhead. In Camp 2, Dan Teters gathered his men in the mess hall and told them to "go about their normal duties" but not to "congregate" anywhere—particularly in the mess hall, where they would be the most vulnerable. Teters later admitted that the CPNAB organization was "not quite set up to take over all work duties as decided upon" in the immediate prewar discussions. "Furthermore," he explained, "we did not know but what [the raid on 8 December] was merely a token bombing." The contractors' superintendent thought that perhaps—just perhaps—the raid of the day before would be the only one, "at least for some time." Teters ordered the contents of the CPNAB store made available to the marines. If a leatherneck needed clothing, underwear, razors, candy, tobacco, cigarettes, or socks, he had only to ask for it.

On Peacock Point, Barninger and his men began the day with hot coffee, a "cheering note to us all." The marines of Battery A set to work improving the shelters and working on the battery position. Barninger inspected his position, in company with Wally Lewis, around 0820. Lewis said his guns were ready "for the day's event." Would the "Nips" continue to attack from a low level, as they had the first day—the least effective height for the defenders because they could not bring their guns to bear on the attacking planes? Or would they go "upstairs"? As Barninger later remembered the conversation, Lewis "believed, and rightly so, that from now on they would go upstairs."

Work to improve positions also engaged the men of Godbold's Battery D; he set them to constructing an emplacement for the height finder. Needing sandbags, however, Godbold sent Corporal Kenneth L. Marvin with a tractor and trailer to Camp 2 to fetch a load of them.

Among the marines at Toki Point, the questions about what lay ahead seemed "even more insistent" on the morning of the ninth. "Whatever happened today," Kessler later wrote, "would cast a well defined shadow over our future. If the Japs didn't come back . . . the events of 8 December were a punishing but one-time affair." If they did, "we were definitely on their list for elimination."

The bombing of the field the previous day had prompted Staff Sergeant Hotchkiss to try to convince Captain Wilson of the wisdom of moving their radio equipment to a safer location. Hotchkiss suggested that they remove the transmitter from the truck and "install it in an empty powder magazine." Wilson did not agree.

As the day progressed, more of Dan Teters's men volunteered to help the garrison's leathernecks. Nine civilians arrived at Battery B, eager to help out "in any way they could." Carpenters George Harris, Ray L. Howard, Arne E. Astad, Vahren Yerman, Lawrence L. Scott, and Thomas Lyall; Tom G. Huskison, a driller's helper; Doris Lee Ralston, a sprayman; and Albert Boutell, a potwasher, expressed their willingness to "do almost anything." Kessler could not issue them rifles (there were no extra Springfields), but there were enough hand grenades to give each man three after he had been thoroughly instructed in their use. They aided in "fetching shells and powder canisters" and in improving the defenses, each knowing the risk if an enemy found a civilian who had taken up arms but willing regardless of the possible cost.

Reinforcements would have been welcome. While Cunningham's garrison was recovering from the first raid, the *William Ward Burrows* had been zigzagging slowly westward toward her original destination, behind schedule because of the detour to pick up the appendicitis patient from the *Sonoma*. One hour into the forenoon watch on 9 December, however, when she was about 425 miles east of Wake, she received a dispatch from ComFourteen, ordering her to return to Honolulu.[30] Apparently, Rear Admiral Bloch, knowing that the transport was unescorted and thus highly vulnerable, deemed it improbable that the *William Ward Burrows* would be able to discharge her cargo "under the . . . circumstances" and thus directed her return.[31]

While the U.S. Navy ship closest to the atoll headed away from it, at the airfield three planes had taken off on the early morning patrol, and Kinney had a fourth, 211-F-8—with its irreparable reserve gas tank—ready by 0900. A test flight proved the plane "o.k." because she withstood a 350-miles-per-hour dive "without a quiver." It had been none too soon, for at 1145 on the ninth, twenty-six *rikkōs* (their number having been reduced en route when one of the twenty-seven that had taken off had had to abort the mission), with a bomb load consisting of 2 250-kilogram and 285 60-kilogram bombs, again under Lieutenant

Commander Matsuda, came in at thirteen thousand feet. Second Lieutenant Kliewer and Technical Sergeant Hamilton attacked straggling bombers and claimed one shot down.

Battery D's number 2 and 4 guns fired one hundred rounds, engaging the enemy as long as they were within range—a broken firing pin prevented the civilian-manned gun 3 from taking part in the battle—and Godbold conservatively estimated that five planes left the skies over the atoll smoking; he thought he saw one explode and crash "some distance from the island." Marine antiaircraft fire damaged twelve (none had been shot down), but the enemy suffered very light casualties: one man wounded in each of the number one planes of the second and third *shōtais* of the third *chūtai*.

Some of the bombs fell near the edge of the lagoon, north of the airfield. One exploded in a foxhole in which the three men of the crew of one of the dispersed gasoline trucks—Sergeants Quince A. Hunt and Robert W. Mitwalski and Corporal William M. Tucker—had sought shelter, killing them instantly.[32] Corporal Marvin, bringing sandbags to Battery D, received a head wound, but prompt work by the pharmacist's mate at Toki Point enabled him to return to duty.

Other bombs damaged a warehouse and a metal shop in Camp 2 and demolished the hospital, killing Coxswain Wolney and Sergeant Robert Zurchauer, Jr. Burning collapsing wreckage threatened to pin down Boatswain's Mate Second Class Ludwick and Seaman First Class Darden until Owen G. Thomas, a seventy-year-old blacksmith, risked his life by forcing his way inside and extricated the two sailors.[33] Doctors Kahn and Shank and their helpers evacuated the wounded and saved as much equipment as they could. Shank carried men from the burning building, courageous work that so impressed Marine Gunner Hamas, trapped nearby delivering a load of projectiles and powder to gun positions on Peale, that he subsequently recommended the doctor for the Medal of Honor.

Under Shank's personal leadership, the medical people moved wounded men and the remaining medical equipment into two reinforced concrete magazines on Wake's eastern shore. Located near the unfinished leg of the airstrip, the magazines served as two twenty-one-bed wards, one under Lieutenant (j.g.) Kahn for the military wounded, the other under Shank for the civilians. The plethora of shrapnel and gunshot wounds, as well as fractures, soon drained the supply of morphine and anesthesia, and in the cramped quarters operations had to be performed in the same room where patients convalesced. One observer noted that despite the crude facilities, the wounded recovered remarkably well and seemed cheerful.

There was little cheer at Peacock Point, however, where a bomb

Private First Class John Katchak, 8 October 1941, the first fatality in the Wake Detachment, First Defense Battalion. His older brother, Sergeant George Katchak, USMC, would be wounded in action at Saipan in June 1944. (USMC)

had exploded near the lip of the foxhole occupied by nineteen-year-old Private First Class John Katchak, USMCR, and had not only killed him outright but nearly buried him. "Surrounded by all the reverence and sympathy men have for a fallen messmate," Barninger "spoke the burial service over him. It was crude, but if ever a body was committed to the earth and a soul to God with more depth of feeling or in closer kinship with the Almighty it was in a similar circumstance." Katchak had died half a world away from his birthplace of Coaldale, a coal town sprawled on a blackened hillside in eastern Pennsylvania. The simple mound of earth that marked his resting place lay in the middle of Battery A's position, constantly reminding his messmates of the task that lay before them and proving "a source of inspiration" to them. The bombing had rendered Battery A's range finder useless, as shrapnel riddled the tube and shattered one of the lenses. The men at the seacoast guns perhaps found their situation more frustrating than did those who manned the antiaircraft batteries. "Taking punishment without a means of retaliation," First Lieutenant Kessler later explained, "is both frustrating and enervating."

Once the bombers had gone, the work of repairs and improving positions resumed. At the airfield, 211-F-8 had been repaired, and, although he had no instruction book, Kinney tried to fix 211-F-9's propeller. That night, a crew of civilians helped load .50-caliber ammunition because the initial bombing had destroyed the power-loading machines.

Despite the destruction wreaked that day by the Japanese bombs, emergency construction soon provided two large shelters and one small one on the beach south of Camp 1, courtesy of Harold E. ("Jim") Jimison, a CPNAB "scraper" operator. Four hundred yards east of the marine camp, workmen built another shelter to serve as Major Devereux's command post. He and his staff moved into it the next day.

That same evening, work crews dispersed food, medical supplies, water, and lumber to various points around the atoll. Typical of such a movement was that undertaken by the men from Battery D, Battery B, and the marines manning the machine guns on Toki Point, who distributed food supplies from the marine storeroom in Camp 1. Dan Teters told his men to vacate Camp 2 and take shelter in the brush, promising that they would be furnished with supplies.

Earlier that day, from his vantage point at Battery E, near the tip of Peacock Point, big, burly Marine Gunner Clarence B. McKinstry, the Wake Detachment's three-inch antiaircraft artillery maintenance officer, had seen one bomber break off from the rest. Surmising that the plane had taken aerial photographs, he suggested that the battery be moved. Consequently, that afternoon, First Lieutenant Lewis received orders to reposition his battery after dark, two of the eight-ton guns at a time—a task difficult enough even in daylight that required folding the four outrigger legs to form the body of the gun, jacking up the gun, and mounting it on bogies to haul to the new position, where the process would be reversed. That night, aided by about a hundred civilians with several trucks, Lewis and McKinstry shifted guns, ammunition, and sandbags some fifteen hundred yards to the northwest and left dummy guns in the old position to deceive Japanese aerial observers.

Also that night, Commander Cunningham met with Dan Teters, Commander Keene, and Lieutenant Commander Greey in the first of what would become nightly war councils in Teters's cottage. They decided to put in operation the plan they had agreed on earlier to employ the CPNAB people in supporting work. Cunningham suggested that Teters "continue to manage the activities of the civilian construction crews" while the CPNAB men who had volunteered for duty with the marines, either with VMF-211 or the defense battalion, would be under the orders of the commander of that unit.[34] Another result of that conference was that Keene moved his headquarters into Teters's; from that point on, "all activities of the civilian crew[s] were carried on with [Keene's] knowledge and consent." The CPNAB cooks would feed the entire population, CPNAB operators would keep the powerhouse and water-distillation plants running; the civilians would drive trucks and repair any equipment (except guns and airplanes) that needed fixing. Over the days that followed, Major Potter, Devereux's executive officer, would telephone Teters and ask him to provide work crews, giving the "number of men and the type of workers desired, and designate the battery commanders to whom they would report." A few men protested, Teters noted later, "but we were able to shame most of them into cooperating."

Both the *Triton* and the *Tambor*, struggling to run at periscope depth because of the ground swells off the island, had observed the latest raid. From their limited periscope's-eye perspective, the former spotted columns of smoke and flames while the latter, patrolling east to west about four miles offshore, noted large fires, one of which burned into the night. Both boats remained submerged until nightfall, when they surfaced to charge their batteries.

The *Tambor*'s officer of the deck (OOD) reported gun flashes at 1840 and ordered the boat taken down. Spuds Murphy, however, ordered her brought up immediately, but by the time he reached the bridge, the flashes had ceased.

Curiously, the *Triton* saw no flashes at that time. When she surfaced, Pilly Lent noted that Wake's radio station did not seem to be on the air so the *Triton* got off a priority dispatch at 2000—shortly before the *Tambor* was ready to do likewise—telling of the latest bombing raid and reporting that she had not been able to raise station NCL by radio. She also reported that she had sighted no enemy ships and asked that she be advised if any American ships had been sent to Wake. She then resumed her vigil off the atoll. Station NCL, the *Triton* noted later, came back on the air an hour before midnight.

"By 10 December," Woodrow Kessler would later write, "we were already attuned to the prospects of war; it was as though it had been going on for ages." For the marines, sailors, Signal Corps soldiers, and civilians on Wake, it indeed must have seemed so.

The submarines operating offshore tried to help. As the *Tambor* patrolled north of Wake on the morning of the tenth, her depth-control officer sighted by periscope what he swore looked like a lone "enemy land plane" (a "queer-looking craft," Spuds Murphy later reported him as saying, "but definitely a land plane") flying in from the southwest at 0610. Murphy himself took a look twenty minutes later but saw no plane. Surmising that the aircraft was reconnoitering from the Marshalls and perhaps photographing the atoll, the submarine tried to warn Wake of its approach but found that the frequency used—4,265 kilocycles—was being "jammed" by the enemy. More than likely, however, the queer-looking plane spotted by the *Tambor* had only been one of the "millions of birds" seen in the course of the patrol that made detection of aircraft by periscope difficult.

On the tenth Marine Gunner McKinstry received orders to report to

Captain Platt, who commanded the Wilkes strongpoint, to take charge of the provisional Battery F, which had four guns but lacked crews, height finder, and director. As a consequence, McKinstry could fire the guns accurately only at short or point-blank range so they were good only to protect the beach. Assisted by one marine and some civilians, the gunner moved his weapons into position just before Lieutenant Commander Matsuda and his twenty-six *rikkōs* flew in at 1042 to drop 275 60-kilogram bombs on the airfield and the batteries at the tips of Wilkes and Peale.

Casualties were light—in Battery L Corporal Paul Tokryman was killed and Private First Class Herbert R. Byrne wounded, while fragments wounded Battery G's Private First Class Wilford J. Lindsay, a searchlight operator, and Adams, a civilian, suffered shell shock—but the positions on Wilkes received considerable damage. One bomb set off 120 tons of dynamite stored by the contractors near the site of the new channel. The cataclysmic blast stripped the three-inch battery of its fresh camouflage, destroyed all ammunition at the guns, knocked over a searchlight (a fragile and conspicuous piece of equipment at best) and shook it up severely, and irreparably damaged the range finder, time-interval apparatus, navy plotting board, pointer scope for gun 1, trainer scopes for guns 1 and 2, as well as batteries and phones at both ends. Fortunately, the supply sheds on Wake yielded two trainer scopes, and the telephones were replaced and the batteries reorganized. Thirty rounds of ammunition were placed at each gun. McKinstry then had the other three guns moved nearer to the shoreline and had them camouflaged with burned brush.[35]

From its new position about a thousand yards northwest of its old one, Battery E managed to hurl one hundred rounds skyward before bombs started hitting near Peacock Point. A direct hit set off a small ammunition dump, and the old position was "very heavily bombed," vindicating McKinstry's hunch about the photo-reconnaissance plane. "The battery would have been out of action," Lewis noted later, "if it had not been moved."

Misfortune befell Battery D just at the instant that lookouts spotted the incoming *rikkōs* when a defective carburetor disabled the battery's power plant, compelling Godbold's gunners to shift to local control. First Lieutenant Kessler watched, fascinated, "as the puffs of smoke broke among the enemy planes as they entered their bombing run" on Toki Point. The nine G3M2s that bombed the battery positions (either the first *chūtai*, under Lieutenant Commander Matsuda and Lieutenant Watanabe, or the second, under Lieutenant Kotani) landed none of their ordnance any closer than the reef off Toki Point, but, their aim appar-

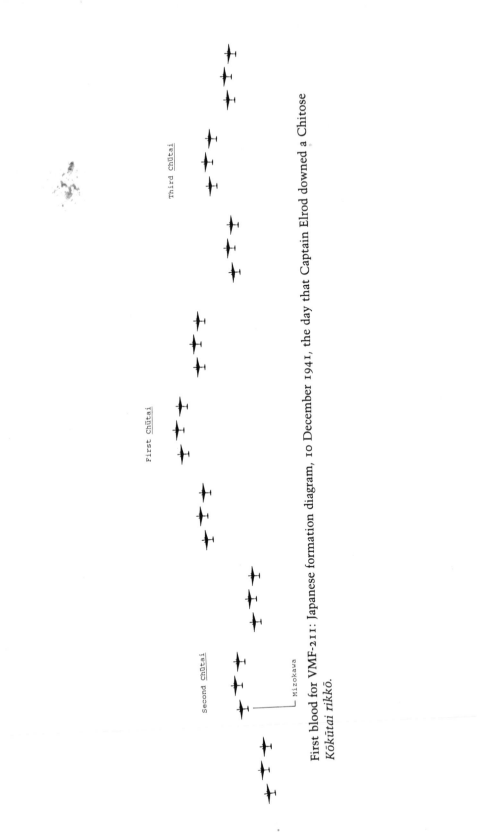

First blood for VMF-211: Japanese formation diagram, 10 December 1941, the day that Captain Elrod downed a Chitose *Kōkūtai rikkō.*

ently thrown off by Battery D's bursting shells, flew off to the north and circled around for a second pass. Battery B's marines, "furious but helpless to retaliate," crouched against their sandbags, stomachs tight in anticipation of the dull "crump" of exploding bombs.

Battery D's frustrations continued unabated. As the *rikkōs* began their second run, Sergeant Bowsher, the gun captain on number 3—the civilian-manned piece—pulled the lanyard only to have it break. A hasty replacement allowed the weapon to continue firing. Fortunately, again, the Japanese accuracy proved poor. In the second attack all of the ordnance splashed harmlessly into the lagoon—a dismal performance duly noted by the *Tambor*, watching by periscope from the waters north of the atoll.

Though they had to fire by local control, Godbold's men claimed hits on two bombers (one of which they said exploded later) out of the 275 rounds fired. Although Captain Elrod, who single-handedly attacked the formation and reported downing two bombers, only one *rikkō*—that commanded by Petty Officer First Class Mizokawa Hiroshi, the number two plane of the second *chūtai*, first *shōtai*—failed to return to its base, splashing sixty-seven miles southwest of Wake at 1104, killing Mizokawa and his crew. Four of the twenty-five remaining G3M2s had been damaged by either the fearless Elrod or three-inch gunfire.

Although the actual damage to the enemy differed from that claimed, Cunningham reported to ComFourteen that two Japanese bombers had been downed, additional damage had been slight, and casualties were few. He also reported that the daily air patrols had spotted enemy submarines southwest of Wake. They may have seen one of the group of three "second-class" submarines from the Twenty-seventh Division (Captain Fukuya Sokichi), the *Ro-65*, the *Ro-66*, and the *Ro-67*, that had sailed from Kwajalein on 6 December. They had been slated to arrive off Wake around 0200 on the tenth and scout out the island, on the alert for reported "torpedo boats."[36]

Captain Elrod had exacted a toll from the aerial raiders, but Kinney's attempt to render 211-F-9 flyable had met with less success. That same day, Kinney had tried to coax the ex-VF-6 machine aloft and needed all five thousand feet of runway to prevent a crash. Concluding that the engine was running overspeed because the propeller pitch had been set too low, he reset it and planned to test it again the following day.

There were still not enough plane shelters to go around, and finding the labor to finish them looked like a difficult task. In the eyes of some of 211's marines, the civilians—with the exception of what seemed to be only a few—had "holed up." The majority, Kinney observed, seemed "to[o] scared to come out." The pilots threatened to "knock off flying" to "drive some needed labor out of the brush."

Living by the airstrip meant that VMF-211 sometimes felt itself at the proverbial end of the line when it came to getting fed. Camp 2 served as the main food distribution center. Hot meals were trucked to designated points on what seemed to be a catch-as-catch-can basis, and Kinney grumbled that the airfield was "sometimes overlooked." With "leaner days" perhaps ahead, 211 dined sparingly from a stock of canned goods. Sergeant Comin, whose wounds had kept him off the flight line but who had refused to stay in the hospital to have them treated properly, helped set up and run a galley for 211—a task at which he persisted for the next fortnight, often in the face of appalling field conditions.[37]

Although temporary repairs had gotten Battery D's power plant back in operation by 1115, Captain Godbold, in the aftermath of the power failure that had crippled his battery's fire control apparatus at a most inopportune time, dispatched a detail to find an auxiliary power source. At 1145, about the same time that permanent repairs had been made to the existing plant, the scavenging party returned with a diesel generator set from Camp 2. Connected to the battery and run continuously during the day, the new generator seemed, in Bob Greeley's estimation, "very satisfactory."

Following the latest raids, Technical Sergeant June and his assistants installed an air warning system—a single line, manned around the clock, to each station on the atoll—which made it easy to warn all units either to take cover or to man antiaircraft batteries. Limited to warning use, the system was not connected to the main switchboard and required no ringing.

The desire to keep the radio equipment intact prompted Staff Sergeant Hotchkiss to approach Captain Wilson again about moving the transmitter to a magazine. This time Wilson assented because the recent near total destruction of the navy radio equipment had caused him to ponder the status of his own. "After some hesitation and considerable thought," Wilson "decided to sacrifice mobility for security." On the night of the tenth, the soldiers, assisted by a party of CPNAB workmen, dismantled the equipment and hauled the transmitter out of the truck and down into one of the concrete magazines, bolstering the "hasty installation with spare bits of equipment" salvaged from the ruined PanAir station. Workmen laid concrete bars, intended for one of the atoll's interrupted construction projects, overhead and dumped about eight feet of coral dirt on top of them, camouflaging the installation with brush. A shortage of sandbags compelled Wilson to use sacks of government-issue coffee to "sand-bag" the entrance. He placed his equipment at the navy's disposal (station NCL moved in the next day) and provided a keying line to the transmitter. Access to the army unit's "continuous, instantaneous communication" to Hickam enabled the navy to reach Pearl. Other than a small navy transmitter with a limited one-hundred-mile range, the SCR-197 constituted Wake's sole means of communication with the outside world. Commander Cunningham soon moved his command post into the refurbished magazine.

Later on the afternoon of the tenth, Battery D received a pair of .30-caliber machine guns. Godbold had them set up on Toki Point to cover the entrance to the lagoon. Soon thereafter, the battery received nine hundred rounds of three-inch antiaircraft and six hundred rounds of three-inch armor-piercing ammunition. The marines and their civilian helpers dispersed the former into the battery magazine and the rest into small dumps nearby.

That evening, the peripatetic Battery E shifted into the "toe" of the "horseshoe" on the lagoon side of Wake. Previous bombing runs had been from east to west and the bombs dropped along the length of the island. To reach it now, the Japanese would have to risk dropping their ordnance into the lagoon.

The shift also compelled Barney Barninger to alter his defensive dispositions: no longer able to count on Battery E to defend the landward side of Peacock Point, he had his men prepare mutually supporting foxholes. With no men to spare, he planned to use his range section as infantry (the range finder had been destroyed on the ninth), with the machine guns, to hold the high ground. His marines would watch the south shore while his civilians would watch the east. "Not an excellent position," Barninger admitted philosophically, "but. . . the best I could devise on the spot with the few men available."

Elsewhere, contractors Jim Jimison, Harry E. Bartlett, and Herman E. Schoningle seemed to work round the clock. Jimison continued to bulldoze more shelters, while Bartlett, normally a laundry helper, and Schoningle, a carpenter, joined Technical Sergeant June and his communications men in trying to repair the breaks in the J-line caused by the bombings. "Repairing and installing new circuits," June noted, posed a problem because much of the work had to be done under blackout conditions.[38] If the lines were laid close to the roads and in the edge of the thick underbrush along the beach, any bombs dropped on the island's main thoroughfares or near the beach positions would knock out that portion of the network nearby. Nighttime operation of lumbering construction equipment posed an equally potent threat to the efforts toward keeping the lines intact.

For First Lieutenant Kessler, the first two nights of the war had not brought restful, regenerative slumber. Watches, patrols, work on the defenses under blackout conditions, and false alarms—when "overly sensitive and imaginative ears picked out the rhythm of heavy motors from the monotony of the surf"—had proved enervating. In the damp blackness of the night of 10 December, however, perhaps finally lulled by the monotonous surf and worn out from stress, he enjoyed his first deep sleep since the Japanese had unleashed war upon Wake Island.

CHAPTER FIVE

"HUMBLED BY SIZEABLE CASUALTIES"

While Wake's lookouts vigilantly scanned the horizon and those of the island's defenders not on duty grabbed what sleep they could, late in the first watch on 10 December the *Triton* was patrolling on the surface on a northeasterly course, ten miles south of the atoll, charging her batteries. At 2315, her bridge lookouts discerned two flashes and then the shape of what appeared to be a destroyer or light cruiser against the backdrop of the heavy clouds that lay abaft the submarine's port beam.

Originally on a parallel course, the strange ship steered toward the *Triton*, which was proceeding at four knots, silhouetted against the rising moon. After his OOD determined the range as six thousand yards, Pilly Lent cleared the *Triton*'s bridge and took her down. The heavy seas, however, running on the starboard bow, required the submarine to change course toward the enemy to get under. Leveling off, the *Triton* detected the ship on her starboard side, seemingly following each move she made. A short time later, with the stranger trailing at slow speed astern of her, the *Triton* planed up to 120 feet and seventeen minutes into the mid watch on 11 December 1941 loosed a salvo of four torpedoes from her stern tubes—the first fired from a Pacific Fleet submarine in World War II.

Although the submariners heard a dull explosion, indicating at least one probable hit, and the propeller noises appeared to cease shortly thereafter, success did not crown the *Triton*'s work. She went to 175 feet and ran silent for a time and later picked up high-speed propeller noises that did not come close. She resumed patrolling off Wake, however, at deep submergence, unfortunately oblivious to what was transpiring on the surface.

Two hours into the mid watch, Captain Wilson's army radio unit on the atoll sent a message from Cunningham to Pearl at 0200 on the eleventh, telling of the casualties in the CPNAB contingent and suggesting early evacuation of the contractors. Upon receiving the message, army communicators on Oahu noted that the Japanese—as they

Rear Admiral Kajioka Sadamichi,
Commander, Sixth Destroyer
Squadron. (U.S. Naval Institute)

apparently had attempted to do concerning the *Triton's* warning the
previous day—had tried to jam the transmission.

The ship the *Triton* had encountered in the heavy seas off Wake's
south coast was probably from the invasion convoy bearing down on
the atoll; one destroyer had been deployed ten miles ahead of the main
body to spot the island and provide information on any opposition. That
convoy pounding up from the south had set out from Kwajalein, in
the Marshalls, on 8 December, under Rear Admiral Kajioka Sadamichi,
commander of the Sixth Destroyer Squadron.

Kajioka, fifty-two years old, had entered the naval service in July 1909
and had been commissioned an ensign in 1912. He had risen steadily in
the Imperial Navy and in the course of his career had commanded the
oiler *Naruto*, the training ship *Kasuga*, and the light cruisers *Nagara*
and *Kiso* before attaining flag rank in 1940. Following a tour as port
director at Yokosuka, Kajioka had been given command of the Sixth
Destroyer Squadron in July 1941.

Just as those who had contemplated a Japanese attack on Wake had
predicted, no capital ships backed up the operations unfolding in the
predawn darkness off the atoll's lee shore. Kajioka's force included his
flagship, the rakish light cruiser *Yūbari*, six destroyers (all of which bore
poetical names)—the *Mutsuki* (January), the *Kisaragi* (February), the
Yayoi (March), the *Mochizuki* (Full Moon), the *Oite* (Fair Wind), and
the *Hayate* (Squall), and two old destroyers reconfigured during 1941 to
launch landing craft, *daihatsu*, down a stern ramp—the *Patrol Boat No.*

32 (formerly *Aoi*) and the *Patrol Boat No. 33* (formerly *Hagi*). Each armored, steel-hulled *daihatsu*, powered by a sixty-horsepower diesel engine, had a crew of seven (helmsman, machinist's mate, anchorman, signalman, and three other men) and could carry seventy troops. Rounding out the invasion force were two armed merchantmen, the *Kongo Maru* and the *Kinryu Maru*, that carried between them four Aichi E13A1 Type 00 reconnaissance seaplanes from the Seventeenth Air Group. In addition, the *Kinryu Maru* carried an antiaircraft gun detachment from the Fourth Base Force; the *Kongo Maru* carried construction equipment, three guardboats from the Sixth Base Force, and six fishing boats.

Scouting ahead were the *RO-65*, *RO-66*, and *RO-67* that had arrived off Wake the previous day. They had reconnoitered the island and proceeded south, where they had rendezvoused with the rest of the force seventy-five miles south of the atoll. The *RO-65* guided Kajioka's ships to their objective while the other two took up patrol stations—the *RO-66* to the northwest, the *RO-67* to the northeast—off the atoll.[1]

To provide additional gunfire support, Vice-Admiral Inoue had also assigned Kajioka the Eighteenth Cruiser Division—the *Tatsuta* and the *Tenryu*—under Rear Admiral Marumo Kuninori. The *Yūbari* and the two venerable light cruisers each mounted shielded 5.5-inch guns, the destroyers (roughly the same vintage as the flagship) and patrol boats shielded 4.7-inch. Their only antiaircraft batteries were open, pedestal-mounted 3-inch high-angle guns (only on board the cruisers) and small numbers of 25- and 7.7-millimeter machine guns. None of the warships could be considered first-line naval vessels; the newest ships were the auxiliaries, which had been converted from modern freighters.

The light cruiser *Yūbari* airing bedding as she lies moored in the Whangpoo River, Shanghai, China, in April 1937. (NHC, NH 82098)

The Japanese plan called for 150 Special Landing Force (SLF) men (specially trained sailors whose mission corresponded to that performed by the U.S. Marine Corps), drawn from the Second Maizuru SLF, to go ashore on Wilkes and 300 on Wake. Lieutenant Uchida Kinichi commanded one company, transported in the *Oite* and the *Patrol Boat No. 32*; Special Duty Lieutenant (j.g.) Itaya Yakichi the other, the latter transported in the *Mutsuki* and the *Patrol Boat No. 33*. If those troops proved insufficient, the destroyers were to provide bluejacket landing forces to augment the SLF. From aerial reconnaissance and intelligence reports the Japanese reckoned some three hundred marines to be on Wake and about one thousand civilians; twelve dual-purpose guns, some mobile; and a large number of coast defense batteries and machine-gun positions. Several fighters appeared to be based on the island, while submarines and torpedo boats purportedly lurked in the vicinity.[2]

Should any American warships appear to contest the invasion, the Japanese ships that sighted them were to lay smoke to cover the retirement of the *Kinryu Maru* and the two patrol boats from the disputed area while the *Yūbari*, *Tenryu*, and *Tatsuta*, supported by the destroyers, would attack the enemy with gunfire and torpedoes. If contrary winds threatened the landing, the SLF would go ashore on the less suitable northern beaches.

Kajioka and his sailors faced less than favorable weather for the attempt to take Wake, but it appeared to have moderated by the eleventh and the force stood toward the atoll's south shore, confident that two days of bombings by the Chitose *Kōkūtai* had rendered the defenses nearly impotent. Kajioka's gray ships had sailed from the Marshalls, his men buoyed by the news of the devastating surprise attack on the American fleet at Pearl Harbor; the comparative ease with which Guam had been captured on 9 December made the Japanese even more optimistic for their chances of success at Wake.

The *Triton* had already encountered at least one of Kajioka's ships, and her sister ship would soon find herself—albeit unknowingly—near the enemy, too. Around 0300, as the *Tambor* was proceeding due west, two miles off Wake's north shore, her OOD spotted "two shapes about one point on the starboard bow." Uncertain as to whether they were buildings or ships, the OOD reasoned that if they were the latter they had the advantage of the moon and had probably already seen the submarine. Spuds Murphy, below, in his bunk, then felt what appeared to be a faint explosion. After the OOD reported soon thereafter that a large smoke cloud appeared to rise from one of the shapes, he sounded the diving alarm and the *Tambor* submerged immediately. During the dive, however, a gasket in the negative tank blow line carried away. Murphy decided to take the boat northeastward, repair the leaking gasket, and await the dawn. Uncertain of the situation, the sub's captain thought that the shapes seen by his OOD were buildings and that the explosions had been ashore. Murphy feared that the current had set the *Tambor* southward during the night and that his boat was in danger of running aground.

Murphy's OOD, however, had indeed seen ships: the *Tenryu* and the *Tatsuta*, which were steaming at twelve knots on an east-southeasterly course off Peale. Sighting what was unquestionably the *Tambor* four thousand meters off the port bow, Marumo's division changed course to roughly north-northeast and increased speed to eighteen knots. The smoke seen by the submarine's OOD probably resulted from the enemy ships' increasing speed to evade the sub. They altered course to due northwest at 0306.

Wake's lookouts, standing their watch in the moist breeze, were becoming convinced—justifiably—that there were ships offshore. From the battery control tower on Wilkes, Second Lieutenant McAlister's marines thought they observed several ships making runs parallel to the beach. Captain Platt, the Wilkes strongpoint commander, had reported ships in the distance; Gunner Hamas, on duty in the new battalion command post, notified Major Devereux. Grabbing night-vision binoculars, Devereux and Major Potter stepped into the night and scanned the horizon to the south. Hamas called Cunningham's quarters, and the island commander ordered fire held until the ships had stood in close.

After he had gotten off the line with Hamas, Cunningham turned to Commander Keene and Lieutenant Commander Greey, with whom he shared the cottage, and told them that lookouts had spotted ships, undoubtedly hostile ones, standing toward the atoll. He then directed the two officers to order an alert and immediately headed for the island's communications center in his pickup truck.[3]

Shortly after 0300, Wake Island went to general quarters. Devereux cautioned the battery commanders not to fire until told to do so—superfluous orders, First Lieutenant Kessler would recall, because it was too dark to see anything. Kessler sent out patrols and stationed extra lookouts, while his men brought ammunition up to the guns.

Don Butler was among the civilians awakened soon thereafter as word circulated that Japanese ships were off the atoll. "The impact of what seemed about to happen," he wrote later, "seemed wrenching." He was thankful for military training because "it help[ed] condition the soldier to the stark reality of impending conflict."

Over near Peacock Point, shouting awakened John Burroughs; he heard his name called and picked up the words "all civilians down on the guns." "In the west," he later wrote, "the sky was slightly less black than total night. I felt the morning mist on my face. Men were emerging

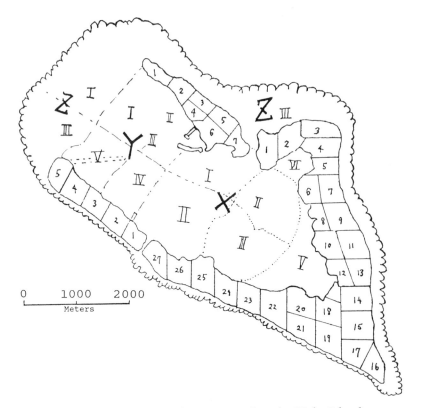

Sixth Destroyer Squadron gunfire support chart for Wake Island,
December 1941.

from the foxholes and running in the direction of Peacock Point." Burroughs followed, "stumbling over the sharp coral boulders."

When he reached the battery, Burroughs saw Barney Barninger dimly
outlined against the sky, standing on his command post roof, trying to
make out the identity of the ships that lay in the darkness offshore.
Gunnery Sergeant Anthony Poulosky, chief of the five-inch artillery gun
sections, meanwhile, put Burroughs in charge of the powder magazine,
telling him, with all the urgency required: "If we go into action, pass
up two shells—one for each gun. Then two powders—understand?"
Turning to John L. Clelan, a CPNAB labor foreman, Poulosky instructed
him on what to do with the shells and powder canisters that Burroughs
passed up to him.

At 0400, informed of the appearance of ships offshore, Paul Putnam put VMF-211 on the alert. Soon thereafter, he and his three senior pilots—Captains Elrod, Tharin, and Freuler—climbed into the cockpits of the four operational F4Fs. Frustratingly, only three of the Pratt and Whitney R-1830-86 engines coughed to life while the fourth Wildcat, as if possessed by a perverse nature, balked. The trio of Wildcats, each carrying a hundred-pound "Wake Model Band" bomb beneath each wing, then taxied into position for takeoff; the fourth similarly armed Wildcat would have to follow when ready. Shortly before 0500, Kajioka's ships began their final run-in. At 0515, "well before daylight," the three F4Fs—flight operations effectively masked by the high ground along which the highway ran south of the airfield—took off into the predawn darkness while Kinney and his ground crew redoubled their efforts to get the plane that constituted one-fourth of Wake's air power aloft.[4]

Meanwhile, on board the *Yūbari*, bucket chain hoists brought up the 38-kilogram shells and the silk powder bags from the magazine to the upper deck near the single mounts and to the central hoist tube into the twin gunhouse. Sailors then brought the ammunition to the guns and loaded them. The silence of the atoll that lay beyond their guns, however, was deceptive, for, fully alerted, Spiv Cunningham's garrison of marines, sailors, soldiers, and civilians crouched coiled and ready for the approaching Japanese. At 0522, the guns on board the *Yūbari* spoke, and her first shells roared toward Wake. At that moment, as twenty-one-year-old Sergeant Robert E. Bourquin, Jr., of VMF-211 later observed, "All hell broke loose."[5]

The marine guns, whose silent mouths pointed toward the enemy, remained so as Kajioka's ships "crept in, firing as they came." The first enemy projectiles set ablaze the oil tanks on the southwest portion of Wake while the *Patrol Boat No. 32* and the *Patrol Boat No. 33* prepared to land the SLF. Those fires soon occupied the full attention of Second Lieutenant Poindexter, who organized and led a damage control party to keep the blaze from spreading to the power plant and water-distilling equipment in Camp 1. As the twin columns of smoke boiled skyward into the darkness, flickering orange flame at their base, the column of dark gray warships advanced westward, still unchallenged by the marine batteries, whose camouflage remained in place. Reaching the western part of Wake proper twenty minutes later, the *Yūbari* closed to within forty-five hundred yards, seemingly "scouring the beach from one end to the other . . . from Peacock Point to the vicinity of Camp 1" with 5.5-inch fire at a rate commensurate with the toil of the laboring, sweating sailors who manually provided the shells and powder bags to do so.[6] At 0600, the light cruiser reversed course yet again and closed the range still further. From the airstrip, the fourth Wildcat roared aloft; the quartet of fighters was to rendezvous at twelve thousand feet over Toki Point.

Only fifteen minutes earlier, about five miles off Wake's north shore, and about two and three-quarters hours after the *Tambor* had unknowingly encountered the *Tenryu* and the *Tatsuta*, Spuds Murphy had squinted through the *Tambor*'s periscope and again estimated his boat's position. Murphy was relieved that he did not have to fear running aground, but his new assessment of his position meant that his OOD had indeed spotted ships some three hours earlier. At 0600, while mulling those thoughts over from his veritable ringside seat, he saw the gun flashes emanating from the Japanese ships and the oil fires on Wake. After determining that the gunfire was coming from what appeared to be three men-of-war shelling the atoll, he ordered the *Tambor* to shape a course to the southwest to "skirt the island and close them."

The *Yūbari*'s maneuvering toward Wake prompted the marines to remove the brush camouflage, and the gunners began to track the Japanese ships. At Battery A, Gunnery Sergeant Poulosky dashed back to the magazine. "All right you civilians," he shouted, "break out those shells." The neophyte shell-passers, who probably had received far less instruction for their task than their sweating counterparts on board the ships that lay offshore bombarding them, began their work, Poulosky's strident exhortations ringing in their ears. "Come on, you God-damned civilians," he bellowed, "hurry up with those shells!"[7]

As the distance decreased and the reports came into Devereux's command post, the major again told Gunner Hamas to relay the word to Commander Cunningham, who had reached his own command post. The island commander, upon receiving Hamas's report, replied: "What are we waiting for, open fire. Must be Jap ships all right." Devereux (who had given his battery commanders a second admonition to hold fire) accordingly gave his disciplined artillerymen the word for which they had been waiting anxiously.

At 0610, the gunpointers at Barninger's Battery A, at Peacock Point, sang out "Fire!" Wake's high ground behind them, the five-inch rifles boomed sharply and sent the first fifty-pound projectiles over their intended target. Adjusting the estimated range quickly, the gunners soon thought they scored hits on the *Yūbari*.

Although Barninger's guns, captained by Platoon Sergeants James F. Boscarino and Howard E. Warren, had unavoidably revealed their location, Kajioka's flagship put only one shell some 150 feet from Barninger's command post. Fragments from the exploding projectile inflicted a slight cut on one of Private First Class Sylvester Gregouire's legs as he manned gun 1 and hit the command post shack, while Barninger dauntlessly continued to direct Battery A's fire from atop the structure. "The [enemy] fire . . . continued to be over and then short throughout her firing," Barninger later reported. "She [the *Yūbari*] straddled continually, but none of the salvoes came into the position." Barninger and his men were fortunate that the Japanese return fire was inaccurate because the battery had not been sandbagged. Battery A's guns damaged the *Patrol Boat No. 33*, killing two men and wounding fourteen (seven slightly, seven seriously) and wounding one of the SLF sailors.

Battery A's civilian ammunition handlers, including John Burroughs, proved invaluable. Without them, Barninger doubted that it could have sustained fire "for any length of time." With only enough marines for the range section and guns' crews down to the second shellman (responsible for keeping the first shellman supplied with projectiles, "taking care to place them in his hands with [the] point of [the] shell toward [the] gun"), there were not enough men to handle the projectiles and powder. "No one could have serviced the guns," Barninger later wrote, "or behaved better than the civilians who chose to remain with us at the position."[8]

Meanwhile, Captain Platt, Wilkes's strongpoint commander, told Major Potter over the phone that since Battery L's range finder had been damaged in the bombing the previous day, Second Lieutenant McAlister, at Battery L, was having trouble obtaining the range. After Platt passed along Potter's order to McAlister to estimate it, Battery L opened fire. After the first few rounds appeared to fall well over the target, McAlister's guns apparently menaced the transports, for three destroyers stood toward them.

Platt, directly in front of the guns and blown about by the muzzle blast, carefully scrutinized the Japanese ships moving offshore. What appeared to be two destroyers standing toward Wilkes at high speed soon captured his attention; beyond them, he could see what were probably the *Kongo Maru* and the *Kinryu Maru*. Correctly perceiving them to be transports, he began searching the dark waters closer inshore for signs of approaching landing boats.

Platt knew Wilkes to be the least developed of the islets at Wake. If material to build fortifications had been sparse on the atoll in general, it was even more so on Wilkes, mainly because material had to be brought from Wake across the boat channel on one "cranky small ferry" whose civilian operator had apparently quit the job abruptly when the bombs started falling on 8 December. "Knowing the conditions at the ferry," Platt later explained, "I did not ask for a great deal of material" but simply made good with what was available.

The dense brush to the east of the new channel had been cleared, but that to the west had not and remained "thick and difficult to negotiate." With the exception of two-man shelters with splinter-proof roofs, the only "field fortifications" of any note completed by Wilkes's marines were foxholes. Platt felt that he had too few sandbags to be worthwhile and decided not to sandbag the guns but to save the bags for foxholes and shelters. And because of the nearly impenetrable brush, Platt had had to place his machine guns very near the water.

Although the defenses of the strongpoint under Platt may have seemed weak, his men's fighting skill—particularly that of John McAlister and his gunners—soon became apparent. McAlister, thin and wiry, blond-haired and blue-eyed, hailed from Mississippi and "was of the mold that has provided fighting men of our country from the days of the early settlers, through the Revolution, to the present . . . the kind of man that made the U.S. Marines the dependable fighting force . . . it is."[9]

McAlister's Battery L had been as ready for war as it could be when hostilities broke with dramatic suddenness on Wake on 8 December. Its 5-inch/.51-caliber guns had been emplaced, oriented, and boresighted. All the marines assigned to the battery had had experience with the 5-inch/.51, but many had not had much practice in the specific jobs they were to perform at Battery L. Use of the men as working parties had left little time for battery drills. Nevertheless, McAlister and his noncoms had taught the men well and drilled them whenever possible.

A control tower stood behind the battery, and all necessary equipment had been installed. A 350-round magazine had been constructed for 300 powder cans and projectiles, as well as for 50 starshells; another magazine constructed near the position held 350 primers. Communications men had established the requisite network between guns, the range section, and the tower. Despite the damage received on the previous day, Battery L still posed a potent threat to the Japanese ships.

To allow the passage of trucks with construction materials and other supplies, the marines had widened trails to roads and improved the existing roads. Owing to the exposed nature of the guns, McAlister had emphasized camouflage; his marines had daubed the guns with camouflage paint, gathered vine seeds from all over the island and planted them, and transplanted shrubs. They had stretched nets over the guns, where they had remained unless the crews were performing drills or maintenance on the weapons. Knowing that the battery's effectiveness required that it be concealed as long as possible, McAlister rigidly enforced the camouflage discipline. As the Japanese steamed offshore on the eleventh, his marines took down the camouflage and prepared for battle.

As Platt peered intently at the waters nearby, McAlister's 5-inchers, ably captained by Platoon Sergeants William D. Beck and Joe M. Stowe, outranged the 4.7-inch guns of the old destroyers dashing in to screen the *Kinryu Maru* and the *Kongo Maru*. They sent three salvos slamming into the *Hayate* (Lieutenant Commander Takatsuka Minoru), the lead ship, just as she turned to parallel the beach. The *Hayate* (Squall) proved aptly named, for the destruction that visited her came as unexpectedly and overwhelmingly as a sudden storm at sea. At the third direct hit, Lieutenant Commander Takatsuka's doomed destroyer exploded, broke in two, and sank with breathtaking swiftness. The deadly shellfire from the marine guns apparently dissuaded the nearby ships from picking up survivors. If any of the *Hayate*'s 167 men had survived the loss of their ship, they perished in the water.

As McAlister's gunners cheered at having sunk a warship the first time they fired their five-inchers in anger, Sergeant Coulson interrupted Platt's search for incoming landing craft (there were none), pointing to two other destroyers that steamed before his gaze. Soon Battery L's guns hammered the *Oite*, which suffered fourteen men wounded (seven seriously, seven slightly) and the *Mochizuki*, which suffered an undetermined number of casualties. Fragments from the exploding shells hurled toward the battery in return hit Platoon Sergeant Stowe in the leg and Corporal John R. Dale in the back, but neither man's wounds warranted hospitalization; both received prompt treatment at the island's aid station. Battery L's equipment emerged from the action unscathed.

First Lieutenant Kessler's Battery B, guns captained by Platoon Sergeants Eugene W. Shugart and Forest Huffman, had its hands full, engaging the destroyers *Yayoi*, *Mutsuki*, and *Kisaragi*, as well as the *Tenryu* and *Tatsuta*, and drew heavy and accurate return fire. Although "their deflection was perfect from the very first," Kessler later wrote of the Japanese gunners, they were off in range, finding the low-lying position difficult to hit with flat-trajectory weapons. The first shells burst in the lagoon with brilliant geysers tinted with blobs of greenish-yellow picric acid. The next ones landed on Peale's north beach. Splitting the straddle, the enemy then centered the next pattern right on the battery; one shell passed between two lines of ammunition passers. Had it been a few feet to either side, it would have wiped out half the crew.

Almost miraculously, Battery B suffered no serious casualties despite the shells bursting in the position. Amid the tumult of battle, a piece of flying shrapnel nicked Kessler's nose, drawing an alarming flow of blood. Pharmacist's Mate Second Class John I. Unger applied a double band-aid to the wound and, after Kessler had wiped his face with a wet rag, thankfully discovered the cut to be minor. On gun 2, the recoil cylinder filling pipe plug blew out, putting it out of action and injuring Corporal Arthur F. Terry, who stayed at his post nonetheless. The crew of the inoperable gun 2 shifted to gun 1 as ammunition passers, however,

Second Lieutenant Woodrow M.
Kessler, ca. 1938; he later commanded
Battery B at Wake. (Brigadier General
Woodrow M. Kessler, USMC, Retired)

and after ten salvos Kessler's remaining gun scored a hit on the *Yayoi*'s
stern, killing one man and wounding seventeen (three seriously, fourteen
slightly) and starting a fire. His gunners then shifted fire to the next
destroyer in column.

The enemy's counterbattery fire against Toki Point, however, had
severed communication between Kessler's command post and the remaining operable gun, and a muzzle blast temporarily disabled the range
finder, which had been positioned—for lack of any other suitable space
in the crowded conditions on that part of Peale—directly in the line of
fire. "A Model 1911 rangefinder," Kessler wryly observed later, "had
never in its previous life aboard ship been called upon to withstand such
mistreatment." Battery B continued by local control, and as the Japanese
warships stood to the south, Kessler's gun hurled two parthian shots
toward a transport that proved to be out of range. Meanwhile, Private
First Class Joseph F. Commers, normally a fire-control specialist, a "serious and dependable young man who got things done with a minimum
of talk," showed his battery commander that he possessed a "minor
. . . knowledge of telephones and wiring" by repairing the battery's
communications lines even before the smoke of battle had cleared.

Kessler later praised his men generously: "The conduct of everyone was superb. They were proud. There was no fear evident as the enemy shells fell about them; it was as though here at last they had been given an opportunity to fight back and they were determined to do so. There was no cheering, but I sensed a feeling of great pride and satisfaction in the relaxed look on their faces. They had been tested and found themselves not wanting." Other than Corporal Terry's bruised side and Kessler's bloodied nose, Battery B's people had fired twenty-five rounds at the enemy and emerged unscathed.

The *Yūbari*'s action record—curiously silent on the matter of damage sustained—proves that though Wake had been pounded by land-based planes, its defenders still had enough coast-defense guns to mount a fierce counterattack and compel Kajioka's retirement toward the Marshalls. And even though the Imperial Japanese Navy had modeled itself after the British Royal Navy, those entrusted with the task of wresting Wake from the hands of the Americans apparently forgot Admiral Horatio Nelson's observation concerning shore bombardments: "A ship's a fool to fight a fort."[10]

Sadly, while the *Triton* had been ineffective as Kajioka's ships had approached Wake, the *Tambor* proved just as impotent as they retired. Running submerged and unable to get close enough to obtain a good look—the enemy seemed to be standing well to the southwest and had withdrawn by 0615—the *Tambor* reversed course and proceeded north, away from the retiring Japanese, to avoid penetrating the *Triton*'s patrol area.

As if the seacoast guns and the weather were not enough to frustrate the Japanese venture—the heavy seas had overturned landing boats almost as soon as they were launched—the enemy, with dead and wounded sailors on board several ships, would soon encounter a new foe after they left the five-inchers astern. While Cunningham's cannoneers under Barninger, Kessler, and McAlister had been trading shells with Kajioka's ships, Paul Putnam's four Wildcats had clawed their way to twenty thousand feet and maintained that altitude until daylight, allowing Putnam to determine whether any Japanese planes were aloft. The sudden formation of a thin but solid cloud layer at a thousand feet, though, prompted him to delay making his attack until the clouds had dispersed almost as quickly as they had formed. As the destroyers that had dueled Battery B opened the range and retired, the Wildcats roared in, attacking, as specified in standard doctrine, in two-plane sections.

Elrod and Tharin opened the aerial onslaught by attacking the *Kisaragi*, and Putnam saw at least one of Elrod's bombs penetrate the ship's vitals. Trailing oil in her wake and smoke above it, the damaged destroyer slowed to a stop but then got under way again, unmistakably

First Lieutenant Henry T.
Elrod while serving in
VMF-2 at North Island
ca. May 1940. (Harold W.
Bauer Collection, MCHC
Personal Papers)

Wrecked Grumman F4F-3s from VMF-211 near the airstrip. The Wildcat
in the foreground, 211-F-11 (BuNo 4019), was flown on 11 December by
Captain Henry T. Elrod in the attack that resulted in the loss of the
Japanese destroyer *Kisaragi*. (NA, USMC Photo 315173)

afire internally. While she crept off to the south, Elrod, his plane's oil line perforated by antiaircraft fire, headed for home. Although he landed 211-F-11 adroitly among the boulders on Wake's rocky south beach, the damage the F4F had suffered compelled Kinney to write it off as a total loss fit only for cannibalization.

Meanwhile, the *Tenryu*—which had shelled what she had reported as the "Wake residential area" and "housing in the west area"—came under attack by Putnam, Tharin, and Freuler shortly before 0730 as she and her sister ship were retiring to the southwest at twenty-four knots. The three pilots strafed the *Tenryu* forward, in the vicinity of her no. 1 torpedo tube mount, wounding five sailors and disabling three torpedoes. Marine fire also wounded five men on board the *Tatsuta*.

The trio of operable Wildcats then shuttled back and forth to Wake, where the busy ground crew rearmed and refueled them as quickly as humanly possible, allowing VMF-211 to carry out a total of ten attacks, expending twenty hundred-pound bombs and about twenty thousand rounds of .50-caliber armor-piercing ammunition. Putnam and Kinney later saw the *Kisaragi*—which had been carrying an extra supply of depth charges in response to the American submarine threat—blow up and sink, taking Lieutenant Commander Ogawa Yoichiro and his entire crew (167 souls all told) with her. Kajioka's chief of staff, Captain Koyama Tadashi, watching from the *Yūbari*'s bridge, saw "a tremendous explosion." Paul Putnam later recalled that "she [the *Kisaragi*] just changed from a ship to a ball of flame . . . within a matter of seconds." After Kinney had witnessed the *Kisaragi*'s fiery demise, he strafed another destroyer before returning to the field.

Putnam, Freuler, and Hamilton braved heavy antiaircraft fire and strafed the *Kongo Maru* (Captain Mizusaki Shojiro), damaging one of the embarked Type 00 reconnaissance seaplanes, touching off barrels of gasoline stowed in one of her holds, and killing three sailors and wounding nineteen. Captain Mizusaki also reported two of his men missing. Freuler managed to land one of his hundred-pounders on the *Kongo Maru*'s stern but, as he modestly observed, the damage he inflicted did not seem to be serious. The damage that Japanese antiaircraft fire inflicted on Freuler's plane in return, however, proved serious—bullets passed through one cylinder and the oil cooler—but did not prevent him from bringing his F4F back to the field. Technical Sergeant Hamilton returned with his plane's tail section well holed.

As Captain Koyama would later observe, not only had the bad weather compelled Kajioka to abandon the attempt to storm Wake, but the losses his force had taken from the "very accurate" seacoast guns and the "three aggressive fighter planes" that it had not been able to

Sergeant William J. Hamilton, naval aviation pilot, 20 January 1938,
Pensacola, Florida. (William J. Hamilton File, MCHC Reference Section)

shoot down helped hurry him on his way as well. The Japanese grudg-
ingly admired the marine pilots' "skill and bravery."

Contrasting with the boldness of the marine pilots was the apparent
timidity of the navy's submariners. The *Triton* had remained at deep
submergence while the island's garrison was repelling the enemy task
force. She had heard what appeared to be several light explosions between
0310 and 0605 and two very loud ones fairly close at 0605. She came
to periscope depth almost three-quarters of an hour later, at 0647, but
could see only empty ocean. She heard distant explosions at 0725 and
two violent ones at 0743 that compelled Pilly Lent to take his boat
down deep again. Closing Wake later, he saw no ships.

Meanwhile, Cunningham hastened down to the south shore of Wake
to congratulate Jim Devereux's gunners, after which time several of the
officers apparently retired to the little officers' mess canteen in Camp
1. There, celebrating with warm beer, the participants in the morning
action reveled that the Japanese had turned tail and steamed off whence
they had come. For the defenders of Wake, the repulse of the Ja-

panese—even if the results were inflated honestly because of the general poor quality of ship recognition in the heat of battle—had a tonic effect. An exuberant Marine Gunner Hamas sought out Commander Cunningham. "You told us to cut loose at them," he declared, "and, boy did we cut loose at the dirty sons of the bitches."[11]

After the last Japanese ships had retired to the south, Cunningham sent a message at 0845 telling of the morning's events. Though shelled at dawn by "several light vessels," Wake had suffered no casualties but sank what were believed to be a light cruiser and a destroyer and sent two transports with an escort of light cruisers and destroyers steaming off to the southwest. That optimistic assessment of the morning's score elicited a "Splendid work" from CinCPac.[12]

The enemy, though, would not afford Wake's defenders their hard-earned respite. John Kinney took off again, in 211-F-12, at about 0915, accompanied by Carl Davidson in 211-F-10—the last two planes in commission—at about the same moment that seventeen *rikkōs* with a combined bomb load of 176 60-kilogram bombs and led by Lieutenant Nakai, one of the Chitose *Kōkūtai buntaichōs*, commenced their bombing runs on Peale's antiaircraft battery. For the first time since the war began, Commander Cunningham was under cover in his command post when the disciplined formations of twin-tail bombers came over, comforted by the concrete and steel roof of the unfinished magazine overhead, to wait out the raid.

The marine pilots acquitted themselves well in a thirty-minute aerial duel. Davidson waded into Nakai's nine-plane *chūtai* as it headed to the southwest while Kinney headed for Yamagata's eight-plane formation, waiting above the antiaircraft fire for an opportune time to strike. Seeing that the bombers' gunners seemed preoccupied, Kinney dove out of the sun and pressed home his attack close to the formation, which soon began to circle north of the island. Attacking again from down-sun, Kinney saw gasoline streaming from the damaged tank of one of Yamagata's *rikkōs*. Suddenly, a bullet passed through his windshield, near the bulletproof glass, through the left side of his goggles, and exited through the turtleback aft of the cockpit, jamming the canopy in the closed position. Descending to the east until he was well ahead of the enemy planes, he pressed home a head-on attack and then turned for home, noting only seven Type 96s instead of eight.

Battery D, meanwhile, although having to use twenty-one-second powder train fuses—the accuracy of which depended on the rate at which compressed black powder burned—that limited the time of firing to a very short time and at a high angle of elevation, hurled 125 rounds at Nakai's bombers. Godbold observed what appeared to be three planes leaving the island trailing heavy smoke and reported that one crashed

"The Marines Have Landed," a Duffy cartoon in the *Baltimore Sun* for 12 December 1941. The fist connecting on the jaw of a Japanese sailor reflects the Wake garrison's turning away the first invasion attempt on 11 December. (*Baltimore Sun*)

into the ocean off Wilkes. Although some of the enemy's sixty-kilogram bombs fell near their target, the Japanese again inflicted neither damage nor casualties.

Carl Davidson, however, had splashed the number one and two planes of Nakai's Second *shōtai*. The former, commanded by Special Duty Lieutenant (j.g.) Sasao Fumio, crashed five miles west of Wake (apparently the one Godbold saw) at 0918 and the latter, commanded by Petty Officer First Class Miyazaki Daisuke, twenty-five miles to the southsouthwest at 0928. John Kinney had holed one plane from Yamagata's *chūtai*, the *rikkō* commanded by Warrant Officer Okabe (who had lost a crewman to Wake's antiaircraft fire on 8 December), killing Petty

Officer Third Class Oda Jiro, one of the observers. Besides Okabe's, thirteen more G3M2s had been damaged by the efforts of Davidson, Kinney, and the antiaircraft batteries. Casualties among the crews amounted to one reserve lieutenant, nine petty officers, and five enlisted men dead, one enlisted man wounded slightly. Returning Japanese aircrew reported optimistically that they had shot down one fighter and sent another off "flying erratically."[13]

At 1050, Cunningham radioed ComFourteen that the latest bombing raid had caused no damage and that two enemy planes had been downed. Three marine fighters remained operable. Shortly thereafter, Colonel Hoppaugh, at Hickam, passed along a message to Rear Admiral Bloch that Cunningham had ordered sent on the heels of the one describing the air raid, this one amplifying his earlier dispatch covering the repulse of Kajioka's ships. Cunningham deemed one light cruiser and one destroyer "definitely sunk" by shore batteries; the island commander thought that Wake's defenders had shot down a total of five enemy bombers.

VMF-211's intrepid pilots had had a good day; they would accomplish more, however, before the day was out. Second Lieutenant Kinney and Technical Sergeant Hamilton took off around 1600, followed some fifteen minutes later by Second Lieutenant Kliewer.

During the attempted landings, the three submarines of the Twenty-seventh Division had carried out their patrols; they remained in the vicinity of the atoll while Kajioka's ships had slunk off to the south after being bested by the five-inch batteries and the Wildcats' slashing attacks. The Triton, running at deep submergence south of Wake, picked up possible propeller noises on her JK gear at 1620, drawing across the bow off north by west. Planing up to periscope depth, Pilly Lent swept the horizon but saw nothing. Unable to identify the noises—she had perhaps heard her own screws in the freakish sound conditions prevailing off the atoll—the Triton resumed her patrol.

One Japanese submarine did turn up shortly thereafter, though, when David Kliewer, at about 1630, spotted what was most probably the RO-66 (Lieutenant Commander Kurokawa Hideyuki) on the surface twenty-five miles southwest of Wake. Kliewer dove from ten thousand feet, out of the sun. Convinced that the submarine was Japanese, he strafed her with his four .50-calibers. Turning to the right, to better his chances of scoring maximum damage on the enemy, he dove again and released his two hundred-pounders at such low altitude that bomb fragments holed his wings and tail surfaces. Emptying his guns into the submarine on his next pass, he looked over his shoulder after he flew over her and saw her submerge.

Major Putnam, flying out later in the gathering darkness, spotted

what appeared to be an oil slick in the area Kliewer had indicated. Upon
landing, Putnam reported what he had seen and declared that it was
"almost certain" that a sub had been sunk. In all probability, however,
Kliewer's bombs had merely set in motion a fateful chain of events for
the *RO-66* and her men, as the morrow would show.[14]

Late that afternoon, Commander Cunningham decided that the time
had come to bury the men who had died during the first few days of
war. Up to that point, they had been lain in a large refrigerator ("reefer
box") in Camp 2. A CPNAB dragline operator dug out a long trench one
hundred yards southwest of magazine 10, alongside and to the north of
the main road, and a burial party laid the dead—marine, navy, and
civilian—to rest in the common grave clawed out of Wake's coral.

Cunningham, Major Devereux, and Dan Teters were there, and four
marines, drawn from one of the machine-gun positions nearby, formed
the squad that fired a salute over the rough site. Because Wake had no
chaplain, John H. O'Neal, a forty-one-year-old carpenter from Worland,
Wyoming, and a lay preacher, prayed over the grave site, committing
the souls of the departed to God's care. A workman with a bulldozer
then covered the dead; camouflage completed the work, and Wake's
living went on with the business of striving to survive. "There was a
terrible feeling inside us when we buried our friends," Technical Sergeant Hamilton of VMF-211 later recalled. The scene would remain
imprinted indelibly on his mind. It was, as Cunningham recorded subsequently, "a sad note on which to end the day" that otherwise had been
one of triumph.

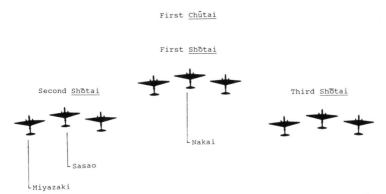

Second Lieutenant Davidson's bag on 11 December 1941 (drawing of
Chitose *Kōkūtai* formation showing Davidson's aerial victories).

Second Lieutenant David D. Kliewer, USMCR, ca. September 1941. (Mrs. Virginia Putnam)

While the mass funeral tempered the euphoria of Wake's defenders, far to the east, at Pearl Harbor, the Pacific Fleet continued to pick up the pieces after the shattering blow the Japanese had dealt it. In his estimate of the situation dated 10 December 1941 (11 December at Wake) Admiral Kimmel, who had underestimated how daring the Japanese would be at the outset, acknowledged that the enemy onslaught had forced him to revise his strategy. Although the loss of his battleships compelled him to fight on the "strategic defensive" until they could again sally forth in strength, "a very powerful striking force"—aircraft carriers, heavy cruisers, and destroyers—had survived, to be operated "boldly and vigorously on the tactical offensive" to "retrieve our initial disaster."[15]

Although CinCPac recognized that defending Wake was one of the important tasks confronting the Pacific Fleet, he and his staff knew that the enemy held an important psychological advantage by placing the fleet on the defensive at the very beginning. The Japanese had proved themselves daring, as well as careful and skillful planners. It would be a mistake to underestimate them again; they had already attacked Wake, and should they capture it, they could readily supply it from the Marshalls. Kimmel acknowledged that even in peacetime, the navy's ability to supply Wake had been difficult. The Japanese would desire to occupy Wake, and he believed it "most probable" that they would raid it from shore bases "with possible minor landing attempts." Deploying the forces that remained, however, not only to protect sea communications, defend the outlying bases (particularly Wake and Samoa), and protect far-flung territory, as well as defend Oahu, called for a wide dispersal of limited forces. By 10 December (11 December on Wake), the scattered positions of his carriers, patrolling the Oahu-Johnston-Palmyra triangle, militated against deploying them in support of Wake.[16]

Ironically, the issue of relieving outlying bases, which had absorbed so much of Kimmel's attention before the Japanese attack on Pearl Harbor, had been rudely thrust to the background in its aftermath. Consequently, the relief of Wake appears first to have come up for discussion on Wednesday, 10 December, when Captain McMorris began to feel concern that repeated Japanese raids on that outlying base would deplete its ammunition supply. Worry over the *William Ward Burrows*'s exposed position (had she not reversed course to pick up the *Sonoma*'s appendicitis case she would have been even farther west when hostilities broke out) had prompted her rerouting to Johnston Island. McMorris considered it improbable that the *William Ward Burrows* could have discharged her cargo and disembarked the marines she had on board so another ship would have to be made available.

The most likely candidate appeared to be the seaplane tender *Tangier* (AV-8), because the *Curtiss*, which had been to Wake in late October, had been damaged by a crashing Japanese plane on 7 December; the *Wright* was at sea, en route to Midway, eliminating her from consideration. The *Tangier* had suffered only very minor fragment damage from near misses from Japanese bombs on the seventh; her cargo-carrying ability was unimpaired. "Although the garrison at Wake was small," McMorris later explained, "it would require a considerable effort on the part of the enemy to take that place." If Wake was to be held "for a prolonged period," relief measures must be expedited. He and his section set to work on just that.

An operation order of 10 December was based on the premise that the garrisons at Wake and Midway needed to be reinforced and that wounded men and a portion of the CPNAB work force must be evacuated. The *Tangier*, after having embarked men and loaded the requisite supplies, would depart Pearl on 12 December escorted by two destroyers. Task Force 12, after fueling, would rendezvous with the *Tangier* and her consorts at a designated time and place and would proceed to rendezvous with the *William Ward Burrows* and head for Wake. Task Force 12 would then cover the unloading and loading of the two auxiliaries "as may be found expedient without undue exposure of this force," after which time the seaplane tender and the transport were to proceed to Pearl with two destroyers in company and then rendezvous with the

Wright and proceed to Midway; the *Wright*, with two destroyers as escort, would then be directed to return to Pearl as well, with the *Lexington* and her consorts operating in the waters north of Midway to cover their voyage "against any enemy that may approach." If, during any of these operations, American forces encountered Japanese, they were to "take offensive action against them."[17]

While such measures were being contemplated, Wake's garrison continued its purposeful toil. Ordered to move Battery D the length of Peale during the night, Godbold reconnoitered the new position that Major Devereux had picked out and at 1745 on the eleventh, after securing all battery positions, began the shift. For the next eleven hours, because the sandbags from the old emplacements were virtually useless, the marines, assisted by nearly 250 civilians, constructed new, smaller emplacements out of cement bags and sand-filled ammunition boxes. Godbold thought the new position looked superior to the old. It required fewer sandbags (which were in short supply), gave more protection to the men, and facilitated the loading of the guns because the ready-service boxes lay closer to the weapons. By 0445 on 12 December, Godbold could again report his guns "manned and ready."

First Lieutenant Kessler had reported one gun out of action so Marine Gunner Borth hurried over to Toki Point and found that the counterrecoil intake tube had blown out and the gun had failed to return to battery. Borth, the noncommissioned officer in charge of five-inch artillery instruction, disassembled the mechanism, repaired it, tested it, and found it serviceable. The following day, Borth would smooth down the shrapnel hits on one of McAlister's guns and in the elevating friction gear plates. He also installed a new scope and bore-sighted the piece, restoring another weapon to operational status. Gunner Hamas and his work party replenished shells and powder at both McAlister's and Barninger's batteries, while a six-man party of civilians led by a man Hamas knew only as Fritz, volunteered to help McAlister on Wilkes. Later, with a few marines and ten civilians, Hamas oversaw the completion of the construction of an air raid shelter in front of the marines' garage in Camp 1.

Meanwhile, from his vantage point offshore, after drafting a report of the day's occurrences, Lieutenant Commander Murphy contemplated sending it but decided that instead of surfacing to transmit it (and thereby risk detection) he would see if Wake was still on the air. The *Tambor* surfaced off the atoll's north shore at dusk, making her presence "conspicuous," and established visual contact with Wake at 1750. "They said they had no message to send," Murphy later reported, "so I assumed they were all right."

When the *Triton* surfaced off Wake's southern shore that night, Pilly

Lent reported to CinCPac that a destroyer or light cruiser had kept her down on station earlier in the day. Detonations heard on board led Lent to believe that ships had shelled the island. Although the presence of American submarines off Wake had obviously concerned the enemy (the *Tambor* had been spotted by Marumo's cruisers before the battle had been joined), neither his boat nor Spuds Murphy's had aided Wake's defenders.

At Peacock Point on the night of the eleventh, Wally Lewis, who never got the chance to use the data he had worked on the night before, allowed all but two men at each gun and the director to get some sleep—the first his men had had in three days.

The Japanese force, meanwhile, "probably humbled by sizeable casualties," as Rear Admiral Ugaki Matome (Admiral Yamamoto's chief of staff) observed candidly in his diary, withdrew to the Marshalls.[18] Back at Pearl Harbor, elements of the Fourth Defense Battalion received orders to prepare for immediate embarkation and began gearing up for an operation whose destination was closely held "but like many such, it was badly kept: 'We're headed for Wake' was the word circulated all day on the 10th." Later that same day, however, word came down for the elements of the Fourth to stand down, to return to their positions, rewarding the marines' "day of special exertion and excitement" with "another night at watch at the guns, waiting for the return of the bombers which it seemed so surely would reappear over Oahu."[19]

Perhaps wearying of the resistance they were encountering in daylight raids from Wake's fighters and antiaircraft guns, those who cast the Chitose *Kōkūtai*'s operations planned a predawn strike. That night, shortly before midnight (Wake time), seven *rikkōs* under Lieutenant Kotani took off from Roi, followed shortly by a second *chūtai* of eight under Lieutenant Watanabe. Unable to find their objective in the dark, however, Kotani and Watanabe aborted the mission, the former's planes reaching Roi at 1000 on the twelfth and the latter's at 1050. Thereafter they would bomb in daylight.

"STILL NO HELP"

At 0739 on 11 December, Pearl Harbor time (0439, 12 December, at Wake) CinCPac sent out an interrogatory message asking Wake to report the status of aviation material there to maintain marine aircraft and patrol planes. Before Cunningham could respond, however, the sound of unsynchronized fourteen-cylinder Mitsubishi *Kinsei* radial engines heralded the approach of Japanese planes shortly before dawn on the twelfth, and Captains Freuler and Tharin took off to intercept. One intruder—a Kawanishi H6K Type 97 reconnaissance flying boat commanded by Special Duty Ensign Nakano Unekichi—dropped its bombs on the edge of the lagoon and then sought cover in the overcast and rain squalls. Tharin chased it and splashed it. Not one of its nine-man crew survived.[1]

The doomed flying boat had been one of five from the Majuro-based Yokohama *Kōkūtai* under Lieutenant Commander Tashiro Soichi that had left Majuro at 2100 the previous night. Three of the Kawanishis, however, had had to abort the mission en route, leaving only Lieutenant Commander Tashiro and Special Duty Ensign Nakano—each plane carrying four 250-kilogram and twelve 60-kilogram bombs—to reach Wake around 0530. Tashiro's flying boat returned whence it had come at 1120 on the twelfth.

At 0735 (Wake time) on the twelfth, Cunningham reported the downing of the flying boat to CinCPac and noted that during the repulse of Kajioka's force the day before the marines had "severely punished" the convoy's train vessel (the *Kongo Maru*). He also said that marine planes had "attacked and believed sunk" a Japanese submarine (Kliewer's attack on what was probably the *RO-66*) and that the enemy had retired to the south-southwest. A little less than two hours later, he informed CinCPac that although Wake could operate two marine squadrons, the only spare parts to be had were from wrecked planes; Wake could support one patrol plane squadron and had 125,000 gallons of gasoline on hand.

Captain Wilson's communicators continued to log in incoming dis-

First Lieutenant Frank C. Tharin while serving with VMF-2 at North Island, ca. May 1940. (Harold W. Bauer Collection, MCHC Personal Papers)

Captain Herbert C. Freuler, ca. September 1941. (Mrs. Virginia Putnam)

patches: less than two hours after the island commander had reported *Wake*'s aircraft handling arrangements to CinCPac, ComFourteen's district matériel officer wanted a report on the ammunition situation, a request that probably mirrored Captain Mcmorris's anxiety over the depletion of the atoll's supply.[2] Later that morning, Cunningham provided ComFourteen with the names of the thirty marines and sailors who had died up to that point.[3]

The daily routine went on. At Battery A, for example, Barney Barninger's men worked on their foxholes, freshened camouflage, cleaned the guns, and, when time allowed, tried to catch up on their sleep. He checked his battery's .50-calibers and found them "well-handled and policed." The machine gunners, he noted, seemed "anxious to get a crack at the enemy and were on their toes as was everyone else."

That same day, despite the primitive conditions at the airfield, Captain Freuler resourcefully solved another problem confronting VMF-211. The bombing and normal usage had exhausted 211's supply of oxygen so on 12 December, he devised a "crude and fragile" contraption "consisting largely of a short length of ordinary water pipe" for transferring welding oxygen from large commercial storage cylinders to the smaller ones used in the planes. Mindful of the danger, Freuler worked alone, generally filling eight small bottles from one large one so VMF-211's pilots could take their F4Fs to "sufficient altitudes to fight effectively."[4] Elsewhere at the airstrip that day, Air Corps Staff Sergeant Hotchkiss and Marine Corps Private First Class Lester C. Byard repaired the field lighting system that had suffered heavy damage on the first day of the war.

Vice Admiral Inoue, meanwhile, was ordering the Twenty-seventh Submarine Division (the *RO-65*, *RO-66*, and *RO-67*) back to Kwajalein, to be relieved by the Twenty-sixth (the *RO-60*, *RO-61*, and *RO-62*). The latter group (Commander Matsue Yorio), which had been held in reserve at Kwajalein at the outset of hostilities, sailed on the twelfth for Wake. One of the Twenty-seventh Division's boats, however, the *RO-66*, did not get the word because radio communication failed—perhaps a result of damage suffered at the hands of David Kliewer the previous afternoon—so while the *RO-65* and the *RO-67* set course for Kwajalein, the *RO-66*, temporarily incommunicado, remained behind.

At dusk on the twelfth, the report of a plane crash north of the island prompted Captain Elrod to scramble to check it out. He returned at dark; the disturbance turned out to have been a flare sent up by the *Tambor* in an attempt to establish visual communication with Wake that night to determine whether the atoll's radio was operating.

Also that same day, in an effort to boost morale, Commander Cunningham, having seen that Camp 2's commissary had provided food only on a catch-as-catch-can basis, designated Ensign Davis as commissary officer. Cunningham instructed Davis to "provide and distribute two hot meals a day" to all hands, according priority to the marines and civilians at the strongpoints, and to use CPNAB men and the sailors not assigned to the Mobile Reserve, as well as naval and contractors' vehicles, in the effort.[5] Working under twenty-nine-year-old Willis C. Stone, the head chef, the CPNAB galley staff (which included one of PanAir's marooned young Guamanians, J. Javana) prepared the meals while men under Gene L. Henderson, a material clerk; Richard A. McKinney, an office clerk; Lester L. Turner, a cost engineer; and Olin L. Skirvin, the ice cream maker, distributed them daily at 0615 and at dusk. "Food thusly prepared," Major Bayler later reported, proved "plentiful, wholesome and of sufficient variety to be appetizing and provide a balance." Gunner Hamas put it more succinctly: "Good 'chow' for all."

As daylight waned on the twelfth, Battery D moved its location. Major Devereux selected the spot, and Captain Godbold and Second Lieutenant Greeley reconnoitered it. While Greeley stayed at the new site, Godbold returned to the old to direct the movement. Approximately three hundred civilians answered the call to help, and Battery D was in position to fire shortly before dawn.

At 1100 on 12 December (Washington time) (0300, 13 December, at Wake), Presidential Press Conference No. 791 had begun in the White House, in the executive office of the president. Responding to a journalist's question, Roosevelt replied: "So far as we know, Wake Island is holding out—has done a perfectly magnificent job. We are all very proud of that very small group of Marines who are holding the Island. We have no further information today. They are holding out. We knew that very early this morning."[6] That night, listeners on Wake heard a stateside radio report praise the atoll's marines. Noting that Radio Tokyo had claimed Wake to be the "most strongly fortified island in the Pacific," the report stated that for security reasons it could not mention the size of the garrison defending the atoll but, perhaps reflecting the president's comments that morning, noted that "we know the number is very small"—an admission that prompted John Kinney to note sardonically in his diary: "Nothing like letting the enemy know our status. . . . Still no help."

Word of the repulse of Kajioka's ships on the eleventh caused the American public to rejoice—it was a welcome ray of light in the post–Pearl Harbor gloom. When the good news reached General Holcomb, the commandant of the Marine Corps, he proudly passed it on (it was "particularly pleasing at a time like this"). Wake's garrison, he wrote, was showing "the sort of determination to do their job which we like to see."[7] "God bless our fine Marines," a friend wrote to Holcomb on 13 December. "What an honor it is to belong to the same nation that contains such men."[8]

The Japanese press reaction to the same event was predictably more muted and did not appear until three days later, on 14 December, in a five-line entry on the front page of the morning edition of the *Japan Times and Advertiser.* "The Imperial Navy shelled Wake Island on December 11," it declared, "and dealt heavy losses to the remaining military establishments of the enemy." The brief blurb concluded with a masterpiece of understatement: "Our side suffered some damage, too."

Wake's defenders, however, were not yet out of the proverbial woods. By 11 December (12 December at Wake) plans to reinforce the garrison had not yet crystallized. Nor could they until the carriers around which any task forces could be formed could be marshaled for the job, and other concerns (the operations of Japanese submarines off Oahu, for example) needed to be dealt with.

In Captain McMorris's estimation, all of the nearly fifteen hundred people on Wake could be accommodated rapidly on board the *Tangier* (Commander Clifton A. F. Sprague) if they either destroyed or abandoned their personal belongings. "She should not go," McMorris wrote, "until air protection is available." If evacuation of Wake was decided upon—and he recommended against it—the "promptest measure" (as the operations plan dated 10 December 1941 intimated) would be to have the *Tangier* assigned to the *Lexington* task force (Task Force 12) then under Vice Admiral Wilson Brown, Commander, Scouting Force, in the heavy cruiser *Indianapolis* (CA-35). Then, accompanied by destroyers, the seaplane tender could evacuate Wake's people while the *Lexington*'s planes provided cover. While plans for her employment were being considered, "Lady Lex" and her consorts, which had been at sea continuously since 5 December, were having difficulties attempting to fuel from the *Neosho* (AO-23) in the very rough sea and moderate gales northwest of Oahu. Kimmel, the events of 7 December fresh in his mind, had wanted Brown to fuel at sea rather than risk being bottled up at Pearl. Ordered to postpone those logistical evolutions, Brown received direction from CinCPac shortly before the end of the forenoon watch to take his force toward Midway "pending more favorable weather."

That same day, 11 December (Pearl Harbor date), Secretary of the Naxy Knox, on a fact-finding mission for the president, arrived at Kaneohe, after which he would visit Pearl. He would spend the next thirty-two hours (leaving late on the twelfth) gathering what information he could—including Kimmel's 10 December 1941 estimate of the situation—so that he could brief the chief executive personally on what had happened at Pearl on the seventh. He arrived in the midst of preparations to launch the expedition to relieve Wake that was, at that point, aimed at reinforcing and carrying on the existing defense—not defeating a Japanese force at sea in a pitched battle.

While the U.S. Navy was evaluating what had happened at Pearl a few days before, the Japanese were assessing what had gone wrong at Wake on the eleventh and how to increase chances of success the next time. In Tokyo, Rear Admiral Nakahara Giichi, chief of the Navy Ministry's Personnel Bureau, wrote in his diary on 12 December about the repulse of Kajioka's force: "Well-protected islands are strong. If such . . . is guarded by any submarines, we shall be [in] all the more disadvantageous position in carrying out our operation . . . and at the same time, the occupation . . . will not be easy if the circumstances were thus that supporting enemy forces are coming there." He lamented, "We have to waste an unexpected amount of our strength in occupying Wake Island."[9]

The Japanese were indeed very submarine conscious. One of the boats whose prescence concerned them, however, the *Tambor*, was experiencing problems of her own. After she surfaced after dark on 12 December, one of her torpedomen inadvertently struck the hand-firing key and fired a torpedo from the boat's number 3 tube when the *Tambor* lurched in the seaway; then, as she was running on the surface within her assigned fifteen-mile semicircle to the north of the atoll, at 0200 on 13 December, the sound gear operator on watch reported propeller noises on the port bow. Visibility in that direction was zero so Spuds Murphy ordered the *Tambor* taken down to carry out a sound attack, but his two best sound operators could not hear anything after the boat submerged. "Freakish" sound conditions had often resulted in the boat's JK operators picking up their own propeller noises "at many points on the dial." Murphy, apparently believing his boat had picked up a false contact, decided to remain submerged and reload the tube accidentally fired the night before. At 0650, the *Tambor* picked up another contact on her sound gear but evaluated it as false, too.

On the morning of 13 December, Kajioka's ships stood in to Kwajalein's lagoon. Soon thereafter, the admiral asked Inoue's chief of staff if additional elements of the Second Maizuru SLF could augment his landing force for the second attempt at Wake. He also requested the seaplane carrier *Kiyokawa Maru*. By later in the day, plans were afoot to provide an additional SLF company, the *Kiyokawa Maru*, as well as the armed transport *Tenyo Maru*. Two destroyers from the Twenty-fourth Division would replace the sunken *Kisaragi* and *Hayate*.

While Kajioka was busy seeking reinforcements, Cunningham was reporting the ammunition situation requested by the district matériel officer the previous day. Wake's magazines at that point held 48 depth charges, 4 1,000-pound bombs, 200 500-pound bombs (all useless for the island's small existing air force), and 250 100-pounders, in addition to 1,000 cases of .50-caliber armor-piercing ammunition and 250 cases of .50-caliber tracer. The defense battalion had 1.5 units of fire of 3-inch, 2 of 5-inch, and 3 each of .50- and .30-caliber, in addition to 2,200 hand grenades.

At the airfield on 13 December, VMF-211 conducted its patrols with the three available aircraft, while work on 211-F-8 continued. Having discovered that the engines on the Wildcats burned on the eighth had not been severely damaged—at least the cylinders appeared salvageable—Kinney removed two cylinders from the engine in 211-F-5 to replace ones on number eight.

The pilot of 211-F-9, who took it aloft on the morning patrol, reported that the engine was running rough. Kinney changed two magneto leads to no avail. Major Putnam, who took the plane up on the noon patrol, reported the same problem. Kinney test-flew 211-F-9 himself that afternoon and found that the engine barely ran in low blower, not at all in high, and rough in neutral. Checking the valves yielded no improvement. Meanwhile, ground crews dragged Captain Elrod's erstwhile mount, 211-F-11, over from the beach and propped it up across the runway as a decoy.

Work on 211-F-8—which had to be done principally during the day—progressed slowly. To provide a place to work on the planes after dark, the contractors had promised Kinney that they would finish the lightproof hanger that night. CPNAB workmen had bulldozed four U-shaped plane shelters along the south side of the airstrip, taking advantage of the slight rise in the ground from the level of the runway southward toward the wooded area. To make a hanger, the workers enlarged one shelter, dug a ramp down below the level of the runway, placed steel I-beams overhead, and covered it all with tarpaulins and lumber. Workers began fabricating a second hangar on the east side of the field, taking advantage of a man-made bluff that had resulted from the clearing of the runway and tie-down areas. With a tarpaulin for a blackout curtain, a Wildcat could be completely housed; work could proceed at night.

Putnam, whom Kinney later wrote "was always unfortunate enough to usually miss the bombers," had failed to detect the prescence of a lone Japanese reconnaissance plane—a Type 1 *rikkō* commanded by Warrant Officer Ota Shoichi—during his midday flight. Overflying Wake at five thousand meters shortly after noon, Ota's observers saw, through a hole in the clouds, one fighter in a revetment west of the runway and thought they saw two aloft. They saw no flying boats. Puzzlingly, Ota, who reached Roi at 1620 on the thirteenth, also reported the presence of a "merchant ship carrying out unloading operations." What he saw is a mystery, unless he mistook the *Columbia* for a merchantman.

That evening, a radio message from Wake to the Hawaiian Air Force headquarters reported that the navy and PanAir radio installations had been destroyed and the army radio unit was the only one remaining, operating from a "basement." Wake reported that it would transmit only at intervals to prevent the Japanese from homing in on the transmissions. The *Tambor* had observed "nothing unusual" during the day. That night, before the boat surfaced to carry out her nocturnal patrol, Lieutenant Commander Murphy talked with his ship's company (half of the crew at a time) in the *Tambor's* mess hall, "to help quiet the nerves" because he believed "everyone had been under a severe strain those first few days."

Despite the strain evident in several quarters, it could not be said that Wake was not on people's minds. "Wake Island," Rear Admiral Bloch wrote to Admiral Stark on 12 December, (13 December, Wake time) "is putting up a magnificent fight. Kimmel is doing his best to devise means for reinforcing it and getting out the civilians."[10]

Devising those means, however, consumed valuable time. That morning (12 December), Task Force 12 (constituted around the *Lexington*) again attempted to fuel. Only the heavy cruiser *Chicago* (CA-29) managed to do so before a submarine scare compelled her to break off the evolution, damaging the *Neosho's* fueling gear in the process and thus further postponing efforts to take on precious fuel because no other ships could do so until the gear was repaired. At the same time, the *Saratoga* (wearing the flag of Rear Admiral Aubrey W. Fitch), which had departed San Diego on 8 December with the destroyers *Waters* (DD-115), *Dent* (DD-116), and *Talbot* (DD-114), had been joined by the heavy cruiser *Minneapolis* (CA-36) and the destroyers *Tucker* (DD-374), *Case* (DD-370), *Selfridge* (DD-357), and *Conyngham* (DD-371) during the afternoon watch on the twelfth. "Sara" continued on toward Oahu, delayed, like her sister ship, by heavy weather.

As efforts proceeded to disprove those of Wake's defenders who despaired of help, rumors circulated at Pearl among Fourth Defense Battalion marines that the marine detachment under Captain Frederick P. Henderson, from the heavy cruiser *San Francisco* (CA-38)—caught on 7 December in the midst of a yard overhaul—had volunteered to be flown out to the embattled atoll. The apparent pluck of the *San Francisco's* marines inspired those who began gearing up—once more—to go to Wake. Admiral Kimmel considered such spirit "inspiring" and, writing to Admiral Stark on 12 December, noted that "Marines, hearing of attacks on Midway and Wake, have insisted on being sent there."[11]

The *Tambor's* patrol that night had taken her well to the west of the atoll when a messenger brought Spuds Murphy a dispatch from ComSubScoFor stating that shore direction-finder bearings "indicated the prescence of an enemy ship or submarine not far to the northeastward of Wake." Approaching the island with the moon ahead, Murphy had the *Tambor* ready to attack any surface ships making a daylight run on the defenses. Seeing no reason to change his plans, the sub's captain ordered her course held. When dawn revealed no enemy men-of-war, the *Tambor* carried out her routine patrol. Murphy kept "one of the two good listeners on watch all the time" because of the heightened expectation of meeting an enemy submersible.

In the meantime, the Japanese maintained aerial pressure. Eleven Type 97 flying boats from the Yokohama *Kōkūtai* under Lieutenant Commander Tashiro had set out from their base at Majuro at 2100 on the thirteenth, each plane laden with four 250-kilogram and twelve 60-kilogram bombs. After one of the flying boats had to abort the mission en route, the remaining ten bombed the island at 0340 on Sunday, 14 December, but did not inflict any damage and returned to Majuro at 0910. Cunningham duly reported the most recent enemy raid (by what the garrison believed was only three planes) to ComFourteen at 0615 on the fourteenth, noting that Wake had emerged unscathed. At 0800 that morning, he amplified that dispatch, saying that the planes that had raided Wake had been "four-engined seaplanes." He also amended his earlier report on the status of the island's aviation gasoline supply as 200,000—*vice* 125,000—gallons.

The *Triton*, south of Wake, had noted "distinct flashes . . . probably from gunfire" at the time of the predawn raid by the Yokohama *Kōkūtai*. She closed the island after sunrise, but a periscope search revealed no ships in sight. While Pilly Lent's boat resumed running at deep submergence—a routine encouraged by the daily visits of Japanese planes (Rear Admiral Withers had fostered a healthy respect for aircraft)—Spiv Cunningham's garrison went about its daily business of improving defensive positions, and the artillerymen replaced the natural camouflage with fresh foliage.

Following the most recent raid, Cunningham reported his garrison's urgent needs in four separate messages sent thirty minutes apart. The five-inch batteries required fifteen gallons of recoil fluid, a twenty-foot range finder, an elevation order recorder, a friction disk housing, and two firing locks. The three-inch batteries needed rammer staffs with brushes, four jacking wrenches, three height finders, four hand fuse-setting wrenches, four generators for data transmission, and, among other items, one radar set. The atoll's .50-caliber battery required barrel packing material, fifty firing pins, and three sets of spares, while the .30-caliber guns required five hundred ammunition belts and ten belt-filling machines. The searchlight battery required one hundred yards of asbestos packing material, a complete elevation receiver, a complete azimuth receiver, two hundred sets of carbons, and three fire-control radars. He also requested new gasoline hoses and a new disk clutch for the gasoline bowser.

Over at the field, at dawn on the fourteenth, two planes (211-F-10 and 211-F-12) were in commission. Kinney reasoned that because 211-F-9 (the one that ComAirBatFor had "sold" them and which had been again rendered flyable on the twelfth) had never had new impeller gear installed, they would have to replace the engine, taking the nose section from the engine in the destroyed 211-F-5 and the main section of 211-F-2's power plant. Tackling the task with gusto, Kinney, Technical Sergeant Hamilton, Corporal John S. Painter, and several civilians were busily engaged at the center of the field, working on the carcass of 211-F-5, when someone said: "I hear planes." Painter scoffed: "Don't be so damned scared, those are our own patrol." Despite that brave reassurance, everybody stopped, cocked an ear, and looked skyward. Suddenly the dull crump of bombs came from the direction of Camp 1.

Restored to full strength by the retrieval of the three planes under Lieutenant (j.g.) Mizuno Yosihisa that had been based at Truk since the start of the war, thirty G3M2s from the Chitose *Kōkūtai* had departed Roi at 0545 on the fourteenth carrying 327 sixty-kilogram bombs. Lieutenant Commander Nakano Chujiro, the group's air officer, who rode in the *rikkō* commanded by the first *chūtai* leader, Lieutenant Watanabe, led the strike. Nakano's presence not only indicated the importance the Japanese high command placed on the mission but reflected its obvious concern that the Chitose *Kōkūtai* have something to show for its efforts. All hands on the airfield sprinted for shelter as Nakano's planes began sowing sixty-kilogram bombs methodically in a southeasterly direction toward them.

One landed close to Kinney and Hamilton, showering them with dirt. Staff Sergeant John F. Blandy, Sergeant Bourquin, and Corporal Trego tumbled into a small foxhole when bombs exploded close by, throwing rocks and shrapnel on top of the sandbags; fifty yards away, south of the airstrip, a bomb exploded and killed Sergeant Robert E. Garr, Jr., and Corporal John F. Double. Shrapnel felled Aviation Machinist's Mate First Class Hesson with a hip wound. Still another bomb exploded in a revetment, setting 211-F-10 afire. Japanese postattack estimates noted "direct hits . . . on the runway, revetments, and one fighter plane set afire."[12] Cunningham dutifully reported the raid at 1320, noting the two fatalities and the one fighter destroyed on the ground but stating that antiaircraft fire had downed two of the enemy force—regrettably only wishful thinking for all Chitose *Kōkūtai* land attack planes returned to Roi.

Hurrying over to the burning 211-F-10 after the raid had ended, Kinney saw that the bomb had hit close to the tail but had inflicted very little damage except to the oil tank and intercoolers. Deciding that this was the best power plant of all the ones that remained more or less intact, Kinney used an International rubber-tired hoist to lift the engine—mount and all. When its rear wheels left the ground, Kinney had six men climb on the hoist to keep it down and had a tractor pull it. At the same time, Technical Sergeant Hamilton and two men scrambled to pull 211-F-9 over to where it could receive its new power plant from the still burning 211-F-10. Kinney later reflected that saving the precious engine consumed his full attention with an intensity that defied prudence. With only the single makeshift hoist, the energetic Kinney and his crew, which included the civilians Yeager, Stevenson, and the two Gibbonses (father and son), then hung the engine from 211-F-9 on a tripod and picked up that from 211-F-10 to install it. They got the mount hooked up by nightfall, fortified only by a gallon of ice cream that Pete Sorenson had thoughtfully brought over. Because the hanger was not yet complete, they had to work quickly to observe the blackout.

Kinney instructed the civilian foreman to call him as soon as the hangar was ready to receive the plane. After sending Hamilton to bed at 0800, he tried to grab some sleep himself but was awakened an hour and a half later. He roused the slumbering civilians who had helped out earlier, and they all trooped over to the hangar and had it ready for the aircraft at 1130 on the fourteenth. Kinney and his helpers finished installing the engine by 0330 on the fifteenth: "a Navy record," Kinney crowed proudly, "even for ideal conditions."

The lack of work on the hangars had irritated Major Putnam. Commander Cunningham differed with his marine subordinates over just how much pressure to apply on the civilians, eschewing the use of armed force in favor of addressing the workers in small groups and appealing to them to lend a hand. Annoyed that Cunningham seemed to be using only "moral suasion"—and not martial law—Putnam, on 14 December, persuaded the contractors to work on the two underground shelters on which no work had been done for the previous twenty-four hours.

While the civilians turned out in force ("about 300 when only 50 could work," Kinney noted), curiosity moved many workers to line the airstrip to watch the takeoff of the evening patrol. The surging crowd prompted Captain Freuler, the pilot of one of the two planes, to ease to the left to avoid hitting any of the men. Suddenly a crane that had been moved across the field to the north side of the strip loomed in front of him. Continuing to the left, Freuler tried to miss the piece of heavy equipment but instead ground-looped 211-F-12 into the "boondocks."

Hauled back to the runway, the wrecked Wildcat, along with the damaged 211-F-11 (which had provided a port elevator for 211-F-8) served thereafter as a decoy. The incident illustrated graphically what those who flew the F4F regarded as one of the Wildcat's weaknesses: if a pilot was not "extremely attentive," the Grumman's narrow-track landing gear made it "prone to [lose] directional control on landing and take-off."[13] That evening, Cunningham radioed ComFourteen that only one plane remained effective.

While Wake's defenders carried on as best they could and John Kinney's hardworking mechanics "worked their hearts out" to get another plane operational, the Japanese were continuing their preparations for a second assault.[14] Because the seacoast guns and VMF-211's Wildcats had foiled the first attempt, Rear Admiral Kajioka asked Vice Admiral Inoue for help in reducing Wake's air power. Inoue in turn sought help from his friend Admiral Yamamoto, who promised to send a portion of the carrier strike force (*Kidō Butai*) under Vice Admiral Nagumo Chuichi toward Wake once it had completed its projected strikes on Midway en route back to Japan.

Strict radio silence had cloaked Nagumo's task force since 8 December as it battled its way through stormy seas tossed by moderate gale-force winds; curtains of rain occasionally obscured one ship from another. On the night of 14 December, Nagumo reported the weather-induced cancellation of the planned homeward-bound Midway strike. In Phase One of the Imperial Navy's operations in the Pacific war, the First Air Fleet was to operate in support of the Fourth Fleet. The inability of the Sixth Destroyer Squadron and supporting units to take Wake the first time around provided the first opportunity for Nagumo's force to support Inoue's command. Early the next morning, Yamamoto radioed the commander of the *Kidō Butai:*

> Twenty Fourth Air Flotilla has made successive air attacks on Wake since the beginning of the war but despite considerable damage to its air power and facilities X Invasion force lost two destroyers to enemy's remaining fighter aircraft force and suspended temporarily that invasion and are at Ruotto planning another attempt X
>
> Carrier strike force at appropriate time will assign a suitable force to reinforce the South Seas Force Wake invasion force to destroy enemy forces at Wake X[15]

Despite the danger posed by continuous use of the radio, messages flew back and forth between the principal Japanese commanders. Inoue expressed the desire to invade Wake between 20 and 23 December and wanted Nagumo's carriers to attack the atoll "with full force" on the twentieth.

Upon receipt of Yamamoto's orders, Nagumo informed the *Kidō*

Butai that enemy fighters had "stalemated" the Wake Island operation, and as a consequence, it would attack Wake after it had been refueled and had proceeded to Truk for conferences (where they were slated to arrive on 22 December) concerning the role the First Air Fleet would play in the reduction of the American defenses. He also informed his sailors that they would not carry out strikes on Midway as had been planned. "We turned south without delay," Lieutenant Commander Chigusa Sadao, executive officer of the *Akigumo*, noted in his diary later that day. "For the sake of supporting the capture of Wake Island," he wrote, "our operation against Midway is cancelled."

North of Wake, the *Tambor's* captain, still hoping to encounter a Japanese submarine, kept a periscope watch as long as light permitted. Only when he was unable to see because of darkness did Murphy order his depth control officer to balance the boat and stop all noise-making machinery to obtain "better listening conditions." Unfortunately, because Murphy had ordered the diving officer not to use the trim pump, the *Tambor* had difficulty maintaining her depth. She sank to 200 feet before Murphy ordered "all ahead standard" to regain control. At that moment, however, the chief electrician's mate in the *Tambor's* maneuvering room heard a rattling noise along the hull—"something . . . dragging against the side"—and recommended against turning over the propellers. After the boat settled a further 70 feet, Murphy ordered the main ballast tanks blown. The *Tambor* eventually reached 310 feet before she "caught" and began ascending, finding "nothing in sight" when she reached the surface. An examination of the boat revealed no "abnormalities" so the *Tambor* resumed her patrol.

While the Japanese were making their plans, Soc McMorris and his war plans people had conceived of a mission for the *Tangier*. Valuable aviation stores—torpedoes, gasoline, and bombs—had to be unloaded before the *Tangier* could take on the equipment necessary for Wake's salvation. She began discharging gasoline to a barge alongside on the thirteenth and began unloading warheads and torpedoes and loading aviation stores for Wake in the predawn darkness the following morning. She later shifted to the Pearl Harbor Navy Yard, where she continued discharging gasoline and unloading torpedoes. As marines embarked on board the *Tangier*, their shipmates on the island bade them "goodbye and give 'em hell!"

The Fourth Defense Battalion's men and matériel on board the *Tangier* included Battery F (three-inch), Battery B (five-inch), a provisional ground and antiaircraft machine-gun detachment (drawn from Batteries H and I), and a provisional headquarters and service detachment drawn from the Fourth Defense Battalion's H&S Battery, consisting of 8 officers and 197 enlisted marines (including three full operating crews for the

The *Tangier* (AV-8) unloading torpedoes onto a lighter alongside at Pearl Harbor, 14 December 1941, part of the time-consuming but necessary process to prepare the ship to take on board supplies and equipment needed at Wake. (NA, 80-G-266630)

three radar sets) and 1 officer and 4 enlisted men (navy Medical Corps). Supplies included 200 tons of dry stores; 2 SCR-268 radars and 1 SCR-270-B radar; 12 .50-caliber antiaircraft machine guns; 2 height finders for 3-inch antiaircraft guns, 1 M-4 director, and 1 range finder for 5-inch guns, as well as the spare parts requested in Cunningham's dispatch. Ammunition included 1,320 5-inch powder charges, 1,200 rounds of 5-inch service ammunition, 120 rounds of 5-inch illuminating, 70 boxes of primers, 12,000 3-inch antiaircraft shells (equipped with 30-second mechanical time fuses, not the virtually obsolete 21-second powder-train variety that equipped Wake's batteries), 360,000 rounds of .50-caliber armor-piercing bullets, 120,000 rounds of .50-caliber tracer; 700,000 rounds of .30-caliber ball, 69,000 rounds of .30-caliber armor-piercing and 69,000 rounds of .30-caliber tracer; and 480,000 .50-caliber links.[16]

The senior marine was Colonel Harold S. Fassett, a forty-nine-year-old Maine native and commander of the Fourth Defense Battalion, a "sound, intelligent, and resourceful" officer whose orders directed him to "temporary duty beyond the seas"—that of island commander at Wake.[17] Fassett's presence perhaps reflected less of a patent disapproval of Cunningham's having commanded the defense up to that point than a recognition of the fact that protecting Wake could be a marine "show" because the Japanese had virtually halted construction of NAS Wake and rendered what few installations had been completed for the naval air facility useless. Certainly, nothing untoward had occurred in how things had been handled up to that point, especially given the weaknesses in men and matériel that had plagued the garrison from the beginning.

At 1231 on 14 December (1001 15 December, Wake time), Task Force 11 (formerly Task Force 12) began clearing Pearl: Vice Admiral Brown's flagship *Indianapolis*, the heavy cruisers *Chicago* and *Portland* (CA-33), destroyers *Phelps* (DD-360), *Aylwin* (DD-355), *Dewey* (DD-349), *Dale* (DD-353), *MacDonough* (DD-351), *Farragut* (DD-348), *Worden* (DD-352), *Monaghan* (DD-354), and *Hull* (DD-350), and the *Neosho*. The question of which oiler to send with which task force would be debated often, mostly from the magnificent vantage point of hindsight and in ignorance of the capabilities of the vessels available. In early December 1941, there were only three oilers at Pearl—the *Ramapo* (AO-12), which had arrived on 5 December; the *Neosho*, which had arrived on the sixth; and the *Neches* (AO-5), which had arrived on the tenth—three distinct types of ships. Of the three, the fastest (and newest) was the *Neosho*, capable of 18 knots; the slowest was the *Ramapo*, which could make 10.7. The *Neches*'s top speed was 12.75. Their speed would obviously limit that of the force to which they were assigned.

Operating experience had shown that the *Lexington* and her sister ship *Saratoga* consumed "copious" quantities of fuel when operating aircraft, the latter using "as much as ten percent of her total capacity in a single day."[18] Because the foray toward the Marshalls required a longer voyage and there was apprehension that Brown's force might have to do battle far away from home, the decision to send the newer *Neosho* with Task Force 11 made eminently good sense. Task Force 14 was not going out with the prospect of fighting a battle, only relieving a siege.

The *Lexington* got under way at 1357 and, after a delay when one of her propellers struck a submerged raft, stood out at 1433, clearing the approach channel and commencing recovery of her air group soon thereafter: twenty-one Brewster F2As, thirty-two Douglas SBDs, and fifteen Douglas TBDs. All planes were on board by 1745, and the *Lexington* and her consorts stood to the southwestward. Upon opening his sealed orders, Brown learned that Task Force 11 was to raid Jaluit, reckoned to be the center of Japanese naval activity in the Marshalls,

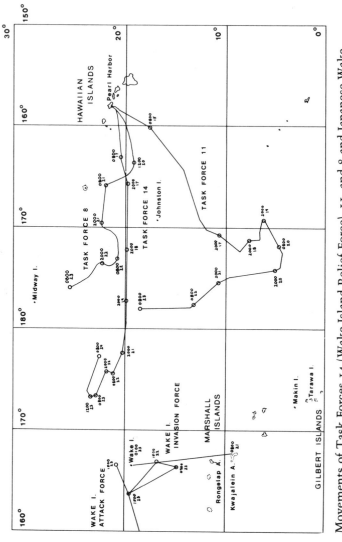

Movements of Task Forces 14 (Wake Island Relief Force), 11, and 8 and Japanese Wake Island Reinforcement Force.

Rear Admiral Frank Jack Fletcher, ca. 1941. (Author's Collection)

creating a diversion to cover the operations of Task Force 14—formed principally around the *Saratoga* and the *Tangier* and under Rear Admiral Frank Jack Fletcher, commander of Cruiser Division (ComCruDiv) Six—which was to sortie the following day.

"Orders were most explicit," Brown recorded in his war diary, "that only one attack would be made, and that on return of planes from Jaluit, Task Force 11 was to retire and return to Pearl Harbor." He was to seize "every opportunity to destroy important enemy forces, particularly carriers or capital ships." As Captain Frederick C. Sherman, the *Lexington*'s commanding officer, noted, however, the orders authorized "Commander Task Force 11 . . . to change objective to other installations and forces in eastern Marshalls or to withdraw without attacking as his judgement and the circumstances dictate." To the fiery Sherman, Brown appeared "exceedingly timid . . . and eager for [an] excuse to call [the attack] off." When one considers, though, that the initial war plan called for a raid on the Marshalls with at best two carriers (Brown had only one) the admiral's caution perhaps becomes more understandable.

Furthermore, Kimmel's choice of Fletcher to command the part of the relief effort that was to see that the *Tangier* reached Wake appears to have been based on Kimmel's high regard for Fletcher's capability and not, as some have argued, on his seniority. A graduate of the Naval Academy Class of 1906, the Iowa-born Fletcher (described by a classmate as a "strenuous son of the Middle West") had been awarded the Medal of Honor for distinguished conduct during refugee-evacuation operations at Veracruz in 1914 and a Navy Cross for his command of the destroyer *Benham* (Destroyer No. 49) on convoy escort duty during World War I. A Naval War College graduate, Fletcher had served as chief of staff to Admiral Montgomery M. Taylor, who was serving as commander in chief of the Asiatic Fleet at the time of the Japanese occupation of Manchuria in 1931 and the Sino-Japanese hostilities at Shanghai in 1932. Kimmel regarded Fletcher, a man with "smiling brown eyes . . . trigger-quick on repartee," who resembled "a finely trained welterweight ready for 15 or more rounds," as strong and vigorous—prized qualities in the immediate post–Pearl Harbor Pacific Fleet.[19] Fletcher would need those qualities in seeing that the *Tangier* reached her objective, which was easier said than done.

Operational attrition had reduced the *Saratoga*'s embarked fighter squadron, VF-3, to only thirteen available Grumman F4F-3s. The *Saratoga* was to launch VMF-221's fighters to fly into Wake while the sea-plane tender was to moor offshore to begin putting ashore reinforcements, ammunition, provisions, and equipment—including the vitally important radars. The *Tangier* was then to embark approximately 650 civilians and all wounded men and return to Pearl. Kimmel and his staff had estimated that the process of unloading and debarkation would take at least two days; embarking all of the people at Wake could be done in less than one. Unfavorable weather, however, could lengthen the time considerably, as those familiar with conditions at Wake knew only too well.

On the morning of 15 December, the *Saratoga* and her consorts passed Pearl's entrance buoys and entered the harbor. The *Saratoga* moored at berth Fox-Nine at 1037; the oiler *Ramapo* moored alongside within a half hour to begin replenishing the carrier's depleted oil bunkers. As that work proceeded, the CNO sent a dispatch to CinCPac authorizing him "at [CinCPac's] discretion, to reinforce Wake and Midway, to restock them with ammunition and supplies," and to remove CPNAB workmen.[20]

Kimmel responded within the hour. Wake, he radioed, must either be supplied with ammunition and reinforced with fighter aircraft or evacuated. He also mentioned a third option: to abandon the garrison and defense workers, totaling about fourteen hundred men. Unloading ammunition and stores and embarking a portion of the CPNAB work force would consume two days, whereas embarking everyone would take one, although he acknowledged that if the weather was unfavorable those times could be "indefinitely increased." Wake could be supplied with enough ammunition for one month at the present rate of expenditure. He informed Stark that he had planned to reinforce Wake, evacuating "about 700 defense workers," indicating that apparently those contemplating Wake's relief did not have a good grasp on exactly how many civilians there were on the island. He went on to state that he was dispatching a convoy that very day and planned a diversionary strike on Japanese positions in the eastern Marshalls.[21] During the afternoon watch, Stark "heartily concurred" with Kimmel's proposal.[22]

On the surface, the infusion of another squadron of marine fighters into the situation at Wake loomed large in the relief efforts. VMF-221 had taken delivery of its Brewster F2A-3 Buffalo fighters that summer. Compared to the F3Fs they had flown previously, 221's pilots generally thought the F2A an improvement ("a good-looking little fighter" that was a "thrill" to fly), but the Brewsters, like VMF-211's F4Fs, were not equipped with self-sealing fuel tanks or armor plate.[23] The F2As had been loaded on board the Saratoga—not flown in—before she left the west coast for Oahu. They had been flown off to Kaneohe and then to Ford Island, but shipboard cranes brought the Buffaloes on board before the expedition sailed. Any landing gear failures at that juncture would have been disastrous.

Brigadier General Ross E. Rowell, commanding the Second Marine Aircraft Wing, knew of 221's manpower and operational deficiencies and lamented having to send "[Major Verne] McCaul's half-baked outfit into that mess" at Wake.[24] Rowell knew that maintaining the temperamental F2As at a stateside air station with all the conveniences had been a chore. Having to operate Buffaloes at an advance base (especially one that had been as badly battered as Wake had been) or at sea in a carrier (where the F2A's performance—especially the failures of its delicate landing gear—was infamous) had all the potential to be a nightmare. It was bad enough that the men who had been sent to Wake at the eleventh hour had been more familiar with SBDs and SB2Us than F4Fs.

On Wake on 15 December, meanwhile, VMF-211 continued to maintain its patrol routine as best it could. Paul Putnam took an F4F aloft that morning and, in his patrol to the southwest of the atoll, spotted a submarine on the surface. Knowing that two American boats were operating near Wake, he sought to identify her before attacking. He noted what appeared to be three arabic numerals on both sides of the bow and a large arabic numeral on the conning tower. On the foredeck, there was a "solid dark orange, almost red-colored, triangle superimposed on a solid white circle." Thinking that the submarine was Dutch, Putnam did not attack.[25] If the submarine was indeed Japanese, she was probably the ill-starred RO-66 because none of the Twenty-sixth Division boats had yet reached their assigned stations.

Late that morning, Cunningham summarized the situation on Wake in a lengthy dispatch to ComFourteen. He noted that the first two Japanese raids, both carried out at low level, had been very effective.

The enemy had inflicted heavy damage with incendiary bullets as well
as bombs. Since those two attacks, the Japanese had remained at high
altitude, apparently respecting VMF-211's fighters and the defense battalion's antiaircraft fire. A large number of bombs had been dropped in
a "ladder" pattern, and "slight deflection errors" had prevented more
extensive damage. His people were "well provided" with shelters, and
sand-covered hangars were being built. Unfortunately, the island's fuel,
aviation gasoline, and water supplies lay virtually naked to the enemy's
bombs.

During the day on the fifteenth, Dan Godbold's men had observed
the usual routine, starting the day at Condition 1 and replacing
the natural camouflage before setting Condition 2 at 0700. His men
completed the shelters near the guns during the day and began work on
the shelter at the height-finder position. Ironically, despite the atoll's
abundance of coral sand, empty sandbags were in short supply, and
Cunningham requested three hundred thousand of them from ComFourteen that afternoon.

Godbold's men knocked off work at 1700 to set Condition 1, but a
half hour later, battery lookouts reported a plane lurking among the low
clouds to the east, and Godbold reported the presence of the intruder
to the island command post. Had his men spotted a snooper? Perhaps.
Earlier that day, at 1230, eight Kawanishi flying boats from the Yokohama Kōkūtai had departed Majuro under Lieutenant Commander Koi-
zumi Sanemiro, whose own plane had had to abort the mission an hour
and a half into it to return to base, thus leaving the lead in the hands
of Lieutenant Yoneyama Shigeru. At 1800, Yoneyama brought the seven
remaining flying boats in at a thousand feet. They dropped their 250-
and 60-kilogram bombs on what their crews thought was the "barracks
area [Camp 2] in the northern part of the island" and also strafed the
area near Batteries D and B; some of the bombs fell across the road from
Battery D, but the strafers inflicted no casualties or damage. Because of
the low visibility, Godbold's three-inchers did not fire. Although the
Japanese rated their bombing as "effective," it killed only one man (a
civilian) and damaged no installations.[26] From his vantage point, Marine
Gunner McKinstry, in Battery E, thought all of the bombs landed in the
ocean. The Japanese planes returned to Majuro at midnight.

Cunningham's dispatches to ComFourteen that evening reported the
presence of the submarine that Putnam had spotted and the good news
that Kinney's engineers had managed to get an additional plane operational and that the most recent raid had inflicted no ascertainable damage to installations.

The next day, the sixteenth, thirty-two G3M2s from the Chitose
Kōkūtai (one had had to abort the mission soon after takeoff) under the

command of Lieutenant Watanabe raided Wake at 1340. The island commander reported it to ComFourteen shortly after the bombs began falling. The marines, however, greeted the Japanese fliers with novel fire-control methods. Kinney and Kliewer, aloft on patrol, spotted Watanabe's incoming *chūtais* closing the atoll at eighteen thousand feet almost ten minutes before they reached Wake's airspace. Next, they radioed their altitude to the gun batteries. The time lag permitted Lewis to crank the data into the M-4 director and pass the solution on to Godbold. Battery D hurled ninety-five rounds skyward; Battery E's first shots exploded ahead of the formation, and Gunner McKinstry reported that the lead *rikkō* in one formation dropped, smoking, to the rear of the formation. He estimated that at least four other planes trailed smoke as they cleared the island. Godbold estimated that four planes had been damaged and one had crashed some distance from the island. Japanese accounts, however, acknowledge neither losses nor damage to their aircraft during the attack that day. Both Kliewer and Kinney attacked the planes, but only one of Kinney's four machine guns worked.

Bombs falling on Peacock Point shook up the machine gunners in their foxholes. That night, civilian work crews aided Barninger's marines in constructing two deep shelters near Battery A that boasted an abundance of cover overhead and three feet of hard coral rock to detonate any direct hits. By morning, the dugouts had been completed, all traces of the night's activity erased so that it could not be seen from the air, and the camouflage replaced.

Just as frustration dogged the aviators and Wake's defenders continued to dig in, misfortune continued to hound the *Tambor*. Soon after she had observed the latest air attack on Wake from her ringside seat off the atoll—during which time her "rattling noise reoccurred in striking fashion"—Lieutenant Commander Murphy received word that a bad leak had developed in the sub's forward torpedo room. Investigating, he saw what looked like a "bubbling spring" in the starboard after corner of the torpedo well develop into a strong spray. Ordering the boat brought up to 120 feet, where the spray momentarily subsided but then burst forth with renewed force, Murphy estimated that a gasket was leaking—a leak that had perhaps been started during the boat's 310-foot descent the evening before.

Repair problems absorbed the energies of the defenders ashore just as they did those on board the submarine, as John Kinney returned to the task of keeping the planes ready to fight with homemade expedients or borrowed gear. The last two gun-cleaning rods had been lost when 211-F-10 was destroyed so Kinney and his helpers fashioned gun-cleaning rods from two welding rods. His battle against the pervasive coral sand—a familiar problem to anyone who had been stationed on

Wake—forced him to borrow a compressor from PanAir (two previous compressors had been "straffed [sic] out of commission") to blow out accumulations of grit with a mixture of air and kerosene.

To help Kinney and Hamilton and the small but dedicated band of marine and civilian mechanics, Aviation Machinist's Mate First Class Hesson ignored doctor's orders and surprised his shipmates by returning to the airfield to resume work. He carried on as effectively as ever in spite of the shrapnel still embedded in one hip, reflecting the courage and devotion to the task that exemplified Wake's defenders. Putnam later recalled Hesson's service as "one of the foundations [Kinney and Hamilton were the others] of the entire aerial defense of Wake Island."[27]

The planes that Kinney, Hamilton, Hesson, and the mechanics strove so mightily to keep in some semblance of fighting trim seemed to acquire personality traits of their own—especially 211-F-8, which figured in one of the few humorous but momentarily embarrassing instances that Kinney would recall. The pilots who flew it knew that it only had one gasoline tank; the other was inaccessible for patching. One day, one of the pilots was aloft in another plane when he noticed that his main tank ran dry at eighteen thousand feet. Forgetting that he was not at the controls of 211-F-8, he brought the Wildcat in to a perfect dead-stick landing. A check of the tanks, however, revealed that he had had about sixty gallons of fuel remaining.

Battery D's men, meanwhile, had spent a portion of 16 December working on the large shelter for the gun crews. That night, a seventy-five-man working party helped Godbold's men finish the large personnel shelter. That work complete, they turned to building a shelter for the men who manned the director. Perhaps because of the dwindling number of operable motor vehicles (half of those on the atoll had been destroyed), Staff Sergeant Ernest E. Short, the detachment's transportation sergeant, could afford to transfer two marines from service at the garage to serve with Battery D, for Private First Class LeRoy N. Schneider and Private Ewing E. Laporte arrived that night for duty with Godbold's unit.

Back at Pearl Harbor, in the lengthening shadows of 15 December (16 December at Wake), the relief expedition began to put to sea soon after Halsey's Task Force 8 entered port. The Tangier, the oiler Neches (the only one, McMorris noted, that was immediately available), and the destroyers Porter (DD-356), Mahan (DD-364), Lamson (DD-367), and Flusser (DD-368) sailed at 1730 on the fifteenth (1500 Wake time, 16 December).

"The twilight sortie," then First Lieutenant Robert D. Heinl, Jr., wrote of the Tangier's sailing, "dramatized the adventure." The ships steamed past somber reminders of 7 December—the beached battleship Nevada and a Douglas SBD Dauntless from the Enterprise lying in the shallows near the channel entrance, the latter shot down by friendly fire off Fort Kamehameha. "The waters beyond sight of Oahu," Heinl observed, "seemed very lonely waters indeed, and those who had just seen the Japanese Navy materialize a crushing surprise-attack out of nowhere were perhaps inclined to credit the enemy with more omniscience or ubiquity than we later learned he possessed . . . Columbus' men, sailing westward in hourly apprehension of toppling off the edge of a square earth, could not have felt the seas to be more inscrutable and less friendly."[28]

Having received the relevant operations orders that afternoon, Rear Admiral Fletcher met with the other task unit commanders and their staffs at 1900 to discuss the broad mission assigned them and the individual missions of each group. Fletcher set zero hour as 1000 the following morning, when the first cruiser was set to pass buoy 18 on her way out of the channel.

On the same day the *Tangier* and her consorts sailed for Wake (15 December, Pearl date) and the relief effort he had fashioned began to unfold, Admiral Kimmel reflected on his own somewhat indeterminate future. Secretary of the Navy Knox, after having seen firsthand the devastation wreaked by the Japanese on the seventh, had concluded that the navy had not been on the alert, and the shadow of an investigation into the disaster loomed across Kimmel. "If I am to be relieved," the CinCPac wrote to Admiral Stark, "I think my relief should be nominated and that he should take over as soon as practicable." Evincing a desire to help his successor, he enjoined Stark to "decide on the basis of what is best for the Country. What happens to me is of no importance."[29]

After allowing that perhaps he "should be relieved," Kimmel suggested that a "strong vigorous man" be appointed to command the fleet. He put forth several candidates, including Frank Jack Fletcher, to whom he had just entrusted a significant portion of the relief effort. The other candidates he suggested were Rear Admirals H. Fairfax Leary, Milo F. Draemel, Robert A. Theobald, Robert L. Ghormley, Royal E. Ingersoll, and Chester W. Nimitz. On the subject of his own relief, Kimmel concluded resignedly: "Do not spare my feelings."[30]

While Wake's defenders doggedly carried on and the man who had set in motion the efforts to relieve their bitter siege seemed reconciled to the uncertainty that lay ahead for him, the appeals for help by Inoue and Kajioka were bearing fruit—although not on the scale originally desired. Nagumo sent a dispatch informing Inoue that the *Kidō Butai* could not "afford full cooperation because of [a] fuel problem." At 1800 on 16 December he informed the anxious admirals that the Eighth Cruiser Division (the eight-inch gunned heavy cruisers *Tone* and *Chikuma*), the Second Carrier Division (the aircraft carriers *Hiryū* and

Rear Admiral Abe Hiroaki, Commander, Eighth Cruiser Division, on board either the *Tone* or the *Chikuma*, ca. April 1942. The Wake Island Reinforcement Force that he commanded performed significant work in helping to reduce the atoll's defenses. (Japan War History Office)

Sōryū), and two destroyers (the *Tanikaze* and the *Urakaze*) would cooperate with the Wake Island invasion force on about 20 December, upon completion of which operations the force would "return to home waters as soon as possible" and make ready for future deployment.[31]

The *Sōryū* and the *Hiryū* combined had lost three Mitsubishi A6M2 Type oo carrier fighters (*kansen*) and four Aichi D3A1 Type 99 carrier bombers (*kanbaku*) in the Hawaiian operation, and twenty *kansen*, twenty-three *kanbaku*, and three Nakajima B5N2 Type 97 carrier attack planes (*kankō*) had received varying degrees of damage over Oahu a week before. On board the two carriers, some pilots, observers, and radio-gunners had yet to see combat, having been embarked as spares in anticipation of heavy losses.

Nagumo entrusted command of the Wake Reinforcement Force to fifty-two-year-old Rear Admiral Abe Hiroaki, commander of the Eighth Cruiser Division, who in 1939–40 had been head instructor and chief discipline officer at Etajima. Abe's air commander was the redoubtable forty-nine-year-old Rear Admiral Yamaguchi Tamon, whose seemingly perpetual but "deceptively sorrowful expression" belied an "impulsive devil-may-care" outlook on life. Despite Yamaguchi's comparatively recent acquaintance with aviation (he had come to the Japanese navy's air arm in January 1940), it was said that his men thought of him as "the greatest invention since the airplane . . . [his naval aviators] considered him one of them."[32] A 1941 description of Yamaguchi in the U.S. Navy's Office of Naval Intelligence called him "rather heavy set and fat. Qualified submarine officer and apparently capable. Specialist in torpedoes. Studied at Princeton and Johns Hopkins. Seems to enjoy bachelor drinking parties. Speaks excellent English. Close mouthed and reserved, but affable and makes [a] good impression."[33]

At 1830 on 16 December, Nagumo detached the ships he had enumerated (the carriers with 118 operational planes between them) from the First Air Fleet and bade Abe good luck. The latter's ships then hastened off to the southwest through the stormy seas, in the darkness, while the rest of the Kidō Butai remained triumphantly on course for Japan.

Shortly before Rear Admiral Abe's ships began heading toward Wake, the Tambor's problem became insurmountable. Murphy's executive officer had urged that they attempt to renew the gasket that night but soon discovered that there was no suitable material on board. In addition, as Murphy later recounted, "no man aboard [sic] felt competent to attempt the job of cutting, fitting, and installing such a large gasket without a pattern." Advised by his two most experienced chief machinist's mates that any attempt to fix it would probably only worsen the situation, Murphy decided against trying. He feared losing depth control and being forced to surface to "meet an ignominious end with no chance of inflicting compensating damage on the enemy." He decided that to take that chance, "on a patrol station where the opportunity to inflict damage was infrequent at best," would amount to "rash heroics." He informed ComSubScoFor of his intentions; Rear Admiral Withers directed him to return via 18 degrees north latitude and 175 degrees west longitude. The Tambor then surfaced at 1809 and "headed for Pearl via the points prescribed," setting course roughly east by south on the first leg of the voyage to Oahu.

As the Tambor was leaving the atoll behind, the Triton received a radio message from Wake's signal station at 2130 on 16 December directing her to search the waters south of Kuku Point. Running in within three miles of the island, she stood roughly southeast by east to parallel the shoreline, Pilly Lent reasoning that anything in that area would be silhouetted by fires burning ashore in the aftermath of the day's air raid. After sighting nothing, the Triton continued her patrol. Subsequently, she received a dispatch from ComSubScoFor: the Tambor had to depart the vicinity, and the *Triton* was to assume the patrol duties for the entire area.

Knowing that reinforcements were on the way, Rear Admiral Kajioka and Rear Admiral Goto, the commander of the Twenty-fourth Air Flotilla, barraged Nagumo and Abe with suggestions for employment of the *Hiryū* and the *Sōryū*. On the seventeenth, Vice Admiral Inoue ordered Abe to cooperate with the invasion between 20 and 23 December. Kajioka's force would assault the atoll on 22 and 23 December.

Coordinating plans with Kajioka and Goto, however, required use of the radio—too much use, in the opinion of the men in Abe's force who were justifiably anxious over the menace posed by American submarines. On the evening of 17 December, Captain Fujita Kikuichi, Abe's chief of staff, lamented sardonically in his diary: "With messages going back and forth, the entire matter became complicated and confused. Additionally, the more *we* use *our* radio, the more dangerous it becomes for *us* because of enemy submarines. . . . *They're* safe at anchor inside Kwajalein Atoll!" When the "irritating radio conference type messages" continued the next day, Abe ended the process by radioing his intentions to Inoue at 0930 on the eighteenth and letting it go at that.[34]

That very day, as if to underscore the danger posed by American submarines possibly homing in on radio transmissions from Abe's ships, the crew of one of the *kanbaku*s on antisubmarine patrol ahead of the force—the *Hiryū* had six aloft that day and the *Sōryū* four, in addition to seven *kankō*s from the latter's attack bomber squadron—thought they spotted one forty miles ahead in their path. "While things were tense for a while," Captain Fujita wrote, "nothing happened."[35]

The Japanese pressed on. Their use of the airwaves, however, had enabled the U.S. Navy's radio intelligence people to surmise on 17 December (Pearl Harbor date) that the operations of "Crudiv 8 [the *Tone* and the *Chikuma*] and Cardiv 2 [the *Sōryū* and the *Hiryū*]" were connected to those of "Airon 24 [24th Flotilla] of the Fourth . . . Fleet."[36]

The expedition to relieve Wake continued on the morning of the sixteenth. That same morning the *Astoria* (CA-34), wearing Rear Admiral Frank Jack Fletcher's flag, sailed as scheduled. Fletcher's flagship had a passenger on board—Rear Admiral Thomas C. Kinkaid, who was slated to relieve Fletcher as ComCruDiv Six. Kinkaid, Admiral Kimmel's brother-in-law, was experienced in the matters of convoy escort, having recently arrived from the Atlantic Fleet. Delayed by the time spent fueling the *Saratoga* from the *Ramapo*, however, the carrier did not stand out until that afternoon. The destroyers *Bagley* (DD-386), *Blue*, *Henley* (DD-391), and *Helm* (DD-388) joined her soon thereafter; the *Jarvis* joined a little over an hour later.

That same day, Admiral Kimmel received a message from OpNav

Vice Admiral William S. Pye, USN, ca. 1942. (NHC, NH 82801)

Martin cartoon depicting the statement that reinforced the story that larger-than-life marines on Wake had requested more "Japs," ca. 17 December. (Col. Arthur A. Poindexter, USMC, Retired)

Sergeant Robert O. Arthur, 2 June
1938. (USMC)

informing him that he was to be relieved imminently by Vice Admiral
William S. Pye. Pye, whose flagship, the battleship *California* (BB-44),
had been sunk at her moorings at Pearl on 7 December, had been Kimmel's adviser since that terrible morning. Kimmel regarded Pye as a
level-headed, extremely competent planner, whom he had "particularly
desired" to serve as commander of the Battle Force because he was
"able, vigorous, and loyal" and an officer he would select "above all
others" for that billet. Although he "did not want to be relieved right
in the middle of [the operation he had set in motion]," Kimmel informed
OpNav that Pye was fully cognizant of the details of the unfolding plan
to relieve Wake.

    Up to that point, daily war communiques had told an anxious Ameri-
can public that Wake was still holding out against the Japanese. On 17
December, however, a story, reportedly circulating in Honolulu,
emerged that navy officials had contacted the marines at Wake (there
had been no public word that a naval officer was in command there)
and asked what they required. "Yes," the marines purportedly replied,
"send us some more Japs." Ensigns Henshaw and Lauff, who encoded
Cunningham's dispatches for transmission from Wake, had in fact used
the words in "padding" a message that would be decoded by their friends
and opposite numbers in Patrol Wing 2 back at Pearl. It was Lauff's
idea, Henshaw noted later, not his. "If there was anything [we] didn't
need," he wrote later, "it was more Japs!"[37] John Kinney noted in his
diary that Kay Kyser, the popular bandleader, had dedicated a song to
the "Wake Marines," and commentators noted that Wake's defenders,
when asked what they required, had said cockily, "Send us more Japs."

"We began to figure out," Kinney sighed, "that the U.S. was not going to reinforce us."[38]

That same day another news item appeared telling of Paramount Pictures' "forthcoming production" of a movie, *Wake Island*, that was to star actors William Holden, Fred MacMurray, Brian Donlevy, Macdonald Carey, and Robert Preston. Hollywood knew a good story when it saw one.[39]

Initially unaware that they had requested more Oriental adversaries, that Hollywood's efforts to relate an account of the events that, at that point, still had no denouement, were getting under way, and as the real-life drama of the relief expedition unfolded tortuously across the Pacific, on Wake 211-F-8, as if it had a vexing spirit of its own, continued to cause problems for Kinney and his hardworking mechanics. It had been hard to start the day before and defied initial attempts to start it on the seventeenth. Kinney checked the valves and replaced the carburetor with no success. Changing the magnetos helped only marginally.

In the meantime, a rotation of the surviving pilots, their strength bolstered by vitamin pills reserved solely for their use by Lieutenant (j.g.) Kahn, flew the dwindling number of planes. Putnam had omitted Staff Sergeant Bob Arthur, who had been wounded in the initial bombing on the eighth, from that rotation. Arthur had stood watch in the ready tent daily, looking on as other pilots took up Wake's Wildcats, aching with frustration at not being able to do what he had been trained to do—fly. On the seventeenth, though, Arthur, who had not flown since before the bombing nine days earlier, asked Major Putnam to let him take his turn in the rotation. Initially, Putnam refused, but he soon learned that the staff sergeant had been experimenting secretly with attaching his bandaged left hand to the throttle of an F4F-3 so he could fly. Moved by the young noncom's eloquent and dogged desire to return to duty, Putnam let him take his hard-earned turn.[40]

Given the desperate straits of the men on Wake, one could perhaps forgive Commander Cunningham's astonishment at a message originated by Rear Admiral Bloch at 1710 on 16 December (1440 on 17 December at Wake). Cunningham had been primarily concerned with defending the atoll and keeping his men alive. Bloch's message stated that it was "highly desirable" to continue dredging the channel across Wilkes and inquired as to the feasibility "under present conditions" of finishing the work with existing equipment—as if Cunningham and his band of defenders did not have enough to be concerned with. Bloch requested an estimated date of completion and concluded by asking about the whereabouts of the tug *Arthur Foss*.[41]

Before Cunningham could respond, the Japanese carried out another nuisance raid on his garrison. Earlier that day, at 1230, eight Type 97 flying boats, again led by Lieutenant Commander Tashiro, lifted off the waters off Majuro, bound once more for the triangular atoll visited thrice before by men of the Yokohama *Kōkūtai*. Beneath the broad parasol wings of the Kawanishis hung an ordnance load of five 250-kilogram and seventy-eight 60-kilogram bombs. Sighting their objective despite low visibility at 1752, about a half hour after sunset, Tashiro's bombers loosed their loads over Peale—their target was the antiaircraft batteries there—three minutes later. Their aim, however, proved poor. Bombs fell near the ruined PanAir hotel and across the road from Battery D, while gunners in the flying boats strafed the battery. All of the Type 97s returned to Majuro at 2315 that night having accomplished nothing more than annoying the defenders. Poor visibility had prevented Battery D from firing in response.[42]

A little over two hours after the last of Tashiro's flying boats had lumbered off into the night, Cunningham radioed ComFourteen, reporting that the most recent raid had caused no damage. By that point, however, he had been able to ascertain the extent of the damage from all of the previous raids. It was discouraging. The principal storehouse with spare parts and contruction materials had been burned to the ground; the machine shop, blacksmith shop, and garage had been demolished; 50 percent of the heavy digging equipment, 50 percent of the motor transport (including trucks), 80 percent of the diesel oil, and the majority of the dynamite had been destroyed as well.

As Wake's defenders continued to improvise their defenses, the three boats from the Twenty-sixth Submarine Division arrived off Wake to take up their stations on the seventeenth, unaware that a sister ship from the Twenty-seventh, the *RO-66*, remained in proximity of the atoll. Consequently, at 2230 on that day, as one boat from the newly arrived group, the *RO-62* (Lieutenant Commander Takizawa Koresuke), entered her patrol area, she rammed and sank the *RO-66* roughly twenty-five miles west-southwest of Wake, causing the loss of Lieutenant Commander Kurokawa and his crew.[43] Admiral Ugaki, writing in his diary on 18 December 1941, deplored the "tragic mishap." Wake, he lamented, was "somewhat of a jinx."[44]

At Pearl on the morning of 17 December, Captain McMorris sent an urgent memorandum to Captain John B. Earle, Bloch's chief of staff, concerning CinCPac's views on the proposed evacuation of Wake Island. "The most desirable situation," McMorris wrote, "would be to have only volunteers remain, but if necessary the number needed will be required to remain." He went on to list the services that Kimmel felt were required there: power plant and utilities, distilling plant, refrigeration plant, truck and tractor operators, mechanics for plants, machinery, and transportation, medical and messing services, and defense-oriented duties such as transporting supplies, ammunition, food, and men. Paramount among the construction projects that had been halted by the coming of war, McMorris specified completion of the cross runway and dredging. He went on to note, however, that because Bloch was most familiar with the "civilian requirements at Wake" CinCPac was providing the memorandum only "for such use and help as it may be to you."[45]

"In order to reduce the possibilities of information regarding the relief expedition reaching the enemy," McMorris cautioned Earle that CinCPac "wishes no radio communications regarding it." If the commandant deemed radio traffic "vital," McMorris added, Kimmel wanted such "sent to him [CinCPac] to release." McMorris then informed Earle that CinCPac was sending a patrol plane to Wake the next day (18 December), "to carry any necessary information and instructions regarding unloading and evacuation of civilians." Although CinCPac was not forwarding any instructions "in the premises directly to Wake," he wanted copies of any orders the commandant issued. "The information and directives which you wish transmitted by this plane," McMorris concluded, "should be delivered to the War Plans Section of the Commander-in-Chief's staff today." The same plane would carry "similar matter" to Midway concerning the *Wright*'s mission and the evacuation of men from that atoll.[46]

Consequently, Rear Admiral Bloch, in his memo dated 17 December 1941, directed that the number of civilians on Wake be reduced to 250 "volunteers if possible." Besides those supervisors and a minimal number of office workers to keep track of "bare essential records such as lists of people, stores on hand, etc.," Bloch ordered the retention of operators of power plants and stationary mechanical equipment, mechanics and machinists to operate trucks and equipment, Caterpillar operators, firemen and oilers, crane operators, tug operators, men to operate the galley, and a nucleus construction crew of skilled tradesmen such as welders, pipe fitters, electricians, and carpenters. He called for the evacuation of unskilled laborers and those in nonessential trades (such as painters) and stated that if any unskilled labor was required, the "military forces" could supply it—a problem that had bedeviled the marines since they had first set foot on the atoll.[47]

ComFourteen urged Cunningham to concentrate on "immediate defense"-related items. He suggested embankments for defenses, rectangular coral embankments approximately eight feet high that could be constructed adjacent to the runways to house planes, and additional magazines from wood, if concrete could not be poured. He suggested boarding up the steel frames of the yet incomplete air station buildings to make them usable, providing a supply of saltwater for fire fighting, filling the cross runway to a minimum of 3,000 by 150 feet, covering gasoline tanks with coral, blasting and digging out coral heads to enlarge the seaplane operating area, providing staggered and well-spaced holding-down anchors in the seaplane parking area, and constructing small nose hangars as necessary to provide shelter for men working on a plane engine. Although the tasks enumerated by Bloch seem unrealistic (Dan Teters deemed them "impossible" at that stage) for an outlying base under constant siege, ComFourteen ordered dredging work in the lagoon halted to conserve fuel, as well as on the new channel, to preserve motor access to the western tip of Wilkes, indicating that Bloch had had second thoughts about the dredging projects that he had ordered continued in his message of the previous afternoon.[48]

"Upon arrival of a vessel with cargo," Bloch concluded, referring obliquely to the *Tangier*, he urged Cunningham to exert every effort "to expedite unloading of cargo and loading of evacuees thereafter" and to "be prepared to execute these orders about 23 December."[49]

At sea, the *Astoria* sighted her convoy one hour into the forenoon watch on the seventeenth; lookouts on board the *Saratoga* spotted at least five ships (which grew to nine as the distance lessened) at 1015. Shortly after high noon, "Sara" joined Task Force 14: the *Astoria, San Francisco,* and *Minneapolis* and the destroyers *Mugford* (DD-389), *Selfridge, Patterson* (DD-392), and *Ralph Talbot* (DD-390), screening the *Tangier* and the *Neches*. Fletcher's task force set course for Wake.

By midafternoon, however, despite Kimmel's apparent appeal to be retained as CinCPac to see his Wake relief operations through, at 1500 on 17 December (1230, 18 December, Wake time), in accordance with orders from President Roosevelt and Secretary of the Navy Knox, and in a perfunctory ceremony at the submarine base, Admiral Kimmel turned over temporary command of the Pacific Fleet to Vice Admiral Pye.[50] Kimmel's designated relief, Rear Admiral Chester W. Nimitz (who would assume the rank of admiral upon assumption of command) would not be on Oahu for over a week.

That same day, at 1745, as McMorris had intimated to Bloch's chief of staff, Ensign James J. Murphy, A-V(N), Ensign Howard P. Ady, Ensign Francis C. Riley, A-V(N), and Radioman First Class (NAP) J. A. Spraggins, VP-23's no. 1 flight crew, received orders to depart for Wake Island the following day. They were to proceed via Midway and "carry mail and equipment" to both places and "return immediately over [the] same route."[51] If anyone could handle the job, it was J. J. Murphy, an experienced pilot whom no one had qualms about flying with. A competent, positive man with an uplifting nature, Murphy could be counted on to deliver the goods and get back home.

Japanese aerial reconnaissance from the Marshalls continued over

Wake in the meantime. Lieutenant Ando, who had overflown the atoll on 4 December, took off from Roi at 0730 on the eighteenth and reached his objective at 1140. After ground observers caught a glimpse of the enemy, Captain Elrod took off in the only flyable F4F, 211-F-9, to try to catch Ando's *rikkō*. The Japanese eluded the determined marine, however, and retired to the Marshalls unscathed, landing at 1500 that afternoon.[52]

About an hour after Ando's overflight of Wake, Cunningham received a message from the port director of the Fourteenth Naval District, prodding him about the whereabouts of the *Arthur Foss*. At 1405 on the eighteenth, Cunningham responded heatedly to Bloch's message of the previous afternoon accusing him of being concerned only with defending the island and preserving lives. He pointed out that blackout conditions militated against any work being done on the channel at night and that the Japanese air raids, which came without warning, limited the workday to six hours. Because Wake's defenders possessed no radar to provide timely warning, noisy equipment could prevent workmen from learning of incoming planes in time to take cover. Furthermore, the contractors' equipment was being whittled down by the bombings, and to complete the remaining projects required the immediate replenishment of diesel oil and dynamite. The morale of the civilian workmen was plummeting, and Cunningham could not predict when the construction projects would be completed. Before he appended word of the date the *Arthur Foss* had sailed, he declared pointedly that "relief from raids would improve [the] outlook."[53]

Cunningham knew that the morale of the contractors was not good. Despite the assistance rendered by the individual civilians who shared VMF-211's lot in life, Paul Putnam was growing weary and exasperated with what he perceived as the general breakdown of the CPNAB organization as a whole. Work, he felt, was proceeding "with unreasonable slowness and confusion." Dan Teters noted that on one of the two occasions (around 18 December) that Putnam had asked Cunningham to use force to round up civilians, the marine squadron commander seemed "in an extremely excited frame of mind" when he and the commander showed up at Teters's dugout. Work on airfield facilities, Putnam complained, was not proceeding "to his satisfaction." If Cunningham would permit it, Putnam said he would use ten armed marines "to enforce civilian labor to do as he ordered." The island commander replied "very calmly" that he did not think such draconian measures necessary; "more would be accomplished," he said, "if [the] civilian workers continued to perform their duties under the general superintendent."[54] He would not proclaim martial law.

Still "steaming with exasperation" after turning the first message over to his coding officers for transmission to Pearl, Cunningham noted in a second dispatch the damage inflicted by the Japanese. He stated that since the outbreak of war, assisting in the defense and salvage operations had fully occupied all of the contractors; of the forty-five CPNAB men who had died thus far, fifteen were unidentified or missing. Describing the contractors' general morale as "extremely low," he considered evacuating them because the large number of them who were not helping in the active defense efforts required subsistence.

The object of the expressed concern by ComFourteen's port director, the tug *Arthur Foss*, had been the last American-flag vessel to leave Wake before the war started. Unable to pick up either of the Honolulu radio stations on the night of the eighth, the crew thought their radio was broken. On the fourth night out, they picked up a Japanese broadcast that gave war news—all of it good for Japan. A concerned Captain Ralsteadt maintained radio silence for ten days until he finally allowed transmission of a simple "O.K." in response to the repeated attempts to contact the tug from Oahu.[55]

At 0610 on the eighteenth (0340, 19 December, Wake time), Ensign Murphy's PBY-5 Catalina (BuNo 2447), 23-P-4, departed Pearl Harbor on the first leg of its flight to Wake. The situation there concerned Vice Admiral Pye, who had inherited an operation about which he would soon harbor many reservations. His concern deepened that day when his radio intelligence unit noted again that "Cardiv 2 and Crudiv 8 continued to be associated with the Fourth Fleet in communications."[56]

While the new CinCPac was digesting the latest disquieting intelligence about the enemy's movements and sending it to Fletcher and Brown, Wake's defenders endured another air raid. On the nineteenth, twenty-seven G3M2s that had departed Roi at 0615 that morning, under the command of Lieutenant Watanabe, came in from the northwest at 1045 and dropped 27 250-kilogram and 182 60-kilogram bombs. Two *chūtai*s of land attack planes bombed the airfield area; one dropped its ordnance on what its crews pinpointed as the gun battery on the eastern point of Wake. Cunningham radioed ComFourteen, reporting the raid at 1050.

Battery D fired seventy rounds at the attacking planes, and both Godbold and Marine Gunner McKinstry reported seeing one plane leaving the sky over the atoll trailing smoke and what looked like one aviator drifting down in his parachute some distance from land. Wake's gunners had actually done far better than they thought, for the three-inch fire had damaged twelve of the twenty-seven land attack planes, and a shell fragment had killed Petty Officer Third Class Kaneki Makoto, the copilot of the *rikkō* flown by Petty Officer Second Class Hisamatsu

Hirosaku, the number three plane of the first *chūtai*.[57] Kaneki was the only casualty suffered by the Chitose *Kōkūtai* that day.

On Wake, the civilians who had proved invaluable continued to serve well. That night, Godbold's Battery commenced work on a second shelter to complement the one they had completed on the seventeenth. A fifty-man working party labored in the building of the second structure, locating it near the first.

In the meantime, Vice-Admiral Pye conferred with Vice-Admiral Halsey and Pye's chief of staff, Rear Admiral Milo F. Draemel, on the morning of the eighteenth about the part Task Force 8 would play in the relief of Wake. He had given Brown information indicating that Japan was establishing an air base in the Gilberts and possessed a submarine force based on Jaluit. Intercepted enemy communications had placed the Yokohama *Kōkūtai* in the Gilberts and the commander of a Japanese submarine force at or near Jaluit. Most disturbing, though, was the news that CinCPac's intelligence people had no definite clue as to where Nagumo's *Kidō Butai* was.

Considering the newly established enemy air bases that he would have to pass en route to Jaluit and having learned that a test firing of five-inch ammunition on board his flagship had yielded twenty-three duds of twenty-three rounds fired, a concerned Brown realized that Japanese air searches might spot Task Force 11 before it could reach its objective. With defective ammunition, the prospects of running into Japanese planes seemed daunting. He directed fueling of his ships to commence on the eighteenth and notified his task force of its objective. Brown completed the fueling evolutions on the nineteenth, then detached the *Neosho*, accompanied by the *Worden*, to stand out of potential danger and mulled over what lay ahead.

Halsey's Task Force 8 sailed from Pearl on the morning of the nineteenth to proceed to the waters west of Johnston Island and south of Midway. Fletcher's Task Force 14 steamed resolutely westward. At noon on the nineteenth, the *Saratoga* and her consorts were 1,020 miles east of Wake. D-Day had been set for the twenty-fourth, the day before Christmas.

Ahead of them, the three boats of the Twenty-sixth Division began deploying to be ready to intercept any approaching American ships. While two boats took up positions to the east, one remained to the south to serve as a guide.

That same morning, encouraging word came from NAS Midway, reporting Ensign Murphy's departure for Wake at 0520, Wake time.[58] It would be the defenders' first direct contact with anyone from outside the atoll in a fortnight.

"VERY SECRET TO EVERYONE
EXCEPT THE JAPS"

Just before the start of the first dog watch on 20 December and "imme-diately scrutinized" by the pilot of the only operable F4F-3 as the Catalina approached the atoll, J. J. Murphy brought in 23-P-4 after an uneventful flight from Midway. Other than the *Philippine Clipper,* which had returned because of word of the Pearl Harbor attack, the Catalina was the first friendly plane to arrive since the war had started. The PBY landed in the lagoon in the midst of a rain squall, but the defenders welcomed the precipitation because it worsened the flying weather and prevented the Japanese from bombing. Commander Keene's sailors moored and fueled the Catalina for the next morning's flight.[1]

Barney Barninger observed that the flying boat's arrival "set the island on end with scuttlebutt." Most men surmised that the civilians would be evacuated. The scuttlebutt was partially correct. The secret orders carried on board the Catalina notified Cunningham that fire-control, radar, and other equipment was being sent, along with reinforcements of men and machines. The orders also instructed him to prepare all but 250 civilians (those to be selected "by specific trades to continue the more important of the projects") for evacuation.[2] Cunningham told Dan Teters to pick those who were to stay without regard for whether they had volunteered for service with the marines.

Among the civilians slated to be taken off Wake were the men who made up the crew of Sergeant Bowsher's gun 3 at Battery D. "The entire gun crew," Godbold later noted proudly, loyally "offered to stay on the Island and serve with the Battery." Dr. Shank volunteered to stay, too, inspiring the five remaining nurses—Daly, Dettra, Gottlieb, Kerr, and Pace—to express a desire to remain as well.

That same gray afternoon, during a few free moments, Putnam's executive officer, Captain Elrod, typed out a letter to his "darling Eliza-beth." Although he confessed little hope that the letter would get out that day, he wrote that "there is little news that you don't have or can't imagine. We are still clinging grimly on to what little that we can call our own. Everything is very secret to everyone except the Japs who seem to know it all before the rest of us."[3]

In his report to Rear Admiral Bloch, Commander Cunningham recounted the events to date. He noted the many air raids that had taken place but reported that most had resulted in few casualties and, except for the initial raids, little damage to installations. Obviously and justifiably proud of the work of the marines under his command, he attributed Wake's escape from more serious damage to the effectiveness of the detachment's antiaircraft fire that had been maintained despite the lack of necessary fire-control equipment. A former fighter pilot himself, he lavished unstinting praise on VMF-211's heroic aviators, who had "never failed to push home attacks against heavy fire." That none of the [marine] planes had been shot down, he marveled, "is a miracle."[4]

Buoyed by the prospects of relief, Cunningham wrote optimistically to his wife and daughter. "We are having a jolly time here," he declared, "and everything is in good shape. I am well and propose to stay that way. Hope you are both in the pink," he continued, "and [are] having a good holiday season. Trust you haven't worried about me, for you know I always land on my feet." Declaring that the situation was "good and . . . getting better," he boasted jokingly that "before long you won't hear of a Japanese east of Tokyo." He described the climate as good, the food not bad, and noted that he had to wash his face only once a day. Baths were scarce, although he did try to "work in a swim now and then" in the lagoon. Before he signed off in an affectionate farewell, he wrote: "You know I am waiting only for the time of our joining. Circumstances may delay it . . . but it will surely come."[5]

The representative of the Bureau of the Budget, Herman Hevenor, wrote his superiors telling them of the siege and praising those who had led the defense. "The Commanding Officer [Cunningham] and his staff, including the marine Officers, have done a big job and an efficient one. Their stand against the Japs has been marvelous and they deserve everything our Government can give them."[6]

Lieutenant Commander Greey reported to the officer in charge of the construction projects in the Fourteenth Naval District that "practically every building and structure on the island has been damaged by either bombs or machine gun fire." Camp 1, he wrote, had been destroyed. Japanese ordnance had badly damaged buildings in the portion of Camp 2 that lay south of the main road on Wake, although the mess hall, laundry, and powerhouse remained intact. That part of Camp 2 north of the road, however, had been largely destroyed; only the central mixing and aggregate plants could be made operable. Although the contractors' warehouse had suffered damage, "its contents [were] still intact." The warehouse planned for squadron stores at the future air station, however, which was a little over 80 percent completed and in which the CPNAB workmen had stored much construction material, had been burned out. Greey estimated that the Japanese had either destroyed or damaged, much of it irreparably, some 90 percent of the materials that had been on the island for construction of the NAS.[7]

Greey reported that since the war had started, "it has been impossible to do any construction work" because the CPNAB men had concentrated almost solely on building dugouts and assisting the marines in the defense work. The men on Wake, he continued, were sheltered "in dugouts scattered throughout" the atoll. Noting the "very low" morale of the construction workers, Greey doubted that they "can again be used advantageously for construction work. Many men," he explained, "now refuse to expose themselves even after the danger of raids is past." Thus he recommended evacuating the civilians and reinforcing the garrison. "The present construction program," he concluded, "will have to be completely revised unless the threats of air raids can be eliminated."[8]

Dan Teters, from his office dugout ("Just like a Mexican General," he joked, "two telephones and an orderly"), wrote to George Ferris, a friend back on Oahu. He informed Ferris that he still had charge of the CPNAB people and had them dispersed in dugouts, which had undoubtedly saved many lives. Some 186 of his men were serving with the marines, and the CPNAB cooks fed the entire garrison. The navy and marine officers had expressed satisfaction with the work his men had done—Commander Cunningham solicited names of individuals for special commendations—and expressed pride in the "excellent work" several of them had done for the defense force. Teters echoed Greey's observations that the workers be withdrawn, strongly urging that step "before I have more mental and shell shock cases than I have now."[9]

"I have written a letter to Florence," he continued, solicitous of his wife's welfare, "addressed to the Halekulani Hotel. I wish you would check into it and see if she receives it. I am worrying about her more than anything else. Any word you can manage to get through to me about her will be greatly appreciated by me, as will anything you can do for her comfort and safety." He hoped he would see Ferris soon and closed with a cheery "I will have a story to tell you."[10]

As word circulated at the airfield that Major Bayler was leaving Wake and had volunteered to deliver personal letters, many scrambled to write to loved ones.[11] Sergeant Robert Bourquin wrote two letters, although he "couldn't say where I was or how things were."[12]

John Kinney sent a letter via his friend Second Lieutenant Robert E. Galer, at Ewa Mooring Mast Field, telling his loved ones that he was "getting some good gunnery practice (aerial) although the targets shoot back. Had my goggles shot off last week when I went in on eight bombers—seven got away. No more news," he concluded, "except that what would be censored."[13]

On a piece of PanAir air mail stationery, Paul Putnam wrote to his beloved Virginia: "Sweetheart: War sure is hell—I've grown a beard! But don't worry, I will shave it off before you get a chance to complain about it in person. Everything not OK, of course, but getting along as well as might be expected. Got a small knick [sic] in the back, but just a knick and it is doing fine—didn't miss a day of work. Not much squadron left, but what there is, is still in there swinging at 'em. Like the Limeys, we may be dumb and slow, but we sure can come up grinning and asking for more. Keep the old chin up, girl. Don't know just when I can get home to see you all, but I surely will get there. Give all my little gals a great big piece of my love, but keep a piece as big [as] all of them for yourself. Take great big pieces—there's plenty of it. Your Paul."[14]

His report of VMF-211's operations sent to Lieutenant Colonel Larkin was less sanguine than his letter to his wife. After recounting the losses suffered by his squadron, both in planes and men, and the damage he believed his men had inflicted on the enemy, Putnam wrote that a large share of the squadron's records had been destroyed the first day, and since then, "parts and assemblies have been traded back and forth so that no airplane can be identified. Engines have been traded from plane to plane, have been junked, stripped, rebuilt, and all but created." Although practically all of 211's gear had been destroyed, VMSB-231's and 232's remained largely intact. Quartermaster property lay scattered about, wholly unaccounted for. "I regret that the only expedient will be to strike off the whole lot," he wrote, "from airplanes to engines to tent pegs."[15]

Putnam praised his men. "All hands have behaved splendidly and held up in a manner of which the Marine Corps may well tell." He could not set any officer or enlisted man apart from the others, for "they all have acquitted themselves with equal distinction." He did, however, single out the "indefatigable labor, the ingenuity, skill and technical knowledge of Lieutenant Kinney and Technical Sergeant Hamilton," saying that "it is solely due to their efforts that the squadron is still operating."[16]

Never suspecting in the morning that he would be able to do so, that evening Talmage Elrod typed out another letter to his wife, his "dearest darling sweetheart." Thankful that Bayler had consented to deliver the missive personally, Elrod wrote that there "isn't a lot of news that I can write about." After expressing how much he missed her and that he, like everyone else, was undergoing "a few *new* experiences," and describing the weather ("nothing to complain about but

I would like to see a good old fashioned typhoon sweep this entire area")—the tenor of his letter changed briefly, as he alluded to the way war had broken out with destructive suddenness upon the unprepared American forces in the Pacific. "I imagine," he wrote, "that there is an awful lot of whitewashing going on in high places. It certainly will be a criminal shame if they succeed in covering over everything."[17]

He was writing "in something of a hurry and under somewhat difficult circumstances." He commented, "I'll think of a million things that I should have said after I have gone to bed tonight. But now I am going to say that I love you and you alone always and always and repeat it a million times or so . . . I know that you are praying for me," he concluded tenderly, "and I have nothing more to ask then that your prayers be answered."[18]

At the airfield, meanwhile, Kinney and his maintenance men strove mightily to keep the Wildcats operational. After 211-F-8 had been difficult to start the previous day, Kinney decided that the ignition harness would have to be replaced. Hamilton and others were laid low by dysentery, and 211's engineer officer and other helpers worked on the plane into the night.

Although the time consumed in mooring and fueling the PBY prevented Ensign Murphy and his crew from inspecting the atoll in detail, Commander Cunningham had taken the pilot and his copilot, Ensign Ady, to his headquarters dugout, a short ride by pickup truck that proved a sobering and eye-opening experience for the two visitors. The island commander noted the expression of incomprehension on the newly arrived aviators' countenances, demonstrating that, "like some of the dispatch writers back at Pearl . . . they had not realized the extent of the damage the Japanese had done us."

Murphy noted that the defenders—"Naval, Marine, and civilian," at least the ones they could see (most were scattered about in small dugouts)—looked tired. Most of the buildings, with the exception of some still standing in the bombed-out contractors' camp, had been either knocked down or burned up. As Murphy later related, with considerable understatement, "The island . . . appeared as a shambles." As night fell, Murphy observed that the marines were manning their guns. He understood that small plane shelters were being constructed and some of the civilian workers (he had been told that 186 or more were helping the Wake Detachment's marines) were constructing more dugouts—a twenty-five-man working party, for example, continued work on Battery D's second shelter that evening. That night, because Commander Keene forbade anyone to remain on board the moored plane, the PBY's crew slept fitfully in dugouts.[19]

Meanwhile, offshore, the *Triton* continued her lonely patrol, her

Lieutenant James J. Murphy, A-V(N), 1943, patrol plane commander of the last PBY out of Wake on 21 December 1941. (USN)

sailors feeling—perhaps justifiably—that they were not alone in the waters off Wake. Three times during the previous day, her JK gear had picked up the sound of "suspected propeller noises." On the third such contact, the *Triton*'s sound gear operators heard the noise for twenty minutes. Taking the boat up to periscope depth to reconnoiter, Pilly Lent could see nothing on the surface. Upon surfacing on the evening of the twentieth, he transmitted an urgent dispatch to Rear Admiral Withers, informing him that Lent believed an enemy submarine was operating in the waters to the south of the atoll.[20]

Before dawn on the twenty-first, "knowing that the Japs liked to make early morning calls," Murphy and his crew arose and trooped down to the PanAir dock only to discover that the boat crew that was to transport them out to 23-P-4 had not yet arrived. "We were getting pretty itchy," then Ensign Francis C. Riley, A-V(N), later recalled, "because we wanted to get away from there before the Japs called."[21] Major Bayler soon arrived and noticed Murphy glancing "from the eastern sky to his wrist watch and back again."[22]

Finally, the boat showed up. After shaking hands with the men who had come down to the dock to see him off, Bayler climbed down into the boat, joining Murphy and his crew for the short ride to the waiting Catalina. The pilots and flight crew wasted no time warming up the flying boat; soon, uncomfortably long after first light, Murphy and Riley taxied the PBY across the lagoon and took off, heading out at low altitude for some distance to avoid detection by any possibly inbound Japanese planes. En route to Midway, Bayler prepared a synopsis of events at Wake up until the day he left. Upon arrival at his destination, he entrusted it to Murphy to deliver to CinCPac headquarters at Pearl.[23]

The arrival and departure of 23-P-4 profoundly influenced the next Japanese move. "For some reason," John Kinney later recalled, "the PBY which came in had broadcast weather reports every hour in plain English. They did so much jabbering . . . that the Japs probably thought a whole patrol squadron was coming in." On 20 December, Rear Admiral Abe had received a report (apparently based on the volume of radio traffic emanating from Murphy's PBY) that planes from VP-23 had advanced to Wake from Midway the previous day, arriving at 1550. Although the worry over the presence of patrol planes was patently disproportionate to the actual size of the force involved (one plane), the prospect of Kajioka's ships being sighted on the way in sufficiently concerned Vice Admiral Inoue that he ordered Abe to advance his attack one day (to the twenty-first) to destroy the elements of VP-23 in question. Consequently, the Wake Island Reinforcement Force increased speed to thirty knots.

On the morning of 21 December, Rear Admiral Kajioka's gray ships stood out from the Ruotto anchorage in the Marshalls for his second attempt at Wake. The ships of his task force were largely the same ones he had had with him on 11 December, the destroyers *Asanagi* (Morning Calm) and *Yunagi* (Evening Calm) having replaced the sunken *Hayate* and *Kisaragi*, and the eight-inch gunned heavy cruisers *Kako*, *Aoba*, *Furutaka*, and *Kinugasa*, under Rear Admiral Goto Aritomo, that had recently taken part in the occupation of Guam, added to provide more weighty gunfire support and operate to the east of Wake to intercept any U.S. Fleet units that might attempt to relieve the atoll. In addition to the Uchida and Itaya SLF companies on board the two patrol craft, the *Kinryu Maru* and the destroyer *Mutsuki*, planners for the second invasion attempt added the SLF company commanded by Special Duty Ensign Takano Toyoji, drawn from the Sixth Base Force SLF. Takano's troops embarked in the destroyer *Oite*, the flagship for the Twenty-ninth Destroyer Division (Captain Setoyama Yasuo). In addition, the seaplane carrier *Kiyokawa Maru*, a converted modern freighter, supported the operation with her complement of reconnaissance seaplanes. Landing exercises had been conducted at Kwajalein. Kajioka's ships set a northward course that would allow them to reach the vicinity of the objective at the start of the mid watch on 23 December.

That same morning, Rear Admiral Abe's force prepared to begin softening up Cunningham's command. At 0545 on the twenty-first, beneath cloudy skies, the heavy cruiser *Chikuma* launched an Aichi E13A1 Type 00 reconnaissance seaplane, her number 1 plane (the same one she had catapulted aloft to reconnoiter Pearl Harbor on the seventh) to scout out the atoll, while the *Tone* launched her number 4 and 5 planes to provide local inner air patrol in the vicinity of the carriers. At 0700, the *Hiryū* and the *Sōryū* turned into the northeasterly wind.

Fourteen Type 99 carrier bombers—a 250-kilogram bomb slung beneath the belly of each *kanbaku*—rolled down the *Sōryū*'s flight deck, from her twenty-first through twenty-sixth *shōtai*s, under Lieutenant Commander Egusa Takashige, the handsome, highly regarded officer whom many of his contemporaries considered "the number one dive-bombing pilot in all Japan" and a born leader. The thirty-two-year-old veteran of combat in China possessed eight years of flying experience. Those who knew Egusa believed him to be courageous and an air tactician par excellence who could grasp intuitively "precisely the right thing to do in flight under almost any set of circumstances." Few in Japanese naval aviation could wonder why he had been placed in charge of training *kanbaku* pilots at the small training field at Kasonohara, near Kanoya, during the working-up period for the Pearl Harbor attack.[24] Once that appointment had been made, "the degree of training suddenly went up and results were amazingly good."[25]

The *Sōryū* contributed nine Mitsubishi A6M2 Type 00 fighters (*kansen*s) from her first, second, and third *shōtai*s, commanded by Lieutenant Suganami Masaji, whose men had wreaked destruction on the marines at Ewa Mooring Mast Field on 7 December. The *Hiryū*'s flight deck was busy: fifteen Type 99 carrier bombers—a total bomb load of sixty-seven 250-kilogram bombs between them—from her twenty-first through twenty-sixth *shōtai*s, commanded by Lieutenant Kobayashi Michio, who had missed the attack on Pearl Harbor because of a balky engine, droned purposefully into the sky, their mission to seek out and destroy barracks, drinking water facilities, and radio transmitters. The *Hiryū*'s nine Type 00 fighters from her first, second, and third *shōtai*s, commanded by Lieutenant Nōno Sumio, took off to escort the bombers while two *kankō*s commanded by Lieutenant (j.g.) Kondō Shōjirō and Petty Officer First Class Toba Shigenobu, from the carrier's forty-third *shōtai*, accompanied the strike's bombers and fighters to guide them to the target.

Lieutenant Commander
Egusa Takeshige, ca. 1941,
led the first carrier air
strikes against Wake on 21
December 1941. (Egusa
family, c/o J. Michael
Wenger)

Bombs explode on Peale (upper right) as planes from the Second Carrier
Division attack Battery D's position on 21 December 1941. (Japan War
History Office)

Egusa's men arrived over Wake around 0900 to find a two-hundred-meter ceiling and, seeing no patrol planes present, circled at fifty to two hundred meters before turning their attention to the shore installations below like eagles with bared talons. Neither antiaircraft fire nor aerial opposition troubled them as they "worked things over a bit" during a part of the forenoon watch and gave the embattled defenders their first taste of dive-bombing. These were no high-level bombers.

"It was only a matter of seconds," John Burroughs later wrote, "until we realized that this was no ordinary raid: the nerve shattering roaring of the engines close overhead was exceeded only by the repetitive swish and scream and crashing crescendo of the falling bombs. Each ear-splitting detonation shook the timbers in the dugout. There was no surcease, no breathing spell between explosions." In the shelter in which he had taken refuge, "the beams rattled and shook, the earth trembled, and dirt and gravel sifted down on us while we lay stiff with fear."

As had happened each time since the beginning of the siege, the blow from the sky fell without warning. It caught Second Lieutenant Kliewer eating breakfast with the crews of the two .50-caliber machine guns at the west end of the field. He admired how they stuck to their guns amid the bombing and strafing, continuing to fire "when other guns on the island [had been] silenced."

The Japanese bombed and strafed Battery D's position ineffectively, and the low altitude at which the carrier-based planes attacked, together with low visibility, prevented Godbold's guns from getting into action. Godbold, however, again reported neither casualties nor damage in the latest attack. Although the three-inchers had not been able to engage the enemy, the marine machine gunners managed to score three hits on two planes from the *Sōryū*—two on a *kanbaku* and one on a *kansen*—the only damage suffered by the attackers as they swooped low over Wake that morning.

The raid caught Major Putnam returning from Camp 2 in a truck. His squadron's only operable F4F, 211-F-9, had not been aloft at that time because he had wanted it available to intercept the usual midday raid. Putnam tried to reach the Wildcat during the attack, but *kansens* from either Suganami's or Nōno's strafing *shōtais* twice forced him to abandon his vehicle. When he finally did reach the field and climbed into 211-F-9, it initially refused to start.

As the last of the Mitsubishis and Aichis were clearing the area, Putnam finally got the F4F started and took off at 1020 to try to follow them back to their ships. Although his long search was not successful, his attempt typified what Commander Cunningham called the "highest order of courage and resolution" that VMF-211's commanding officer had displayed throughout the siege and reflected David Kliewer's recollection that Putnam apparently desired to fly every combat mission himself. During the time between the end of the attack and Putnam's attempt to find the Japanese flattops, Cunningham radioed word of the morning's raid to CinCPac and ComFourteen.[26]

Later that same day, thirty-three *rikkōs* (again under Lieutenant Commander Matsuda) bombed Wake at about 1430, centering their attention on the airfield, gun batteries, and "barracks." The marines' antiaircraft fire, however, forced them to drop their 16 250-kilogram and 290 60-kilogram bombs from a higher altitude than before (18,000 feet as opposed to 13,000). As the guns of Battery D fired at one formation of Type 96s, bombs from a second group of Mitsubishis fell thick about the position. One scored a bull's-eye on the director emplacement, killing Platoon Sergeant Johanlson E. Wright, wounding Staff Sergeant Stephen Fortuna, Corporal James R. Brown, and Private First Class Leonard G. Mettscher, and knocking the range officer, Second Lieutenant Greeley, unconscious. The M-4 director, although destroyed by the bomb, deflected the full force of the explosion from Greeley and saved his life.

Wright, the firing battery officer, had been known for his cheerfulness and boundless vitality. Although told to take cover during past raids, he had remained at his post, calmly giving the necessary orders and disregarding the bombs that often seemed to rain around him. His efforts to improve the efficiency of the battery had often been rendered without rest or sleep.

Staff Sergeant Fortuna, whose "initiative and industry" had been a big factor in maintaining the battery's fire-control instruments, had kept his men at a "high state of efficiency." Like Wright, Fortuna seemingly spurned both cover and slumber. From his position in the open, he spotted and adjusted the fire of the three-inch guns, apparently heedless of the bombs that fell around him. Ignoring his wounds, he insisted on staying at his post; at about 1445, Godbold ordered Fortuna evacuated forcibly, along with Greeley, who regained consciousness a few minutes later, Corporal Brown, and Private First Class Mettscher.[27] Although Dan Godbold believed he saw one plane quitting the skies over Wake trailing smoke, all of Matsuda's G3M2s returned undamaged to Roi.

At Peacock Point, a bomb had hit close to the shelter for Barninger's number 2 gun crew, tearing and blocking the entrance and blowing the sides in. Fortunately, no one was hurt. "The bomb hitting the shelter," Barninger wrote later, "was the only one close to the guns." The resulting crater, as well as others nearby, were the largest he had ever seen. Although he and his men spent the rest of the day repairing the damaged shelter, most of the marines decided they preferred foxholes. "Although we didn't lose a man," he ruminated, "it was a close thing and with the heavy caliber bombs the shelter is too light. For that reason we are all back in the foxholes."

That evening, Cunningham dutifully recounted the damage wreaked by the two Japanese raids on the twenty-first. He reported that the gun director had been destroyed, that only one four-gun three-inch battery was effective, and that the power plant had been damaged and additional diesel fuel storage had been hit and both buildings and equipment demolished. There had been no further carrier raids.[28]

The previous day, Major Devereux had ordered Marine Gunner McKinstry to keep the two guns of Battery F firing to attract the enemy's attention from Battery E. On the twenty-second, McKinstry's gunners put on a fine performance although they had neither director nor height finder. Firing by the expedient of "lead 'em a mile" ("and without any hits except on clouds," as Barninger observed), the two guns of the provisional Battery F served to keep the enemy guessing as to which group possessed fire-control equipment.

All of the planes that had been launched from the *Hiryū* and the *Sōryū* that morning had alighted on the decks from which they had come. Those returning aircrew who had flown in the Hawaiian operation reported the antiaircraft fire as "very slight" in comparison to what they had encountered over Pearl. "The enemy," Rear Admiral Abe reflected upon being informed of his pilots' reports, "seemed to lose their fighting spirits." Once the planes were recovered, Abe's force steamed south to be in a position two hundred miles off Wake the next day to provide an antisubmarine screen for Kajioka's ships. What strikes Yamaguchi's pilots would fly against Wake on the twenty-second would depend on the target information gathered by floatplanes launched from the *Chikuma* and the *Tone* the next morning.

As Abe's ships neared Wake from one direction and Kajioka's from another, the *Triton* was leaving the atoll behind. That morning, she had again picked up "definite propeller noises" on the JK gear. Again unable to see anything on the surface, Lent assumed that he had heard an enemy submarine. He reported that she would continue on station even though there was trouble with the lower packing gland for her number 2 periscope. With the relief operations well under way, however, and U.S. ships nearing Wake, at 2030 on 21 December, the *Triton* received Rear Admiral Withers's directive that she return to Pearl. Pilly Lent ordered the course changed accordingly, and within a half hour the *Triton* was skirting the atoll around which she had been patrolling since late in November. An hour later, she transmitted a priority dispatch to CinCPac in her last attempt at contributing to the defense of Wake: "Enemy submarine believed south of Wake approaches island from southwest daily about 0100 GCT [noon, local time] for observation."[29]

Barrel-chested Sergeant Clarence B. McKinstry, Hilton Head, South
Carolina, in 1938, later (as a marine gunner) distinguished himself at
Wake throughout the siege. (Charles A. Holmes Collection, MCHC
Personal Papers)

Owing to her proximity to Wake and potential enemy ships, the
Triton submerged at 0509 the next morning, headed for Oahu. Like her
sister ship, the *Tambor*, which had had to quit Wake because of the
irreparable leak, the *Triton* had done nothing for the atoll's defenders.

In the meantime, Wilson Brown's Task Force 11 was proceeding on
course toward the Marshalls, gearing up for action. Cruiser and carrier
planes maintained inner and intermediate air patrols, while by the end
of the nineteenth the *Lexington* had ready twenty-seven SBDs, nine
TBDs, and twenty-one fighters. Under overhaul on board "Lex" were

an additional four SBDs and six TBDs. With the topping-off of the *Chicago* by the *Neosho* by the end of the day, all of Brown's ships had been fueled to capacity. Although he had considered the contingencies, he still deemed "a crippled ship . . . a lost ship." At 1241 on 20 December, Brown disseminated his operation order to Task Force 11. On board the *Chicago*, Lieutenant Ward Bronson wrote in his diary that his ship was to support the *Lexington* when she raided the Gilberts. "Admiral Brown told [the] men to keep calm and shoot straight." The attack, Bronson noted, would take place on the twenty-second.

Back at Pearl Harbor, however, Vice Admiral Pye digested Cunningham's dispatch reporting the carrier raid with concern. The Japanese had unexpectedly inserted a new and dangerous factor into the equation. All three of the Pacific Fleet's carriers were at sea. In view of the weakened state of army defenses on Oahu and the reduction in battleship strength, Pye deemed it essential "to insure [the] defense of the [Hawaiian] islands."[30] He evidently believed that the carriers constituted the best insurance of that defense.

After he considered the evidence of increased Japanese air activity in the Marshalls, with one or perhaps two carrier groups in proximity, as well as "evidence of extensive offshore lookout and patrol," he decided that Task Force 11's projected surprise raid on Jaluit could not be carried out successfully. Pye thus reluctantly canceled Brown's proposed carrier raid. He allowed the efforts to relieve Wake to continue but warned Fletcher not to get within two hundred miles of the atoll and directed Brown to move north with Task Force 11 to support Task Force 14. He radioed OpNav of his decision at 1617 on 20 December. He then radioed Cunningham on the morning of the twenty-second (twenty-first at Pearl Harbor), asking him to report the condition of the landplane runways and to inform him immediately if their status changed.[31]

As the Japanese ships steamed inexorably toward Wake from two directions, the need to have at least one complete operable antiaircraft battery compelled the virtual dismemberment of Battery D. At 1500 on the twenty-first, Dan Godbold had received orders to transfer the only height finder on the island—the one Sergeant Box and his crew had operated with courage and skill—over to Wally Lewis's Battery E, along with the power plant, one gun, and the necessary men to serve as crew; the rest of his three-inchers were to be moved to provide beach defense.

Because Battery D's director had been knocked out of commission, Lewis ordered a quarter-inch-thick piece of steel cut out to fit the top of Battery E's M-4. That simple expedient, he reasoned, would provide some protection for the equipment from plunging machine-gun fire. That action typified the ingenuity that was so often in evidence during the siege, as did the cannibalization of equipment when Battery E obtained parts from Battery F's crewless weapons. Lewis, too, had had small dugouts constructed near the guns, with entrances that would allow the crews to take cover speedily when the bombs began falling too close for comfort. In addition, after the battery's power source failed after three days, Battery E had run a cable to the hospital generator. Not having the noisy motor nearby greatly improved the gun crews' ability to hear approaching planes.

Godbold and his command got ready to move their equipment, but when they had completed those preparations, they paused for a brief burial serivce at 1630. After committing Platoon Sergeant Wright's body to Peale's soil, where he had fallen in battle, they resumed work. Beginning at 1730, Godbold transferred gun 2, the height finder, and the power plant to Battery E and guns 3 and 4 to their new positions along the beach, west of the hospital building that had been under construction for the naval air station. During the night, a 125-man working party turned to, to help make emplacements, and completed the necessary arrangements at 0100 on 22 December. Six hours later, Battery D's marines resumed work on improving the emplacements for guns 3 and 4 and fabricated dummy guns in the old positions.

As efforts proceeded to give Wake the first full-strength antiaircraft battery since the siege had begun a fortnight before and Battery D's marines acclimated themselves to their new surroundings, other elsewhere were interested in conditions on the atoll. As 22 December dawned, Rear Admiral Abe realized that the heavy seas would prevent the launching of floatplanes from the *Chikuma* and the *Tone*. Abe reported his ships to Kajioka for duty, and both carriers prepared to put planes aloft for local patrols. The *Sōryū* launched four *kanbakus* at 0630; the *Hiryū* sent up four to relieve her sister ship's at 0930, ten minutes before the *Sōryū*'s planes queued up to begin recovery operations.

Because the planes from the *Hiryū* and the *Sōryū* had not encountered any aerial opposition the previous day, Abe contemplated suspending the attacks planned for the twenty-second. Soon thereafter, however, the Japanese task force commander received word that returning Chitose *Kōkūtai* aircrews, perhaps wearying of the warm reception accorded them daily by the tenacious Wildcat pilots, had reported being fiercely opposed by fighters—they may have spotted Putnam—the previous afternoon. Consequently, planning for strikes from the carriers resumed.[32]

At 1100 on 22 December, the *Sōryū* began launching her second *shōtai* of three *kansens* under Lieutenant (j.g.) Fujita Iyōzō and seventeen *kankōs* (the forty-first through forty-sixth *shōtais*) under Lieutenant Abe Heijirō. The *Hiryū* commenced flight operations eight minutes later, putting aloft her sixteenth *shōtai* of three *kansens* under Lieutenant Okajima Kiyokuma and sixteen *kankōs* (the fortieth through the forty-second and the forty-fifth through the forty-seventh *shōtais*) under Lieutenant Commander Kusumi Tadashi. While the *Tone* launched her number 3 plane to cooperate with the attack group, the thirty-nine carrier planes ascended and headed for the gray skies above the beleaguered atoll, most of the crews apparently expecting to meet American fighters.

Kusumi, leading the strike and flying a *kankō* from the *Hiryū's* fortieth *shōtai*, had been the man whose bomb had triggered the cataclysmic magazine explosion that had blown the battleship *Arizona* into oblivion at Pearl Harbor a fortnight before. Nearly every man of the ill-fated *Arizona's* marine detachment was a casualty that morning.

In the path of the enemy, a cheerful and eager Second Lieutenant Davidson took off from Wake at 1000 in 211-F-9, cranked up his landing gear with the requisite thirty-two turns, and set out on the regular midday patrol. Engine trouble in the chronically temperamental 211-F-8, however, prevented Captain Freuler from getting aloft until 1030.

Shortly after noon, Davidson, patrolling north of Wake, radioed Freuler, then south of the atoll, and reported sighting Kusumi's oncoming planes, which reached Wake at 1210. In spite of the odds, both marines unhesitatingly gave battle.

As dictated by standard doctrine, Freuler took on the enemy's lead element—the *shōtai* consisting of the three *Sōryū kankōs* led by Lieutenant Abe, whose men had bombed the battleships *West Virginia* (BB-48) and *Tennessee* (BB-43) a fortnight before. Commander Genda Minoru, on Vice Admiral Nagumo's staff, would subsequently laud *kankō* pilots as the "least complaining and most gallant men of the Japanese Navy" because their mission required them to fly undeviating courses to drop their torpedoes or bombs accurately, depending upon their appointed task.[33] Other than the single 7.7-millimeter machine gun in the hands of the radio-gunner in the third seat, the *kankō* pilots and plane commanders needed to rely on the fighters to protect them in the event of aerial opposition.

That December day, defense of the *kankōs* lay in the hands of Lieutenant Okajima and his wingmen (Petty Officer First Class Muranaka Kazuo and Petty Officer Third Class Tahara Isao) from the *Hiryū* and Lieutenant (j.g.) Fujita and his wingmen (Petty Officer First Class Takahashi Sōsaburō and Petty Officer Second Class Okamoto Takashi) from the *Sōryū*. Unfortunately for their shipmates in the *kankōs*, all six *kansens* were deployed above and in front of the attack planes. Fujita, Takahashi, and Okamoto apparently were more out of position to deal with the two marines than Okajima and his wingmen (they spotted the two Wildcats but did not engage them) so the latter trio went to the aid of the embattled *kankōs*.

Before the *kansen* pilots could deploy their nimble fighters to ward off the slashing attacks of the Wildcats and defend the comparatively vulnerable Nakajimas, however, Captain Freuler dropped the Type 97 commanded by Petty Officer Third Class Ōtani Sueyoshi out of formation, trailing smoke and slanting toward the sea below, on his first pass. None of the three-man crew—Ōtani, Seaman First Class Kurita Teruaki (pilot), and Seaman First Class Okami Akimada (radio-gunner)—exited the plane or survived the crash in the unyielding ocean.

As the group of Nakajimas appeared to break up—they had apparently just deployed from cruising formation to an attack formation shortly before the two Wildcat pilots intercepted them—Freuler snapped his F4F around, made an opposite approach, and flamed a second Type 97 that suddenly blew up in an expanding ball of fire about fifty feet beneath 211-F-8, killing Petty Officer First Class Kanai Naburo (plane commander), as well as Warrant Officer Satō Haruo (pilot) and Petty Officer Second Class Hanada Yoshiichi (radio-gunner).[34] As the fiery wreckage of Kanai's *kankō* tumbled into the sea and his own controls responded sluggishly while his badly scorched F4F's manifold pressure plummeted, Freuler glanced back past his plane's turtleback toward Wake. Davidson seemed to be engaging six enemy planes.

In an instant, however, Petty Officer Third Class Tahara, Okajima's number three wingman, brought his *kansen* in astern of Freuler's already damaged Wildcat and opened fire. Bullets penetrated 211-F-8's fuselage, both sides of the vacuum tank, bulkhead, seat, and parachute, inflicting back and shoulder wounds. After his plane was hit, Freuler threw his F4F into a steep dive—Tahara did not follow, apparently satisfied that he had shot down the marine. Fresh from knocking Freuler out of the fight, Tahara then went to the aid of the six *kankōs* Davidson was engaging and shot him down.

Tahara having rendered hors de combat the last of the Wildcats, the carrier planes dropped their bombs on Wake unhindered, the *Sōryū's* pilots assessing their attacks as "very effective." The marines, however, considered the accuracy of the *kankō* formations much worse than that displayed by the *kanbaku* pilots the previous day—perhaps to be expected because a dive-bomber pilot could normally deliver his ordnance with more precision.

Battery D's gun 1 fired seven rounds by local control. Marine antiaircraft fire damaged two Type 97s from the *Sōryū's* forty-second *shōtai* commanded by Lieutenant Nakajima Tatsumi, who was piloting one of the Type 97s. The damaged planes were his wingmen's—those flown by Seaman First Class Fujiwara Karoku (one hit) and by Seaman First Class Komatsuzaki Teruo (two hits). Komatsuzaki, his observer, Petty Officer Third Class Suzuki Takahisa, and the radio-gunner, Shimada

Kiyohasu, were seeing their first combat, having been "spares" at Pearl Harbor. In addition, antiaircraft fire scored one hit among four *kankōs* from the *Hiryū*—three from her lead *chūtai* (Lieutenant Commander Kusumi's, Petty Officer First Class Kobayashi Masamatsu's, and Petty Officer Third Class Sato Shigeharu's) and one from her forty-second *shōtai*, Lieutenant Sumino Hiroharo's. Damage suffered at the outset of the action compelled Lieutenant Abe (who had lost both of his wingmen to Freuler's good gunnery) to ditch his *kankō* near the task force, where a screening ship picked up Abe, Warrant Officer Kasahara Jisuke (pilot), and Petty Officer First Class Ono Toshi (radio-gunner).

Herb Freuler, meanwhile, after escaping from Petty Officer Third Class Tahara, managed to nurse his Wildcat home, putting his wheels down and landing with the canopy stuck in the closed position. Ground crews extricated him and rushed him to the hospital bunker.

Kinney surveyed the battered 211-F-8; Putnam could see that it showed "unmistakeable evidence of having been through intense fire and having encountered solid objects." Because the defense of the atoll depended on Wake's planes keeping the sky, the F4F had to be repaired, and it was wheeled into the covered hangar. That particular Grumman, however, which had so often been regarded as possessing a personality of its own, was "now in very sad shape." It was one "cat" that had used up its nine lives.

Planes could be repaired or replaced, but it was not so easy to replace people. Carl Davidson, whose unwavering high spirits Paul Putnam believed had been a major factor in maintaining VMF-211's morale throughout the siege, never returned. Rear Admiral Abe later paid homage to the two marine pilots who had challenged his planes, lauding them as having resisted fiercely and bravely.[35]

Tahara, the victor over the two Wildcats, received not only congratulations from his shipmates for that achievement but a scolding for his poor landing technique from Lieutenant Matsumura Hirata, who was overseeing the flight deck operations when the *Hiryū* air unit returned from the strike. In his exuberance, Tahara had landed too fast and too hard, nearly wrecking his plane.

Released from the hospital at his own request late on the morning of the twenty-second, Bob Greeley returned to Battery D. Arriving after the day's raid, he found that the battery's remaining gun (number 1) had been retained—like Battery F—in the old position, along with the dummies, "to invite bombing." Greeley noted that the ruse apparently worked, for a good many bomb craters in the vicinity of the old position bore mute testimony to the effort the enemy had expended in trying to destroy the still troublesome antiaircraft guns.

The *Hiryū*'s and the *Sōryū*'s planes provided air cover for Kajioka's

Second Lieutenant Carl R.
Davidson, ca. September 1941,
VMF-211's assistant gunnery
officer. (Mrs. Virginia Putnam)

The aircraft carrier *Saratoga* (CV-3), one of the main elements of Task
Force 14, ca. September 1941; Douglas TBD-1s and SBD-3s can be seen
on deck, while a *Mahan*-class destroyer steams astern as plane guard.
(NA, 80-G-21191)

ships until sunset, when the two carriers landed their respective broods and commenced preparations for the following morning's operations. Initially, the loss of the two *Sōryū kankōs* to the defending Wildcats had prompted Rear Admiral Abe to contemplate launching a second attack against Wake, but when he learned that the accompanying *kansens* had apparently shot down the last two airborne F4Fs, he canceled it. Any Japanese planes flying over Wake now could do so unhindered by Wildcats.

The loss of the last two flyable planes proved a matter of concern for the atoll commander. At 1320 on 22 December, Cunningham radioed CinCPac that a "combined land and carrier based plane attack" had occurred earlier that day and that his fighters had engaged the attackers. He reported the loss of Davidson and the wounding of Freuler but noted that they had apparently shot down "several" planes. Facilities and installations on the atoll had suffered "no further damage."

As Barney Barninger later recounted: "Dive bombers [sic] again—the carriers must still be in the vicinity. . . . Things are getting tense. Rumor continues to fly about relief, but the dive bombers [are] also present. Things go on in the same manner as before. All that can be done is being done, but there is so little to do with." Gunner Hamas had an "insecure feeling" that night. Defending the island without planes, he reflected sadly, seemed "impossible."

The same heavy seas that had prevented Abe from launching his floatplanes that morning to reconnoiter Wake also bedeviled Frank Jack Fletcher's Task Force 14 as it pressed westward at a speed of 12.75 knots, the best the *Neches*'s engineering force could do. Ordered to fuel to capacity before giving battle, late during the morning watch on 22 December Fletcher began fueling his ships from the *Neches* in the turbulent seas. Although the wind ranged from a moderate to a strong breeze, the long, rolling swells, hampered the operation. The *Bagley* came alongside at 0704, but the heavy seas made it impossible to secure her alongside the *Neches* until forty-five minutes later; the hoses went across at 0752 and the oiler commenced pumping at 0805. The process took a little over an hour to complete, both ships steaming at twelve knots, and the destroyer cast off at 0916. Compelled by the rough sea to slow to seven knots, the *Neches* refueled the *Ralph Talbot*, the *Henley*, and the *Jarvis* in succession; lines parted during the fueling of the *Ralph Talbot*. The whole evolution (from the *Bagley* to the *Jarvis*) took ten hours, and only four destroyers were fueled.

Not only had Fletcher not been able to have all of his destroyers fueled, but VF-3, having begun the war cruise with only thirteen Wildcats, suffered the loss of one during the forenoon watch on 22 December. Shortly after he had been launched with the relief combat air patrol at

1021, Lieutenant (j.g.) Victor M. Gadrow attempted an emergency landing but splashed off the *Saratoga*'s port quarter. As the plane guard
destroyer *Selfridge* rushed through the heavy seas toward the scene,
Gadrow's F4F sank, entombing the pilot with it.

Fletcher's ships' fuel capacity may have been fine for routine or
economical cruising such as was often practiced before the war, but
with combat in the offing, it was neither the time nor the place for
conservation and proceeding at an economical pace. Before the war,
computations of cruising radius and endurance had been based on fuel
allowances for engineering scores. Those allowances had been established for peacetime operating conditions, when each ship practiced
rigid fuel economy to obtain a high score. Fleet and force commanders
consequently planned their operations with an eye toward conserving
fuel. Strategic and tactical situations—not economy—dictate wartime
task force speeds and compel individual ships to "maintain maximum
safety and readiness to meet sudden heavy demands while operating
under relatively unfavorable conditions." Rarely could ships use single
or reduced boiler operation, cruising turbines, and other fuel-saving
measures.[36] In short, if Fletcher was expected to fight, his ships had to
have enough fuel to maneuver at high speed if required. He resolved to
top off the rest of his destroyers the following day (23 December).

Meanwhile, to the eastward, one hour into the second dog watch on
21 December (1630, 22 December, Wake time), the PBY that had borne
Major Bayler (the "last man off Wake Island") from the atoll and depos-
ited him at Midway reached Oahu. Ensign Murphy's description of
Wake's desperate plight, dictated to a CinCPac stenographer soon after
the pilot arrived at Pearl, moved Pye deeply. His staff, most of whom
had served Admiral Kimmel, pleaded with Pye's chief of staff, Rear
Admiral Milo F. Draemel, to continue the relief attempt.

On the basis of Murphy's report, Pye declared later, "the situation
at Wake seemed to warrant taking a greater chance to effect its reinforcement even at the sacrifice of the *Tangier* and possible damage to some
major ships of Task Force 14." The admiral therefore removed the restrictions on Fletcher's operations—the *Tangier* was to be detached with
two destroyers to run in to Wake to begin evacuating the contractors
and reinforcing the marines. He also lifted the restrictions on the operating areas of Halsey and Brown to allow them to give more support
to Cunningham's command.[37]

Those from Kimmel's old CinCPac staff who had pleaded for the
relief force to continue toward Wake, who included Captains Walter F.
DeLany, Lynde D. McCormick, and Vincent R. Murphy and Lieutenant
Colonel Omar T. Pfeiffer, felt vindicated by Pye's decision that night.
"Those of us who lived in the [bachelor officers' quarters] at the Subma-

rine Base walked home together," Pfeiffer recalled, "and we felt that we were walking on air, we were so happy."[38]

Far from the euphoria felt by the members of Kimmel's old staff that the Wake relief expedition would be allowed to proceed, the atoll's defenders continued doggedly improvising their defenses. At 1500, Dan Godbold began transferring his battery command post from a dugout located near the new hospital building to the navy mess hall to the west of that incomplete edifice, completing the move an hour later. At 1700, Battery D's men began to move gun 1 from its old position to a spot near the commissary building, where they finally emplaced it midway into the first watch on the twenty-second.

Meanwhile, with Commander Cunningham's approval, Paul Putnam, with no flyable planes left—211-F-8 was beyond help—reported his remaining men to Major Devereux for service as infantry. The detachment commander ordered Putnam to retain his squadron where it was located, at the airfield, and await further orders. John Kinney, however, would not be with 211's "infantry." Badly fatigued and racked by dysentery, he reported to the hospital, having reached the limit of human endurance. No one had done more to keep VMF-211 in the air over the previous two weeks than he.

"THIS IS AS FAR
AS WE GO"

Driven before rainy gusts, the surf continued to crash and pound on Wake's rocky shore. As the first watch ended, Rear Admiral Kajioka's flagship, the *Yūbari*, led two columns of gray ships through the heavy seas toward the atoll, the strong wind whistling through the rigging. The passage had been stormy. "Only the white foam of the waves could be seen across the sea," Japanese war correspondent Ibushi Kiyoshi later recounted, "where even the silhouette of our escorting ship could not be recognized in the wild and windy night." The destroyer *Mutsuki*, with eighty men from the Uchida Company's machine-gun platoon, began steaming on a northwesterly course as the mid watch began, followed by the *Patrol Boat No. 32* and the *Patrol Boat No. 33*. Almost simultaneously, the destroyer *Oite*, with the 210-man Takano Company, altered course to the northwest, too, followed by the *Kinryu Maru*.

The bad weather that prevented the marines from seeing their approaching foes likewise hindered the Japanese, who found the sea conditions nearly identical to those that had bedeviled them on the eleventh. Determination, though, sometimes spawns daring. The Japanese had a healthy respect for Battery A and wanted to beach the two patrol boats at twelve knots to ensure that the troops got ashore, although some of those entrusted with planning the operation feared that the ships would capsize once they hit the coral. If the surprise landing failed, plans called for the cruisers and destroyers to put ashore bluejacket landing forces. "The orders were to seize Wake Island at all costs," Captain Koyama later recounted, "beaching the destroyers if necessary."

As the mid watch opened, Barney Barninger thought he saw flashing lights "way off the windy side of the island," a sight his Naval Academy classmate First Lieutenant Kessler likened to heat lightning on a sweltering summer night in Indiana. Barninger telephoned Major Devereux, who replied that he too had seen it. He told Barninger to keep his eye on it and emphasized that the lee shore posed the most possibilities for danger.

Kajioka's operation plan apparently called for the landings to occur one hour into the mid watch—0100. Conditions of wind and wave, however, forced a change in the schedule. Lookouts on Wake noted irregular flashes of light—like gunfire—at about that time, but, curiously, no shells hit the atoll. Wary of Battery B, the light cruisers *Tenryu* and *Tatsuta* were steaming off the northeast side of Wake, heading northeasterly—probably firing at what their spotters thought was Peale but was only empty ocean and perhaps equally unaware that the landings were not occurring at that time. At 0100, at about the moment the two warships turned to the north, a lookout shook Bob Greeley awake. Greeley saw the lights off to the northeast and reported them to Devereux, then awakened Battery D's men.

At 0145, however, a report came into Devereux's command post over the J-line that seemed, at least to those who received it, to indicate an enemy landing in progress at Toki Point. Private First Class Robert E. Cooper, Kessler's rangefinder operator and a "very reliable man," reported "bobbing lights" and what he believed to be small boats "off the north shore." Devereux alerted the detachment and told Kessler to send out a patrol either to confirm or deny the earlier report.

Meanwhile, out in the gusty, wet blackness, the Japanese operation began to unfold as the "angry waves," war correspondent Ibushi, in one of Kajioka's men-of-war, observed, "tossed the ships around as if they were toys . . . the hardships encountered in lowering the landing barges were too severe even to imagine." As the patrol from Battery B was reconnoitering Toki Point's north beach, seventy men from a rifle platoon from the Itaya Company were disembarking from the *Patrol Boat No. 33* into a *daihatsu*, while from the *Patrol Boat No. 32*, the Third Rifle Platoon from the Uchida Company, under Warrant Officer Horie Kiroku, plus thirteen men from the embarked antiaircraft unit, about seventy men in all, formed the *kesshitai* ("do-or-die force") that clambered into another *daihatsu*. The landing craft, launched over four thousand meters offshore, soon began having difficulty in the long swells and squalls keeping up with the *Patrol Boat No. 32* and the *Patrol Boat No. 33* as the two former destroyers headed for the beach on a northeasterly course.

On Wilkes, meanwhile, Platt directed McAlister to move two of Battery L's five-inch gun sections (equivalent to two rifle squads) to the shore of the lagoon, west from the area of the new channel being dredged across the island. The fire-control specialists and headquarters men under McAlister, who had established his command post near the searchlight section of the battery, moved into positions they had readied along the south shore of Wilkes, between Battery F and the new channel. Hand grenades had been issued to all. On Peacock Point, Private First Class Jesse E. Nowlin, Barninger's runner, rousted out John Burroughs from a fitful sleep. Pulling on his shoes, Burroughs hurried to awaken the other civilians nearby. Near Camp 1, Staff Sergeant Ralph E. Johnson, the detachment's mess sergeant, awakened John Valov, who had been relieved of beach sentry duty at midnight, in his dugout. "Get up, Valov," he said urgently, "they [the Japanese] are here. Let's go."

Kessler, whom Devereux had asked to confirm or deny the veracity of the information he had received earlier about the landing at Toki Point, received a negative report from the patrol he had sent out. He reported no landing in progress but that he, too, when he had personally reconnoitered with Platoon Sergeant Huffman, had seen the lights off-shore.

On the strength of what meager information he possessed, Cunning-ham, at 0145, radioed ComFourteen, reporting "Gunfire between ships to northeast of island."[1]

With Wake thus alerted, Second Lieutenant Poindexter, at Camp 1 with the Mobile Reserve (predominantly marines assigned to supply and administration duties and fifteen sailors under Boatswain's Mate First Class Barnes), heard the talker in his command post repeating the message concerning Toki Point. Taking the phone, he heard the word for himself. Knowing that there were no marines available to man the four .30-caliber machine guns on Toki Point, Poindexter ordered steady, taciturn Sergeant "Q" "T" Wade to get his men on the two trucks assigned to his unit, along with four .30-caliber Brownings, ammunition, and accessory gear. Wade, a small, red-haired marine with a florid com-plexion, immediately complied.

Poindexter then called the detachment command post and asked to speak with Devereux personally. When the major came on the line, Poindexter asked if he could take his people to Toki Point. Devereux asked him whether he could see anything offshore. After taking a quick look outside, the Mobile Reserve's commander responded in the nega-tive. "Very well," Devereux replied, "go ahead."

Poindexter and his men were soon jolting down the road that ran alongside the lagoon side of the airfield in the black night. As the two trucks rumbled up to a point nearly abreast Devereux's command post, however, a marine stepped out into the road ahead of them, signaling them to stop. The major, the marine said over the noise of the idling engines, had told him to have the Mobile Reserve hold up there. Poin-dexter dismounted from the running board of one of the trucks, telling his men to stay put. Keep the engines running, he told the drivers. He then hurried toward the command post.

Almost two and a half hours into the mid watch, marines at Peacock Point barely glimpsed the dark shapes of the two patrol boats as they steamed toward the reef off the airstrip. At 0230, practically unseen,

Major Arthur A. Poindexter, in a postwar view. (USMC)

the *Patrol Boat No. 32* grounded. On board was the Uchida Company, containing elements of the company headquarters, a portion of the Anti-aircraft Platoon (35 men) and the First and Second Rifle Platoons plus "attached units" (125 men). Ten minutes after the ship that had disembarked them ran aground, Warrant Officer Horie's seventy-man *kesshitai* reached the beach west of Peacock Point, to the "loud, unpleasant, scraping reverberations" of the *daihatsu*'s double bottom scraping the coral.

Ten minutes later, at 0250, the *Patrol Boat No. 33* joined her sister ship on the rocky shore; on board was the 40-man landing force headquarters unit (with Commander Tanaka Mitsuo, the *Yūbari*'s executive officer, as the overall force commander), 6 men from one section of the antiaircraft platoon of the Uchida Company, men from the Itaya Company headquarters element plus the remainder of the rifle platoon that had disembarked earlier (30 men), a second rifle platoon, and a machine-gun platoon (plus "attached forces")—some 140 men in all. Commander Tanaka's landing force soon descended the rope ladders dangling down the sides of the patrol boats into the surf and went ashore.

The *daihatsu* slated to follow the *Patrol Boat No. 33*, bearing the rifle platoon and elements of the headquarters unit of the Itaya Company, had lost sight of the ship in the squally darkness. Apparently, her helmsman lost his bearings and headed almost due east on a course that would take him a little way beyond Peacock Point.

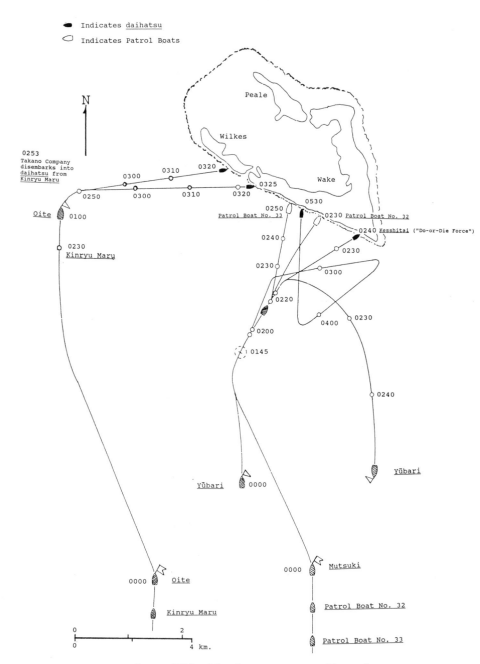

Japanese approaches to Wake Island, 0000–0325 23 December 1941.
(adapted from chart in *Senshi Sōsho*, vol. 38)

Reports from observers along the beach soon reached Devereux's command post, where he and his executive officer, Major Potter, would attempt to keep abreast of events. Gunner Hamas relayed the information to Cunningham at his command post to the north. Cunningham radioed ComFourteen at 0250: "Island under gunfire X Enemy apparently landing."[2]

While the Uchida and Itaya Companies were establishing their beachheads at 0253, the Takano Company's 210 men disembarked from the *Oite* into two *daihatsu* provided by the *Kinryu Maru*. Retained on board the transport was the Uchida Company's antiaircraft platoon in addition to a paymaster unit (30 men) and elements of the Itaya Company (70 men). Meanwhile, the two landing craft steered northeastward through the swells; the one carrying Special Duty Ensign Takano headed toward Wilkes, the other toward the western end of Wake. The former grounded and began disgorging troops at 0320.

On Wilkes, Gunner McKinstry called to Captain Platt and told him that he thought he heard the noise of motors over the boom of the surf. At 0325, McKinstry ordered one of his .50-caliber guns (gun 10) to open fire into the darkness in the direction of the sound. Apparently, this action was moderately successful because Captain Koyama later admitted that in the landing on Wilkes "the troops suffered damage before reaching the beach." About fifteen minutes later, McKinstry sought permission to illuminate, and the searchlight emplaced on Wilkes near the eastern end of the islet struck arc. Although the light snapped off just as suddenly as it had shone forth—it had not worked well since it had been blown over and badly shaken up in the bombing on 9 December—its momentary brilliance pinpointed what appeared to be a landing boat aground on Wilkes's rocky shore and, beyond, two "destroyers," beached on Wake. Soon, from his vantage point at Peacock Point, John Burroughs heard the "clamor of machine guns, periodically punctuated by the hollow sound of our three-inch guns."

McAlister immediately ordered forty-one-year-old Platoon Sergeant Henry A. Bedell, chief of Battery L's five-inch artillery range section, to detail two men to go down to the water's edge and hurl grenades into the beached *daihatsu*. Bedell volunteered himself and, accompanied only by nineteen-year-old Private First Class William F. Buehler, a fire-control man, set out bravely into the blackness toward the sound of the booming surf. Ten minutes later, Buehler limped back to the marine lines with a foot wound, reporting that Bedell had been killed. Neither man had been able to get close enough to carry out their mission.

McKinstry's men manned Battery F's three-inchers, but because of the steep, sloping beach the guns could not be depressed far enough. Cutting the fuses to practically muzzle blast—the shells set to explode

Platoon Sergeant Henry A. Bedell,
24 June 1940, the first fatality of
the final fighting for Wake Island.
(USMC)

Albin Henning's artist's conception of marine machine gunners firing on
the Japanese as they swarm ashore in the darkness on 23 December 1941.
The only obvious inaccuracy is the barbed wire along the beach; none
had been placed there because of the lack of holding ground for the
stakes upon which it could be strung. (NA, USMC Photo 307142)

about two seconds after leaving the gun—the marines held their position until Special Duty Ensign Takano's men approached close enough to begin lobbing grenades. Occidental and Oriental grappled tenaciously in the darkness, hand to hand, before McKinstry's gunners, after removing the firing locks from the three-inchers and "acting under orders previously given," pulled back to take up infantry positions in the brush. The marines' stiff return fire kept the majority of Takano's men from venturing beyond the perimeter of the emplacement they had overrun and contained them there.[3]

Some Japanese sailors, probing west toward Battery L, ran into heavy fire from gun 9, a well-camouflaged .50-caliber Browning operated by twenty-year-old Private First Class Sanford K. Ray, some seventy-five yards to the west of where the enemy had first landed. Ray kept the enemy no closer than forty or fifty yards from him, while his proximity to the beach allowed him not only to harass the foe but report on his movements. Having been informed that the Japanese had Ray's sandbagged emplacement nearly surrounded, Platt ordered Sergeant Coulson to keep the .50-calibers in action "as long as possible."

Poindexter, who had stepped into Devereux's command post, learned of the latest developments. After hearing the reports of what appeared to be a landing barge approaching Wake's south beach, Devereux ordered Poindexter to set up his machine guns in a position "between Camp 1 and the western edge of the airstrip." At 0325, the second *Kinryu Maru daihatsu* carrying the other half of the Takano Company pushed its bow up onto the coral and began putting troops ashore. To that point, none of the landing boats had beached where they were supposed to.

His eight marines and their civilian helpers had remained in the trucks, along with the four machine guns, and Poindexter and his Mobile Reserve soon retraced their route along the inshore side of the airfield. As they sped along, they heard gunfire emanating from the south beach and, after about ten minutes, began setting up their weapons in a position commanding the road that ran along the south shore as well as a critical section of beach there. John Valov was helping Private First Class Charles E. Tramposh set up one of the .30-caliber Brownings when he heard Poindexter tell Mess Sergeant Gerald J. Carr to detail a man to challenge anyone coming down the road from the direction of the airstrip. Ominously, flares began blossoming overhead in the predawn darkness.

Carr detailed Valov, who set off by himself down the road about seventy-five yards, armed with a slingless Springfield. The thirty-seven-year-old laundry helper did not have long to wait for action. He soon spotted a large group of men emerging stealthily from the scrub less than fifty yards away. He called out: "Who goes there?" When the shadowy intruders did not answer and instead took cover, Valov, his suspicions rightly aroused, squeezed off a round, calling out for supporting machine gun fire from Tramposh. Mess Sergeant Carr, though, heard Valov's alarm and opened fire, discomfiting the SLF troops, who had trouble distinguishing their own flares from the red and green tracers of the defenders. Soon thereafter, Poindexter's Brownings opened up on the grounded *Patrol Boat No. 33*.

At Camp 1, meanwhile, men from Battery I and the sailors who had been serving as lookouts manned the four .30-caliber machine guns there. To Poindexter, the enemy appeared confused and disoriented (they may have been because they were plagued by communication failures caused by wet or otherwise damaged radios, and the unit's leader was on Wilkes), shouting and discharging flares. The marines surmised that the pyrotechnic displays were perhaps for "control and coordination," but they signified that "we have succeeded in landing against enemy opposition." In the initial phase of the firefight, Assistant Cook Pershing "B" Bryan, one of Poindexter's two runners, became the Mobile Reserve's first casualty, but the young messman shrugged off his slight shoulder wound, "declined the opportunity to retire to the aid station," and remained at the front.

In the meantime, forced to retain Battery B intact to deal with surface threats and Battery E (which, by that point, had a full complement of guns and crews along with the only height finder and a director) to deal with enemy planes, at 0300 Devereux directed Godbold's Battery D, which had only two operational guns and no fire-control gear, to send one section of nine men to the detachment command post to man the three-inch antiaircraft gun emplaced as an antiboat weapon on the beach near the airfield. Godbold detached the crew of gun 3 under Corporal Leon A. Graves for the task; they climbed on board a contractors' truck and moved out.

The invaders, however, would not allow Graves's experienced marines to reach the three-incher that had been deployed on the landward side of the beach road, on a slight rise between the road and the oiled tie-down area at the airstrip commanding that section of the beach, and operate it effectively. The exigencies of war dictated that those who would man it would be largely novices.

As the *Patrol Boat No. 32* and the *Patrol Boat No. 33* had stood toward Wake's south shore, well inside the arcs of fire for the five-inch batteries that had so vexed the enemy on 11 December, Second Lieutenant Hanna, from his dugout command post in the coral on the south beach, clearly perceived the unfolding threat. Knowing that the three-inch antiboat gun had no crew and having had previous service in Battery D (three-inch) of the Second Defense Battalion, he sought and received permission to man it. Accompanied only by Corporal

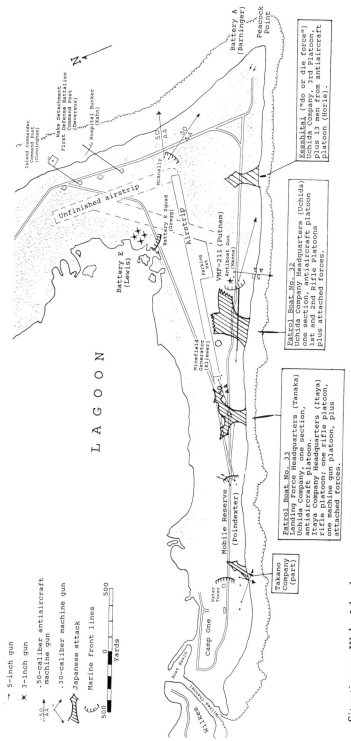

Situation on Wake Island, 0400, 23 December 1941. (adapted from Map 4 in Heinl, *The Defense of Wake*)

Lieutenant Colonel Robert M. Hanna, 1949. Although he commanded a machine-gun battery at Wake, he gained deserved fame for his tenacious defense of his three-inch antiboat gun position at Wake on 23 December. (USMC)

Paul J. Gay, Jr., CPNAB canteen clerk, ca. 1940. (*A Report to Returned CPNAB Prisoner of War Heroes and Their Dependents*, via Stan Cohen)

Holewinski, who normally commanded a machine-gun section, and three civilians—Paul J. Gay, Jr., a canteen clerk, Eric H. Lehtola, a shore laborer, and Robert L. Bryan, an engineering clerk—Hanna set off at a dead run for the gun.

Up to that point, Major Putnam's VMF-211 and its remaining ground support unit, including the faithful civilian volunteers, had awaited orders. As Hanna and his scratch crew sprinted to the unmanned three-inch gun, Devereux, not knowing how much time it would take for Graves's squad to reach the position, ordered Putnam to support the antiboat gun.

With Captains Elrod and Tharin and Second Lieutenant Kliewer the only officers left, Putnam took stock of his forces. There were Technical Sergeant Bailey and Corporal Trego from Major Bayler's erstwhile air-ground team; Staff Sergeant Blandy; Sergeant Edwin M. Ackley; Technical Sergeant Joseph L. Everist; Corporal Page; Corporals Walter J. Gruber and Hugh L. Boyle; Private First Class Taylor; and Staff Sergeant Paul F. Hemmelgarn. Staff Sergeant Arthur, his left hand still useless, was determined to fight with his one good hand holding a .45. Sergeant Comin, his wound still not properly healed, could barely walk. Aviation Machinist's Mate First Class Hesson was there, too, ready and willing. Each man knew the odds against them and what probably lay ahead.

The squadron's civilian auxiliaries wanted to go along, too. Putnam tried to advise those stalwart men, whom he had come to regard as indispensable, to seek security in the rear, but they would not hear of it. "Major," Pete Sorenson asked him, "do you think you're really big enough to make us stay behind?"[4] "Their participation in the resistance to the enemy landing was not only voluntary," Putnam later recounted with grateful admiration, but in "humorous defiance" of his advice. Leaving behind Second Lieutenant Kliewer and five enlisted men (Blandy, Bourquin, and Trego among them) to hold two dugouts and mine the airfield if necessary, Putnam gathered the rest of his men—leatherneck and civilian alike—and headed for the south beach.

Kliewer, along with Blandy, Bourquin, and Trego, the three marines who had operated the surviving gasoline truck that had fueled 211's fighters for much of the siege, manned the post that Putnam had assigned them on the west end of the airfield, near the beach. They had a gasoline-powered generator hooked up to the mines laid on the field; if the enemy attempted to use the airstrip, they were to blow it up. Losing contact with the rest of the island around 0300, though, Kliewer and the three enlisted men, peering out into the murk, soon became aware of the beached *Patrol Boat No. 33* on their right and the *Patrol Boat No. 32* on their left. The Japs, Kliewer later noted, appeared to be surrounding them.

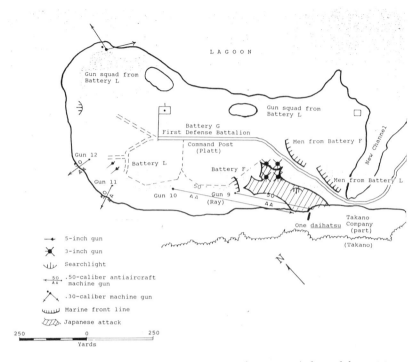

Japanese landing on Wilkes, 0320, 23 December 1941. (adapted from Map
6 in Heinl, *The Defense of Wake*)

Two .50-caliber guns situated just north of the airstrip covered Kliewer's position. At the eastern end of the strip lay the guns manned by
Corporal Winford J. McAnally, along with six marines and three civilians
and supported by a small group of riflemen. The gunners enjoyed a
perfect, unobstructed, field of fire—the airstrip itself.

About 0300 events began to develop with menacing rapidity as the
Japanese pushed ashore on Wilkes and Wake. Devereux lost touch with
Camp 1, Putnam's platoon, Hanna's command post, and Battery A probably because Uchida's or Itaya's advancing troops had found the communication lines and cut them. Devereux's last situation reports from those
units before the lines went dead painted a bleak picture. If Cunningham
received less than encouraging reports from his marine commander,
he received equally disheartening news from CinCPac. After he had
attempted to direct a submarine toward the Japanese invasion force,
Captain Wilson informed him of the latest message from Pearl that had
arrived at 0319. Both the *Triton* and the *Tambor* were returning to Pearl,

he was told; "no friendly vessels should be in your immediate vicinity today." CinCPac asked to be kept informed of developments.[5]

Hanna and his small band, meanwhile, had reached the three-inch antiboat gun, which, to operate most efficiently, normally required a crew of six, exclusive of ammunition passers, and soon excited the begrudging admiration of their adversaries and caused one Japanese observer to regard that position as perhaps "the most important" on Wake.[6] Anxious hands fumbled in the darkness for ammunition while Hanna squinted down the bore—the gun lacked sights—at the beached *Patrol Boat No. 32* that lay less than five hundred yards away. The first high-explosive round tore into the bridge, inflicting serious head wounds on both the captain and navigator, killing two sailors (Seaman First Class Inagaki and Seaman Second Class Kamitake), and wounding five. Hanna's gun then hurled fourteen more rounds on target, some projectiles evidently touching off a magazine, for the beached warship began to burn. Poindexter, from his vantage point, noted "a tremendous blaze" that "momentarily illuminated the beach for several hundred yards." In addition, marine gunfire wounded two officers and eleven enlisted men on board the enemy ship.

Not only did the pulsating flames on board the wrecked *Patrol Boat No. 32* reveal her sister ship, the *Patrol Boat No. 33*—which Hanna and his hardworking tyro gunners holed as well—they also allowed Poindexter to see SLF troops on the beach in front of them as well as advancing past the west end of the airstrip into the thick, tangled undergrowth that sprawled in front of the Mobile Reserve's positions. Poindexter, after ordering one machine-gun section to keep firing into the brush to interdict that movement and protect his flank, then heard the stutter of machine-gun fire from Camp 1, behind him.

Wanting to see for himself if more Japanese landing craft were coming ashore to his rear, Poindexter, accompanied by Private First Class Herman L. Rasor, his other runner, left the front in Sergeant Wade's capable hands and hurried back to the camp. Unable to see the target on which his neophyte navy machine gunners were expending their ammunition, Poindexter, exasperated that the sailors seemd to be firing at shadows, asked each to point out his target. Two could not—they had opened fire only because the other two had done so—but a third pointed to a dimly visible "large landing barge on the order of a self propelled artillery lighter." The lieutenant walked down to the water's edge to get a better idea of what lay out there, but when a *daihatsu* seemed to materialize out of the murk menacingly close at hand, Poindexter scampered back to his machine guns "like a striped-ass baboon" and breathlessly ordered fire resumed on what proved to be the *Kinryu Maru*'s landing craft thirty

A postwar view of the nearly impenetrable underbrush, which aided friend and foe alike in the battle near the airfield on Wake. (Mrs. Virginia Putnam)

yards offshore, twelve hundred yards east of the entrance to Wilkes Channel.[7]

The enemy helmsman, however, appeared to be having difficulty backing the unwieldy landing craft off the beach, and the gunwales seemed to be deflecting the .30-caliber bullets peppering them. Poindexter called for volunteers to pick their way down the rocky beach to the water's edge to lob grenades into the boat. After quickly organizing two two-man teams—Mess Sergeant Carr and Raymond R. "Cap" Rutledge, a forty-five-year-old office clerk, who had reputedly served in the army in France in World War I (and whom John Hamas regarded as a "real morale booster") in one, Poindexter and the unflappable Boatswain's Mate First Class Barnes in the other—the grenadiers sallied forth while the machine guns behind them momentarily checked fire. Barnes, taking cover behind coral heads, remained hidden until the surf appeared to sweep the barge ashore again. Then, exposed to enemy fire, he hurled several grenades toward the landing craft; he believed that he had landed at least one inside.

That valiant effort, however, had little effect on the Japanese, for the *daihatsu* had already put its troops ashore and they were moving inland.

Shortly before wire communication with Devereux's command post failed, Poindexter reported the result of his sally to the water's edge. A bit later, a civilian workman—perhaps unnerved by the sound of the Japanese shouting and firing and letting off flares—made his way to Devereux's command post and blurted out that Japanese troops had overrun Camp 1 and were bayoneting Poindexter's gunners. Lacking any way of verifying that account, Devereux had to accept it at face value.

Having received the report of red flares arcing skyward from a point near the air station on Peale, Dan Godbold sent out a patrol of three men from Battery D along the lagoon shore toward the naval air station and ordered First Lieutenant Kessler to send out a two-man patrol from Battery B toward the ruins of the PanAir facility. Neither patrol encountered any enemy troops, meeting empty-handed at about 0330. A half hour later, shortly before his patrol returned, Godbold established an outpost at the bridge connecting Peale and Wake with three marines, one armed with a Browning automatic rifle.

As those events unfolded, Barney Barninger debated whether he should remain in position and fight the guns if surface ships came within range or try to help defend the airfield. Lacking much information, and losing touch with the command post in the darkness, he decided to stick with his primary mission.

After word of the enemy landing reached Pearl Harbor, Vice Admiral Pye convened a meeting of his staff. In the deliberations that ensued, the interim CinCPac's chief of staff, Rear Admiral Draemel, asked: "Can the forces at sea, *in fact*, relieve Wake?" If the *Tangier* landed everything, lock, stock, and gun barrel, it would afford only temporary relief for the beleaguered defenders; a series of operations would be necessary to hold Wake. If that could not be carried out, Wake "eventually must capitulate." He allowed that Wake had been weak even before the enemy had assaulted it. Would Wake even be in a condition to receive the aid brought from Hawaii? The Japanese might have been successful in their efforts—the marine pilots taking off from the *Saratoga* needed to know that beforehand.

Furthermore, the central issue, at least to Draemel, was not so much the relief of Wake per se but how to deal with the Japanese forces apparently gathered there. If the Japanese were unaware that Pye's carriers were at sea and attempting to relieve the island, they might have inferior forces in the vicinity of the atoll. Yet if they correctly deduced the Pacific Fleet's mission, the Japanese could be "fully prepared and ready for action" to defeat any attempt to relieve Cunningham's garrison. Japanese forces, Draemel thought, "are undoubtedly strong, or what he considers strong enough to do the job." Noting the weakness in the plan then being carried out—Task Force 14's fueling en route—Draemel observed that a "major engagement" could develop if Fletcher encountered the Japanese. Was Pye willing to accept that—especially "at this distance from our base—with an uncertainty in the fuel situation?" With no reserves, and with "*all* our forces . . . in the area of possible operations," Draemel counseled "caution—extreme caution." Pye had either to abandon Wake or "accept the risk of a major engagement."

By 0700 on the twenty-second (Hawaii time) (0430, 23 December, on Wake), Pye had received word of recent developments at Wake. Consequently, he estimated that relief of the island looked impossible and suggested that the *Tangier* be diverted to the east. With the relief mission abandoned, should his forces attack what enemy forces lay in the vicinity of Wake or be withdrawn to the eastward? He feared that the timing of the Japanese carrier strikes and the landing then in progress indicated that the enemy had "estimated closely the time at which our relief expedition might arrive and may, if the general location of our carrier groups is estimated, be waiting in force"—a prospect Draemel had considered. American forces could inflict extensive damage upon the Japanese, Pye believed, *if* the enemy did not know of their presence. But the Americans were untested in battle, and no one could underestimate the danger of having ships damaged two thousand miles from the nearest repair facilities—"a damaged ship is a lost ship," Brown had commented in Task Force 11's war diary. Damage to a substantial force could leave the Hawaiian Islands open to a major enemy thrust. "We cannot," Pye declared, "afford such losses at present."

Two possible courses of action existed—to direct Task Force 14 to attack Japanese forces in the vicinity of Wake, using Task Forces 8 and 11 only to cover Task Force 14's retirement, or to retire all forces without any attempt to attack the enemy force (of unknown size) concentrated near the atoll. If American forces hit the Japanese ships off Wake and suffered the loss of a carrier air group in the process, Pye, knowing that the *Yorktown* was due in the Pacific within two weeks, thought the "offensive spirit" shown by the navy perhaps worth the sacrifice.

In the midst of those deliberations, shortly after 0736 (0506, 23 December, Wake time), Pye received a message from the CNO which noted that recent developments emphasized that Wake was a "liability " and authorized Pye to "evacuate Wake with appropriate demolition." Because Japanese forces were on the island, Pye felt that capitulation was only a matter of time. Should the navy risk the loss of a carrier group in an attempt to attack the Japanese force off Wake? Radio intelligence from the previous day linked "CruDiv 8 . . . CarDiv 2" and, erroneously, "BatDiv 3" (consisting of two battleships) with the forces off Wake. A pair of *Kongo*-class fast battleships, supported by carriers and heavy cruisers, could make short work of Task Force 14.

Captain McMorris knew that one Japanese carrier, perhaps two, was in proximity to Wake. No hard evidence indicated any more. The vague and limited information at hand—some from partially decrypted enemy message traffic—prevented any conclusions on the number of Japanese carriers, although he suspected (rightly) that most of those that had been in the mid-Pacific were homeward bound. Although he still believed that Wake should be relieved, because the Japanese had already landed there, relief or abandonment assumed "secondary importance." The main issue was that "there is an enemy force (possibly weaker) that we can get at"—a situation that, ironically, Kimmel had hoped to precipitate—with American forces at sea that were "scattered but converging."

After positing that relieving Wake must either be delayed or abandoned—the question of evacuation would have to wait until the situation could be clarified—McMorris weighed four alternatives. Withdrawing, the first, seemed "unduly cautious" because he believed that Fletcher's force by itself outweighed the enemy force arrayed against it. Attacking the forces threatening Wake, the second option, offered "the greatest chance of damaging the enemy" because the Japanese did not know the exact location of Fletcher, Brown, and Halsey even if they knew they were at sea. "The enemy cannot have superior forces in all directions," McMorris reasoned, "we *know* where part of them are." The one carrier known to be near Wake was the "10,000-ton" *Sōryū* with forty to fifty planes. McMorris believed that Fletcher's force could conduct a limited patrol while attacking the Japanese because the *Saratoga* had two fighter squadrons embarked. "The odds," he wrote, "are strongly in her favor."

Evidently, McMorris, in his optimism, was unaware of the weakness of the *Saratoga*'s squadron (which had suffered the loss of one plane it could ill afford to lose the previous morning) and the inexperience of the "half-baked outfit" (VMF-221) that Brigadier General Rowell lamented having had to send. CinCPac's war plans officer deemed it "improbable" that the *Saratoga* would be attacked while her own planes were off attacking the Japanese, and though he allowed that the enemy might search for Task Force 14, the odds were "against rather than in favor" of it being detected.

Japanese triumphs off Malaya and at Pearl Harbor did not cause McMorris to concede them any "assured" success against the *Saratoga* and her consorts. "Reports from [the] Far East as well as from Oahu and from Wake," he wrote, "indicated [that] the enemy aircraft are very vulnerable to fighter attack." All of the foregoing, McMorris believed, offered a "great chance of success" of piecemeal destruction of the Japanese force off Wake. "Even though the enemy [may] be encountered in superior strength the chances of falling back without serious loss are excellent."

A third course of action—having Fletcher, Brown, and Halsey search for the Japanese—"temporizes and merely postpones the vital decision," he wrote, because in "playing for complete safety we would stand to lose a golden opportunity through wasted time." The fourth, concentrating the three task forces and then driving off the enemy, necessitated a delay that, he reasoned, "probably removes the advantage of surprise" because that "gives the enemy further chance to learn as much of you as you do of him." It also gave the enemy a chance to withdraw or accomplish his objective at Wake.

McMorris urged Pye to adopt the second course, to seize the opportunity because it seemed "unlikely to come again soon." "We are in great need of a victory," he declared, adding that success in the venture would "tremendously" strengthen Oahu's defenses.

Far to the west, as McMorris was recommending that the relief expedition press on—a course he had advocated from the beginning—the *Yūbari*, *Tenryu*, and *Tatsuta* had begun shelling Wake, while the enemy continued to press steadily toward 211's position around Hanna's three-inch antiboat gun, taking heavy casualties in the process. In the confusion near the beach, three SLF sailors managed to get close enough to attack Hanna's exposed position. In the ensuing fight, Hanna coolly shot and killed all three with his .45 and resumed operation of his three-incher.[8]

A sniper's bullet had penetrated Putnam's jaw on the left side, severing the facial artery and nerve before entering his neck well forward on the left side, emerging just above his sternum. As blood from the would stained the backs of the snapshots of his little daughters that he carried in a breast pocket, he resolutely formed his final line. "This," he said, determination etched on his face, "is as far as we go." After daylight, Hanna located the sniper endangering 211's position and killed him with his .45.

Putnam had placed the fearless Talmage Elrod in command of one flank of VMF-211's line, situated in dense undergrowth. In the predawn darkness, impenetrable beyond twenty feet, the squadron executive officer and his men—most of whom were unarmed civilians who willingly acted as weapons and ammunition carriers until weapons became available—conducted such a spirited defense that repeated attacks by SLF troops could not dislodge them. Each time he heard Japanese troops massing for a probe at 211's position, Elrod interposed himself between the enemy and his own men and provided covering fire to enable his detachment to keep supplied with guns and ammunition. Shortly before dawn, however, a few yards west of Hanna's gun, a Japanese sailor who had hidden himself among the heaps of casualties in the vicinity of the three-incher shot and killed the gallant captain, who, ironically, had once written of a romantic notion of death "upon the jagged spears of some rocky shore, by the angry waves of a turbulent sea."[9]

Sergeant Comin, whose galley had helped sustain VMF-211 during the siege, had stubbornly refused to go to the rear as the fighting neared the airstrip. Armed with only a .45-caliber pistol, he hobbled bravely toward the sound of the guns at the front lines. There he held his little patch of ground, turning back several rushes by enemy troops, until he was slain.

Also killed in the ebb and flow of combat around Hanna's gun and at the airfield that morning were Corporal Boyle and Private First Class Taylor. Several civilians died, too, as they fought alongside the squadron's marines: Pete Sorenson, Harry Yeager, Doc Stevenson, and George Gibbons, who had been with 211 since the beginning of the siege; Rex D. Jones, a steelworker; David E. Lilly, a welder; Don K. Miller, a steelworker's apprentice; Robert H. Lancaster, a carryall scraper operator; Ralph Higdon, a structural steel worker; and Jack F. McKinley, a steel sash worker. Of the eighteen CPNAB contractors who fought with 211's marines in the proximity of Hanna's three-incher, only three—Fred Gibbons (George's father), structural steel foreman Charles E. McCulley, and Mick D. "Mickey" Johnson, a truck driver, who had been wounded—survived the morning's action. Paul Putnam later wrote, with obvious gratitude and admiration for their courage: "No mere words can ever express what is owed."

Captain Tharin, in charge of a group of marines on the left flank of 211's line, delivered covering fire for the unarmed ammunition carriers attached to his unit, which repulsed several assaults on his position. Japanese sailors penetrated the defenses at one point, but in the counterattack that drove out the enemy, Tharin captured an enemy automatic weapon and used it "successfully and effectively against its former owners."

The indomitable Aviation Machinist's Mate First Class Hesson had armed himself with a Thompson submachine gun (a weapon that permitted "one man to deliver an accurate, fully controlled, long-sustained . . . fire of great stopping power within its range"[10]) and some grenades. Although sorely wounded by rifle fire and grenade fragments, he singlehandedly drove back two concerted rushes by Uchida's men—killing several and preventing them from overrunning 211's flank. He remained in his position, his dungaree legs soaked in his own blood.

"There are only twenty meters left to go," Lieutenant Uchida had

Sergeant Howard D. Comin,
9 January 1940. (USMC)

Lieutenant Commander James F.
Hesson, ca. 1949. (Mrs. Hilda
Hesson)

told his men as they advanced toward Hanna's gun. No sooner had he spoken those words when a bullet pierced the officer's forehead, between his eyes. Despite the heroic efforts of Putnam's embattled platoon, though, the sailors of the Uchida and Itaya Companies advanced with equal gallantry "over the dead bodies of their comrades" into the triangle bounded by Peacock Point, the south beach, and the south side of the airstrip.[11]

Corporal Graves's squad from Battery D, meanwhile, clambered down off their truck somewhat north of their intended destination (two hundred yards south of the airstrip rather than six hundred). Soon after they headed toward VMF-211's position, however, they encountered machine-gun fire that killed Private Ralph H. ("Hezzie") Pickett—an "excellent Marine," Godbold later wrote, "[who had] performed his duties most capably." After being pinned down for a time, Graves and his men managed to extricate themselves from their predicament and retire northward.

Upon reaching Devereux's command post, Graves surmised that he had encountered friendly fire. Major Potter, however, was not so sure that the corporal's men had been fired on by other marines: "Owing to the blackness of the night, the absence of land marks and relative unfamiliarity with [the] vicinity," Potter doubted "that even Graves would have had more than an approximate idea of his own location." Potter felt that Graves had not been gone long enough to have made the trip as far as Putnam's position. If it had been SLF machine guns (the Itaya Company forces landed had included a machine-gun platoon) that had turned back Graves's patrol, it reflected the enemy's swift penetration of the region, for apparently neither Kliewer and the .50-caliber guns nor the Hanna–VMF-211 group had obstructed their advance for very long.

Devereux soon received word from one of the few positions that had retained wire contact with his command post—Corporal McAnally's .50-caliber machine-gun section at the eastern end of the airstrip. McAnally reported the Japanese advancing up the shore road, apparently intent on launching a thrust up the other prong of Wake. With the Uchida unit besetting Putnam's at the airstrip, Special Duty Lieutenant (j.g.) Itaya's troops and Warrant Officer Horie's *kesshitai* were apparently skirting Putnam and Hanna and plunging into the triangular end of Peacock Point.

McAnally, establishing contact with the .50-caliber machine guns on the east shore of Wake some four hundred yards south, carried on a "resolute, well-coordinated defense" and, perhaps more important, served as Devereux's eyes and ears to the Japanese efforts to consolidate their gains. McAnally's gallant defense, however, stymied the enemy in his immediate vicinity.

Elsewhere on Wake, Wally Lewis noticed what looked like flares arcing into the murk between Wilkes and Peale, about 0430. After reporting the phenomenon to Devereux, Lewis posted sentries. Because the battery position lay only about thirty yards from the lagoon shore and his men had heard "unidentified noises" coming from that direction, Lewis deemed his concern well-founded.[12]

Over on Wilkes, where Private First Class Ray's defense of his position equaled that of McAnally on Wake, Captain Platt—out of communication with his own posts and with the detachment command post—set out on a personal reconnaissance around 0430. He crawled through the thick underbrush and picked his way along the edge of the rocky beach until about 0500, when he came to a place east of gun 10 where he could see Japanese sailors massed in or about Battery F's silent weapons. He scampered back to gun 10.

Over a century earlier, in his classic study *On War*, Major General Carl von Clausewitz had praised the commander who led by example, declaring that in discouraging situations the responsibility for motivating the defenders rested "on the will of the commander," who could, "by the spark in his breast, by the light of his spirit," kindle, afresh, "the spark of purpose, the light of hope" in his men.[13] Such a leader of troops was Wesley Platt. The energetic South Carolinian ordered Sergeant Coulson to gather two .30-caliber Brownings and crews from Kuku Point (where they had been sent during the false alarm earlier that morning), along with the searchlight crew from there and anyone else he could find, and return to gun 10. The Japanese apparently were unwilling to venture out from the captured battery, and the marines would take it back.

Despite the gallant actions of the defenders, the Uchida and Itaya Companies, in addition to Warrant Officer Horie's "do-or-die force" and that part of the Takano Company that had landed there, could now move at will on Wake in the areas they had captured and consolidated. At his command post, Devereux, isolated and in the dark (literally) as to what was going on on Wilkes and in the vicinity of Camp 1, apparently kept the island commander informed of events from his limited point of view. Cunningham thus had no knowledge of the way the fighting was going in those areas. At 0500, about the time Platt was reconnoitering the Japanese position on Wilkes, Cunningham was radioing ComFourteen, borrowing a phrase he had remembered from reading Anatole France's *Revolt of the Angels* some sixteen years before: "Enemy on island X Issue in doubt."[14]

Poindexter, satisfied that Camp 1 was being defended as well as

Captain Wesley M. Platt relaxes in Honolulu, 18 September 1945, en route home after his release from captivity. (NA, USMC Photo 135550)

possible and was taking advantage of the spare machine guns stored there, proceeded to the Mobile Reserve gun positions in place to the west of the field. Japanese machine-gun fire and projector-launched grenades, accompanied by "much shouting" and "numerous pyrotechnic flares," began to fall around those positions—too "darn close for comfort" John Valov recalled later—disabling one machine gun. As the sky over Wake began to lighten with the dawn, Poindexter, concerned not only about the accurate fire coming from those enemy positions but that the enemy troops infiltrating the woods on his left—where there were poor fields of fire—might outflank the Mobile Reserve, ordered a retirement toward Camp 1.

As the disabled section moved back along the edge of the road, Private First Class William T. Schumacher, one of the detachment's ordnance mechanics, resourcefully kept his section in action during the move-ment, one group displacing the other, "leap-frog" fashion. The sections thus alternated in covering each other throughout the movement, main-taining a steady volume of fire. Reaching Camp 1 after daylight, Poin-dexter established a north-south line astride the shore road east of the water tank.[15] Ironically, the Japanese infiltration into the scrub saved the Mobile Reserve from annihilation. "The Japanese had . . . cover and concealment," Poindexter later wrote, "but we had better control and mobility along the beach and roadway."[16]

The movement had not been made without casualties. As John Valov was carrying some equipment back to one of the trucks, Frank R. Mallo, a CPNAB laborer and one of the other civilians attached to Poindexter's unit, yelled "Look out!" The surprised Valov felt something hit the back of his head as a grenade exploded some distance behind him, some fragments of which shredded the light raincoat he was wearing. He thought the wetness he felt on the back of his head and down his back was merely perspiration—not the blood that it was.

While Poindexter was reflecting on his situation, Japanese movement up the east shore road put increasing pressure on Corporal McAnally's group east of the airfield—a predicament he soon communicated to Devereux's command post. Hand grenades and small arms fire made life difficult for McAnally's band, but it refused to budge and broke up several assaults.

Wally Lewis finally got the chance to use the data he had formulated before Kajioka's ships had showed up on 11 December. After Devereux called for prearranged concentrations of air bursts over Wake's south beach, Battery E sent three-inch rounds exploding and showering shrap-nel over the target area in the gray dawn. Unable to communicate with any friendly units, Lewis had no way of knowing how effective his fire was. Japanese war correspondent Ibushi, however, later testified to the effectiveness of Battery E's barrage. "Shells burst directly over our heads," he recounted, "and there was a continuous and intense hori-zontal fire from the high-angle guns. . . . We hugged so close to the ground that our helmets dug into the earth."

At about 0530, as dawn was breaking, fresh troops entered the fray on Wake, although perhaps feeling the effects of almost six hours in an open, pitching and rolling landing craft. The *daihatsu* from the *Patrol Boat No. 33*, bearing the rifle platoon from the Itaya Company, landed on the south beach almost midway between the two grounded patrol boats. Its eight-knot odyssey had taken it within five hundred meters of Peacock Point at about 0330, at which point it had turned and begun shaping a course to the southwest, opening the distance to almost four thousand meters shortly after 0400. A little while later, the boat had turned again, this time on a straight northerly course that ultimately took it to its objective almost three hours after the first Japanese had splashed ashore.

Soon thereafter, Devereux told Major Potter to form a final defensive line astride the north-south road being threatened from the south by the advancing Japanese. Potter consequently called up Godbold and told him "to prepare to move to the CP by truck." After Devereux and his executive officer conferred, Devereux called Battery D's commander back and urged him to hurry because daylight would bring the inevitable carrier aircraft that could now raid the island with impunity because VMF-211 possessed no more flyable planes; both Devereux and Potter feared that Godbold would then be strafed en route. In summoning Godbold's Battery D into the battle, Devereux committed his last reserve troops. Aware of Corporal McAnally's predicament, Devereux ordered the corporal's group to withdraw toward the command post to join Potter's detachment.

At about that time, on Wilkes, Sergeant Coulson rejoined Captain Platt with two machine guns and crews and eight additional marines. The booming surf that had masked the approach of the invaders now worked to the advantage of the hard-pressed defenders as it, together with the sputter and crackle of gunfire along the south shore of Wake, kept Takano's sailors from discovering Platt briefing his men for the assault. Platt had no idea of the location of McAlister and McKinstry and so instructed his men to "shoot only at targets identified as Japanese." Squeeze off short bursts, he told his marines, and keep moving.

"Discipline," George Washington had written to the captains of the Virginia regiments in 1759, "makes small numbers formidable; procures success to the weak, and esteem to all."[17] In the waning darkness, Platt and his disciplined men crept silently toward the unsuspecting enemy, reaching a point less than fifty yards away from them. On Platt's signal, his two machine guns opened fire, and his skirmishers charged forward and soon began engaging the Japanese, who, spurning security toward Kuku Point, had been taken completely by surprise. Their only light machine guns were facing toward the old channel, inside the position itself.

Almost simultaneous to, but uncoordinated with, Platt's assault, McAlister (who had lost contact with Platt shortly after the enemy had landed) and his men surprised a three-man enemy patrol on the beach ahead of them at one end of the enemy's flank, killing one before the other two scampered behind a coral boulder. While flanking fire pinned down the two Japanese, Gunner McKinstry started forward to clean out that pocket of resistance. McAlister, however, stopped him and told him instead to ask for volunteers. Before the warrant officer could do

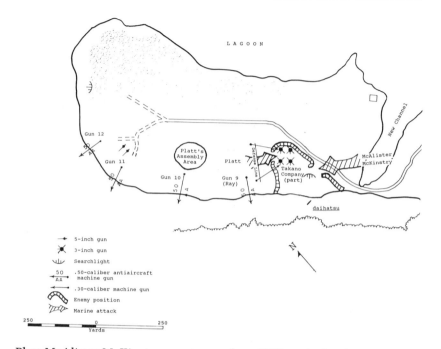

Platt-McAlister-McKinstry counterattack on Wilkes, daybreak on
23 December 1941. (adapted from Map 7 in Heinl, *The Defense of Wake*)

so, though, Corporal "Whitey" Halstead, whom Platt would later praise
as "quiet, efficient, and completely reliable," told McKinstry confidently: "I've got it, Gunner." Halstead jumped atop the rock and shots
rang out as he dispatched the two Japanese.

That task having been accomplished, McKinstry suggested to
McAlister that they form a skirmish line, which they did. Platt's and
McAlister's disjointed coordinated assault—the latter comprising three
elements consisting of McAlister and a group of men on the left flank,
McKinstry and a party of men at the center, and Corporal Alvey A. Reed
bringing up the right flank—then cleaned out the Japanese in the three-
inch gun position. A few of the enemy had played dead and waited
for the marines to close in before rising up to bayonet the attacking
leathernecks.

McAlister and McKinstry—the latter having been supplied enthusi-
astically with hand grenades by civilians "Chuck" Smith, Forrest D.
Read (a CPNAB scraper operator), John E. Schultz (a yard foreman), and

three others throughout the action—then reorganized their units and, in the course of the search for any enemy troops who might have escaped, encountered no further resistance.[18] They took two prisoners, who had been wounded and had been among those who had feigned death. The gun sections that met on the lagoon side of the island reported killing a single Japanese officer whom they encountered before dawn.

All told, Platt estimated that the Japanese had lost at least seventy-five to eighty-five enlisted men and four officers (including the one killed near the lagoon shore); at least thirty of those lay around or under the searchlight truck. Japanese records, however, admit casualties among the Takano Company as three officers (including Takano) dead and one wounded, fifty-five enlisted men dead and thirty-one wounded, the majority of the dead undoubtedly slain on Wilkes. The victory, though, had not come cheaply for the defenders; Platoon Sergeant William A. Gleichauf, who had captained one of the five-inchers, as well as Corporal "Whitey" Halstead—hit squarely in the chest by a burst of Japanese automatic weapons fire—and Privates First Class Gordon L. Marshall, Ernest M. Gilley, Jr., and Clovis R. Marlow lay dead; Private First Class Wiley W. Sloman had been wounded.

Platt then ordered McAlister to keep ten men and mop up the position and tear down all of the flags—probably put up for the benefit of the expected close air support—that had delineated the enemy's limits of penetration. "In general," Captain Koyama later lamented understatedly, "that particular phase of the operation [the landing on Wilkes] was unsuccessful."

They also enjoyed no success against a very small but very determined quartet of marines near the airfield. At about that time (shortly before dawn), Japanese troops—perhaps from the freshly landed (but probably bedraggled) elements of the headquarters unit and the rifle platoon from the Itaya Company that had just disembarked from the *daihatsu* from the *Patrol Boat No. 33*—surrounded Kliewer's position. Armed with only two Thompsons, three .45-caliber pistols, and two boxes of hand grenades between them, the four marines tenaciously held their ground, backed up by the two .50-caliber machine guns 150 yards behind them, repelling repeated assaults even as the sky began to lighten to the east.

Shortly after daybreak, Japanese mortar shells began bursting in the vicinity of Battery E and Battery A, and both received small-arms and machine-gun fire as well. As the latter increased in intensity, Barninger deployed his range section, with two .30-caliber Brownings, as infantry, to the northwest, to hold the high ground to the rear of the five-inchers. He kept the crews of his main battery largely under cover in the vicinity of their guns because there were no Japanese ships within range. Bursts of machine-gun fire, however, swept the unprotected weapons, keeping the sergeant in charge of gun 1 at his post on the disengaged side of the mount, in contact by wire with the battery commander and protected only by the barrel and carriage of the gun itself.

Lewis, whose battery's three-inch air bursts had silenced an automatic weapons position in the thick undergrowth southwest of his position, received permission from Devereux to send out one of his crews to cover his battery. With orders to "take the position from which the Japanese were firing . . . and to hold this ground," bullnecked Sergeant Raymon Gragg and his men advanced until SLF sailors, firing from across the cleared area near the airstrip, pinned them down as they reached the edge of the thick brush about fifty yards beyond the perimeter.[19]

On Peale, after Godbold and the last marines of Battery D departed toward Devereux's command post on Wake, First Lieutenant Kessler became strongpoint commander. At dawn, he scanned the other islets. On Wilkes, across the lagoon, he discerned Japanese flags—one particularly large one flying where Battery F had been emplaced near the shore (flags Platt's men would remove shortly thereafter). Kessler's ominous report prompted Devereux, who had not heard a word from Platt since around 0300, to fear that Wilkes had fallen.

As he scanned Wake around 0600, however, Kessler, from his ten-foot perch in the battery control tower, observed the masts of the *Patrol Boat No. 33* off the south shore of Wake. Receiving permission to do so but admonished to avoid firing into friendly troops, Kessler "took several readings with a wet finger" and ordered his five-inchers to open fire. Unable to spot in the more traditional manner ("short" shots could endanger friendly forces on Wake, and the ocean was not visible from Kessler's vantage point), Kessler's "Kentucky Windage" proved accurate enough—despite the amusement of Sergeant Huffman and the other men who witnessed their battery commander's unorthodox methods.

The first salvo clipped off the mainmast; then Battery B's sightsetters, who could see only the funnel tops over the intervening island, received new data from the rangekeeper to place the ship in the pattern. Twenty-five minutes later, at 0625, the command post ordered Battery B to cease fire, the target having been "demolished." Twenty minutes later, though, a new enemy hove into view, as Kessler observed what was probably Rear Admiral Goto's Wake Invasion Operation Support Unit—the heavy cruisers *Aoba, Kinugasa, Kako,* and *Furutaka*—off Heel Point, moving westward and insolently standing out of range, their eight-inch guns silent. The Japanese held their fire, though, apparently unable to distinguish friend from foe ashore because of "poor liaison with shore observers."[20]

More Japanese forces, of a different nature, were soon headed for Wake. At 0612, to the northwest, the *Sōryū* had turned into the wind and launched the twenty-fourth, twenty-fifth, and twenty-sixth *shōtais* of her bomber squadron—six *kanbakus* under Lieutenant Ikeda Masatake, each armed with a single 250-kilogram bomb—and the eleventh and twelfth *shōtais* consisting of six *kansens* under Lieutenant Suganami. The day's air operations in support of Kajioka's invasion force had begun, the Aichis and Mitsubishis the first of five groups of planes that Yamaguchi's carriers would hurl into battle. En route, at 0651, less than twenty-five minutes from Wake, they spotted what appeared to be a commercial ship but soon discovered it to be the *Kiyokawa Maru*, on her way toward Wake to conduct supporting operations.

Throughout the battle to that point, Devereux had apparently kept Cunningham informed of its progress. While the marines, assisted by the sailors and civilians, had been attempting gallantly to stem the tide, most of the tidings trickling into Cunningham's command post boded ill. Captain Wilson's communicators erected the antenna that would allow them to transmit; consequently, at 0652 (0922, 22 December 1941, Pearl Harbor time), Cunningham informed CinCPac of Wake's situation: "Enemy on island X Several ships plus transport moving in X Two DD aground X"[21]

Twenty-four minutes later, Lieutenant Ikeda's *kanbakus* from the *Sōryū* arrived over the island, Lieutenant Suganami deploying his fighters as a CAP. The presence of Japanese planes overhead rendered further use of Wake's radio nearly suicidal because the erected antenna—which would not be put up again—would have drawn them to its location. Shortly thereafter, even before a bomb had been dropped by the first wave of Japanese carrier planes, the *Hiryū* began launching the second wave at 0700: six *kanbakus*—each Aichi carrying a pair of sixty-kilogram bombs—from the twenty-second and twenty-sixth *shōtais* under Lieutenant Kobayashi and six *kansens* of the eleventh and eighteenth *shōtais* under Lieutenant Nōno to carry out ground-support operations.

While the *Hiryū*'s planes were droning toward Wake, Lieutenant Ikeda's pilots began bombing "shipping" in the lagoon—perhaps mistaking the *Pioneer*, the *Justine Foss*, or even the *Columbia*, for warships—and promptly drew fire from Battery E, the only effective antiaircraft battery on Wake. Lewis's three-inch guns scored no hits, but neither apparently did the Japanese, and although they did not report the antiaircraft fire as the cause, returning Japanese aircrew reported that it had not been easy to confirm the effectiveness of their bombing.

Back at Pearl Harbor, Vice-Admiral Pye was concluding that if Task Force 14 encountered anything but a weaker force, the battle would be fought on Japanese terms in range of shore-based planes and American forces had adequate fuel for no more than two days of high-speed steaming. Like Brown, Pye believed that a damaged ship was a lost ship, especially two thousand miles from Pearl. Pye's stewardship of the fleet demanded that he prudently husband its resources—the war had just begun and there was no prospect of a conflict of short duration. It would have been foolhardy to commit scattered forces to battle an enemy of unknown strength.

Given the present level of enemy activity, Pye reasoned that Wake could neither be relieved nor evacuated. Even if Task Force 14 got near enough to allow the *Saratoga* to hurl a strike on enemy ships in the vicinity of the atoll, Wake could not be saved. "One such attack might destroy enemy transports and light forces," Pye posited, "but except for morale value would or could do little to support Wake." The relief expedition, he reasoned, had been a "desperate move to give reinforcements to the gallant defenders, and I was willing, if no enemy activity other than bombing was in progress, to sacrifice the *Tangier* and several destroyers in the attempt."[22]

"From the point of view of the local situation," he later stated, "everything pointed to the first chance to damage the enemy in naval action. Such . . . would comply with the spirit of the offensive [something near and dear to Kimmel's fighting sailor's heart] and might conceivably result in considerable loss to the enemy. To fail to support the gallant defense of Wake seemed pusillanimous and could we spare the force that might conceivably be lost, it would have been." From the "broader point of view, the situation was different. To insure the defense of other points, even the Hawaiian Islands, it was necessary to conserve our forces. If there was a chance to surprise the enemy, quite a risk was justifiable provided it led to a reasonable hope of reinforcing Wake. Such reinforcement being impossible in view of the landing attack, the primary reason for the accepted risk vanished."[23]

Weighing the immediate attack, Pye and his advisers considered several factors: if the Japanese lost the ships involved in the Wake operation, he posited, it would have a negligible effect on "the enemy's future operations." If Task Force 14 suffered heavy losses, though, that could "seriously decrease the effectiveness" of future operations for the navy. If each side sank one of each other's carriers, the United States would emerge at a disadvantage because it possessed fewer than the Japanese. If Task Force 11 rushed to support Task Force 14, "it might lead to a major action . . . nearly 2,000 miles from a single entrance base of limited industrial capacity." Although Pye believed in the "principle of the offensive" and empathized with Wake's garrison, "I could not but decide," he later explained, "that the general situation overbalanced the special tactical situation, and that under the conditions the risk of even one task force to damage the enemy at Wake was unjustifi-able." He therefore directed Fletcher and Brown to retire; Halsey was to cover the *Wright*'s voyage to Midway.[24]

Frank Jack Fletcher, meanwhile, was right on schedule and farther west than Pye knew. His ships fully fueled—the *Neches* had topped off the *Selfridge*, the *Mugford*, the *Patterson*, the *Helm*, and the *Blue* in succession—and ready for battle, Fletcher planned to detach the *Tangier* and two destroyers for the final run-in to Wake, while the pilots on board the *Saratoga* prepared for the fight that lay ahead. "Although delayed one day by fueling, this task force was in position," he later wrote, "and expected to carry out the mission and have the *Tangier* and planes arrive [at] Wake on D-day in accordance with [the operations plans]."[25]

When word of the recall reached him on board his flagship *Astoria*, however, Fletcher, not a man to shirk a fight, snatched his cap from his head and disgustedly flung it to the deck in anger. "Jake" Fitch, Fletcher's air task commander, likewise felt fist-tightening frustration. Captain Archibald H. Douglas, the *Saratoga*'s commanding officer, "urged Fitch to contact Fletcher . . . and request permission for a raid on Wake the next morning."[26] Fitch retired from the *Saratoga*'s flag bridge when the talk there reached "mutinous" proportions. He later said that "he had never seen, in his entire naval career, such intense indignation and resentment as was displayed" that day.[27]

Elsewhere on board the *Saratoga*, Captain James L. Neefus, VMF-221's ordnance officer, felt dejected at not being able to get at the Japa-nese; he saw some of his shipmates weep in frustration. Master Techni-cal Sergeant Robert L. Dickey, 221's only enlisted pilot, felt let down but resigned himself to the recall orders. Such changes in plan, he later observed philosophically, were part of "routine military happen-stance."[28] "Nearly every man," observed Lieutenant Donald A. Lovelace of the *Saratoga*'s VF-3, "had been thriving on the idea of getting into some quick action." To Lovelace, "the set-up seemed perfect for those of us who did not have the complete picture of the strategical situation." While others complained bitterly, Lovelace felt—correctly—that some-one who possessed a bigger picture of the action had compelled the higher-ups to order the change in plan. "No doubt," he confided to his diary on 23 December, "the broader scope of the situation dictated this action."[29]

Pye's recall order had left latitude for neither discussion nor disobedi-ence; those who later felt that Fletcher should have used the Nelsonian "blind eye" obviously failed to realize that at least off Copenhagen the British admiral could see his opponents (who were also in the harbor at the time); 425 miles east of Wake, on schedule with the operation plan, neither Fletcher nor Fitch could see theirs. They had no idea of the forces they might encounter, as "Soc" McMorris put it later: "We had no more idea'n a billygoat" about what Japanese forces lay off Wake. The message traffic linking cruisers, aircraft carriers, and battleships with land-based air painted a formidable picture of what might be encountered by a single U.S. Navy carrier task force well out of supporting range of a second. The Japanese had won the race to Wake, but they still had to claim their prize—something Cunningham's garrison was not about to give them without more of a fight.

"A DIFFICULT THING
TO DO"

While deliberations proceeded to determine the fate of the relief efforts, Wake's defenders fought on. Shortly after 0715 Wake time (0945, 22 December, at Pearl), the two trucks bearing Battery D's men, under Second Lieutenant Greeley and Captain Godbold, respectively, reached Devereux's command post. Almost simultaneously, First Lieutenant Kessler shifted Battery B's attention to a column of what looked like three destroyers off Kuku Point. Four salvos appeared to damage the lead ship so he shifted his attention to the second.

With the Sōryū's planes overhead and the Hiryū's on the way, Major Potter's final defense line beset by increasingly heavy enemy rifle and machine-gun fire, the Japanese still probing and vexing VMF-211's embattled remnant near the airstrip, and Wilkes having apparently fallen, Major Devereux, out of communication with the stubborn defenders of Wilkes and Camp 1, had no way of knowing which of his units were still carrying on the battle. At about 0730, Commander Keene picked up the telephone in the contractors' headquarters and found Commander Cunningham and Major Devereux, both men undoubtedly bone-tired from lack of sleep, engaged in conversation. The latter reported being hard-pressed at his command post and did not believe that the marines could hold out much longer. Cunningham told Devereux that if he did not feel that he was able to continue fighting, he should surrender. A discussion then ensued. "You know," Devereux stated during that time, "Wilkes has fallen." Cunningham answered that he did. Devereux then stated that he did not feel he should make the decision to surrender but that the commander of the island's defenses should decide the matter.

Never would the loneliness of command be more evident than it was to Spiv Cunningham on 23 December 1941. In a position best likened to that of the captain of an imperiled ship at sea, he found himself alone, having the "most difficult and demanding assignment in the Navy"—command—that could not be shared.[1] As his subordinate, Jim Devereux, had said, the decision to surrender was his, and his alone, to make. Pausing for a moment, Cunningham told Devereux that he authorized surrender and to take the necessary steps to carry it out. Uncertain of his ability to get in touch with the Japanese commander, Devereux asked Cunningham to attempt to make contact with the enemy as well, to which the latter responded: "I'll see what I can do."

Soon after Godbold reached the detachment's command post, he asked Potter: "Where do you want me? What position shall I take?" Potter deployed the new arrivals in a thin defensive line across the island encompassing the area that had been partially cleared for the construction of a runway. Although thinly defended in manpower, it was well covered by Battery E and by Potter's guns. Godbold's men, who included the civilians of Sergeant Bowsher's gun 3—armed with a variety of weapons that ranged from Browning automatic rifles to hunting rifles, shotguns, and two .22s—took up their positions astride the road, to the south of Devereux's command post. Marine Gunner Borth, meanwhile, established a defensive line near the command post with two .30-caliber guns and their crews, all of the men assigned to the command post, and a few from Battery D.

Soon thereafter, John Hamas ducked inside and sought out Devereux, who was just finishing his phone conversation with Cunningham. Hamas reported the arrival of Godbold and his force, told Devereux of their dispositions, and asked for further instructions. Devereux, who, like Cunningham, had spent the battle within the confines of his command post, looked at the veteran warrant officer sadly. "John," he said solemnly, his voice betraying emotion, "it's too late. Commander Cunningham has ordered me to surrender. Prepare a white flag of truce, go outside and give the order to 'cease firing.'" Although he was momentarily stunned, the ingrained instinct of obedience prompted Hamas to do as he was ordered.

Surrendering, however, would take time. Owing to the chaotic state of communications, not everyone learned of the decision right away. On Wilkes, Platt had returned to Battery F around 0800. Taking charge of the two wounded Japanese McAlister's men had found, Platt ordered McAlister to man his guns and open fire on the ships southwest of Wilkes. Platt's crude attempts to interrogate one prisoner, using sign language, gleaned the information that the Japanese were apparently not going to land any more boats. He immediately tried to reach Devereux over the warning net but managed only to contact someone at the Camp 1 motor pool. The marines there, however, could not contact the command post because the lines had been severed by the enemy.

McAlister soon discovered that the ships he had been told to fire on were out of range and, more important, one of the five-inch/.51s would not train and fragments from the bombs dropped during one of the dive-bombing attacks (that were still continuing) had holed the other's recoil cylinders. Informed of that situation, Platt then ordered McKinstry to take fifteen men and contact the .30-caliber machine-gun positions near the old channel and report on their status. McKinstry reached them by telephone from the searchlight position and found that they had not been attacked. With that flank secure, Platt ordered Sergeant Coulson to inform him immediately if he say any more landing boats standing in.

The Japanese close air support operations continued. Between 0800 and 0807, the *Sōryū* launched nine *kankōs* (the forty-fifth, forty-sixth, and forty-seventh *shōtais* from her attack bomber unit), each carrying a pair of 250-kilogram bombs, under Lieutenant Nagai Tsutomu, and two *kansens* from her thirteenth *shōtai*, flown by Warrant Officer Tanaka Hiroshi and Seaman First Class Doikawa Isao.[2]

One wave of Japanese planes had completed its attacks, a second was just commencing to attack, and a third was about an hour away. Devereux contacted the remaining units he could still reach. On Peale, around 0800, Kessler's talker turned apprehensively to his battery commander and said: "They say to stop firing the 5-inch guns, we are surrendering the island." A request to repeat what he had just said yielded the same answer. In disbelief, Kessler rang up the command post himself but got no response. Finally, he obtained confirmation from Barninger at Peacock Point. As the surf pounded relentlessly in the background, the marines at Battery B remained at their posts, stunned and silent. Some wanted to disregard the order and keep up the fight.

"We have to carry out our orders," Kessler explained, "we have no idea what the terms of surrender might be, and we might endanger the lives of those already in Jap hands." He told Platoon Sergeant Huffman to remove the firing locks from the guns and hurl them into the sea; Huffman fired off all the remaining primers, too. He also broke the lenses of the gunsights and poured sand in the elevating and traversing mechanisms and in the threads of the breech blocks.

At Battery E, Lewis recalled Sergeant Gragg's squad to destroy their gun. Lewis's men then removed and smashed the firing locks and, when stuffing blankets into the muzzles and firing a round did not do sufficient damage, rolled grenades down the barrels; they smashed equipment and chopped up electrical cables. Unholstering his .45, Lewis fired twenty rounds and destroyed the optics and electromechanical parts of the height finder and director. Another marine firing into the height finder accidentally wounded one of his batterymates—the only casualty from Battery E that day. Lewis then marched his men as a unit, under a white flag, to Devereux's command post.

At Peacock Point, still under fire, Battery A prepared to surrender. Only one casualty occurred that day, when a ricocheting bullet struck

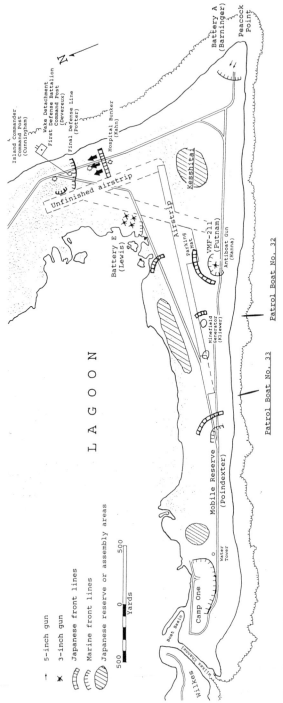

Situation on Wake Island at the time of surrender, 0800, 23 December 1941. (adapted from Map 5 in Heinl, *The Defense of Wake*)

Barninger's runner, Private First Class Nowlin, on his helmet and knocked him unconscious. Barninger order the five-inch firing locks broken and buried and the telescopes and rangekeeper smashed. Running up a white flag soon thereafter, he ordered everyone, including the civilian ammunition handlers, to eat as much as they could because no one knew how much food the enemy would allow their captives. Then they sat down to await the arrival of the victors.

On Toki Point, First Lieutenant Kessler, uncertain of how the Japanese would approach them, ordered his men to retain their rifles. If the enemy reneged on the surrender accords, he wanted to be able to return the fire; stories of how the Japanese had used defenseless Chinese for bayonet practice sprang to mind. He then asked for a count of how many five-inch shells remained and discovered that the cease-fire order had been almost superfluous—only five rounds remained. Kessler then ordered a white bedsheet rigged on a pole, which was done in the nick of time, for a Japanese plane buzzed the position but withheld fire. "Maybe," Kessler thought, "they would play by the rules."

Like Barney Barninger, Kessler had no idea how long it would be before he and his men would be fed. The men of Battery B broke out all of the food—including candy bars—that they had been hoarding and gorged themselves. When they had finished their reluctant repast, Kessler ordered them to pick up any trash, reasoning that when the Japanese did show up, "at least they wouldn't be able to say that we lived in a pig pen."

While surrender preparations were going ahead on one side of Wake and in the positions Devereux had been able to reach by telephone, Poindexter's Mobile Reserve had established itself along a line at the edge of the clearing east of Camp 1 and set up ten .30-caliber machine guns to cover the entire front with interlocking fields of fire. Occasional low-flying planes strafed their positions (probably the Hiryū's kanbakus, under Lieutenant Kobayashi, or the Hiryū's kansens, under Lieutenant Nōno), but gunfire from the front proved ineffective.

When Poindexter sent Private First Class Rasor back to Camp 1 to roust out all "special duty personnel" to join the reserve as riflemen, however, the summons failed to galvanize the men into action. It fell to a gentle, slight, bespectacled quartermaster clerk, Corporal Cyrus D. Fish, to break the tentative silence. "Well," he said bravely, "what are we sitting on our asses for?" He clambered out of the dugout and led a group of men forward under fire.[3]

By 0900, the enemy having shown no inclination to attack him, Poindexter, who, like Wesley Platt, exuded a brand of personal leadership that inspired those who served under him, ordered a counterattack toward the airstrip. Dividing his men into three ten-man squads with a

Corporal Cyrus D. Fish, San
Diego, California, ca. 1941
(Mrs. Marylee Fish)

Nakajima B5N2 Type 97 carrier attack plane over the reef off Peale,
while bombs explode near the seaplane ramp for the yet-to-be-completed
NAS Wake. (Japan War History Office)

noncommissioned officer in charge of each, he decided to attack within a front extending from the beach into the brush on the north side of the road, about twenty-five yards in. Corporal Fish distinguished himself in the ensuing fight when his squad, using grenades and small-arms fire, wiped out small groups of SLF sailors who had sought cover in bomb craters along the beach. Poindexter's force had wrested control of the territory between Camp 1 and the road junction west of the airstrip from the enemy's grasp.

Meanwhile, unable to reach the hospital by telephone—the enemy had already captured it, killing one patient and wounding two when they fired into the entrance—Devereux, accompanied by Sergeant Donald R. Malleck, who held aloft a white rag attached to a swab handle, began trudging down the north-south road along the eastern shore of Wake to contact the Japanese. As he passed marines still in action, he ordered them to cease firing.

An SLF sailor emerged from the brush along the road and halted Devereux's progress, covering the two marines as they took off their "iron kelly" helmets and laid down their weapons. The Japanese, who spoke no English, motioned them toward the hospital bunker, where Devereux found an enemy officer who spoke some English. Soon thereafter, Commander Cunningham, who had changed into his blue uniform for the occasion, arrived to arrange the details of the surrender. Devereux and Malleck, accompanied by a Japanese officer, then began the sad journey toward those marines who still stubbornly held out ahead of them.

Back at Cunningham's command post, Captain Wilson's men, having maintained their equipment up to the end, burned what codes remained, dismantled the cipher devices and hurled the parts into the ocean off Wake, and wrecked the transmitter by burning out the power transformer and smashing the meters. All that remained was to surrender.

Meanwhile, the stubborn resistance put up by Hanna and VMF-211 had prompted the Japanese to call for close air support. The third wave, from the *Sōryū*, was soon on hand to provide it. At 0910, while seven *kankōs* awaited further orders and remained aloft at altitude, Lieutenant Nagai, the leader, and a wingman, Petty Officer Second Class Mori Juzō, descended to reconnoiter. Marine antiaircraft fire, however, hit both planes—Nagai's twice and Mori's four times—as they roared low over Wake. The two *kankōs* would be the only ones in the third wave to be hit, showing that Cunningham's garrison still had fight left in it.

The *kankōs* were not equipped with fixed, forward-firing weapons so one of Nagai's pilots overflew the embattled three-inch antiboat gun at low altitude, permitting his observer to fire on the position with his flexible-mount 7.7-millimeter machine gun. The strafing killed two of

Hanna's civilian volunteers, Paul Gay and Bob Bryan, and wounded Hanna and Corporal Holewinski, as the men sought cover under the pierced aluminum plate of the three-inch gun platform. One of the *Kiyokawa Maru*'s planes flew low over Wake on a strafing run at 0929. The *Hiryū* was completing the launch of the fourth wave that had started at 0905: nine Type 97s under Lieutenant Matsumura (the forty-first, forty-third, and forty-fifth *shōtais*) and three *kansens* under Lieutenant (j.g.) Shigematsu Yasuhiro from the twelfth *shōtai*. Some of the men getting their planes aloft from the *Hiryū* had not yet seen combat. Seaman First Class Nagayama Yoshimitsu had flown at Pearl, but his observer, Petty Officer Second Class Sukeota Kaoru and his radio-gunner, Petty Officer Second Class Suzuki Mutsuo, had been spares when the war started; Pearl Harbor spare Lieutenant Kikuchi Rokurō, who had flown his first combat only the day before, flew a plane with two veterans, observer Warrant Officer Yumoto Noriyoshi and radio-gunner Petty Officer Narasaki Hironori, as his crew. They would reach Wake's airspace at 1018.

When Devereux finally reached the airfield at around 0930, he found that the Japanese had taken cover behind the revetments, pinning down Hanna's men and the remainder of 211's embattled band who still tenaciously held their positions. The major ordered Captain Tharin, the only officer who had not been seriously wounded, to cease fire. Of the ten men at the position, all—including the gallant Aviation Machinist's Mate First Class Hesson—bore wounds suffered in the last-ditch fighting.

Even as elements on Wake still held out, Vice Admiral Pye was informing the CNO that the island could not be evacuated. Japanese forces had landed, supported by cruisers and destroyers, and, potentially, had a covering force close by. The "gallant defense of Wake," Pye stated, "has been of utmost value, but hereafter Wake is a liability." In view of the "extensive operations" then under way, Pye was forced to conclude that risking one carrier task force to attack enemy forces in the vicinity of Wake was "not justifiable." The two westernmost task forces (14 and 11) had been ordered to retire toward Pearl. The third (Task Force 8) was ordered to cover the *Wright*'s progress toward Midway. Apprehensive that Wake's fall meant that various "crypto channels" then in use would be compromised, Rear Admiral Withers changed the *Triton*'s route back to Pearl "to avoid [an] enemy trap."[4]

On Wake, Second Lieutenant Kliewer, seeing the Japanese flags all along the beach, decided to blow up the airfield and fall back in the confusion generated by the explosions. Unfortunately, the rain had drowned out the generator motor and with it, the last chance to deny the victorious enemy use of the airstrip that the Japanese had so assiduously avoided damaging. At 1015 Kliewer saw men carrying a white flag coming down the beach. Major Devereux was among them, with a group of what appeared to be Japanese officers, who stopped about fifty feet from their trench and ordered them to lay down their arms. Blandy, Bourquin, and Trego counseled against giving up: "Don't surrender, lieutenant. The marines never surrender. It's a hoax." "It was a difficult thing to do," Kliewer wrote later, "but we tore down our guns and turned ourselves over."

After seeing the white flag flying back at the detachment command post, Bob Greeley returned there and learned of the surrender. He waited there until the first SLF troops arrived. Stripped of his clothes and watch, he was marched to the hospital and confined there.

About one hour later, around the time (1045) that a plane from the *Tone* was radioing its parent ship that Wake apparently had been captured, Devereux's melancholy procession reached the Mobile Reserve's positions. One of Poindexter's men shouted that a "large group of Japs were coming down the road toward us with a white flag." Poindexter could see no Americans in the group and, after ordering his men to hold their fire, stepped out into the road, rifle at the ready. Cautioning his men not to fire unless the enemy fired at him, he walked toward the group, then discerned Devereux shouting to him that Wake had been surrendered. Poindexter's confident grin melted.

Dropping his rifle and grenades in the road, Poindexter joined Devereux, who told him to return to his unit and order his men to drop their weapons and stand up. SLF troops, bayonets fixed, began to rush the positions they had been exchanging fire with, only to be stopped by a Japanese officer who interposed himself between the two sides. As Poindexter and his men trudged toward the airstrip, the large numbers of enemy troops emerging from the brush and falling in along the road confirmed his suspicions that they were established in force in that region.

Later, Poindexter speculated that the Japanese had been able to land troops on the lagoon side of Wake. Reflecting on the heavy losses that his own men and Hanna's had inflicted on the enemy at that part of the island, the many SLF troops he saw in that region at the time of the surrender prompted him to think that another sizable force might have been able to get ashore without even having to face gunfire. None of his men had seen rubber boats or other landing craft within the lagoon proper, although a corpsmen later recounted that he and another man had thought they had seen small landing craft moving eastward at about the same time the captains of the two patrol boats were grounding their ships on the south shore. Marine working parties later reported the prescence of rafts near the eastern end of the lagoon.

Devereux progressed to Camp 1, still held by Poindexter's machine-gun sections. A Japanese sailor climbed to the top of the water tower observation post and cut down the Stars and Stripes that had been flying throughout the battle. Elsewhere at Camp 1, in one of the last measures of defiance to the victorious foe, Gunnery Sergeant John Cemeris, the Wake Detachment's machine-gun maintenance sergeant and the second in command of the Mobile Reserve, unaware of the surrender, fired briefly at a low-flying floatplane, which soon began trailing smoke and flew off out of sight. Cemeris's target may have been one of the four aircraft (two Mitsubishi F1M Type 00 reconnaissance seaplanes and two Nakajima Type 00 E13A1 reconnaissance seaplanes) that the *Kiyokawa Maru* had launched to reconnoiter and, each plane carrying two sixty-kilogram bombs, to bomb Wake. Three of the *Kiyokawa Maru* air unit planes had to make emergency landings; two landed off Wake proper around 1045, a third at sea at 1133, perhaps attempting to reach the ship, where the *Kinryu Maru* hoisted it on board at 1224. Antiaircraft fire also apparently damaged a floatplane from the *Chikuma* so badly that it capsized upon landing and had to be abandoned.

Cemeris, however, was not alone in his defiance. Marines on Wilkes, ignorant of the surrender, still carried on the fight. During the course of the bombing and strafing of Wilkes, Sergeant Coulson, who had exhibited coolness under fire throughout the siege, kept his gun in operation for nearly two hours while near misses shook his emplacement and strafing tore up the ground nearby.

The *Hiryū*'s three *kansen*s from her seventeenth *shōtai* and nine *kankō*s from the carrier's fortieth, forty-second, and forty-sixth *shōtai*s under Lieutenant Commander Kusumi made up the fifth and last wave of planes hurled against Wake (they carried out their low-level mission between 1150 and 1306). At about 1230 the marines at Battery L spotted small boats standing toward the channel between Wilkes and Wake and what appeared to be several transports and warships lying about four thousand yards out.

Sergeant Coulson informed Captain Platt, who then ordered McAlister, McKinstry, and Coulson to round up all available men and the two .30-caliber Brownings and start out for the old channel and engage the Japanese as soon as possible. As the marines set off in that direction, Platt spotted a destroyer—possibly the *Yunagi* or the *Oite*—standing in, about two thousand yards off the channel entrance. After inspecting the three-inch and five-inch guns and finding that "none would shoot," Platt headed for the channel himself. *Kankō*s from the *Hiryū*, however, dropped sixty-kilogram bombs in the vicinity; one killed twenty-year-old Private First Class Robert L. Stevens while Platt's men were en route to their new positions. Stevens, who was greatly respected by his messmates for his "intelligence, devotion to duty, and quick response to unusual situations,"[5] was the last combat casualty suffered by the marines on Wake Island.

About 1300, Devereux reached Wilkes; soon a destroyer stood in and began shelling the island, but after a flurry of urgent signals, the ship checked fire. Almost a half hour later, at a point between the old and new channels, Devereux spotted "a few grubby, dirty men who came out of the brush with their rifles ready." They were Platt's men, and they laid down their arms in reluctant obedience and surrendered. By 1400, eleven hours after the first Japanese sailors had splashed ashore, Wake lay in the hands of the enemy, and Rear Admiral Kajioka got to see the place that had been the scene of "one of the most humiliating defeats" the Imperial Japanese Navy had ever suffered just twelve days before.[6]

The victorious Japanese began rounding up the Americans—marines, sailors, Captain Wilson's small communications detachment, and civilians—and herded them toward the airfield; as the occupation proceeded, the last of Abe's planes returned to their ships, Lieutenant Commander

Sergeant Raymond L. Coulson, 25 November 1940, one of the heroes of the fighting on Wilkes. (USMC)

Kusumi's group landing on board the *Hiryū* at 1415 to wind up the day's close-support activities. The honor of conducting the last flight operations also fell to the *Hiryū*, when, at 1705, she started recovering the four *kanbaku*s that had carried out local air patrols over the task force. Of the fifty planes from the *Hiryū* and the *Sōryū* engaged (the crew of one had suffered wounds), ten had returned to their respective carriers with holes in them.

From his vantage point atop his command post, Barney Barninger watched the Japanese rounding up prisoners at the airfield and saw the victors strip their captives and bind them with wire. He could also see the invasion fleet arrayed around the atoll—twenty-seven ships, he estimated—particularly impressed by what looked like a division of heavy cruisers some three thousand yards off, "beautiful new ships," probably Rear Admiral Goto's.

As dusk neared, Barninger and his men still awaited the victorious Japanese. Not wanting still to be in the position at night and have the Japanese come to them, Barninger had his men fall in and, under a white flag, marched to the airfield, where he saw men still alive whom he had feared dead. Explaining why he left the position, he reasoned: "The Nips were too excitable, and I didn't trust such a turnover in the dark." Waiting until the Japanese arrived "seemed like a very bad thing" to do. The SLF troops relieved Battery A's men of their gear when the marines reached the airfield but allowed them to retain their clothing—a

Private Robert L. Stevens, ca. 1941, the last battle casualty at Wake. (USMC)

great concession, Barninger thought, especially in view of the treatment he had seen accorded the prisoners taken earlier.

John Hamas was among those captives ordered into the hospital dugout, which soon became "crowded to the point of suffocation." Standing near the door, Hamas, who had picked up a few words of the language while he had been stationed in Shanghai, asked an elderly Japanese naval officer if Dr. Kahn's hands could be untied so he could attend to the casualties. The enemy officer soon released both Kahn's and Hamas's hands. Later, when Hamas saw the same officer and showed him the swollen hands of the men around him, the Japanese allowed Hamas to loosen the wires. Soon thereafter, the enemy approved the release of all wire, produced some cigarettes, and allowed First Lieutenant Lewis and Hamas to gather up some of the clothes that the marines had been forced to leave alongside the road. A few hours passed, and the Japanese herded their prisoners to the airfield, where the men, insufficiently clad and unprotected from the rain and wind, dug into the hard coral with their bare hands, seeking protection from the chill easterly breezes. Small portions of bread and water were their only fare. John Valov, at the cost of being kicked and pummeled by his captors, hung on to the battered raincoat he had been wearing when he had been wounded and shared it with Sergeant Wade, the two huddling together in the cold.

Some distance away to the east, other marines would feel a gnawing discomfort of another sort. On board the *Tangier,* during the voyage out from Pearl Harbor, Fourth Defense Battalion marines had paid "minute individual attention to weapons," honed their bayonets, studied every chart and map available, and designed "improvised forward-area sights" so that the three-inchers could provide direct fire on ground targets, while the machine-gun detachment commander prevailed upon the ship's force to "construct slings with which his .50-caliber machine guns could be hoisted from ship to barges in the full ready position to ward off enemy attacks while unloading." Matters of disembarkation and unloading proved a topic of much discussion en route; one last-ditch scenario included beaching the *Tangier* to ensure delivery of men and matériel. Around sunset on the twenty-third, those marines topside noticed "that the ship's shadow fell in the wrong direction." Soon thereafter, as the realization dawned that the task force was heading east, not west, "a physically tangible sense of futility and failure took possession of marines who had already come to identify Wake's survival with their own."[7]

On board the *Astoria,* Frank Jack Fletcher talked with his "makie-learn" passenger, Tom Kinkaid. Fletcher told Kinkaid that members of his staff had urged him to ignore the recall order earlier that day but that he felt duty bound to obey it. "I could do nothing else," Fletcher said, "could I?" Kinkaid, as he later remembered the conversation, answered clearly, distinctly, and conclusively: "No."[8]

Kinkaid later praised those "sound decisions [reached] in those very difficult circumstances." Although he "deeply regretted" the suffering and hardships suffered by Wake's defenders, Kinkaid believed that neither Pye nor Fletcher could have prevented it; they had, instead, prevented what Kinkaid considered the "useless sacrifice of valuable ships which later saw action with our enemy in circumstances of vital importance." Later, Kinkaid talked with Vice Admiral Pye about the latter's reasons for recalling the Wake relief expedition. "With an apologetic expression on his face," Kinkaid recounted, "he said that he and his staff had carefully considered all of the circumstances in light of the information available" in deciding to recall Fletcher. "He did not know whether or not that was the correct decision, but it was in accordance with his best judgment." Pye's decision reminded Kinkaid of an axiom he had heard early in his career: "Sometimes it takes more nerve to turn back than it does to keep going." Pye's orders to Fletcher, Kinkaid concluded, "followed the intelligent and courageous course rather than the one most likely to be popular."[9]

On board the *Enterprise*, in Task Force 8, the ship that had ferried VMF-211 to Wake a little over three weeks before, Ensign James G. Daniels III, of VF-6, wrote in his diary: "Heard that Wake has been lost. It's a damn shame with 3 carriers out here that we haven't been able to help them out."[10] Fighting Six's scribe put it less delicately: "Everyone seems to feel that it's a war between the two yellow races. Wake was attacked this morning and probably surrendered with the *Saratoga* but 200 [she was 425] miles away and us steaming in circles east of the 180th [meridian]. No reports on the news about it as yet. If only the *Sara* would hit Wake."[11] On board the heavy cruiser *Chicago*, screening the *Lexington*, one of her officers bitterly lamented Wake's fall. "Too little and too late," Lieutenant Ward Bronson confided bitterly to his diary, "The old American way."[12]

The *Japan Times and Advertiser* crowed, "Island of Wake Occupied by Japanese Navy Force," in its evening edition on 24 December. The announcement, released at 1100 that day, proclaimed that the invaders had landed "in defiance of high seas and [a] violent gale" and had overcome "fierce enemy resistance" to attain their goal. An Imperial Navy spokesman admitted the loss of two destroyers in the engagement. A further report on the landings two days later mentioned that the captured garrison had been under a Commander "Cumming," not, as American

SLF sailors pay homage to the memory of Lieutenant (j.g.) Uchida Kinichi, whose unit lost two officers and twenty-nine enlisted men killed and thirty-four wounded in the attack on Wake. (NA, USMC Photo 315175)

press reports soon declared, under Major Devereux.[13] Japanese press reports called the island "one vast fort" but soon belittled the defenders, declaring that "it was not so much the magnificent fighting put up by the defenders . . . as the natural elements which exacted the price of two destroyers."[14] Ironically, in stating who was in command of the garrison, the Japanese press reports proved more accurate than the American.

That same day on Wake, 24 December, the Japanese allowed the defenders to bury their dead. Captain Tharin and Gunner Hamas volunteered to located the bodies, and a detail of thirty marines trudged out on their sad errand. They committed the remains of the men who had perished in defense of the airfield—four marines (including Captain Elrod) and twelve civilians—to the soil they had fallen in defense of, with only a two-foot mound of gravel and sand as a marker. Of the roughly 900 men who came ashore on Wake on 23 December from

Kajioka's ships, 8 officers and 103 enlisted men had been killed; 5 officers (including Commander Tanaka, the landing force commander) and 92 enlisted men had been wounded.

That afternoon, Gunner Hamas accompanied First Lieutenant Lewis over to the ruins of Camp 1 and gathered up two seabags of clothing to bring back to the "rockpile." After their return, they and their fellow defenders learned of the proclamation that had been issued stating "that the entire islands of Wake, are now the property of the Great Empire of Japan." Said empire, the public notice went on, "who loves peace and respects justice has been obliged to take arms against the challenge of President Roosevelt. Therefore, in accordance with the peace-loving spirit of the Great Empire of Japan, [the] Japanese Imperial Navy will not inflict any harms to those people—though they have been our enemy—who do not hold hostility against us in any respect. So, they be in peace!" Turning over the proclamation, however, one read: "But, whoever violates our spirit or whoever are not obedient shall be severely punished."

While Wake's erstwhile defenders grimly sat under the gaze of their guards, on board the *Kiyokawa Maru* as she steamed toward the atoll of Taongi in the northern Marshalls, Warrant Officer Nemeto Kumesaka, of the seaplane carrier's air unit, contemplated the fate of the captives. "Tomorrow is Christmas Day for foreigners," he confided to his diary on 24 December, "the hearts of the defenders of Wake and their families who have been defeated just before the day must be full of deep emotion. I feel sympathetic despite the fact that they are our enemy. There is an old saying: 'love your enemy.' They were defeated after they had done their best. . . . I hope the best thought will be given to the defeated officers and allow them to spend their last Christmas night in comfort. Pity your enemy," he concluded, "but hate his deeds."[15]

Whether or not the Japanese did so out of pity, at sundown on Christmas Day on Wake, they marched the prisoners to the contractors' barracks in Camp 2, segregating the officers into the cottages near Heel Point. Cunningham, assigned John D. Rogge, a twenty-one-year-old CPNAB clerk, as a personal aide, shared the guest cottage with Captain Platt, Captain Wilson, and Herman Hevenor; Devereux shared the contractors' cottage with Dan Teters, Commander Keene, and other officers from the defense battalion. After moving the captives to the CPNAB cantonment, the Japanese provided medical care to the sick and wounded and began issuing food—"mostly stews made from beef heart and liver with some bread, butter, and tea with sugar." The enemy took Major Putnam and Captain Tharin to their headquarters and questioned them.

On 26 December, the Japanese detailed the majority of the civilian prisoners to begin the work of clearing debris, building gun emplacements, and setting up barbed wire entanglements. Almost miraculously in view of the small size of the atoll, two CPNAB men—forty-five-year-old Fred J. Stevens, a sheet metal worker, and fifty-year-old Logan Kay, a carpenter—remained at large on Wake for seventy-seven days until, finally despairing of the arrival of American forces to recapture the atoll, they gave themselves up.

On Christmas Day at Pearl Harbor (26 December on Wake), after having been delayed by bad weather on the west coast, Rear Admiral Chester Nimitz arrived to assume command of the Pacific Fleet. Out of touch with developments concerning the efforts to relieve the siege of the atoll, he asked about the relief efforts as soon as he reached Pearl but had to be told the sad news—a gloomy beginning to his tour.

"Probably all of our people on Wake are gone by this time," Lieutenant Colonel Larkin wrote to Brigadier General Rowell that same day, "we can get no information other than wild rumors . . . Putnam's outfit to the last really lived up to the best traditions of the Marine Corps, and certainly their fight should go down in history as one of the outstanding events of this war." Undoubtedly with a heavy heart, Larkin concluded "We all, out here, feel their loss more than I can say."[16] He soon embarked upon a campaign to see that the men from MAG-21 received appropriate decorations for valor, with Rowell "upping the ante" to recommend strongly that Paul Putnam be awarded the Medal of Honor.

Over the next several days at Wake, the victors questioned the vanquished. Rear Admiral Kajioka and members of his staff interrogated Cunningham principally about the location of arms, munitions, and mines. Cunningham spoke at length one evening with one commander who seemed "mostly concerned with Japan's moral justification for launching the war." At one point in the conversation the Japanese officer asked the man who had commanded Wake during the siege whether he had sent the "Send us more Japs" dispatch. "I did not claim the honor," Cunningham replied, to which his interrogator said, "In any case, it is damn good propaganda."

Japanese war correspondent Ando Akiro inspected Wake soon after its capture. Mirroring the thoughts of Japanese military men, the state of the island fortifications prompted Ando to speculate that "if the occupation [of Wake] . . . had been delayed for two or three months," the Japanese would have had to employ greater forces and suffered greater casualties. He noted the excavations for the seaplane and submarine base and the concrete foundations for "barracks, hospitals, hotels, warehouses," and other buildings. "Dredgers . . . numerous tractors, caterpillars, cranes, and cement mixers" abounded, as did "several thousand tons" of iron and lumber. He described the CPNAB barracks in Camp 2, styled as "temporary" structures, as "grand and not inferior to our first-rate hotels." He marveled at the water distillation and purification systems, the water coolers, the washrooms, and the plumbing—even the screened windows. "It is indeed America," he reported, "there is a drifting scent of America's pride in modern living." Although many of the oil and gasoline storage facilities at Wake had been destroyed, "mountains of canned goods" remained. He noted the weapons that had been emplaced at Wake, the fire-control devices, the "air raid shelters, batteries, and trenches."[17]

In the course of his visit to Wake, Ando saw the beached patrol craft on the south shore, ropes and lines dangling into the surging surf. Rushing waves washed the stern of a boat that lay partially submerged, its plating "unsparingly perforated by numerous bullets." He took note of the beach, with its "bullet-marked rocks to which our brave soldiers [sic] clung," the defenders' dugouts and trenches, and the abundance of personal gear. He saw "numerous cartridge cases" in the vicinity of each battery—mute testimony to the ferocity of the fighting that had taken place. He noted bloodstains, too. He saw the tomb of Lieutenant Uchida, the fragrance of the wood still fresh.[18]

The rolling aftershocks from the disaster at Pearl Harbor continued to be felt throughout the month of December 1941. Five days after Wake fell, Admiral Kimmel testified before the commission chaired by Supreme Court Associate Justice Owen J. Roberts when it met to investigate what had happened on 7 December and the chain of events that had led up to it. When the questioning touched Wake Island, Kimmel's defensive responses betrayed a noticeable sensitivity to the fact that Wake had fallen. He vigorously defended his strategy of building up the outlying base in hopes of compelling the Japanese to expose their fleet units to attack by the Pacific Fleet. Although he remained convinced of the soundness of that strategy, he admitted that "after this affair here [the Japanese attack on Pearl] the picture change[d] considerably from what we anticipated" regarding the ability to follow through on those plans that had been so carefully crafted during 1941. The Japanese had simply not wanted to play the role that Kimmel wanted them to in his scenario for the opening of the Pacific war. He had suspected that the enemy would try to capture Wake, but he had come to discount the possibility that that enemy would attack his fleet's home base as a prelude.[19]

Even while Kimmel was defending his stewardship of the fleet, the men he had hoped to help, Wake's erstwhile defenders, were still hoping fervently that a U.S. Navy task force would show up to liberate them. Some thought of ways to escape, and most nurtured the hope that they would be rescued. For some of the prisoners of war, however, the rigors of captivity at the hands of a cruel enemy, even for a comparatively short period, proved too much to bear. On 3 January 1942, dysentery claimed thirty-five-year-old Joe McDonald, the contractors' recreation director, who had been one of the last CPNAB men to arrive at Wake on board the *Wright* on her last visit to the atoll and whom Cunningham would later commend for his work during the siege maintaining shelters for the hospital staff. The same disease claimed the life of Private First Class Alexander B. Venable, Jr., of Battery E, on 7 January. A second civilian died on the eleventh. The rest were told on 12 January 1942 that they were to prepare to embark on board the *Nitta Maru*.

Wake's prisoners of war (POWs)—with the exception of those either still too badly wounded or too sick to travel or CPNAB men chosen for their specific trades (such as heavy equipment operators)—were ferried out to the former *Nippon Yusen Kaisha* (*NYK*) liner to be transported out. The *Nitta Maru*, originally built for the European trade, had been hastily converted to a troop transport. She had sailed from Yokohama to Kure, to proceed thence on a special mission that, at the outset, was not disclosed to her crew.

The commander of the prisoner escort issued draconian regulations that threatened death to anyone who disobeyed them. Those infractions included "disobeying orders and instructions . . . showing a motion of antagonism and raising a sign of opposition . . . disordering [disobeying] the regulations by individualism, egoism, thinking only about yourself, rushing for your own goods . . . talking without permission and raising

Sightseeing Japanese sailors visit one of the two underground hangars at the airfield on Wake; inside sits 211-F-8, flown by Captain Herbert C. Freuler when he splashed two *kankōs* from the *Sōryū* on 22 December 1941. (NA, USMC Photo 315177)

Japanese photo of 3-inch/.50-
caliber M3 antiaircraft gun
on M2A2 mount. Note
camouflaged barrel and
unpainted recoil area. The
gun may be from the
provisional Battery F
(Wilkes), around which
fighting raged on the
twenty-third, or from
Battery E (Wake), the only
fully operational antiaircraft
battery by the end of the
battle. (D. Y. Louie)

Aerial view of Camp 2 on Wake, looking roughly northeasterly (north
beach of Wake is at top, lagoon at right) probably take around the time of
the Japanese capture of the island. Note bomb-demolished barrack units
to left of center, aggregate plant (top), and storehouses. (NA, USMC
Photo 315179)

loud voices. . . . walking and moving without order . . . carrying unnecessary baggage in embarking . . . resisting . . . touching the boat's
[ship's] materials, wires, electric lights, tools, switches, etc. . . . climbing ladders without order[s] . . . showing action of running away from
the room or boat . . . trying to take more meal than given to them . . .
using more than two blankets."[20]

Noting that the ship was not well equipped and her "inside being
narrow," the Japanese explained that the food was scarce and poor. They
enjoined the prisoners not to lose patience; those who did would be
"heavily punished." They also instructed the prisoners to finish their
"Nature's call," evacuating their bowels and urinating, before embarking. The prisoners were to be fed twice a day; one plate was to be
given each man. Prisoners called by the guard would distribute the meals
as "quick as possible and honestly," while the remaining men stood in
their places "quietly and wait[ing] for [their] plate." Those moving from
their places or reaching for their plate without orders would be "heavily
punished." The same orders pertained after the meal was over.

The regulations stated that toilet facilities would be placed in each
corner of the prisoners' compartment; once the buckets and cans used

Civilian contractors march off to captivity after the Japanese captured
Wake. (NA, USMC Photo 315174)

The smiles masking their depression, Wake POWs, including Dan Teters and Commander Cunningham (foreground) and Commander Keene and Lieutenant (j.g.) Kahn (standing, behind Teters and Cunningham), try to look cheerful for their captors, Yokohama, 18 January 1942, on board the *Nitta Maru*. (*Freedom*)

Technical Sergeant Earl R. Hannum, 31 July 1941, one of the two marines and three sailors beheaded on board the *Nitta Maru* on 23 January 1942. (USMC)

for that purpose were filled, a guard would appoint a prisoner to take the buckets to the center of the compartment, whence the filled containers would be hoisted topside and disposed of. Toilet paper would be provided and the prisoners were told that "everyone must cooperate to make the room sanitary." Men who were "careless" would be "punished."

The regulations concluded by stating that the "Navy of the Great Japanese Empire will not try to punish you all with death. Those obeying all the rules and regulations, and believing the action and purpose of the Japanese Navy, cooperating with Japan in constructing the 'New Order of the Great Asia' which lead to the world's peace will be well treated." The Japanese hoisted the captives on board in cargo nets and confined the officers to the ship's mailroom and the remainder—enlisted men and civilians—on the same deck level in the hold. Upon embarkation, the Japanese forced Cunningham and the others to run a gauntlet while the enemy crewmen kicked, pounded, or slapped them and relieved them of any items they had carried on board. Cunningham and the other officers, including Herb Freuler, whose shoulder wound (suffered in combat on 22 December) had become badly infected, remained closely confined in the same compartment, forbidden on pain of immediate death from talking, moving about, using tobacco, or washing or bathing. Captain Platt violated the rules by talking one day; but instead of death, he was taken from the compartment and beaten severely. Cunningham and the others heard the beating in progress nearby but could not see what was happening.

Japanese propagandists took pictures at Yokohama showing smiling prisoners of war—Cunningham, Dan Teters, Campbell Keene, and Gus Kahn. Cunningham later explained that he and the others had exhibited "the appearance of being in a happy frame of mind" so as not to give their captors the satisfaction of knowing that they were, in fact, depressed and feeling keenly their mistreatment.[21] Upon arrival at Yokohama, Japanese authorities removed Major Putnam, Second Lieutenant Kliewer, Technical Sergeant Hamilton, Staff Sergeant Arthur, and Corporal Gruber from VMF-211's contingent. The five would remain in Japan for the duration of the war.

For those who remained in the *Nitta Maru*, events took an uglier turn. Two days out, Lieutenant Saito Toshio, chief of the guard unit, singled out five men at random and ordered them removed from the hold in which they had been detained—Technical Sergeant Hannum, who had labored with such diligence as VMF-211's leading line chief until felled by dysentery, Technical Sergeant Bailey, one of Major Bayler's radiomen, and three sailors, Seamen Second Class Franklin, who had gallantly worked with VMF-211, Roy J. Gonzales, and John W. Lambert—and taken to B deck, blindfolded, bound, and then decapitated.

Ultimately, the *Nitta Maru* reached Shanghai, and the rest of the prisoners were taken ashore for confinement.

For the vanquished, whatever lessons there were to learn from the loss of Wake would have to be discussed in detail after the passage of years. Commander Cunningham attempted unsuccessfully to escape in March 1942. Major Devereux, however, managed to transmit a cryptic message dealing with the loss of Wake, what guns the Japanese had moved in before his departure, and recommendations concerning offensive and defensive tactics, as well as brief advice for future landing operations, via Lieutenant D. E. Kermode, Royal Naval Reserve, in late 1942. Kermode delivered it to the Royal Navy's intelligence department, which in turn passed it along to General Holcomb, and thence to Admiral Ernest J. King in January 1943.[22]

One immediate effect of Wake's fall on the American war effort was to hamper further deliveries of heavy bombers to the besieged Philippines. It also necessitated "the immediate development of an alternate trans-Pacific route" that employed airfields at Christmas and Canton islands, a route already under consideration and under construction before Pearl Harbor, as well as at Fiji and New Caledonia. Until completion of the necessary facilities along the way, deliveries of B-17s, Consolidated LB-30s, and B-24s had to take place via Miami, Florida, Brazil, equatorial Africa, and India, through Sumatra to Java and Australia. The Japanese occupation of Sumatra in January 1942, however, closed off that route.[23] The fate of the CPNAB workers confirmed the problem of having civilians in a war zone, an issue already addressed by the formation, in October 1941, of the first incipient construction battalion (CB, or "Seabee" unit).

The Japanese pondered several aspects of their conquest of Wake. Surmising that the marines anticipated their attack on the south shore of Wake by concentrating the defenses there, Japanese observers declared that a plan of attack used previously should not be used again. They emphasized that their "method of operation be bound only by the progress of the battle" and that they must take the enemy by surprise. One enemy observer wrote, "There are many cases where it is necessary for the soldier to value speed more than finesse." They alluded to the success of the opening air attack but attributed rising losses to the marines' antiaircraft fire becoming "better and better organized."[24]

Apparently, the Japanese—who also praised the defenders for strengthening their defenses during the period—had not realized that the marines had learned to anticipate about when the midday air raid would arrive. "Their original raid [on 8 December] was tactically well conceived and skillfully executed," Paul Putnam wrote later, "but thereafter their tactics were stupid . . . the best that can be said of their skills is that they had excellent flight discipline. The hour and the altitude of their arrival over the island was almost constant and their method of attack invariable, so that it was a simple matter to meet them . . . they invariably arrived within an hour of noon at approximately 20,000 feet and in a single, tightly packed formation."

Despite the apparent almost slavish adherence to a set time and place of carrying out the bombing of Wake Island, the overall "issue of victory," wrote one Japanese, lay in the "maintenance of the offensive spirit." The Japanese attributed their success to the "fact that . . . the offensive spirit was continuously displayed and all hands fought without regard for their own lives." The enemy praised the "spirit of self-sacrifice" displayed by the SLF on Wilkes and Wake and attributed the collapse of the defenders to that very spirit, apparently ignoring the fact that Platt's men on Wilkes nearly annihilated Takano's landing force. "The factor deciding the final victory," declared one Japanese, "was spiritual strength."

The Japanese assessed the need, when landing on a "very strongly defended strategic island," to make detailed preparations to simplify operations plans and prevent confusion. Their organization and equipment had to allow troops to fight independently in the daytime. Evidencing a hearty respect for the seacoast batteries, those Japanese who evaluated the Wake Island occupation wrote that when the "enemy's main batteries . . . cannot be captured before daybreak," it was "often impossible to get fire support from the ships during the day."

In silencing heavy guns—perhaps alluding to the fire laid down on Peacock Point on the twenty-third—Japanese evaluators lauded the effectiveness of hand grenades and grenade throwers at night. For daytime action, the Japanese deemed it necessary to have ample supplies of machine guns and "infantry cannon" available.

Those who evaluated the Wake Island operation recommended that the landing of the "first line fighting strength" had to be made "at once." As American amphibious planners learned later, "it often happens that motor boats used in the first landing become stranded and cannot be used for another trip."

When landing on a defended shore, Japanese evaluators opined, "it is absolutely essential to complete the landing before daybreak." The earlier the landing, the more effective it would be. Although the Japanese (with the exception of the elements of the Itaya Company that landed near daybreak) had stormed ashore on Wake and Wilkes four hours before sunrise, the old saying that "the hours of the night are short" proved only "too true." Evaluators urged allowing extra time to allow for delays in launching landing craft—as occurred at Wake. Nevertheless, the Japanese ability to get ashore under the conditions that prevailed in the predawn darkness of 23 December impressed their adversaries. "The overall impression I had," observed Major Potter subsequently, "is that they were highly trained troops who worked very well under those particular circumstances; they executed the landing very well against dispersed opposition on a pitch black night with about a 30-knot wind blowing from the northeast—both factors in their favor."[25]

In assessing their landing boats and the speed of the shoreward movement, the Japanese felt that the approach should be made at "half speed," or low speed, until the objective could be seen. Admitting the danger involved in such a course, those who evaluated the Wake operations felt that once the objective was in sight, speed should be increased. They believed that the speed with which the landing had been carried out had confused the defenders. Although the *Patrol Boat No. 33* had been under fire on the run-in, the Japanese deemed the handling of the searchlight "unskillful" (they had no way of knowing that it had not worked well since the bombing of Wilkes early in the siege) and that the machine-gun fire either overshot or struck near the ship's stern. The Japanese also admitted that "it is easy to mistake the landing point at night" because none of the four landing craft "arrived at the appointed time or place."

The Japanese reiterated the absolute necessity for a surprise attack once the SLF reached shore. They counseled against rifle fire that drew "fierce" machine gun fire; in the Wake operation, an observer wrote, "the landing force hardly fired a shot until daybreak," relying instead on "enveloping attacks and hand grenades." The Japanese should eschew firearms for hand grenades and grenade throwers, which proved particularly effective, in their estimation, against machine-gun nests and trenches. The fondness for stealth, Major Potter opined, may have cost the Japanese dearly: "In more than one instance, their inclination to use the bayonet rather than a bullet cost them their lives."[26]

The durability of Wake's defenses impressed the Japanese. They acknowledged the difficulty of destroying the land (i.e., seacoast) batteries with ships' gunfire, as well as by aerial bombing. They urged more direct cooperation, particularly the use of spotting planes (none were launched over the island on 11 December to spot the fall of shot because none of the ships were capable of operating aircraft) and deemed such cooperation "absolutely essential." They allowed, however, that "detailed reconnaissance" of an enemy's positions by air to be "extremely difficult." They also acknowledged the problems of bombarding air bases from the sea, noting that the shoreline on Wake prevented them from seeing airplanes operating from the airstrip.

Communications failures plagued the Japanese almost as much as they did Wake's defenders. Radios were rendered inoperable by water or "severe shocks" and could not be used for communicating between ship and shore. Water ruined rockets and Very pistols, and the Japanese found it difficult to distinguish between the flares that did work and the tracers from the defenders' machine guns. The evaluators stressed the need for simple communications, perfecting them "to maintain [a] close liaison" between the SLF troops on shore and the ships offshore. At Wake, the complete severance of such communication "between the landing force and the sea forces . . . caused great difficulties in the conduct of the operation."

Evaluating American tactics, the Japanese observed that the defenders had put two or three men in front of the position who would fire at approaching enemy troops and then fall back, drawing the SLF up to their position. Those who evaluated those tactics may have had in mind the operations of Captain Elrod in protecting the ammunition carriers at the airfield; he operated out ahead of his men.

Second Lieutenant Hanna's defense of the antiboat gun on Wake's south beach apparently impressed the Japanese, as a diagram shows an antiaircraft gun surrounded by men armed with machine guns, rifles, and pistols—an adequate description of the emplacement defended with such vigor on 23 December. The Japanese recounted taking "great loss" in battle in their frontal assault, so they advised encircling such a position and lobbing grenades into it in future battles.

They also noted how the Americans posted skirmishers some two to three hundred meters ahead of the position, armed with a light machine gun (probably a Thompson), who would fire a burst and then withdraw to a nearby trench, remaining concealed until the Japanese had passed by. Then the Americans would open fire and throw the enemy's rear into disorder.

To deal with that, the Japanese advocated dividing the landing force into assault troops and a mopping-up force. They recounted "bitter fighting" as the result of pockets of resistance being overlooked (Ray's, McAnally's, and Kliewer's positions; Poindexter's counterattack; and perhaps the battle on Wilkes). A mopping-up force would see to it that positions to the assault force's rear would be grenaded (two or three in each place), thus "thoroughly occupying the ground and firmly securing our rear."

The Japanese had noted numerous American positions scattered throughout the heavy brush, as well as the well-dispersed ammunition so that if the guns were moved they could continue the fight from any position. The "great many" small machine gun nests formed the backbone of the defense and "cleverly utilized the terrain and natural cover," making it difficult to detect them from either aerial or frontal observation. Unless an American moved around, he could not be seen.

A similar situation obtained from the defenders' viewpoint, as Potter later remarked: "Due to their [the Japanese] expert use of camouflage and concealment they were hard to locate individually after daybreak."[27]

The American machine guns had inflicted great losses upon the attacking Japanese in frontal assaults, while the unfamiliar terrain made maneuvering difficult. Once the Japanese had penetrated the thick brush, the cover it provided allowed them to consolidate their forces as, for example, the SLF force Poindexter noted assembling after his unit near Camp 1 had surrendered. The Japanese also noted that the Americans rarely, if ever, counterattacked—obviously the efforts of Platt's and Poindexter's forces made no lasting impression upon them. As a lesson learned, one enemy observer opined that that was something that the Japanese could capitalize on later.

The Japanese did, however, apparently notice the skill with which Private First Class Schumacher and his section had carried out their displacement toward Camp 1, for the "lessons learned" carries the notation that even while changing positions, the defenders conducted a "sweeping fire." One American intelligence analyst who read the "lessons learned" from Wake opined that the Japanese respect for the .50-caliber machine gun was born at Wake Island. Japanese observers noted the "extremely high rate of fire" of the American weapons. "Even if it is at short range," one enemy analyst wrote, "one should not disdain the accuracy and effect of their fire." While the Japanese noted that "spiritual strength" overpowers firepower, they did note that "all American soldiers [sic] make much good use of their firearms. Their manner of fighting," they concluded, "is extremely stubborn." The "rank and file," the Japanese observed—presumably referring to the CPNAB workmen as a whole—possessed "absolutely no fighting spirit," but the "fighting spirit" of the American military men "seems fairly high."

Joint operations between land and naval air forces needed work. "The first principle of cooperation between land and air forces in an attack against a land position," one Japanese evaluator wrote, "is to make certain proper recognition of friend and enemy." Strict attention had to be paid to marking the front lines. "Unsatisfactory" recognition markings rendered adequate cooperation difficult. While the "relative inexperience" of the aircrew from the *Hiryū* and the *Sōryū* may have been a factor, the Japanese felt that "in the future it appears necessary to demand more attention be given" to close air support by carrier planes. The Imperial Army's air-ground communication system possessed too many detailed rules; the navy, for its part, needed to develop "simple visual signals" to solve that problem. And unless "definite preliminary arrangements" were made, joint operations with navy planes performing "urgent and unforeseen" missions, such as those carried out by the

Hiryū and the *Sōryū* pilots, would be "most difficult." The *Hiryū* aircrew considered their missions to have been "very effective," but the *Sōryū*'s seemed to be less certain of how much damage they had inflicted.

The Japanese concluded that the carrier-based "Zero fighter" seemed "superior" to the Wildcat in both speed and fighting ability. There were reasons for the disparity in performance. "VMF-211's tactics," Paul Putnam later wrote, "due to the extremely limited number of airplanes, were largely individual." The pilots' lack of experience in the F4F-3, when coupled with the "home workshop repairs" that Kinney and his engineering staff had to carry out, meant that each plane possessed different performance characteristics (and quirks, as pilots of 211-F-8 could undoubtedly attest). Consequently, Putnam instructed his pilots to "fight individually to the best of their and their airplane's ability." His pilots disseminated and discussed information and combat experiences but no attempt was made to carry out any "combat control." The fight that VMF-211 had put up against the enemy convinced Putnam that if he could have "given the squadron 25 hours of tactical training, including gunnery, the results achieved in combat could have been improved several fold."

In summing up, the Japanese military appeared to be afflicted by the "victory disease" that infected their military as a result of its achievements at that stage of the war. Those enemy analysts who evaluated the Wake operation declared that "the enemy forces are, after all, easily beaten. Although they had forces equal to the invasion force and were in a fortified position, they were defeated in a half day's fighting." The "inescapable conclusion" that the Japanese drew from Wake was that "the American soldiers [sic] are at the beginning like lions but at the end are gentle like virgins."

The Americans, however, exhibited little gentleness toward Wake. U.S. Navy reconnaissance planes overflew the atoll in January and February of 1942, noting changes in gun positions and the addition of weapons brought in to strengthen the defenses and installed with conscripted CPNAB labor and equipment. Wake, or, as the Japanese renamed it, Otorishima, or "Bird Island," was first raided when planes from the *Enterprise* bombed the facilities there on 24 February 1942; ships from Rear Admiral Raymond A. Spruance's Cruiser Division Five also shelled the atoll.

Although the bombing and shelling hurt none of the wounded POWs confined on Wake or any of the CPNAB workmen, Japanese antiaircraft fire downed one plane from the *Enterprise*. The Japanese captured the crew, Ensign Percy W. Forman, A-V(N), and Aviation Machinist's Mate Second Class John E. Winchester and interrogated them before they were embarked in the freighter *Chichibu Maru* for transportation back to Japan. Unfortunately, they never reached their destination, for the submarine *Gar* (ss-206) torpedoed and sank the enemy merchantman off the entrance to the Inland Sea on 13 March 1942.

Eventually, barbed wire and tank traps ringed the island, the latter transversing it as well. Slit trenches, rifle pits, and roughly two hundred steel, concrete, and coral pillboxes took shape as the weeks passed. Eventually, the wire entanglements rusted away, and the remaining sharpened stakes, like abattis of old, pointed out to sea. Workers also built two fire-control centers of concrete, an additional concrete magazine (to go with the seven captured in December), twenty-five bombproof dugouts, and fifteen command posts. To beef up the seacoast battery, the Japanese brought in four 8-inch guns, four 6-inch guns, as well as four twin 5-inch dual-purpose mounts, six 4.7-inch guns, and a dozen twin 25-millimeter antiaircraft machine gun mounts. In addition, about half of the original battery of 5-inch seacoast and 3-inch antiaircraft guns could be made operational. "The guns and their fire control apparatus," one observer wrote, "represented a heterogenous collection which was too diversified, difficult to shoot with accuracy and a nightmare for the supply of spare parts and ammunition.[28]

In September 1942, the last group of CPNAB men were transported off Wake, leaving about one hundred—principally heavy-equipment operators and a division of labor that seemed to reflect that which Com-Fourteen had laid out in the plans to evacuate the contractors in the *Tangier*. Dr. Shank volunteered to remain with them to provide medical care. The virtual blockade of Wake, however, made routing shipping to the atoll a dangerous proposition.

Captain Sakaibara Shigemitsu, who had relieved Captain Kawasaki Susumu as island commander on 13 December 1942, subsequently ordered one CPNAB worker, charged with stealing food, beheaded in July 1943. Three months later, after two days of attacks by an American task force (5 and 6 October 1943), Sakaibara, on the night of the sixth, fearing that the strikes portended a landing and that one of the prisoners might escape and communicate the weaknesses of the defenses and the disposition of his garrison, ordered the remaining CPNAB men executed. One CPNAB man who had escaped before the massacre was eventually hunted down and caught ten days later, at which time Sakaibara personally slew him with his sword. "Riotous conduct among [the] prisoners," Sakaibara radioed his superiors to justify his actions. "Have executed them."[29]

The rest of Wake's POWs, military and civilian alike, persevered in prison camps in occupied China and in Japan for the duration. Some attempted to escape. Commander Cunningham (twice) and the imperturbable Sergeant Coulson failed, but others, such as Lieutenants Kinney and McAlister, succeeded. Some POWs—marines, sailors, soldiers, and civilians—perished as the result of the brutal mistreatment that was the hallmark of incarceration in Japanese camps, but most survived. They would forever bear the mental and physical scars of their imprisonment.

The war took a toll of the Japanese naval officers who led the *rikkō* or the flying boat raids on Wake or flew from the *Hiryū* or the *Sōryū*. Among them, from the Chitose *Kōkūtai*, Matsuda, who had led many of that group's raids, died on board the carrier *Shōkaku* while serving as her air officer during the Battle of the Philippine Sea on 19 June 1944; Nakai died attacking the carrier *Enterprise* on 1 February 1942 during the "Big E's" raid on the Marshalls; Kotani died on 8 August 1942 attacking Rear Admiral Turner's task force off Guadalcanal; Tashiro, of the Yokohama *Kōkūtai*, fell at Tulagi on 7 or 8 August 1942. Of the carrier pilots, Nōno died attacking a formation of British Blenheim bombers over the Indian Ocean in April 1942. On 4 June 1942, Kusumi, who had risen to become the *Kaga*'s air unit commander, died on board his ship at Midway, and a Wildcat splashed Lieutenant Kobayashi after his planes had stopped the *Yorktown* dead in the water with three bomb hits out of seven dropped. Lieutenant Kikuchi was shot down by marine fighters at Midway.

Rear Admiral Kajioka took part in the occupations of Rabaul, Lae and Salamaua, and Tulagi but apparently never forgot the air attacks on his ships off Wake, for he evinced great concern that fighter planes be based at Lae and Salamaua soon after the landings there in early March 1942. The planes were not deployed, and aircraft from the *Yorktown* and the *Lexington* sank the *Kongo Maru* while planes from the *Yorktown* damaged the *Kiyokawa Maru*—two Wake Island operation veterans. In addition, planes from those two carriers damaged his flagship, the *Yūbari*, and enough other ships to hamstring Japanese amphibious operations in that theater for some time. Assigned a shore command in September 1942, he was ultimately assigned the Sixth Escort Fleet in April 1944. Kajioka was killed in action on 12 September 1944 and was posthumously promoted to vice admiral.

A grandiose plan to recapture the island developed during 1942 was—fortunately—never attempted for it involved not only an amphibious assault, backed up by carrier air strikes and surface ship bombardments, but paratroop landings as well. No amphibious operation to recover Wake from the Japanese was ever mounted. Instead, Wake was isolated and bypassed. Passing task forces bombarded the island, and carrier planes used it for practice bombings; patrol planes from Midway and later from Kwajalein and Eniwetok (after the capture of the latter places in 1944) bombed the atoll frequently.

The war that had descended with such destructive suddenness on Wake on 8 December 1941 ended in mid-August 1945. On 3 September 1945, shortly after the signing of the surrender accords in Tokyo Bay, Rear Admiral Sakaibara surrendered Wake to Brigadier General Lawton H. M. Sanderson, commander of the Fourth Marine Aircraft Wing, on board the destroyer escort *Levy* (DE-162). At that time, 609 soldiers and 653 sailors made up the Japanese garrison. During the war, bombs and shells from American planes and warships had killed an estimated 600 Japanese; malnutrition and disease killed an estimated 1,288 and prompted the evacuation of a further 974 men. On the day of the surrender, Wake's hospital held some 405 patients, 200 of them bedridden. On hand for the raising of the Stars and Stripes was then Colonel Walt Bayler, whose unceremonious departure in December 1941 forever marked him as the "last man off Wake Island."

An occupation force of 15 naval officers and 126 enlisted men, 1 army officer, and 11 enlisted men arrived at Wake on 12 September, simultaneously with a marine detachment of 2 officers and 54 enlisted. Inspectors found the east-west landing strip in good condition (although no support facilities existed) and marked out the old PanAir seaplane lanes, with an assured depth of five feet at all locations. In the brush near the airstrip, the Americans discovered the broken remains of VMF-211's Wildcats. Three mooring buoys were planted during the early occupation period as well. Commander William Masek assumed command of the naval air facility at Wake.

Early on, the occupation forces removed the Japanese from Wake to Wilkes (army) and Peale (navy), from which 726 Japanese departed on 4 October in the hospital ship *Tachibana Maru*. The Americans confined the remaining Japanese on Peale. On 9 October, Captain Earl A. Junghans, who had flown gunfire spotting missions for the heavy cruiser *Northampton* during the February 1942 raid on Wake, relieved Bill Masek as officer in charge of the naval air facility and became atoll commander. On 30 October, the hospital ship *Hikawa Maru* arrived and embarked 519 Japanese, sailing on 1 November for Japan. The destroyer *Soley* (DD-707) arrived on 5 November, embarked Sakaibara and Colonel Chikamori Shigeharu, the senior Japanese army officer in the island garrison, a dozen other officers, and two enlisted aides, who had been questioned about the fate of the ninety-seven remaining contractors, then sailed for Kwajalein, arriving there on 10 November.

By the end of October, a naval air base organization was in place and a gasoline system ready for operation. The net-tenders *Sandalwood* (AN-32) and *Suncock* (AN-80), which had arrived during the last week of that month, soon began the work of lifting and replanting ship moorings and assisting in clearing obstacles from the boat basin. On 1 November 1945,

One of the 5-inch/.51-caliber seacoast guns on Wake, ca. September 1945. (Mrs. Virginia Putnam)

Wake was activated as an island command and a naval air base with Captain Junghans as island commander and commander, Naval Air Base, Wake.

On 25 November, a joint survey party arrived to look over naval facilities for prospective use by Pan American World Airways and departed the following day. By month's end, five of the fourteen-thousand-barrel gasoline tanks were complete, and work had commenced on the foundations for a Quonset hut to serve as a passenger terminal for the first of the Army Transportation Service flights that were to commence staging through Wake from Hickam Field to Tokyo on 2 December. Early the following month, the salvage vessel *Shackle* (ARS-9) arrived to begin salvage of the ill-starred *Columbia*, after which she would tow it to Pearl Harbor for overhaul.

War crimes trials that commenced at Kwajalein on 21 December 1945 soon revealed what had happened at Wake, and Sakaibara and two of his key subordinates (one of whom hung himself) were charged with the deaths of American civilians "in violation of the dignity of the United States of America, the International Rules of warfare and the moral standards of civilized society." Sakaibara took full responsibility for the deaths of the remaining prisoners. He was found guilty of murder and sentenced to death. Although the sentence for his surviving subordinate was commuted to life imprisonment, Sakaibara was hung on Guam on 18 June 1947, believing to the last that military necessity had compelled him to do what he did and that his trial and proceedings were "entirely unfair."[30]

No submarine or seaplane base was ever built on Wake, but it did serve as an air transport terminal for several years and briefly as the meeting place for General MacArthur and President Harry Truman during the Korean War; soon afterward, the chief executive sacked the general for insubordination. Some of Wake's marines—Godbold, McAlister, Hamilton, Kessler, and Gragg, among others—served in the Korean War and evidenced the same devotion to duty that they had exhibited amid the scrub and coral. Platt ultimately attained the rank of colonel; on the staff of the commander of the First Marine Division, he was inspecting the front in Korea on 27 September 1951 when a Chinese mortar shell exploded nearby. Seriously wounded in the neck and shoulder, he died at an army evacuation hospital later the same day.

Wake in the postwar years was a stop on commercial aviation routes on the itinerary of those aerial arteries to Asia once pioneered by PanAir (later known more familiarly as PanAm). One writer called Wake "earth's remotest service station," sandwiched between seemingly endless miles of sea and sky; some thirty planes a day used Wake's airstrip, about eleven thousand a year by the late 1950s. Wake's importance for commercial aviation dwindled with the coming of far-reaching jets and the establishment of the shorter polar routes.

What occurred there in December 1941, however, will be remembered as long as deeds of valor are recounted. Outnumbered and outgunned, doomed by the devastating way that the Japanese had unleashed the dogs of war in the Pacific, Wake's men had fought well, impressing their adversaries with their tenacious bravery as the first to turn back an attempted landing on American soil. Wake's defense had been one of the few bright spots of the first months of war in the Pacific, providing a shining example of heroism that Americans would take to heart. President Roosevelt awarded the first-ever Presidential Unit Citation to Major Devereux and Major Putnam and the defense forces at Wake, an oversight—in not mentioning Commander Cunningham, who had actually commanded the defenses—that would lead to bitterness after the close of hostilities and into decades thereafter as both Devereux and Cunningham sought to justify their place in history that their unvarnished deeds would have assured them anyway. (See Appendix 1.)

Sometimes overshadowed by the story of the battle for Wake is the work performed by the CPNAB workmen under Dan Teters before the tides of war engulfed the atoll. From the beginning, Teters's contractors had impressed the navy's resident officers in charge of the project with their efficiency. Quality-conscious, CPNAB maintained a strict schedule of detailed inspections for the workmanship of all buildings and structures; the inspections carried out by Lieutenant Butzine and Lieutenant Commander Greey found the work to be performed "in an efficient and workmanlike manner in accordance with plans and specifications." "It may be said," one progress report disclosed, "that the men are becoming more and more efficient" and that "some of those not so highly skilled are gaining valuable construction experience, many new men of ability are being discovered." Commander Dierdorff called the Wake project "the prettiest piece of teamwork I have ever seen."[31]

The same words might be applied to the defense of Wake. It conformed to the scenario that U.S. Navy and Marine Corps planners contemplated well before 8 December 1941: an understrength marine defense battalion, augmented by men from a marine air unit, men assigned to a naval air station, and civilians defending the base against an attack by a comparatively modest Japanese force made up of light cruisers and destroyers, supported in the end by carrier aviation. Despite the gallant efforts of the defenders, the enemy captured the island and garrisoned it. Wake's defense had truly been "a magnificent fight." That the crown of victory was not to be the defenders' in no way diminishes the bravery with which they sought to attain it.

THE CUNNINGHAM-DEVEREUX CONTROVERSY

Those persons overseeing the development of outlying Pacific bases gave much thought to the question of command. The dominant installation on places such as Midway and Wake was the naval air station, to operate both naval and Marine Corps aircraft; the defense battalions and defense battalion detachments existed to defend the air stations. Kimmel's study of the defenses at the outlying installations indicated that the base commander was to be a naval officer, a captain in Wake's case. Subordinate commanders were to advise the base commanders in their areas of expertise.

Brigadier General Charles F. B. Price, commander of the Department of the Pacific, during an autumn 1941 inspection, heard complaints that naval officers at outlying bases such as Midway, Wake, and Johnston were commanding marine officers who were their seniors. Price must have heard of the prospective situation at Wake because the station there had not yet received its commanding officer.[1]

On 8 December 1941 a naval officer, Commander Winfield S. Cunningham, commanded the overall base defense, and Major Devereux served as a "tactical and technical advisor" in "matters affecting [his] own forces." Major Putnam had orders only to "do what was appropriate" upon arrival at Wake and to report to neither Cunningham nor Devereux—a point to which he steadfastly adhered.

The issuance of the Presidential Unit Citation on 5 January 1942 to the Wake defenders mentioned only Devereux and Putnam but, in a most unfortunate oversight, not the island commander, who had been entrusted with coordinating the overall defense. Postwar attempts by Cunningham to get the wording changed to reflect the true command relationship failed because of the statute of limitations and the death of President Roosevelt.

The wartime American press concerning Wake largely ignored Cunningham; Devereux emerged as the hero. After the war, Devereux's articles in the *Saturday Evening Post* and his subsequent book gave short shrift to Cunningham, as did the official Marine Corps monograph,

Commander and Mrs. Winfield Scott Cunningham at a press conference, Washington, D.C., 7 October 1945; the latter's face reflects her determined efforts during the war to attain recognition for her husband's role in the defense of Wake, a role that was downplayed into nonexistence by wartime propaganda. (NA, 80-G-700886)

The Defense of Wake, by Colonel Heinl, who had been in the *Tangier* during the unsuccessful relief attempt. Critics praised *The Defense of Wake*—it was a ground-breaking study—but the marine historian apparently made no effort to interview Cunningham and emphasized the roles of the marines who did the fighting.

Commander Cunningham apparently did exercise command, according to the classic definition of "command"—which suggests the official exercise of authority—throughout the siege, but the wartime publicity accorded Devereux eventually came to be regarded as fact. Cunningham's irritation simmered over the years, and his book, *Wake Island Command,* came out well over a decade after his subordinate's. Both men showed an obvious concern for how posterity would view them and their actions.

Devereux set out to present "simply . . . a record of what happened on the island from my point of view as well as from the point of view of my subordinates." He had "no intention of presenting a historical document," even calling his book, *The Story of Wake Island,* a "romance

. . . not a history." Devereux admitted that a "ghost writer did the book after gathering a certain amount of information from me and from a number of my officers and men." Unhappy with the original result, he "toned [it] down a great deal."[2]

When asked who actually exercised command at Wake, John Kinney responded to interviewers in July 1945: "Commander Cunningham . . . actually exercised command. Major Devereux was in charge of the defense of the island, but he took his orders from Commander Cunningham. . . . Usually the top man gets credit in a military operation," he went on, "but this case seems to be different." Mrs. Cunningham, he noted, was "quite annoyed about it."[3]

Colonel Walt Bayler, when questioned on the subject in a 12 June 1947 interview, however, waxed "vitriolic" concerning Commander Cunningham. Bayler stated "emphatically" that Cunningham had caused Devereux "much hardship" and that "I was damned glad we had someone like Devereux out there. We couldn't have lasted a half-day with Cunningham as commander. We were always in a God-damn hole. The only time we saw Cunningham was each day when the fight was over and then, all he wanted to know was how much ammunition was expended; how many shells were fired—nothing else." Bayler was "noncommittal" on the subject of his own book, *Last Man Off Wake Island*, saying that "he was only a co-author" of the volume.[4] Bayler intimated that Cunningham spent a good deal of time in his command post, which was precisely where he was supposed to be. Both Cunningham and Devereux spent all of their time on the last day of the siege, 23 December, in their respective command posts. Neither man fit the image of the fire-eating leader, nor would that have been appropriate.

The truth was that the garrison *did* hold out with Cunningham in command. His decisions were not always popular (particularly with Paul Putnam, who twice urged the commander to declare martial law and allow him to use force to get cooperation from the CPNAB workers when he desired it).

Dan Teters thought the marines had given Cunningham "a bad time" and stopped corresponding with Devereux after reading some statements the colonel had made in the press. Devereux's serialized articles concerning Wake's defense in the *Saturday Evening Post* drew fire from civilians who felt (rightly) that their role was slighted. Devereux responded that the Navy Department had told him to downplay their contribution, but *The Story of Wake Island* did not do much better on that score. "I have never," Teters wrote Cunningham, "seen any legitimate grounds for Devereux getting such a hell of a play. You were in command, Keene was your second, and I could never see where that point was open to argument."[5]

Campbell Keene, whose character was impeccable, agreed. "You certainly did exercise actual command over the island as far as I could see," he wrote Cunningham. "In fact, I felt at the time that you were rather dictatorial in your decisions, which, of course, was your right, in that you did not call officers, like Major Devereux, Major Putnam, and myself, into conference . . . I am quite certain that no one wanted to assume your command perogatives [sic] . . . during the period of Japanese bombing," he continued, "because I am sure that neither Major Putnam, Major Devereux, nor myself envied your position." He recollected that Cunningham had been urged to declare martial law and had been criticized for not having done so. That fact alone indicated to Keene that Cunningham had "exercised actual command over [Wake Island]."[6]

Heinl, who prepared the official Marine Corps monograph on the battle for Wake, believed that Cunningham had agitated the command controversy. First, Heinl called it "a matter of personalities." Second, he noted that the controversy arose from the "inherently contradictory rank and command situation . . . whereby command of a defense fell unexpectedly (by virtue of rank) upon a Navy officer unfamiliar with land or amphibious warfare who was superimposed upon a well-trained Marine Corps unit within his command, in turn commanded by an officer qualified by local and professional experience to exercise such a command in combat."[7] Heinl seems to have ignored the plans that placed the naval officer in command of the defenses of island bases.

Heinl claimed that the situation at Midway was altogether different. During the battle, overall command of the defense forces lay in the hands of Captain Simard (who had been "spot-promoted" by Admiral Nimitz in May 1942), while the ground forces were under Colonel Harold D. Shannon (also the recipient of a spot-promotion by Nimitz). Simard, Heinl wrote, "recognized his own professional limitations in the field of ground operations and confined himself to the administrative functions of overall island command, as well as to those of air operations (in which he was well qualified), leaving tactical decisions where they belonged by common sense, namely, in the hands of Shannon."[8]

The same situation apparently occurred at Wake in December 1941. As Cunningham himself wrote, "a commanding officer should allow his subordinates as much freedom of action and decision as was commensurate with his own responsibilities." The concept of a commander who "threw his weight around simply to demonstrate that he was a head man" had never appealed to him. The function of command, he declared, "was to listen as well as act; to approve as well as disapprove; to let each specialist run his part of the show as long as he did a satisfactory job, and coordinate the over-all picture." Devereux, he wrote, "knew the details of ground defense and artillery tactics better than I, just as some sergeant in his battalion no doubt knew how to operate a direction finder more skillfully than he; Putnam knew his planes and the men who operated them."[9] Unquestionably, Devereux and Putnam conducted the defense under Cunningham's overall command, much as division officers on board a ship carry out their specific duties under the commanding officer of that vessel.

Cunningham, finding himself in unfamilar waters (according to Heinl), "appears to have taken refuge from his own lack of experience and technical capacity by enveloping himself in authority. He *attempted* [Heinl's emphasis] to supervise every detail of the defense exactly as the captain of a man-of-war would fight his ship," which was his job as coordinator of the overall defense operation. Heinl declared (but did not enumerate) that Cunningham issued "ill-timed, inapplicable, and sometimes erroneous" orders and that regardless of what the island commander directed, Devereux "actually conducted the defense as he saw fit and in light of his own professional knowledge," intimating that Devereux was, in that case, nothing less than insubordinate. Heinl declared that a "vacuum" in leadership existed at the top.[10]

Cunningham did not possess a monopoly on bad decisions, however, for as Paul Putnam candidly admitted after the war, his own decision not to try further to disperse VMF-211's eight planes on the ground on 8 December 1941 was "inevitably" the "wrong" one.[11] Furthermore, Devereux took credit in at least one instance for the ideas of others—it was apparently Marine Gunner McKinstry's idea, for example, to suggest moving Battery E on 9 December, not Devereux's. That he changed his story of the order of events of 11 December may reflect an attempt to take credit for a strategy that did not exist and that, if carried out, would have endangered the only air power Wake possessed.

"As a result of the fact that the Marine officers, Devereux and Putnam, actually conducted the defense," Heinl declared in a memorandum on 10 December 1948, "the public has in fact been by no means misled by the amount of favorable publicity accorded both." The author of the Marine Corps monograph on Wake felt it "inevitable and understandable that Cunningham should resent this" because of what Heinl called disparagingly the naval officer's "hyper-sensitive personality." The marine historian went on to decry the "aggressive" campaign Mrs. Cunningham waged during the war (even to the point, he claimed, of writing "insulting personal letters" to the Devereux family). Heinl called the controversy "inherently one-sided," adding that Devereux had never (other than privately) "spoken critically of Commander Cunningham," whereas Putnam, "although he has commented rather pointedly in official reports on some of the difficulties experienced with Commander Cunningham had since taken every possible step to keep his skirts clear of controversy."[12] Favorable publicity is one thing, but a total lack of it is altogether another, for Cunningham emerged from the war, as suggested by a character in a different theater of war, as "the man who never was."

Heinl declared that the "documentary evidence" of Cunningham's had been "ex post facto in character as well as self-serving." The documentary evidence "on which our [the Marine Corps monograph's] conclusions were based was largely contemporaneous with the events narrated, internally consistent as between various individuals, and not originally written with a view to use in connection with this controversy," which, he averred, had not yet reached "public status." Heinl disparaged Cunningham's sources as of the "Palace Guard" character—"Navy staff officers who remained at his [Cunningham's] rear headquarters, and the civilian construction superintendent." Material supporting the conclusions in The Defense of Wake and Samuel Eliot Morison's "unofficial" history of the navy's operations in World War II came, Heinl noted, from "marine officers, the preponderance of whom are personally known to all of us, and whose powers of observation and veracity are susceptible of accurate assessment." Heinl disparaged the only marine (Gunner John Hamas) whom Cunningham cited as "the least reliable of the Marine witnesses (on all grounds), with a bad previous record for internal contradictions and failure to jibe not only on this but on other aspects of the defense."[13] One might be tempted to observe with a cynical eye that the reason why he proved the least reliable in Heinl's eyes was that his account did not follow the line of argument that all the others had—in which there was, however, nothing inherently wrong.

Unfortunately, Heinl ignored the basic fact that the material he sought for his monograph consisted of recollections four years removed from the events that occurred, the same distance from the events that existed in what he decried as the "Palace Guard" evidence. Cunningham was responsible for the big picture, the marines for the basic work of defense. A careful reading of the reports of the "marine officers . . . whose powers of observation and veracity" were "susceptible of accurate assessment" shows inconsistencies (as well as, in light of Japanese records) outright inaccuracies; they acknowledged readily that the reports were done from memory after the passage of almost four years of grueling captivity at the hands of a foe not known for generosity and mercy.

In the end, then, Spiv Cunningham indeed appears to have been treated unfairly by the predominant publicity accorded his subordinates—the fault of incompetent Navy Department public relations. The interservice controversy that emerged is unfortunate because it casts a slight pall over the conduct of what had indeed been "a magnificent fight" carried out with resolution and courage by all concerned. There was enough glory for all.

DECORATIONS FOR VALOR AWARDED TO WAKE DEFENDERS

Medal of Honor: Captain Henry T. Elrod.*

Navy Cross: Staff Sergeant (NAP) Robert O. Arthur, Commander Winfield S. Cunningham, USN, Second Lieutenant Carl R. Davidson,* Major James P. S. Devereux, Captain Herbert C. Freuler, Second Lieutenant Robert M. Hanna, USMCR, Aviation Machinist's Mate First Class James F. Hesson, USN, Major Paul A. Putnam, Dr. Lawton E. Shank, M.D.*

Silver Star: Boatswain's Mate First Class James E. Barnes, USN; Sergeant Howard D. Comin,* Second Lieutenant David D. Kliewer, Second Lieutenant John A. McAlister, Captain Wesley McC. Platt, First Lieutenant Frank C. Tharin.

Gold Star in Lieu of Second Silver Star: Second Lieutenant John A. McAlister.

Bronze Star: Sergeant Robert S. Box, Sergeant Raymond L. Coulson, Richard E. Elliott, William L. Fairey, Corporal Cyrus D. Fish, Sergeant Stephen Fortuna, Captain Herbert C. Freuler, Laurence G. Frosberger, George W. Gates, Fred S. Gibbons, George F. Gibbons,* Technical Sergeant Earl R. Hannum,* Ralph Higdon,* Walter N. Hokanson, Malcolm D. Johnson, Rex D. Jones,* Master Gunnery Sergeant John W. Krawie, Robert H. Lancaster, Charles E. McCulley,* Jack F. McKinley,* Marine Gunner Clarence B. McKinstry, Don K. Miller,* Herschel L. Peterson,* Second Lieutenant Arthur A. Poindexter, USMCR, William H. Ray, Chester A. Riebel, Leal H. Russell, Private First Class William T. Schumacher, Joe D. Smith, Clinton L. Stevenson,* Willis C. Stone,* Nathan D. Teters, Platoon Sergeant Johanlson E. Wright,* Harry Yeager.*

Air Medal: Second Lieutenant Carl R. Davidson,* Captain Herbert C. Freuler, Technical Sergeant (NAP) William J. Hamilton, Second Lieutenant David D. Kliewer.

---

* Indicates posthumous award.

Gold Star in Lieu of Second Air Medal: Captain Herbert C. Freuler, Technical Sergeant (NAP) William J. Hamilton, Second Lieutenant David D. Kliewer.

Legion of Merit: First Lieutenant Clarence A. Barninger, Jr., Captain Bryghte D. Godbold, Technical Sergeant (NAP) William J. Hamilton, Aviation Machinist's Mate First Class James F. Hesson, USN, First Lieutenant Woodrow M. Kessler, First Lieutenant William W. Lewis, Major George H. Potter.

WAKE ISLAND'S WILDCATS

For VMF-211, the transition from one Grumman product (the F3F) to another (the F4F) had apparently been generally smooth, marred only by Second Lieutenant Robert "J" Conderman's ground-looping BuNo 3972 (the first Wildcat that 211 had received in August) at Ewa Mooring Mast Field on 16 October 1941 and Second Lieutenant Frank J. Holden's bad landing in BuNo 4035 during qualification landings on board the *Lexington* on 19 November 1941, coming to rest in "Lex's" after port five-inch gun gallery. The twelve Grumman F4F-3 Wildcats that ended up on Wake Island with VMF-211 were ordered from Grumman under Contract No. 75736 and were powered by Pratt and Whitney R-1830-86 engines.[1] All (except BuNo 3988, 211-F-9) were flown on board the *Enterprise* on 28 November by marine pilots.

The Wildcats arrived on board the "Big E" in nonspecular light gray finish overall. They were repainted at sea on 3 December, however, the upper surfaces camouflaged with "non-specular blue gray lacquer, specification M-585." The under surface color carried up over the front of the cowling. The demarkation line appears to have been soft-edged, or "feathered." Squadron identifying markings (211-F-x) were in low-contrast black block characters, one foot high, on the fuselage. No numbers appear to have been painted on the wing root upper surface or on the cowling, as was the standard practice for carrier-based planes. National insignia consisted of four red-centered blue and white stars (both fuselage sides and atop the port wing and beneath the starboard). Propeller hubs and cuffs were natural metal; blades were black with blue/red/yellow tips.

211-F-10

BuNo 3980 (engine no. 14179) was shipped on 19 July 1941. On 25 July 1941, during its ferry flight to the west coast, Lieutenant (j.g.) Noel A. M. Gayler exhibited what investigators deemed poor technique in landing it into the wind on a dirt runway at the Trans-World Airways Airport at

Kingman, Arizona, and ground-looped it, damaging its left wingtip and aileron. Eventually, the plane arrived at the Battle Force (BatFor) pool, San Diego, California, on 31 July—the only one of the twelve Wake Wildcats to have received actual airframe damage before the start of hostilities. Transferred to the BatFor pool at Pearl Harbor on 10 September, it was received on 1 October and assigned to VMF-211 on 10 October. Second Lieutenant Carl R. Davidson flew it on 8 December on combat air patrol (CAP) while Japanese planes from the Chitose Kōkūtai were bombing the atoll. Davidson flew the plane in action on 11 December, when he shot down two Type 96 rikkōs. The plane was destroyed in a bombing raid on 14 December, but its engine was saved and installed in 211-F-9.

211-F-9

BuNo 3988 (engine no. 14193) was shipped to San Diego and the BatFor pool on 28 July 1941 and received on 7 August. Over the next two months, the plane went from VMF-211 to VF-3 on board the Saratoga and wound up in the BatFor pool at Pearl Harbor, where it was received on 11 October. A little under one month later, on 7 November, the plane was assigned to the Enterprise and was received by VF-6 on 19 November. Nine days later, on 28 November, it was reassigned from VF-6 to VMF-211. It was flown by Captain Henry T. Elrod on 8 December on CAP while Japanese planes from the Chitose Kōkūtai were bombing the atoll. It was reengined (to no. 14179) at Wake on 14–15 December and flown by Major Paul A. Putnam in his unsuccessful attempt to find the Japanese carriers Hiryū and Sōryū on 21 December. Second Lieutenant Carl R. Davidson flew it in aerial combat on 22 December, when it was shot down by Petty Officer Third Class Tahara Isao of the Hiryū and crashed at sea, killing the pilot.

211-F-11

BuNo 4019 (engine no. 14236) was shipped 23 August 1941 to the BatFor pool at San Diego and was received there on 4 September. Assigned to VF-3 on board the Saratoga on 8 September and received by that squadron the same day, it was transferred to VMF-211 on 21 October. It was flown by Second Lieutenant John F. Kinney on 8 December on CAP while Japanese planes from the Chitose Kōkūtai were bombing the atoll. It was flown by Captain Henry T. Elrod on 11 December in the action that sank the Japanese destroyer Kisaragi. Damaged in that action, it was subsequently used as a decoy. Its port elevator replaced the damaged port elevator of 211-F-8 about 14 December.

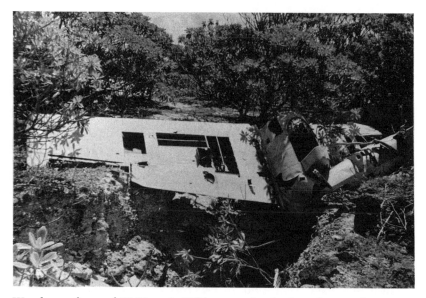

Wreckage of one of VMF-211's Wildcats in the thick undergrowth near the airfield on Wake after World War II. (Mrs. Virginia Putnam)

211-F-12

BuNo 4020 (engine no. 14229) was shipped the same day as BuNo 4019 (23 August 1941) but was received on 3 September, a day ahead of it. Like BuNo 4019, it was assigned to VF-3 in the *Saratoga*, but not until 10 September. Records indicate that it was not received until 3 October and was reassigned to VMF-211 on 20 October. It was flown by Technical Sergeant (NAP) William J. Hamilton on 8 December on CAP while Japanese planes from the Chitose *Kōkūtai* were bombing the atoll. Later that day the pilot, Captain Frank C. Tharin, taxied it into an oil drum and damaged the propeller. It was again damaged on takeoff on 14 December (ground-looped when the pilot, Captain Herbert C. Freuler, missed hitting the crowd surging onto the runway to watch takeoff of the evening patrol). Like 211-F-11, it was then used as a decoy.

211-F-8

BuNo 4022 (engine no. 14230) was shipped on 28 August 1941 and was received by the BatFor pool, San Diego, on 8 September. Ordered shipped two days later to the *Saratoga* at Pearl Harbor, it was received by that ship on 3 October, then reassigned to VMF-211 on 10 October. After the bombing and strafing of 8 December, two damaged cylinders were replaced by two undamaged cylinders from 211-F-5 on 13 December. The plane had chronic starting problems. It was flown by Captain Herbert C. Freuler in aerial combat on 22 December during which he splashed two *kankōs* from the *Sōryū*; it was heavily damaged by the explosion of his second "kill" and by Petty Officer Third Class Tahara Isao of the *Hiryū*. Freuler, wounded in the shoulder, flew the plane back to Wake, where the Japanese captured it the following day.

211-F-1

The career of BuNo 4024 (engine no. 14249) paralleled that of BuNo 4022; it was shipped to the BatFor pool and received by that unit the same day. Ordered shipped to the BatFor pool at Pearl Harbor on 10 September, it was received on 1 October and reassigned to VMF-211 on 10 October. It was irreparably damaged by bombing and strafing on 8 December.

211-F-2

BuNo 4027 (engine no. 14232) was shipped 29 August 1941 to the BatFor pool at San Diego and was received on 8 September. Like BuNo 4924, it was ordered shipped to Pearl Harbor on 10 September, was received at the BatFor pool on 1 October, and was reassigned to VMF-211 on 10 October. It was irreparably damaged by bombing and strafing on 8 December.

211-F-3

BuNo 4028 (engine no. 14242) was shipped to the BatFor pool at San Diego the same day as BuNo 4027 but was not received until 10 September. Ordered shipped the same day to the BatFor pool at Pearl Harbor, it was received on 10 October and transferred the same day to VMF-211. Sometime during October the plane's engine was changed (to no. 14200), one of two of Wake's twelve Wildcats to have had a documented engine change before the alterations performed during the siege of Wake. It was irreparably damaged by bombing and strafing on 8 December.

211-F-4

BuNo 4030 (engine no. 14257) was shipped to the BatFor pool at San Diego on 30 August 1941 and was received on 9 September. Assigned the following day to the BatFor pool at Pearl, it was received on 1

October. Nine days later, on 10 October, it was transferred to VMF-211. It was irreparably damaged by bombing and strafing on 8 December.

211-F-5

BuNo 4032 (engine no. 14251), like BuNo 4030, was shipped to San Diego on 30 August and was received on 9 September. Assigned to the BatFor pool at Pearl on 10 September, it, too, was received on 1 October and transferred to VMF-211 on 20 October. It was irreparably damaged by bombing and strafing on 8 December. Two cylinders of the engine replaced two damaged cylinders in 211-F-8 on 13 December.

211-F-6

BuNo 4037 (enging no. 14212) was shipped to San Diego on 3 September 1941 and was received by the BatFor pool there six days later, on 9 September. Shipped to the BatFor pool at Pearl the following day, it was received on 1 October and transferred to VMF-211 on 10 October. Sometime in September or October it, too, underwent an engine change (to no. 14213). It was irreparably damaged by bombing and strafing on 8 December.

211-F-7

BuNo 4041 (engine no. 14245) was shipped to San Diego on 5 September 1941 and was received by the BatFor pool on 9 September. Shipped the following day to Pearl Harbor, it was received by the BatFor pool there on 1 October and was transferred to VMF-211 on 10 October. It was irreparably damaged by bombing and strafing on 8 December.

All twelve of Wake's Wildcats were stricken from the list of naval aircraft on 13 January 1942, having been lost to enemy action. Wreckage of the Wildcats was evident on Wake in 1945, but only the cowl ring of one was salvaged for a museum artifact. Would that there had been foresight to preserve more than just the piece of a cowling!

WAKE ISLAND, THE MOVIE

In the autumn of 1942, the movie that Hollywood had been contemplating even before the Japanese took the atoll, *Wake Island*, was released. Filmed beside California's Salton Sea with hearty Marine Corps cooperation and featuring spectacular special effects, *Wake Island* was perhaps understandably inaccurate. To many, the tag line that the film used "official Marine Corps records" lent it an air of authenticity.

Although the moviemakers employed Wildcat fighters and a 5-inch/.51-caliber gun, the story line differed from reality. To begin with, "Commander Roberts" (Walter Abel), the navy island commander, greets "Major Caton" (Brian Donlevy) upon his arrival at Wake in a PBY flying boat, not a ship. The senior marine aviator is a "Captain Patrick," while a "Captain Lewis" (perhaps a play on Major Walter Louis John Bayler—the "last man off Wake Island") is the marine officer selected to return to Pearl Harbor in a PBY with vital information on Japanese tactics.

Perhaps the most obvious fabrication is that Commander Roberts dies as the result of wounds suffered in the first bombing raid on Wake, thus conveniently leaving the defense of the island in Marine Corps hands. The movie depicts civilian contractors as virtual nonentities with the exception of the superintendent, "McCloskey" (Albert Dekker), who first appears as a two-fisted brawler contemptuous of the "brass hats" who are to defend the island but eventually comes around to see their side. At one point in the film, the civilians are portrayed as looters (some, sadly, apparently were), when McCloskey confronts two contractors who are helping themselves to liquid refreshments in what probably is meant to be the bar in the wrecked PanAir hotel.

Stock footage of Japanese twin-engine bombers was interspersed with live-action shots of single-engine "Japanese" fighters—modified Ryans—open-cockpit, fixed-gear planes dogfighting the Wildcats. The Japanese landing occurs in broad daylight, and, much in the tradition of Custer's Last Stand at the Little Big Horn, the marines go down to the last man, the movie ending with Major Caton and McCloskey manning a .30-caliber Browning machine gun as a grenade is thrown at them, leaving the viewer to speculate (but not for very long) as to what follows.

NOTES

ABBREVIATIONS

AK	Cargo ship
AKS	Stores issue ship
AO	Fleet oiler
AP	Transport
AT	Oceangoing tug
AV	Seaplane tender
A-V(N)	Naval Aviator (Reserve)
BB	Battleship
BuAer	Bureau of Aeronautics
BuNo	Bureau number
CA	Heavy cruiser
CEC	Civil Engineer Corps
CinCPac	Commander in Chief, United States Pacific Fleet
CinCPacFlt	Commander in Chief, United States Pacific Fleet
CL	Light cruiser
CNO	Chief of Naval Operations
CO	Commanding officer
Com14	Commandant, Fourteenth Naval District
ComInCh	Commander in Chief, United States Fleet
ComSubScoFor	Commander Submarines, Scouting Force
CPNAB	Contractors, Pacific Naval Air Bases
CV	Aircraft carrier
DD	Destroyer
14thND	Fourteenth Naval District
LCMD	Library of Congress Manuscript Division, Washington, D.C.
Ltr	Letter
MC	Medical Corps
MCAS	Marine Corps Air Station
MCHC	Marine Corps Historical Center, Washington, D.C.
Msg	Message
NA	National Archives
NAS	Naval Air Station
NHC	Naval Historical Center, Washington, D.C.
NHF	Naval Historical Foundation, Washington, D.C.
OiC	Officer in charge

Opcom	Operating Committee (CPNAB)
Opnav	Office of the Chief of Naval Operations
Panair	Pan American Airways
PHA	U.S. Congress, *Hearings Before the Joint Committee on the Investigation of the Pearl Harbor Attack*
RDO	Resident district officer
RG	Record Group
SecNav	Secretary of the Navy
SS	Submarine
USMC	United States Marine Corps
USMCR	United States Marine Corps Reserve
USS	United States Ship
VP	Patrol Squadron
WPD	War Plans Division (later Strategic Plans Division)

CHAPTER ONE: "A Land Reserved to Those Who Fly"

Sources on the early history of Wake (1568–1899): Amherst and Thomson, eds., *Discovery of the Solomon Islands*; Votaw, "Wake Island," 52; Ward, *American Activities in the Central Pacific*; Wilkes, *Narrative of the United States Exploring Expedition.*

On the coming of Panair: Civil Aeronautics Board Docket Nos. 851 et al.; Pan American Airways, Inc., "History of Transpacific Air Services to and through Hawaii," 5–8; "Wake Remembered," Pan American Airways, *New Horizons*, February 1942, 16–17; Scheppler and Anderson, "Martin Clippers," 174–76.

On the Pickett and Pefley Survey: Pickett and Pefley, "The Defenses of Wake," 2, 16–18, 41, in MCHC Archives; Updegraph, *U.S. Marine Corps Special Units of World War II*, 62.

On the coming of CPNAB: U.S. Navy, *Building the Navy's Bases in World War II*, 1:27–31; Woodbury, *Builders for Battle*, 56–57, 59–66, 243, 256; Dierdorff, "Pioneer Party," 499–508; "The Story of the U.S.S. *William Ward Burrows* before the War."

1. Pan American Airways System travel brochure, ca. 1940, McCrae Papers, LCMD.

2. Bywater, *Sea-Power in the Pacific*, 270–89. As Edward S. Miller points out, "Wake and the other BLUE [the color for the United States] atolls had to await the air age for serious consideration" in an ORANGE war plan (*War Plan Orange*, 102–3).

3. Picking, "Wake Island," 2075.

4. Ibid.

5. Entry for Saturday, 16 March 1935, in "Record of Events," in Yarnell Papers, NHC Operational Archives.

6. Memo from Lt. J. G. Johnson to CNO, 10 January 1935, Box 104, SecNav General Correspondence, RG 80, NA Military Reference Branch.

7. Memo, Lt. Willis E. Cleaves to CNO, "Pan-American Airways Pacific Expedition—Report on," 31 July 1935, in Box 41, General Correspondence, 14th ND, Commandant's Office, Folder Eg 12-1/Eg 60, Midway-Wake (1), RG 181, NA Pacific-Sierra Region.

8. Ibid.

9. Hollywood dramatized the flight in the 1936 motion picture *China Clipper*, starring Pat O'Brien and Humphrey Bogart. Interestingly, the navigator on board

the *China Clipper* was Fred Noonan, later lost with Amelia Earhart Putnam in July 1937.

10. Memo, Chief, WPD [RAdm. William S. Pye] to CNO, Subj: "Development of Midway and Wake Islands for Naval Use," 12 December 1935, in Box 41, General Correspondence, 1912–41, 14th ND, Commandant's Office, Folder Eg 12-1/Eg 60, Midway-Wake (1), RG-181, NA Pacific-Sierra Region.

11. Ibid.

12. U.S. Congress, House of Representatives, *Report on Need of Additional Naval Bases to Defend the Coasts of the United States, Its Territories, and Possessions*, 26.

13. "Statement of Admiral William D. Leahy, United States Navy, Chief of Naval Operations," in U.S. Congress, *Hearings Before the Committee on Naval Affairs of the House of Representatives on Sundry Legislation Affecting the Naval Establishment, 1939*, 52.

14. Woodbury, *Builders for Battle*, 56–57.

15. Ibid., 59–65.

16. "Statement of Admiral Harold R. Stark, Chief of Naval Operations," in U.S. Congress, *Hearings Before the Committee on Naval Affairs on the House of Representatives on Sundry Legislation Affecting the Naval Establishment, 1940*, 3381, 3391–92.

17. Ibid., 3381, 3391–92.

18. CO, VP-26 to CNO, Subj: "Patrol Squadron Twenty-Six—Ferry Flight, Pearl Harbor, T.H., to Cavite, P.I., and return," 22 July 1940, World War II Action Report File, NHC Operational Archives; see also BuAer *Newsletter* No. 128 (15 August 1940); 11–12, NHC Aviation History Office and Archives.

19. Ltr, Bloch to Stark, 1 October 1940, Box 3, Stark Papers, Series I, Correspondence, Semi-Official and Personal, 1939–41, NHC Operational Archives.

20. Affidavit, Nathan Dan Teters, 24 November 1945, 1–2, in Box 4, Cunningham Papers; also Woodbury, *Builders for Battle*, 256.

21. Dierdorff, "Pioneer Party," 499–508.

22. The *Chaumont*'s visit to Wake on her return trip was even shorter: only seventeen minutes between stopping engines and transferring cargo and mail before going ahead. She was probably hurrying because she was carrying a cargo of gold bullion from Manila to San Francisco, convoyed by the light cruiser *Trenton* (CL-11) (*Chaumont* [AP-5] deck logs, January–March 1941, RG 24, NA Military Reference Branch).

23. 1904 *Lucky Bag*, 52.

24. Ltr, Col. Harry K. Pickett to Maj. Gen. William P. Upshur, 25 February 1941, in WPD files, MCHC Archives.

25. Com14 ltr Ser 0302, 2 April 1941, referred to in [Captain Harry W. Hill] Memo for the Director, WPD, Subj: "Wake Island—Policy in Regard to Construction on and Protection of," 28 May 1941; see also [Captain Charles J. Moore] Memo for the Director, WPD, Subj: "Wake Island," 24 May 1941, which refers to the CNO ltr to Com14 Ser 048812, 2 May 1941; both memorandums in Box 97, Strategic Plans Division Records, Subject Files, 1937–41 (Series V), QG Pacific file, NHC Operational Archives.

26. Ltr, CinCPac to CNO, Ser 029W, "Wake Island—Policy in regard to construction on and protection of," 18 April 1941, Box 12, Folder 3a, Miscellaneous Reports, Hawaii, Accession No. 63A-2534, MCHC Archives.

27. Ibid.
28. Heinl, "Marine Coast Artillery: The Defense Battalions," MCHC Reference Section.
29. CinCPac ltr, 18 April 1941.
30. Hill memo, 28 May 1941.
31. Ibid. Interestingly, Captain Hill did not address the question of supplying the civilian contractors.
32. "Study on Defenses and Installations at Outlying Pacific Bases," Encl A to CinCPac to CNO ltr EG61/(86) Ser 090W, 21 October 1941, in Box 1, Commandant's Special Interest Records, 1940-44, Folder A16-1/Eg 61, 1940-41, RG-181, NA Pacific-Sierra Region.
33. Moore memo, 24 May 1941.
34. Memo, CinCPac to CNO, Subj: "Survey of Conditions in Pacific Fleet," 26 May 1941, PHA, 22:361.
35. Ibid., 364.
36. Hill memo, 28 May 1941.

CHAPTER TWO: "An Uninviting Low-Lying Atoll"

For the activities of the ships mentioned in the narrative: deck logs for Blue (DD-387), Castor (AKS-1), Chaumont (AP-5), Curtiss (AV-4), Jarvis (DD-393), Kanawha (AO-1), Regulus (AK-14), Seminole (AT-65), Sirius (AK-15), Sonoma (AT-12), and William Ward Burrows (AP-6) in RG 24, NA; CO, Narwhal (SS-167) to ComSubScoFor, Subj: "Report of War Patrol," 2 December 1941, and CO, Regulus (AK-14), "Voyage Report," 11 June 1941, World War II Action Report File, NHC Operational Archives; "The Story of the U.S.S. William Ward Burrows before the War."

On the CPNAB activities: Teters Affidavit, Cunningham Papers; Whitney, Guest of the Fallen Sun; Donald W. Butler, "Statement . . . Concerning His Actions during the Defense of Wake Island, World War II," 29 September 1980, MCHC Archives; "Technical Report and Project History, Contracts NOy-3550 and NOy-4173," Chapter XI (Wake), A-502, NAS Wake Island, World War II Command File, NHC Operational Archives.

On the activities of the Wake Detachment, First Defense Battalion: Muster rolls, August-November 1941, MCHC Reference Section; Kessler, To Wake and Beyond; William C. Halstead letters of 22 August, 10, 19, and 20 September 1941, in Halstead Papers; Poindexter and Winslow interviews; Col. James P. S. Devereux, USMC, "Wake Island Report, Marine Detachment First Defense Battalion," 18 March 1946, in MCHC Archives.

On the ferrying of army bombers to the Philippines: James, Years of MacArthur, 1:589; U.S. Army, Chief of Staff, Biennial Report of the Chief of Staff of the United States Army, July 1, 1941 to June 30, 1942, to the Secretary of War, 3-4; Edmonds, They Fought with What They Had, 3; Brereton, Brereton Diaries, 15-16; Mitchell, In Alis Vicimus.

On the U.S. Army Detachment, Wake Island: "U.S. Army Detachment, Wake Island, North Pacific Ocean," [February 1942], courtesy of Clifford Hotchkiss; Hotchkiss interview and correspondence; William Ward Burrows (AP-6); Terrett, Signal Corps: The Emergency, 142, 159; Thompson, Signal Corps, 19.

On the Kurusu visit (9-10 November 1941): "Saburo Kurusu," Current Biography:

Who's News and Why, 1942 (New York: H. W. Wilson, 1942), 476; "Rush from Japan," Pan American Airways, *New Horizons,* December 1941, 10; Devereux, *Story of Wake Island,* 28–31; Gandt, *China Clipper,* 10–11.

1. Hill memo, 28 May 1941.

2. WPPac-46 is printed in its entirety in *PHA,* 33:986–1018. A discussion of the War Plans formulation is contained in Richardson, *On the Treadmill to Pearl Harbor.* Those portions of WPPac-46 quoted are found in *PHA,* 33:1000.

3. Lewis A. Hohn Biographical File, MCHC Reference Section; also Lt. Gen. Victor H. Krulak, USMC (Ret.), response to author's questionnaire, received 12 October 1993.

4. Krulak response to questionnaire; also Wesley M. Platt Biographical File, MCHC Reference Section; telephone interview with Col. Arthur A. Poindexter, USMC (Ret.), 5 June 1993.

5. Poindexter interview; interview with Sgt. Maj. Robert E. Winslow, USMC (Ret.), MCHC, 25 February 1994.

6. Heinl, "Mobility of Base Defense Artillery," 24. The quote about the mobility of the guns is from Kessler, *To Wake and Beyond,* 31.

7. Ltr, Kimmel to Stark, 12 August 1941, in Box 3, Stark Papers, Series I—Correspondence, Semi-Official and Personal, 1939–41, NHC Operational Archives.

8. Ltr, Turner to Stark, 21 August 1941, ibid.

9. Ltr, CinCPac to CNO, Ser 078W, "Defenses at Wake," 26 August 1941, in Box 12, folder 3a, "Miscellaneous Reports, Hawaii," Accession No. 63A-2534, MCHC Archives.

10. Ltr, Bloch to Hohn, 27 August 1941, in Box 181-58-3402 (V9509), General Correspondence (formerly classified), 14th ND Headquarters, RG 181, NA Pacific-Sierra Region.

11. Ibid.

12. Ibid.

13. Woodbury, *Builders for Battle,* 152.

14. Seno, "A Chess Game with No Checkmate," 26–39.

15. Ibid., 32–33.

16. Ibid., 34.

17. Ltr, Bloch to Stark, 10 October 1940, Box 3, Stark Papers.

18. Ltr, Capt. Elmer B. Greey (CEC), USN to Historical Section, Division of Public Information, Marine Corps Headquarters, Subj: "Monograph, 'The Defense of Wake Island'—Comments on," 26 February 1948, Wake Monograph Comment File, MCHC Archives.

19. Among the pilots in the flight was Captain Colin P. Kelly, Jr., who would be awarded the Medal of Honor for heroism over Luzon in December 1941.

20. Ltr, Kimmel to Stark, 12 September 1941, *PHA,* 16:2248–49.

21. Ltr, Brig. Gen. Alexander A. Vandegrift to Brig. Gen. Charles F. B. Price, 13 September 1941, in Box 2, Vandegrift Papers, Folder 30 (July–December 1941), MCHC Personal Papers Collection. The Marine Corps was not the only service bedeviled by manpower shortages. Within two months, Admiral Kimmel would be complaining that the detachment of "personnel and material" to the Atlantic had "dangerously reduced [the] efficiency" of the Pacific Fleet (ltr, Kimmel to Stark, 15 November 1941, *PHA,* 16:2253). On Oahu, the army's Hawaiian Department required the Thirty-first Bombardment Squadron (U.S. Army Air Force) to provide men to guard warehouses and other facilities in Honolulu, a task that interfered with gunnery training and

drained the manpower pool for combat aircrew (Arakaki and Kuborn, 7 *December 1941*, 38).

22. Halstead ltr, 20 September 1941. Halstead's salary was about $64 a month.

23. Whitney, *Guest of the Fallen Sun*, 16.

24. "Study on Defenses and Installations at Outlying Pacific Bases."

25. Ibid.

26. Ibid.

27. Ltr, CNO to CinCPac, Ser 0119612, Subj: "Employment of Defense Battalions," 17 October 1941, in Box 82, Strategic Plans Division Records, Serial Files 1938-47 (Series IV), October 1941 Serial File.

28. Devereux, in his report of events, states that he relieved Major Hohn on 15 October; the October 1941 muster roll for the Wake Detachment, however, shows that the turnover apparently took place on the twelfth.

29. Poindexter and Winslow interviews.

30. Cunningham, *Wake Island Command*, 30-31.

31. "Technical Report and Project History, Contracts NOY-3550 and NOy-4173," A-496-A-497.

32. Ltr, Com14 to CinCPacFlt, "Study on Defenses and Installations at Outlying Pacific Bases," 17 October 1941, in Box 64, Series III, Strategic Plans Division Records.

33. Ltr, Kimmel to Stark, 17 October 1941, *PHA*, 16:2214-15.

34. Dispatch, CNO to CinCPac, 17 October 1941, *PHA*, 5:2160.

35. [CNO] Memo for the Chief of Staff, Subj: "Flights of B-17 Airplanes to [the] Philippine Islands," 20 October 1941, in Box 82, Strategic Plans Division Records, Serial Files 1938-47 (Series IV), October 1941 Serial File.

36. Msg, CinCPac to ComSubScoFor 170354, 17 October 1941, *PHA*, 17:2478.

37. Msg, Com14 to NAS Midway, NAS Johnston, NAS Palmyra, MarDet at Wake 170356, 17 October 1941 in *PHA*, 17:2478.

38. Ltr, Bloch to Stark, 23 October 1941, Harold R. Stark folder, Box 4, Bloch Papers.

39. *Narwhal* "Report of War Patrol."

40. Winslow interview.

41. Updegraph, *U.S. Marine Corps Special Units of World War II*, 65.

42. Brereton, *Brereton Diaries*, 16.

43. Muster Roll, Wake Detachment, First Defense Battalion, November 1941.

44. Devereux's comparatively charitable description of Kurusu is quite different from that given by Secretary of State Cordell Hull: "Neither his [Kurusu's] appearance nor his attitude commanded confidence or respect. I felt from the start that he was deceitful" (Hull, *Memoirs*, 2:1062).

45. "What, if anything except camouflage, Japan hoped to gain by his mission, and how much—again, if anything—he knew about his country's plans for the near future, who can say with complete authority?" writes Prange (*At Dawn We Slept*, 357). Devereux's perception of Kurusu's apparent sincerity is mirrored in the interview Ferdinand L. Meyer, an old acquaintance of Kurusu's, had with the envoy in Washington on 6 December 1941 (*PHA*, 20:4528-37).

46. Biographical Material on Lieutenant (j.g.) Gustave M. Kahn from Officer Biography Files, NHC Operational Archives Branch. See also Kessler, *To Wake and Beyond*, 28.

47. Muster Roll, Wake Detachment, First Defense Battalion, November 1941.

48. The orders (a copy of which was provided to the author by Clifford Hotchkiss)

are dated 31 October 1941 and specify that upon completion of their tour of temporary duty they would be returned "via Government airplane to their proper station."

CHAPTER THREE: "Like the Fatted Calf"

On the sending of VMF-211 to Wake: CinCPac to ComAirBatFor and ComPatWing 2, "Naval Air Station Wake and Naval Air Station Midway—Basing of Aircraft at," 10 November 1941, CinCPac Flag Files, July–December 1941 folder, NA Military Reference Branch (transferred from NHC Operational Archives in 1991); Ltr, Larkin to Rowell, 18 November 1941, Larkin Papers, MCHC Personal Papers Collection; *Wright* (AV-1) deck logs, RG 24, NA; Ltr, Putnam to Cunningham, 15 June 1948, Subj: "Monograph Entitled 'The Defense of Wake,'" Wake Monograph Comment File, MCHC Archives; Interview of Lt. Col. John F. Kinney by Lt. Col. Robert D. Heinl, Marine Corps Air Station, Quantico, Virginia, 12 March 1947, MCHC Archives; John F. Kinney Diary, Kinney Papers, MCHC Personal Papers Collection.

For the activities of the various ships mentioned in the narrative: deck logs for *Sonoma* (AT-12), *Triton* (SS-201), *William Ward Burrows* (AP-6), and *Wright* (AV-1); CO, *Triton* (SS-201) to ComSubScoFor, "Report of War Patrol," 3 January 1942, NHC Operational Archives; "The Story of the U.S.S. *William Ward Burrows* before the War."

On the movement of VMF-211 on board the *Enterprise* (CV-6): Halsey, "Life of Admiral W. F. Halsey," 303; Lt. (j.g.) James G. Daniels III, USN, "War Diary"; "War Record of Fighting [Squadron] Six," *Enterprise* (CV-6) Ship History File, NHC Ships' Histories Branch; Lt. (j.g.) Wilmer E. Rawie, Diary; Report of Lt. Col. Paul A. Putnam, USMC, to Commandant of the Marine Corps, "Report of VMF-211 on Wake Island," 18 October 1945, MCHC Archives.

On the CPNAB activities: "Technical Report and Project History, Contracts NOy-3550 and NOy-4173."

On the activities of the Wake Detachment, First Defense Battalion: Muster rolls, August—November 1941; Kessler, *To Wake and Beyond*; Poindexter and Winslow interviews; Devereux, *Story of Wake Island*, 40.

On the U.S. Army Detachment, Wake Island: "U.S. Army Detachment, Wake Island, North Pacific Ocean;" Ltr, Clifford E. Hotchkiss to author, 5 June 1993.

On Litvinov's visit to Wake (3–4 December 1941): Cunningham, *Wake Island Command*, 45–46; "Back to Earth Ambassador," Pan American Airways, *New Horizons*, January 1942, 31; Poindexter interview; on his diplomatic skills: Hull, *Memoirs*, 1:293–94; description: *Current Biography 1941*, 518–19; details of career: Schulz, Urban, and Lebed, eds., *Who Was Who in the USSR*, 352–53.

1. Ltr, Bloch to Stark, 14 November 1941, in Box 4, Harold R. Stark folder, Bloch Papers.

2. Ltr, William C. Halstead to Ray Halstead, 14 November 1941, Halstead Papers.

3. Ltr, Lt. Cdr. Richard H. Best, USN (Ret.) to author, 17 September 1983.

4. Com14 to BuNav, Subj: "NAS, Wake Island—Officer Personnel, requested allowance," 18 August 1941, in Box 181-58-3402 (V9509), folder NA 39 (Wake), RG 181, 14thND Staff Headquarters, General Correspondence, NA Pacific-Sierra Region.

5. Ltr, Lt. Cdr. George H. Henshaw, USN (Ret.) to author, 17 January 1994.

6. Cunningham, *Wake Island Command*, 25.

7. 1927 *Lucky Bag*, 324.

8. 14thND Circular Letter No. 64-41 [21 November 1941], quoted in "History of the Marine Corps Air Station, Ewa, Oahu, T.H., 1941–1944," 40, MCHC Reference Section.

9. Msg, CNO to CincPac 270038, 26 November 1941, PHA, 17:2479.

10. "Testimony of Captain Charles Horatio McMorris, War Plans Officer, United States Navy," 30 December 1941, PHA, 22:526.

11. "Testimony of Rear Admiral Husband E. Kimmel, United States Navy," 27 December 1941, ibid., 325.

12. "Testimony of Vice Admiral William Ward Smith, 2 June 1945," PHA, 36:207.

13. PHA, 5:2124–25.

14. Memo, CincPac to CNO, Ser 0114W, 2 December 1941, Subj: "Defense of Outlying Bases," PHA, 17:2481–82.

15. Ibid., 2481.

16. Ibid.

17. "Final Report of Training," 11 June 1929, in Paul A. Putnam Service Record Book, National Personnel Records Center, St. Louis, Missouri. Used with oral permission of Mrs. Putnam.

18. Cunningham, Wake Island Command, 42.

19. Encl to Lt. (j.g.) Norman J. Kleiss, USN, Diary, December 1941.

20. Ironically, Allen would be shot down over Pearl on the night of 7 December 1941 by American antiaircraft fire; he would die of his wounds the following morning. Like Allen's, Frank Holden's war would be short, too, as will be seen in the next chapter.

21. Ltr, Col. Milo G. Haines, USMC (Ret.), to author, 22 September 1993.

22. Maj. Robert O. Arthur, USMC (Ret.), response to author's questionnaire, June 1993.

23. Howard W. Masterman, "Chronicle of the American War of 1941," unpub. MSS, NHF.

24. Ltr, Henshaw to author, 17 January 1994.

25. Memo from Capt. Campbell Keene, USN, to SecNav, Subj: "Activities of Task Group 9.2 (Wake Base Detachment) at Wake Island, November 29–December 23, 1941, report on," in MCHC Archives.

26. Maj. Walter L. J. Bayler, USMC, to CinCPacFlt, "Wake Island Report on. Period of the 7th to 20th December 1941" (7 January 1942), in Box 1722, World War II Action Reports (Individual Personnel, A–B), NHC Operational Archives; also Wright (AV-1) deck log, 29 November 1941. Bayler's report states that he and Conderman came ashore on the twenty-ninth, which is disputed by the Wright's deck log, which shows that Bayler and Everton came ashore first. Cunningham's Wake Island Command mentions that a scouting squadron's gear went ashore first and had to be lightered back to the Wright, at which point the fighter squadron's equipment was lightered ashore.

27. "Memo for the Commander in Chief, Steps to Be Taken in Case of American-Japanese War within the Next Twenty-Four Hours," 30 November 1941, PHA, 17:2714.

28. The muster roll lists Cooper as still in the dispensary in December when the war started.

29. VMF-211 had received its first F4F-3 (BuNo 3972) on 21 August 1941, its second (BuNo 3977) on 24 August, and its third (4019) on 9 October. Not until 10

October, however, would the squadron receive a substantial number of Wildcats, when it took ten on charge (Aircraft History Cards, National Air and Space Museum). See Appendix 3 for further information on the individual planes that VMF-211 took to Wake.

30. Telephone interview with RAdm. Wilmer E. Gallaher, USN (Ret.), Garrett Park, Maryland, February 1981.

31. Ltr, Best to author, 17 September 1983.

32. Memo, CinCPac to CNO, "Defense of Outlying Bases," 2 December 1941, *PHA*, 33:1284–85; Ltr, Com14 to CinCPac, 17 October 1941, Box 64, Series II, Strategic Studies, Strategic Plans Division Records.

33. Memo, CinCPac to CNO, "Defense of Outlying Bases," *PHA*, 33:1284–85.

34. Ibid.

35. Ltr, Cunningham to Bloch, 3 December 1941, in Box 42, A12-1(0)–A12-1(3) file, 14th ND files, RG 181, NA Pacific-Sierra region.

36. Ltr, Putnam to Larkin, 3 December 1941, Putnam Papers.

37. Of the gift, Rawie wrote: "Gave one of 'em [the marine pilots] my bottle of Scotch—bet he puts that to good use." Kinney revealed that he was the recipient but that he never got the chance to open it, in ltr, Brig. Gen. John F. Kinney, USMC (Ret.) to author, 27 May 1993.

38. "War Record of Fighting Six," 4.

39. Iwaya, *Chūkō*, 223.

40. Memo for Adm. H. E. Kimmel, U.S. Navy, from RAdm. P. N. L. Bellinger, U.S. Navy, in *PHA*, 17:2722. Devereux's "ready for anything" comment comes from an undated newspaper clipping in James P. S. Devereux Biographical File, MCHC Reference Section.

41. "Memo for the Commander in Chief, Recommended Steps to Be Taken in Case of American-Japanese War within the Next Forty-Eight Hours," 5 December 1941, *PHA*, 17:2714–15.

42. Putnam, in his report, stated that after a "perfunctory argument" he gave VMF-211 a holiday, as Devereux and Teters had done, but Kinney's diary disputes that.

43. Maj. Clarence A. Barninger, Jr., USMC, Memo to Lt. Col. James P. S. Devereux, USMC, 8 October 1945, no serial. Subj: "Defense of Wake Island," MCHC Archives.

44. Ltr, Herman P. Hevenor to Colonel [?] Clark, 20 December 1941, MCHC Archives. Reference to Hevenor's report concerning the bauxite supply can be found in Box 82, Strategic Plans Division Records, Serial Files, 1938–47 (Series IV), August 1941 folder, NHC Operational Archives.

45. 1934 *Lucky Bag*, 136; Frank C. Tharin Biographical File, MCHC Reference Section.

46. Carl R. Davidson Biographical File, MCHC Reference Section.

47. Kinney Diary, 7 December 1941; Ltr, Maj. Herbert C. Freuler, USMC, to Lt. Col. James P. S. Devereux, USMC, Subj: "Report of Activities on Wake Island," 9 October 1945; 2nd Lt. David D. Kliewer, "Personal Diary of Second Lieutenant David D. Kliewer, U.S. Marine Corps Reserve (Repatriated Prisoner of War), from 7 December 1941 to 23 December, 1941," Encl A to ltr, Kliewer to Lt. Col. James P. S. Devereux, USMC, 23 October 1945, in MCHC Archives.

48. Kessler, *To Wake and Beyond*, 38.

49. The direct route had been the consequence of the late fitting out of one of the midget submarine elements in the Pearl Harbor attack plan (Hashimoto, *Sunk*, 3-7).

50. PacFlt Confidential Ltr No. 2CL-41 (Revised), 14 October 1941, Subj: "Security of Fleet at Base and in Operating Areas," *PHA*, 22:341.

51. Kimmel's comment concerning Wake's being "vulnerable" is taken from his testimony in *PHA*, 22:397.

CHAPTER FOUR: "I'll See That You Get a Medal as Big as a Pie"

The basic source for Pacific Fleet strategy: War Plans, CinCPac Files, "Captain Steele's Running Estimate and Summary, 7 December 1941 to 31 August 1942 ['CinCPac Greybook'\]," December 1941, NHC Operational Archives.

Message traffic concerning the bombings of Wake Island: Msgs, Wake to Com14 07 2359 Dec. 1941; 08 0840 Dec. 1941; 09 2359 Dec. 1941, in Encl E to Com14 to CinCPacFlt, Subj: "Wake Action, 7 December, 1941 to 24 December 1941," 6 January 1942, in Action Report, CinCPacFlt Ser 01488 of 22 May 1942, World War II Action Report Files, NHC Operational Archives.

On Japanese aerial operations: Chitose *Kōkūtai Kōdōchōsho*s (unit combat logs), December 1941, Japan War History Office, Tokyo; Iwaya, *Chūkō*, 223-24; Japan War History Office, *Senshi Sōsho*, 38:156, 160; Tsuji, "An Account of the Aerial Bombing of Wake Island," in "Hawaii-Malaya Naval Operations," Allied Translator and Interpreter Section, South West Pacific Area, Enemy Publications, No. 6, 27 March 1943, MCHC Archives; "Professional Notebook of an Ensign [Nakamura Toshio] in the Japanese Navy," Joint Intelligence Center, Pacific Ocean Area Item 4986, 25 February 1944, in *PHA*, 13:558.

On the activities of VMF-211: Kinney Diary, 8-10 December 1941; Putnam, "Report of VMF-211 on Wake Island," 4, 8-9; Arthur, response to author's questionnaire; Bayler, "Wake Island, Report on"; Freuler, "Report of Activities on Wake Island."

On the activities of the Wake Detachment, First Defense Battalion: Kessler, *To Wake and Beyond*, 38-41, 45, 47-49, 62-63; and the following narratives in the MCHC Archives: Barninger, "Defense of Wake Island;" Capt. Bryghte D. Godbold, USMC, ltr to Lt. Col. James P. S. Devereux, USMC, Subj: "Report of 'D' Battery Commander (Wake Island, 8-23 December 1941)," 9 October 1945; 1st Lt. Robert W. Greeley, USMC, ltr to Lt. Col. James P. S. Devereux, USMC, Subj: "Informal Report of Action on Wake Island during the Period 7 December to 24 December 1941," 9 October 1945; 2nd Lt. John Hamas, USMC, ltr to Col. James P. S. Devereux, USMC, Subj: "Report on What Happened . . . Wake Island during the Period 7 December to 24 December 1941," 12 October 1945; 1st Lt. Robert M. Hanna, USMC, ltr to Lt. Col. James P. S. Devereux, USMC, Subj: "Report on Wake Island," 11 October 1945; MSgt. Randolph M. June, USMC, ltr to the Director, Division of Public Information (Historical Section), Subj: "Defense of Wake Island," 11 March 1947; Capt. Woodrow M. Kessler, ltr to Lt. Col. James P. S. Devereux, USMC, Subj: "Report on Wake Island operations 7 December to 24 December 1941," 11 October 1945; Maj. William W. Lewis, USMC, ltr to Lt. Col. James P. S. Devereux, USMC, Subj: "Report on Action on Wake Island from 7 December 1941 to 24 December 1941," 9 October 1945; Mar. Gun. Clarence B. McKinstry, USMC, ltr to Lt. Col. James P. S. Devereux, USMC, Subj: "Action during Period 7 December to 23 December 1941," n.d. but ca. October 1945; Lt. Col. Wesley M. Platt, USMC, Subj: "Informal Report on the Defense of Wilkes [Island]," n.d. but ca. October 1945; 2nd Lt. Arthur A. Poindexter, USMC, "Informal Report of Operations of the .30 Caliber MG Battery and the Mobile Reserve" (received at Headquarters, Marine Corps, 8 April 1947); Col. George H. Potter, USMC, ltr to Col. James P. S. Devereux, USMC, Subj: "Brief of Events at Wake Island, Period 7–24 December 1941," 13 October 1945.

On Cdr. Cunningham's activities as island commander: Capt. Winfield Scott Cunningham, USN, "History of Wake Island Defense," 9 January 1946, 4–6, World War II Interviews and Statements File, NHC Operational Archives; Cunningham, *Wake Island Command*, 12, 56, 59, 68.

On the activities of the U.S. Army communications detachment: Maj. Henry S. Wilson, Signal Corps (Army Air Force), to Commanding General, Army Air Forces, War Department, "Report of Operations, Army Air Forces Communications Detachment, Wake Island, December 7 to 22, inclusive, 1941," 13 November 1945, Records of the Provost Marshal, RG 389, NA Military Reference Branch; Thompson, *Signal Corps*, 19–20; "Army Detachment, Wake Island."

On the CPNAB activities: Teters Affidavit, 2–4; Whitney, *Guest of the Fallen Sun*, 17–18; Burroughs, "Siege of Wake Island," 65; Butler, "Statement."

On PanAir activities: "History of Transpacific Air Services," 43–44; "Escape from Wake," Pan American Airways, *New Horizons*, January 1942, 20–21; and "Memorandum for [14th Naval] District Intelligence Officer, Subj[ect]: Midway and Wake Islands," 8 December 1941, Encl A to Com14 to CinCPacFlt, "Wake Action, 7 December, 1941 to 24 December, 1941," 6 January 1942; memorandum, Ensign William W. Moss, Jr., A-V(G), USNR, to Intelligence Officer, Twelfth Naval District, Subj: "Japanese Bombing of Wake Island," 12 December 1941, World War II Action Reports, Individual Personnel, Box 1730, NHC Operational Archives; Schlepper and Anderson, "Martin Clippers," 178–79.

On the activities of the U.S. Navy submarines off Wake: *Tambor* (ss-198) "Report of First War Patrol," 24 December 1941; *Triton* (ss-201) "Report of War Patrol," 3 January 1942; Priority Dispatch 090900, ComTaskUnit 7.2.4 [CO, USS *Triton* (ss-201)] to CinCPac, Com14 and ComTaskFor 7, Encl A to ComSubScoFor to CinCPacFlt, "Information Concerning Attacks on Wake Island," 29 December 1941, NHC Operational Archives; *Triton* deck logs, December 1941.

1. Ugaki, *Sensoroku*, 32.

2. The two PBYs had already taken off from Midway, flown by Consolidated Aircraft ferry crews. They were recalled to Midway, where VP-21 commandeered them. Both were damaged during the Japanese bombardment of Midway later that same evening.

3. Wilson, "Report of Operations."

4. Ibid. Captain Wilson's postwar recollections have him awakening Major Devereux with the word, not, as Devereux remembered it, interrupting his shaving.

5. Barninger, "Defense of Wake Island."

6. *William Ward Burrows* (AP-6) deck log, 8 December 1941; also Hand, "Old Timer," 1, USS *William Ward Burrows* (AP-6) Ship History File, NHC Ships' Histories Branch.

7. Lieutenant Commander Lent, the *Triton*'s captain, noted that he could see the water tower from at least eight miles away at periscope depth. "When close in," he added, "the ship's position was quite accurately fixed with tangents and a bearing

on this tower." The chart of Wake that had been furnished the boat did not show any landmarks (*Triton*, "Report of War Patrol").

8. Elmer Greey later recalled that, to the best of his knowledge, the matter of placing the J-line underground (which would have increased the scope of the contract, which was beyond his authority to negotiate) never came up until after Wake fell (Capt. Elmer B. Greey, CEC, USN, ltr to Historical Section, Division of Public Information, Marine Corps Headquarters, Subj: "Monograph, 'The Defense of Wake Island,' Comments on"). Wesley Platt, however, recalled after the war that such a buried and camouflaged system had been discussed but that "neither the material nor manpower was available to put it into practice" (Platt, "Informal Report").

9. John Hamas Biographical File, MCHC Reference Section.

10. Just how many planes were involved in the dawn patrol is a mystery. Kinney's diary mentions his taking off at 0530 and landing at 0730; postwar statements by both Webb and Freuler refer to a two-plane patrol, and Webb recalled specifically that he and Major Putnam flew the dawn patrol themselves (Kinney Diary, 8 December 1941; 1st Lt. Henry G. Webb, ltr to Lt. Col. James P. S. Devereux, USMC, 19 October 1945, MCHC Archives; Freuler, "Report of Activities on Wake Island").

11. Whitney, *Guest of the Fallen Sun*, 17-18.

12. The defenders suspected that Japanese submarines may have homed in the bombers, but the *RO-65, RO-66,* and *RO-67,* from the Twenty-seventh Submarine Division, did not arrive on station until 10 December (U.S. Army, Far East Command, Military History Section, *Submarine Operations, December 1941-April 1942,* 30).

13. Although the Chitose Kōkūtai was also equipped with thirty-four Mitsubishi A5M4 Type 96 carrier fighters (*kansens*), none accompanied the bombers because of the long distances involved (Hata and Izawa, *Japanese Naval Aces and Fighter Units in World War II,* 103-5).

14. Holden had already sent Christmas presents home to his family; his parents, Mr. and Mrs. Dermot F. Holden, received a silver service together with a "letter full of confidence" that arrived at their Tenafly, New Jersey, home five days after Pearl Harbor; his sister Alice, a nurse in a Brooklyn hospital, received an "emerald-studded gold bracelet" the same day. The news of his death arrived before the presents he had sent (*New York Times,* 25 and 30 December 1941).

15. Darden, *Guests of the Emperor,* 77-78.

16. Ltr, John N. Valov to Lt. Col. James P. S. Devereux, USMC, 15 April 1946, Box 1, Wake Civilians, Personal Letters, Devereux Papers.

17. "Escape from Wake," 20-21.

18. Thompson, *Signal Corps,* 19.

19. Kessler, *To Wake and Beyond,* 45.

20. The matter of the departure of the *Philippine Clipper* raises questions. Commander Cunningham, on 29 January 1946, declared that he had assented to Captain Hamilton's plan to evacuate the PanAir employees on board the flying boat. In a letter to Captain James T. Alexander, however, written 27 August 1946, in response to Alexander's concern about the plight of the Guamanians left behind by PanAir, Cunningham emphasized that the *Clipper* "left without my prior knowledge or assent" (ltr, Cunningham to Alexander, 27 August 1946, in Box 2, Cunningham Papers).

21. Ltrs, Alexander to Cunningham, 1 August 1946; Alexander to U.S. Employees Compensation Commission, 1 August 1946; and Cunningham to Alexander, 27 August 1946, Box 2, Cunningham Papers. Although Cunningham denied that an agreement had been concluded, he informed Alexander that he would "be prepared

to do whatever I can to further the project of securing compensation for the Guamanians, to the extent of confirming Mr. Cooke's assertions in an affidavit. It is a notorious fact," Cunningham allowed, "that the mental faculties tend to atrophy during long imprisonment, and there is no doubt that Mr. Cooke's recollection of the events subsequent to the first Japanese attack are likely to be more correct than mine" (Cunningham to Alexander, 27 August 1946).

22. Although seriously handicapped by his wounds and in intense pain, the thirty-three-year-old Hannum supervised the maintenance of available aircraft for the next ten days, until, exhausted by the exertion that would have been strenuous enough for a well man, he collapsed and had to be evacuated to the hospital (ltr, CO, VMF-211 to SecNav, Subj: "Recommendation for the Silver Star Medal, case of Sgt. Howard D. Comin, USMC [Deceased]," 25 October 1945, and ltr, CO, VMF-211 to SecNav, Subj: "Recommendation for the Navy and Marine Corps Medal, case of TSgt. Earl R. Hannum, USMC," 25 October 1945, Putnam Papers).

23. 1st Lt. John F. Kinney, USMC, "The Last Days of Wake Island" [interview with Capt. W. H. Goodman, USMC, and Joel D. Thacker at Historical Division, Headquarters, Marine Corps, 23 July 1945). Putnam later praised Davidson not only for his part in the rescue work but for his effective assistance in reorganizing the squadron (ltr, CO, VMF-211 to SecNav, Subj: "Recommendation for the Silver Star medal, case of Second Lieutenant Carl R. Davidson, USMCR [Deceased]," 25 October 1945, Putnam Papers).

24. L. A. Hutnich, "Marine NAP, Visitor Here, Tells of Wake Capture, Prison Horror," Windsock, 2 [interview with TSgt. William J. Hamilton] in undated newspaper clipping in William J. Hamilton Biographical File, MCHC Reference Section.

25. Ltr, Haines to author, 22 September 1993.

26. Godbold, "Report of 'D' Battery Commander."

27. Ltr, Valov to Devereux, 15 April 1946, Devereux Papers.

28. Ltr, Harry L. McDonald to Lt. Col. James P. S. Devereux, USMC, 5 February 1946, Box 1, Devereux Papers.

29. Cunningham, "History of Wake Island Defense," 12; Keene, "Activities of Task Group 9.2."

30. CO, William Ward Burrows (AP-6) to Com14, "Enemy Action against Johnston Island, December 15, 1941—report of" (18 December 1941), NHC Operational Archives; "The Story of the U.S.S. William Ward Burrows before the War."

31. McMorris testimony, PHA, 22:530. McMorris erroneously referred to the William Ward Burrows, a transport, as a "cargo ship."

32. The corpses of the three were not discovered until several days later. Someone had stolen a sidearm from one of the dead marines' holster: "A fine Bunch of ghouls in the bush," Kinney wrote (Kinney Diary, 14 December 1941). Corporal Cyrus D. Fish, who apparently discovered the badly decomposed remains, never forgot the horrible sight. He experienced "recurring nightmares" for years thereafter (ltr, Mrs. Marylee Fish to author, received 21 June 1993).

33. Darden, Guests of the Emperor, 86.

34. Teters later recalled that "Devereux never sat in on the nightly staff meetings that we used to hold in my house, and, as a matter of fact, he complained to me rather bitterly that you had not called him in to those meetings and also that you had not reviewed all of the dispatches between Wake and Pearl with him" (ltr, Teters to Cunningham, 27 July 1948, Appendix G to "Narrative of Captain W. S. Cunningham, U.S. Navy, Relative to Events on Wake Island in December 1941 and

Subsequent Related Events," in Box 1723, World War II Action Reports [Individual Personnel, C-Edginton], NHC Operational Archives).

35. Whether the shell-shocked civilian identified only as "Adams" was Andrew F., Henry O., or James O. Adams, all of whom were employed on Wake by CPNAB at that time, is not specified.

36. "Operations of the 7th Submarine Squadron" in *Submarine Operations, December 1941–April 1942*, 30; also "Japanese Capture of Wake Island," Interrogation of Captain Koyama, Tadashi, Chief of Staff of the Sixth Torpedo [Destroyer] Squadron, in U.S. Strategic Bombing Survey [Pacific], *Interrogations of Japanese Officials*, 2.

37. "Recommendation for the Silver Star Medal, case of Sgt. Howard D. Comin, USMC," Putnam Papers.

38. June, "Defense of Wake Island."

CHAPTER FIVE: "Humbled by Sizeable Casualties"

The basic source for Pacific Fleet strategy and planning for relief efforts: "CinCPac Greybook," 8, 18; McMorris testimony, *PHA*, 22:529–30.

Message traffic concerning the bombings of Wake Island: Msgs, Wake Island to OinC Pearl, 10 1500 Dec. 1941, Wake to Com14 10 2145 Dec. 1941, Wake to Com14 10 2350 Dec. 1941, HQ, HawDept to Com14 re: Msg, Wake to Col. Hoppaugh 11 0025 Dec. 1941, as Encl E to Com14 to CinCPacFlt, Subj: "Wake Action, 7 December, 1941 to 24 December 1941," 6 January 1942.

On the activities of VMF-211: Kinney Diary, 11 December 1941; Putnam, "Report of VMF-211 on Wake Island" and "Notes on the Sinking of a Japanese Cruiser [*sic*] off Wake by VMF-211" [1st Lt. Edna Loftus Smith, USMCWR, interview with Lt. Col. Paul A. Putnam, 19 October 1945], MCHC Archives; Bayler, "Wake Island, Report on"; Freuler, "Report of Activities on Wake Island"; Hutnich interview with TSgt. William J. Hamilton.

On Japanese aerial operations: Chitose *Kōkūtai Kōdōchōsho*s, December 1941; Iwaya, *Chūkō*, 223–24; *Senshi Sōsho*, 38:166–67, 171; "Professional Notebook of an Ensign [Nakamura Toshio] in the Japanese Navy," *PHA*, 13:560–61.

On the operations of Rear Admiral Kajioka's force: Koyama Interrogation; "Wake Island Invasion Force" File, Prange Papers; "Professional Notebook of an Ensign [Nakamura Toshio] in the Japanese Navy," *PHA*, 13:560–61; Dull, *Battle History of the Imperial Japanese Navy*, 24; Eighteenth Cruiser Division Detailed Action Report, 8–29 December 1941, WDC 161510, Japanese World War II Records Seized in Post War Japan, in Japanese on Microfilm Reel JD-18, NHC Operational Archives; *Yūbari* Action Record and *Tenryu* Tabular Record of Movements/Action Record, translated on Microfilm Reel JT-1, NHC Operational Archives.

On the activities of the Wake Detachment, First Defense Battalion: Barninger, "Defense of Wake Island"; Warrant Officer Harold C. Borth, USMC, ltr to Col. James P. S. Devereux, USMC, Subj: "Report of Activites for the Period 7 December to 24 December 1941, at Wake Island," 23 October 1945, MCHC Archives; Burroughs, "Siege of Wake Island"; Butler, "Statement"; Godbold, "Report of 'D' Battery Commander"; Hamas, "Report on What Happened . . . Wake Island"; Kessler, "Report on Wake Island Operations," and Kessler, *To Wake and Beyond*, 21, 41, 53; Lewis, "Report on Action at Wake Island;" 1st Lt. John A. McAlister, USMC, "Report of 'L'

Battery, 5" Art[iller]y, Wake Island Det[achment], during the Period 8–23 December 1941," MCHC Archives; and Platt, "Informal Report."

On Commander Cunningham's activities as island commander: Cunningham, *Wake Island Command*, 92–93, 96.

On the U.S. Navy submarines off Wake: *Tambor*, "Report of First War Patrol"; *Triton*, "Report of War Patrol"; and Msg, Task Unit 7.2.4 to CinCPac 110905 of December 1941, Encl A to ComSubScoFor to CinCPac, "Information Concerning Attacks on Wake Island."

1. The composition of the invasion force arrayed off Wake matched well the October 1941 estimates discussed in Chapter 2. Kajioka's force contained three light cruisers (the October 1941 study estimated four), six destroyers (as the October study had predicted), two destroyer-transports, and two auxiliary vessels. The study had underestimated the number of auxiliaries the Japanese would deploy (it estimated only one logistics ship) and overestimated the number of carriers. Other than the planes carried on board the *Kongo Maru* and the *Kinryu Maru*, none were involved in the attempt to take the atoll; no carrier had been assigned to Kajioka's force. The number of troops was also 50 percent less than the Americans believed would be deployed.

2. Commander Uchida Shigeshi, a member of the Operations Section, First Bureau, Naval General Staff, noted in his diary for 7 December 1941: "News also came in that at Wake Island 12 aircraft were on the land airdrome and 6 flying boats were also at Wake" ("Extracts from Diary and Duty Book of Capt. Shigeshi Uchida," in Goldstein and Dillon, eds., *Pearl Harbor Papers*, 84).

3. Grey, "Monograph, 'The Defense of Wake Island,' Comments on."

4. The issue of when VMF-211 took off to deal with Kajioka's force on 11 December 1941 is best resolved by looking carefully at the statements made by VMF-211 pilots. None of the contemporary (December 1941) reports mention the tactic that Devereux claims as his own: asking that the planes not take off until the seacoast guns had opened fire, even if that meant drawing the Japanese ships into "point blank" range. Most historians appear to have uncritically accepted Devereux's tactics and ignored the reports of the pilots who flew the mission. Putnam, in an interview with First Lieutenant Edna Loftus Smith, USMCWR, on 19 October 1945, stated that VMF-211 took off "well before daylight." Captain Frank Tharin, upon his release from prisoner-of-war camp in October 1945, described the time of takeoff as "just before dawn." Because daylight was around 0530, the 0515 time seems to fit. Although Brigadier General John F. Kinney admitted to the author (ltr, 28 May 1993) that the times in his reconstructed diary might be off, the sequence of the events he recounts is significant: three VMF-211 planes take off, Japanese guns open fire, marine batteries open fire in return, a fourth VMF-211 plane takes off. Devereux himself was not clear on the sequence of events. His "Wake Island Report" (18 March 1946) states that the Japanese cruisers opened fire at 0530; "Four planes took off at this time" and at 0615 he gave the order to open fire, thus establishing the sequence as follows: Japanese fire, VMF-211 takes off, seacoast batteries open fire. In his 12 February 1947 interview with Lieutenant Colonel Robert D. Heinl at Quantico, Virginia, however, Devereux was "emphatic that VMF-211 launched aircraft *at the time the 5-inch batteries commenced firing, not before*" [emphasis added], thus contradicting his earlier recollection. Since the VMF-211 pilots were intimately involved in the action (especially Putnam and Tharin, who flew the mission), I have accepted their statements as more

logical. For Cunningham and Putnam (who were aviators) to have done what Devereux (who was not) claims to have suggested they do, thereby exposing the only air power Wake possessed to ships' battery fire, would have been foolhardy.

5. Sgt. Robert E. Bourquin, Jr., Diary.

6. Barninger, "Defense of Wake Island."

7. Burroughs, "Siege of Wake Island."

8. Barninger, "Defense of Wake Island."

9. According to *Ship and Gunnery Drills, United States Navy* (Washington, D.C.: U.S. Government Printing Office, 1927), 123, the standard crew for a 5-inch/51-caliber bag gun consisted of a gun captain, a pointer, a trainer, a sight setter, a plugman, a trayman, a rammerman, first and second shellman, first and second powdermen, and ammunition passers. If sufficient people were not available, the gun captain would act as the plugman.

10. Quoted in Robert D. Heinl, *Dictionary of Military and Naval Quotations* (Annapolis: Naval Institute Press, 1969), 295.

11. Maj. John Hamas to Capt. Winfield S. Cunningham, third endorsement, 8 March 1948, Subj: "The Defense of Wake," Appendix C(1) to "Narrative of Captain W. S. Cunningham, U.S. Navy, Relative to Events on Wake Island in December, 1941, and Subsequent Related Events," World War II Action Report File, "Individual Personnel, C-Edginton," Box 1723, NHC Operational Archives.

12. Quoted in USS *Enterprise* (CV-6) War Information Bulletin No. 2 [11 December 1941], in Rawie Diary, December 1941.

13. Although Paul Putnam later credited Kinney and Davidson with one plane apiece, the Japanese records indicate that Carl Davidson should get credit for both planes shot down.

14. The date Second Lieutenant Kliewer attacked the submarine varies among the postwar accounts by Wake survivors. Kliewer himself recalled the incident as occurring late on the fourteenth; some reconstructed diaries put it on the eleventh, others on the twelfth. Definitive proof, however, is found in Msg, CO Wake to Com14 11 2035 Dec. 1941: "Submarine attacked and believed sunk by fighters five thirty GCT eleventh [0530 GCT 11 December 1941 = 1630 local time 11 December 1941], Encl E to Com14 to CinCPacFlt, Subj: "Wake Action, 7 December 1941 to 24 December 1941," 6 January 1942, NHC Operational Archives. There is no proof, however, that Kliewer actually sank the *RO-66* on that date.

15. "CinCPac Greybook," 8.

16. Ibid., 15–16, 18.

17. Ibid., 41–44. A handwritten notation appears on the upper right corner of that draft (dated 10 December 1941): "Revised and issued for Task Force Fourteen." Other portions of the order dealt with operations to support Johnston and Palmyra. Although it was never issued as such, it is useful because it reflects the thinking concerning the relief of Wake at that time.

18. Ugaki, *Sensoroku*, 47.

19. Heinl, "We're Headed for Wake," 35.

CHAPTER SIX: "Still No Help"

The basic source for Pacific Fleet strategy and planning for relief efforts: "CinCPac Greybook," 45, 67, 75; McMorris testimony, *PHA*, 22:530–31; Kimmel testimony, ibid., 456.

Message traffic concerning the bombings of Wake Island: Msgs, Wake to Com14 11 2035 Dec. 1941; Wake to CinCPac 11 2230 Dec. 1941; [OiC] Wake to Navy Yard, Pearl Harbor 12 2032 Dec. 1941; Wake to Communication Office [Hickam Field], 14 Dec. 1941; Wake to Com14 13 1915 Dec. 1941; Wake to CinCPac, 13 2100 Dec. 1941; Msgs, Wake to Com14 13 2000, 13 2030, 13 2300, and 13 2130 Dec. 1941; Wake to Com14 14 0220 Dec. 1941; Wake to Com14 and CinCPac 14 0715 Dec. 1941; RDO Wake to Com14 15 0750 Dec. 1941; Wake to Com14 14 2359 Dec. 1941; Wake to Com14 15 0216 Dec. 1941; RDO Wake to Com14 15 0750 and 15 0815 Dec. 1941; Wake to Com14 16 0245 Dec. 1941; Wake Island to Com14, 17 0901 Dec. 1941; OiC Wake to Com14, 18 0324 Dec. 1941; Wake to Com14, 18 2350 Dec. 1941; all as Encl E to Com14 to CinCPacFlt, Subj: "Wake Action, 7 December, 1941 to 24 December 1941," 6 January 1942.

On the relief expedition: *Tangier* (AV-8) deck logs, December 1941; Heinl, "We're Headed for Wake," 37; Headquarters and Service Battery, Fourth Defense Battalion, Fleet Marine Force, muster roll, December 1941, MCHC Reference Section; and the following War Diaries in the NHC Operational Archives: Commander, Scouting Force [Task Force 11] and *Lexington* (CV-2); also Vice-Admiral Frederick C. Sherman Diary, NHC Operational Archives.

On VMF-211: Kinney Diary, 12–20 December 1941; Bayler, "Wake Island, Report on"; Freuler, "Report of Activities on Wake Island."

On Japanese operations: Chitose and Yokohama *Kōkūtai Kōdōchōshos*, December 1941; Iwaya, *Chūkō*, 223–24; *Senshi Sōsho*, 38:170; "Professional Notebook of an Ensign [Nakamura Toshio] in the Japanese Navy," PHA, 13:560.

On the operations of the Nagumo and Abe forces: Chigusa Sadao, "Conquer the Pacific Ocean Aboard Destroyer *Akigumo*: War Diary of the Hawaiian Battle," in Goldstein and Dillon, eds., *Pearl Harbor Papers*, 197–99; Task Force Signal Order No. 30, ibid., 230; "War Diary of the First Destroyer Squadron, 1–31 December 1941," ibid., 249; "War Diary of the Fifth Carrier Division 1–31 December 1941," ibid., 231; "War Diary of the Eighth Cruiser Division from 1 Dec. 1941 to 31 Dec. 1941," translated MSS in Prange Papers; *Senshi Sōsho*, vol. 10 and vol. 38.

On the Wake Detachment, First Defense Battalion: Barninger, "Defense of Wake Island"; Godbold, "Report of 'D' Battery Commander"; Greeley, "Informal Report"; Hamas, "Report on What Happened . . . Wake Island"; Lewis, "Report on Action at Wake Island"; McKinstry, "Action during Period 7 December to 23 December 1941."

On Commander Cunningham's activities: Cunningham, *Wake Island Command*, 109.

On the U.S. Navy submarines off Wake: *Tambor*, "Report of First War Patrol," and *Triton*, "Report of War Patrol."

On CPNAB activities: Teters Affidavit, 4.

On the Army Communications detachment: "Army Detachment, Wake Island."

1. CO, VMF-211 to SecNav, Subj: "Recommendation for the Distinguished Flying Cross, case of Capt. Frank C. Tharin, USMC," 25 October 1945, Putnam Papers.

2. Msg, District Material Officer to NAS Wake 11 2359 Dec. 1941, Encl E, to Com14 to CinCPacFlt, Subj: "Wake Action, 7 December 1941 to 24 December 1941," 6 January 1942.

3. Msg, Wake to Com14 12 0000 Dec. 1941, Encl E to Com14 to CinCPacFlt, Subj: "Wake Action, 7 December 1941 to 24 December 1941," 6 January 1942. Cunningham amplified that dispatch at 0945 on the fourteenth, adding Coxswain Wolney's name

to the list and including a message to George Youmans, of the CPNAB OpCom, from Teters, that a list of the known dead contractors would follow in plain language once a check was completed (Msg, RDO Wake to Com14 13 2245 Dec. 1941, Encl E to Com14 to CinCPacFlt, Subj: "Wake Action, 7 December 1941 to 24 December 1941").

4. CO, VMF-211 to SecNav, Subj: "Recommendation for the Navy and Marine Corps Medal, case of Capt. Herbert C. Freuler, USMCR," 25 October 1945, Putnam Papers.

5. Greey, "Monograph, 'The Defense of Wake Island,' Comments on."

6. *Complete Presidential Press Conferences of Franklin D. Roosevelt*, vols. 17–18, 1941, 364.

7. "Memorandum for the Secretary of the Navy," 11 December 1941, Folder 58, Thomas Holcomb Papers, MCHC Personal Papers Collection.

8. Ltr, RAdm. Henry E. Lackey, USN (Ret.) to Holcomb, 13 December 1941, ibid.

9. "Diary of Rear Adm. Giichi Nakahara, Extracts, 11 August 1941–1 January 1942," in Goldstein and Dillon, eds., *Pearl Harbor Papers*, 74.

10. Ltr, Bloch to Stark, 12 December 1941, Box 4, Bloch Papers.

11. Ltr, Kimmel to Stark, 12 December 1941, *PHA*, 16:2257.

12. "Professional Notebook of an Ensign [Nakamura Toshio] in the Japanese Navy," in *PHA*, 13:563.

13. Ltr, Haines to author, 22 September 1993.

14. Ltr, Fred S. Gibbons to Devereux, 2 March 1946, in Box 1(D), Wake Civilians, Personal Letters, 1945–46, Devereux Papers.

15. *Senshi Sosho*, 10:415.

16. Col. Harry K. Pickett, USMC [Commanding, Marine Forces, Fourteenth Naval District] "Memorandum for Chief of Staff, Fourteenth Naval District, Subject: Personnel, Ammunition, Material, etc., for Wake," 15 December 1941, MCHC Archives.

17. Fassett's personal characteristics are derived from his Bronze Star citation, the award he received for leadership at Vella Lavella when his battalion landed there and "speedily and efficiently" installed antiaircraft batteries that repelled numerous Japanese air attacks between 14 August and 31 October 1943.

18. Wildenberg, "Chester Nimitz and the Development of Fueling at Sea," 56.

19. Ltr, Kimmel to Stark, 15 December 1941, Box 3, Series I—Correspondence, Semi-Official and Personal, 1939–41, Stark Papers. Biographical material on Fletcher from Officer Biography Files, NHC Operational Archives and U.S. Naval Academy Archives; the quotes describing Fletcher are from the *Seattle Times*, 22 November 1942, and the 1906 *Lucky Bag*, 82.

20. Msg, OpNav to CinCPac 15 2149 [December 1941] in "CinCPac Greybook," 50.

21. Msg, CinCPac to OpNav 15 2301 [December 1941], ibid., 50–51.

22. Msg, OpNav to CinCPac, 16 0050 [December 1941], ibid., 51.

23. Col. James L. Neefus, USMC (Ret.), responses to author's questionnaire, February 1982, and Col. Charles W. Somers, USMC (Ret.), response to author's questionnaire, 23 September 1981. The F2As would not be equipped with self-sealing tanks or armor plate until after their arrival at Midway shortly after Christmas of 1941.

24. Ltr, Rowell to Larkin, 23 December 1941, Larkin Papers.

25. In his postwar report, Putnam claimed that the island commander had informed him of the possible prescence of Dutch submarines near Wake. Cunningham denied it. The foredeck marking may have been a red ball on a white rectangle, an

identification marking known to have been applied to Japanese submarines. G. W. Stowe's article, "Queen's Navy at War: Operations of the Royal Netherlands Navy in the Southwest Pacific during the Invasion of the Philippines, Malacca, and the East Indies," *U.S. Naval Institute Proceedings* (March 1950), 289–301, does not refer to any Dutch submarines traversing the Pacific at that time in the vicinity of Wake.

26. Although Godbold's postwar account placed the raid that dropped bombs near Battery D on the sixteenth, the Yokohama *Kōkūtai's Kōdōchōsho* places the raid on the fifteenth—the timing is also identical.

27. CO, VMF-211 to SecNav, Subj: "Recommendation for the Distinguished Service Medal, case of James J. [*sic*] Hesson, AMM1c, USN," 25 October 1945, Putnam Papers.

28. Heinl erroneously described the wrecked plane on the reef as Japanese. The only plane that could have been at that spot was a Douglas SBD-3 Dauntless from Scouting Squadron Six that had been shot down on 7 December 1941 by gunfire from the Fleet Machine Gun School at Fort Weaver (Cressman and Wenger, *Steady Nerves and Stout Hearts*, 35–38).

29. Ltr, Kimmel to Stark, 15 December 1941, Stark Papers.

30. Ibid.

31. *Senshi Sōsho*, 10:417.

32. Prange, *At Dawn We Slept*, 110–11.

33. "Individual Records of Japanese Navy Flag Officers . . . ," Intelligence Report Serial 57-41 [8 November 1941], in Box 1, Office of Naval Intelligence Japan Desk Files, RG 38, NA Military Reference Branch.

34. Excessive use of the radio incident to the Wake Island operation bothered Rear Admiral Kusaka Ryunosuke: "But those fleets which did not appreciate the actual situation the Task Force was confronting sent in such long negotiated telegrams as to compel us to send back telegrams against our will. I was extremely embarrassed by them and forced to send back telegrams breaking the restriction [radio silence]" (*Rengo Kantai* [extracts], in Goldstein and Dillon, eds., *Pearl Harbor Papers*, 166).

35. At that time, three American submarines were en route to the waters off the Japanese homeland—the *Gudgeon* (ss-211) (departed Pearl 11 December 1941), *Pollack* (ss-180) (departed 13 December), and *Plunger* (ss-179) (departed 14 December). None reported contacting any ships en route to their respective patrol areas.

36. "CinCPac Greybook," 67.

37. Ltr, Henshaw to author, 7 July 1993.

38. A careful search of news media for the period failed to turn up any reference to the "Send us some more Japs" message before 17 December, suggesting that Kinney's reference to the message in his reconstructed diary may be off by a few days.

39. *New York Times*, 17 December 1941. Holden and MacMurray were not, however, among the actors who were among the actual cast of the film.

40. CO, VMF-211, to SecNav, Subj: "Recommendation for the Navy Cross, case of SSgt. Robert O. Arthur, USMC," 25 October 1945, Putnam Papers.

41. Msg, Com14 to OiC, Wake, 17 0340 Dec. 1941, Encl E to Com14 to CinCPacFlt, Subj: "Wake Action, 7 December 1941 to 24 December 1941," 6 January 1942.

42. Godbold's narrative places the attack on the sixteenth, but the Yokohama *Kōkūtai* records show no mission flown against Wake on that date. Because the objective of the flying boats and Godbold's report (given an adjustment in dates) complement each other, I believe it most likely that the attack occurred on the seventeenth.

43. U.S. Army, Far East Command, Military History Section, *Imperial Japanese Navy in World War II*, 241.

44. Ugaki, *Sensoroku*, 52.

45. Memo for Chief of Staff, 14th ND from War Plans Officer, CinCPac Staff [Captain C. H. McMorris], Subj: "Personnel to Be Evacuated from Wake," 17 December 1941, in Box 181-58-3237 (V 2037), 14th ND Staff Headquarters, General Correspondence (formerly classified), folder NA-39, RG 181, NA Pacific-Sierra Region.

46. Ibid.

47. Com14 to CO, NAS Wake, Subj: "Evacuation of personnel and unloading," 17 December 1941, ibid.

48. Ibid.; also Teters Affidavit, 4.

49. Com14 to CO, NAS Wake, Subj: "Evacuation of personnel and unloading," 17 December 1941.

50. Memo, Kimmel to Stark, Subj: "Conditions in Pacific Fleet," 26 May 1941," *PHA*, 16:2234.

51. Ltr, Ens. James J. Murphy, A-V(N), USNR to ComPatWing Two, Subj: "Flight to Wake Island and Information Concerning Activities on Wake Island—Report on," 28 December 1941, as Enclosure to Action Report, Commander Fleet Air Wing Two, Ser 01, 1 January 1942, World War II Action Report File, NHC Operational Archives. Comments that it was felt that the crew was expendable because it contained three ensigns do not recognize the fact that the flight crew was the best in VP-23, not the most expendable.

52. Kinney gives the date as the seventeenth, but Chitose *Kōkūtai* records do not list a reconnaissance mission on that date, but on the eighteenth. Bayler's account, more contemporary than Kinney's reconstructed (February 1942) diary, agrees with two Japanese sources (Ensign Nakamura's notebook and the Chitose *Kōkūtai Kōdō-chōsho*), thus leading me to conclude that the action most likely occurred on the eighteenth and not the seventeenth.

53. Msgs, Com14 (Port Director) to OinC, Wake, 18 0130 Dec. 1941 and OinC, Wake to Com14 18 0305 December 1941, Encl E to Commandant, 14th ND to CinCPacFlt, Subj: "Wake Action, 7 December 1941 to 24 December 1941," 6 January 1942.

54. Teters Affidavit, 4.

55. Woodbury, *Builders for Battle*, 320–22. When praised later for his steadfastly pressing on to Honolulu–the *Arthur Foss* reached her destination three days after Christmas of 1941 with the two barges in tow—Ralstead simply replied: "There was nothing else to do but come home, and that is what we did." The port director at Honolulu logged in the *Arthur Foss*'s arrival at Honolulu at 1500 on 28 December 1941 (14thND War Diary, Box 431, World War II War Diaries, NHC Operational Archives).

56. "CinCPac Greybook," 67.

57. Details on this raid from both sides are sparse. Kinney's diary indicates one plane in commission that day, 211-F-9. One Japanese source contains reference to one fighter engaging the bombers, but no American source mentions that any attack occurred.

58. Msg, NAS Midway to NAS Wake 19 2010 Dec. 1941 in Encl E to Com14 to CinCPacFlt, Subj: "Wake Action, 7 December 1941 to 24 December 1941," 6 January 1942.

CHAPTER SEVEN: "Very Secret to Everyone Except the Japs"

Sources for the relief expedition: ComScoFor [Task Force 11] War Diary, 19 December 1941; Lt. Ward Bronson Diary, 20 December 1941, World War II Command File, NHC Operational Archives.

On Cunningham's activities: Cunningham, "History of Wake Island Defense," 8–9; Cunningham, *Wake Island Command*, 113, 115.

On VMF-211's operations: Kinney Diary, 20–22 December 1941; Kinney, "The Last Days of Wake Island"; Freuler, "Report of Activities on Wake Island"; Kliewer, "Personal Diary"; Putnam, "Report of VMF-211 on Wake Island," 14; ltr, Putnam to Cunningham, 15 June 1948.

On defense battalion operations: Barninger, "Defense of Wake Island"; Burroughs, "Siege of Wake Island"; Godbold, "Report of 'D' Battery Commander"; Greeley, "Informal Report"; Hamas, "Report on What Happened . . . Wake Island"; Lewis, "Report on Action at Wake Island"; McKinstry, "Action during Period 7 December to 23 December 1941."

On CPNAB activities: Teters Affidavit, 4.

On Japanese operations: *Kōdōchōsho*s for the *Hiryū* and the *Sōryū* for 21–22 December 1941; Chitose *Kōkūtai Kōdōchōsho*, 21 December 1941; "War Diary of the Eighth Cruiser Division," Prange Papers; *Senshi Sōsho*, 38:201; Iwaya, *Chūkō*, 225.

On U.S. submarine operations: *Triton*, "Report of War Patrol"; ComSubScoFor War Diary, 20 December 1941, NHC Operational Archives.

1. Murphy, "Flight to Wake Island."

2. Cunningham stated that 350 civilians were to be evacuated; the memorandum from Bloch to Cunningham stated 250.

3. Capt. Henry T. Elrod to Mrs. Elizabeth Elrod, 20 December 1941, Elrod Papers, MCHC Personal Papers Collection.

4. Ltr, CO, NAS, Wake, to Com14, 20 December 1941, Encl B to Com14 to CinCPacFlt, Subj: "Wake Action, 7 December 1941 to 24 December 1941," 6 January 1942, NHC Operational Archives.

5. Cunningham, *Wake Island Command*, 115.

6. Ltr, Mr. H. P. Hevenor to Col. Clark, 20 December 1941, MCHC Archives.

7. Ltr, ROiC Noy 4173 Wake to OiC Noy 4173 Pearl, Subj: Wake Island, 20 December 1941, Encl D to Com14 to CinCPacFlt, Subj: "Wake Action, 7 December 1941," 6 January 1942.

8. Ibid.

9. Ltr, Teters to George Ferris, 21 December 1941, quoted in Woodbury, *Builders for Battle*, 323–24.

10. Ibid.

11. The word apparently did not reach everyone, for Barninger later complained: "I didn't know it [the PBY] was going out or I would have tried to include some message" (Barninger, "Defense of Wake Island"). "It was physically impossible for me to play Mercury for all marines and civilians," Bayler later wrote, "much as I would have liked to" (Bayler, *Last Man off Wake Island*, 134).

12. Bourquin Diary.

13. *Spokane* (Washington) *Review*, 18 March 1942, clipping in Putnam Papers.

14. Maj. Paul A. Putnam to Mrs. Virginia Putnam, 20 December 1941, Putnam Papers.

15. Ltr, CO, VMF-211 to CO, MAG-21, 20 December 1941, MCHC Archives.

16. Ibid. In a marginal note to this report by Putnam upon his return from prisoner-of-war camp in Japan in October 1945, he added Aviation Machinist's Mate First Class Hesson's name to those of Kinney and Hamilton.

17. Capt. Henry T. Elrod to Mrs. Elizabeth Elrod, 20 December 1941, Elrod Papers.

18. Ibid.

19. Murphy, "Flight to Wake Island." Several marines commented that the pilots seemed annoyed at the lack of accommodations. "The crew of the patrol plane," Kinney recalled, "came in with suitcases and all sorts of gear as though they were going somewhere for a weekend. They seemed surprised when they saw that the [PanAir] hotel was gone and everything burned to the ground. They suddenly decided that they did not want to stay too long" (Kinney, "Last Days of Wake Island"). Writing some years after the event, Lieutenant Commander Francis C. Riley, USN (Ret.), who had been Murphy's first pilot on the mission to Wake, did not recall anyone asking where the PanAir hotel was ("We took 'The Last Man off Wake Island'—21 Dec. 1941," written recollections [ca. 1989] provided to James C. Sawruk in March 1994). PanAir had furnished excellent lodging for transpacific PBY flights in 1939 and 1940. As Cunningham had noted perceptively, although Murphy's men may have known that Wake had been under siege since 8 December, they probably had little idea of the extent of the destruction wreaked by the Japanese over the previous two weeks. Messages emanating from Pearl Harbor also reflected an obvious lack of appreciation for the difficulties being encountered by Cunningham's garrison.

20. Msg, CTU 7.2.4. to CTF 7 [RAdm. Thomas Withers, ComSubScoFor], 206050 December 1941, Encl A to ComSubScoFor to CinCPac Ser 01133, Subj: "Information concerning attacks on Wake Island," 29 December 1941, NHC Operational Archives.

21. Riley, "We Took 'The Last Man off Wake Island'."

22. Bayler, Last Man off Wake Island, 135.

23. The arrival of 23-P-4 at Midway, as Riley later recalled, surprised that garrison because the departure report Murphy furnished Wake to provide Midway, so that the PBY would not have to break radio silence, had not been sent. Japanese carrier planes arrived on the morning of the twenty-first before Wake's communicators had had a chance to send it (Riley, "We Took 'The Last Man off Wake Island'").

24. Prange, At Dawn We Slept, 197.

25. Goldstein and Dillon, eds., Pearl Harbor Papers, 35.

26. Msg, OiC Naval Activities, Wake to Com14 and CinCPacFlt, 20 2300 December 1941, Encl E to Com14 to CinCPacFlt, Subj: "Wake Action, 7 December 1941 to 24 December 1941," 6 January 1942.

27. Bronze Star citations for Fortuna and Wright.

28. Msg, Wake to Com14 21 0715 December 1941, Encl E to Com14 to CinCPacFlt, Subj: "Wake Action, 7 December 1941 to 24 December 1941," 6 January 1942.

29. Priority dispatch 211100 of December 1941, CTU 7.2.4. to CinCPac, Encl A to ComSubScoFor to CinCPac Ser 01133, Subj: "Information concerning attacks on Wake Island," 29 December 1941.

30. Msg, CinCPac to OpNav, 21 0147 December 1941, in "CinCPac Greybook," 73.

31. Msg, CinCPac to RDO Wake 21 2145 December 1941 in Encl E to Com14 to CinCPacFlt, Subj: "Wake Action, 7 December 1941 to 24 December 1941," ibid.

32. The Chitose *Kōkūtai* aircrew must have held a healthy respect for the marine pilots. No American source recounts any attacks that day, and only one plane—Putnam's—was operable. Abe, however, and his air task commander, Yamaguchi, must have discounted the extent of the fighter opposition encountered by the land attack planes because they assigned only six fighters to escort the attack planes on the twenty-second.

33. Goldstein and Dillon, eds., *Pearl Harbor Papers*, 35.

34. In recent years Kanai has been mistakenly credited with dropping the 800-kilogram bomb that destroyed the *Arizona* at Pearl Harbor on 7 December 1941. Kanai, from the *Sōryū*, most likely bombed the *Tennessee* (BB-43) or the *West Virginia* (BB-48). The *Arizona* was hit by bombs from *kankōs* from *Hiryū* and *Kaga*, the fatal missile being dropped by a *Hiryū* plane commanded by Lieutenant Commander Kusumi. An excellent analysis by David Aiken and John DeVirgilio of what caused the destruction of the *Arizona* is in Stillwell, *Battleship Arizona*, 274–78.

35. Tahara, who had undergone flight training between October 1938 and May 1939, was killed in action near Hainan Island on 19 April 1944 (Hata and Izawa, *Japanese Naval Aces and Fighter Units in World War II*, 414). Davidson's F4F was the one that Vice-Admiral Halsey had given VMF-211 en route to Wake to bring the squadron up to full strength.

36. U.S. Fleet, Headquarters of the Commander in Chief, "War Service Fuel Consumption of U.S. Naval Surface Vessels," FTP-218, 1, NHC Ships' Histories Branch.

37. "Testimony of Vice Admiral William Satterlee Pye, United States Navy, Commander Battle Force, United States Fleet," 9 January 1942, in *PHA*, 23:1063. Soc McMorris, in an interview with Samuel Eliot Morison (undated) that Morison provided Lieutenant Colonel Robert D. Heinl, Jr., described the pilot of the PBY as "jittery as hell." Lieutenant Commander Riley's recollections ("We Took 'The Last Man off Wake Island'") clearly reflect an anxiety over being caught at Wake by a Japanese raid, as does Bayler's account, in *Last Man off Wake Island* (135) of Murphy's apparently glancing nervously at his watch. Then Lieutenant Colonel Omar Pfeiffer, a war planner on Vice-Admiral Pye's staff, remembered: "We talked with these two pilots, both of them very, very young and inexperienced, [and] the main word I remember hearing in their replies was 'Grim, grim, grim'" ("Major General Omar T. Pfeiffer, USMC [Ret.], Oral History Transcript," 178, MCHC Oral History Collection). Pfeiffer did Murphy a disservice, though, because he was one of the most experienced pilots in the squadron. Murphy had been awarded his wings on 20 October 1939 (Officer Biography File, NHC Operational Archives). Five of VMF-211's pilots who had been at Wake when the war started (Davidson, Kliewer, Webb, Conderman, and Holden) had had their wings for less time.

38. Pfeiffer Oral History.

CHAPTER EIGHT: "This Is as Far as We Go"

For the operations of the defenders: Barninger, "Defense of Wake Island"; Burroughs, "Siege of Wake Island"; Devereux, *Story of Wake Island*, 158; Godbold, "Report of 'D' Battery Commander"; Greeley, "Informal Report of Action on Wake Island"; Hanna, "Report on Wake Island"; Kessler, "Report on Wake Island Operations," and *To Wake and Beyond*, 66; Kliewer, "Personal Diary"; Lewis, "Report on Action on Wake Island"; McAlister, "Report of 'L' Battery"; McKinstry, "Action during Period

7 December to 23 December 1941"; Platt, "Informal Report"; Poindexter, "Informal Report of Operations of the .30 Caliber MG Battery and the Mobile Reserve"; Potter, "Brief of Events at Wake Island, Period 7–24 December 1941"; Putnam, "Report of VMF-211 on Wake Island," 4, 10; ltr, Valov to Devereux, 15 April 1946.

On Japanese operations: Koyama Interrogation; Ibushi, "A Detailed Report on the Capture of Wake Island," in "Hawaii-Malaya Naval Operations," Allied Translator and Interpreter Section, South West Pacific Area, Enemy Publications, Document No. 6 (27 March 1943), in MCHC Archives; *Kōdōchōshos* for the *Sōryū* and the *Hiryū*, 23 December 1941; *Senshi Sōsho*, 38:211.

On the deliberations concerning the relief of Wake (pages in "CinCPac Greybook" in parentheses): "Decision by Admiral Draemel as to action regarding enemy investing Wake. 0700, 22 December" (82); "Estimate by Admiral Pye as to Action re[garding] enemy investing Wake—0700—December 22, 1941" (77–78); "Estimate by Captain McMorris as to action regarding enemy investing Wake 0800 Dec[ember] 22" (79, 81).

1. Msg, Wake to Com14 22 1445 Dec. 1941, Encl E to Com14 to CinCPacFlt, Subj: "Wake Action, 7 December 1941 to 24 December 1941," 6 January 1942.

2. Msg, Wake to Com14 22 1550 Dec. 1941, ibid.

3. Ltr, Wesley M. Platt to Charles D. Halstead, 6 January 1949, Halstead Papers.

4. Toland, *But Not in Shame*, 99. Toland claims that Sorenson was twenty years older than Putnam. A CPNAB roster shows Sorenson's birth date as 17 February 1901; Putnam's was 16 June 1903.

5. Msg, CinCPac to NAS Wake, 22 1619 Dec. 1941, Encl E to Com14 to CinC-PacFlt, Subj: Wake Action, 7 December 1941 to 24 December 1941, 6 January 1942. In his postwar statement, Cunningham wrote that he attempted to contact the submarine operating offshore; there is no record of that dispatch in the collected message traffic sent from Wake.

6. In 1942, Lieutenant Colonel Stanton Babcock, Cavalry, U.S. Army, while interned at the American Embassy in Tokyo, prepared "A Study of Land Operations in the Far East, December 8, 1941 to June 8, 1942, Based on Japanese Sources." Based entirely on material obtained from the Japanese press, radio, and published personal experiences of officers and enlisted men, the study contained a description of the Wake Island operation. On page 60 there appeared the following: "Japanese accounts are loud in the praise of the way in which the Americans handled the two six-inch guns, mounted near the beach, whose installation was far from complete. According to the report of the commander of the Japanese landing party, the fire control apparatus for the shore defense battery had not yet been set up, and during the action the guns were trained by opening the breech and sighting down the bore. The destruction of the two enemy war vessels and the damaging of a transport by two guns fired in this slow awkward manner excited the admiration of the Japanese officers, and all of the personal experience stories referred to this extraordinary feat in the terms of glowing praise. It is interesting to note, however, that later accounts published by the Japanese propaganda ministry belittled the efforts of the defenders, characterized the defense of the islands as negligible, and made every effort to convince the Japanese public that the Americans had behaved in a cowardly manner." Is the account Babcock reported of the five-inch or three-inch batteries? I believe that, allowing for exaggeration and inaccuracies in oral tradition, the incident to which Babcock refers is most probably that of Hanna's antiboat gun—note the admiration for artillerymen firing

their gun, mounted near the beach and for which no fire control existed, without sights and destroying two enemy ships (Memo to Commandant of the Marine Corps, from Col. M. H. Silverthorn, 1 October 1942, USMC, in Folder 3C, "Miscellaneous Reports of Jap[anese] Forces, Wake," in MCHC Archives). The reference to Hanna's position being the most important comes from Ibushi, "A Detailed Report on the Capture of Wake Island," 28.

7. Poindexter interview.

8. CO, VMF-211 to SecNav, "Recommendation for the Navy Cross, case of Second Lieutenant Robert Melton Hanna," Putnam Papers.

9. Ltr, Henry E. Ramsey to author, 20 September 1993. Another perspective on Elrod's death came from Paul Putnam. "If you are in contact with Betty," Putnam wrote his wife from Zentsuji (he had arrived at that prison camp on 29 January 1942), "tell her to be very proud of Talmadge [sic]. He did very well indeed and died fight[ing] strongly" (Putnam to Mrs. Virginia Putnam, [n.d. but probably ca. February 1942], Putnam Papers).

10. Thompson submachine gun advertisement, ca. 1938.

11. Ibushi, "A Detailed Report on the Capture of Wake Island," 28

12. Lewis, "Report on Action on Wake Island."

13. Tsouras, *Warrior's Words*, 167.

14. Msg, Wake Island to Com14 22 1800 Dec. 1941, Encl E to Com14 to CinC-PacFlt, Subj: Wake Action, 7 December 1941 to 24 December 1941, 6 January 1942; Cunningham, *Wake Island Command*, 134.

15. Although Poindexter referred to Schumacher as a corporal in his postwar reports, the man in question is carried on contemporary muster rolls as a private first class.

16. Poindexter, "Our Last Hurrah on Wake Atoll," 67.

17. Tsouras, *Warrior's Words*, 139.

18. The "Chuck" Smith referred to is not recorded. There were two Charles Smiths employed by CPNAB: Charles E., a reinforced-steel worker, and Charles R., a truck driver.

19. Gragg earned a Bronze Star during the Korean War for his untiring service as an artillery forward observer in June 1951, in which he exhibited determination, courage, and initiative—qualities he evidenced on Wake.

20. The "Records of the 6th Cruiser Division," WDC No. 160977, Group 55, NHC Operational Archives, refer to the ships of the divison firing at Wake. The tabular records of movements for the four ships, however, mention no firing that day. The distance given in the "Records of the 6th Cruiser Division" also refer to the ships being ten kilometers offshore, which would have placed them within the effective range of Battery B.

21. Msg, Wake Island to CinCPac 22 1952 Dec. 1941, Encl E to Com14 to CinC-PacFlt, Subj: Wake Action, 7 December 1941 to 24 December 1941, 6 January 1942.

22. Pye testimony, *PHA*, 23:1063.

23. Ibid.

24. Ibid. In his oral history recollections, Major General Pfeiffer bitterly complained that Pye had made his decision to recall the Wake Island relief force "without any reference being made to any of Admiral Kimmel's old staff members" (Pfeiffer Oral History Transcript, 178–79), but Pye sought the counsel of McMorris, who, as Kimmel's war plans officer, had been involved intimately in planning the relief of outlying bases even before the attack on Pearl Harbor. On the matter of inflicting

damage on the enemy, Pye and his staff may have been overly cautious. The Lae-Salamaua Raid of 10 March 1942 (by the *Yorktown* and the *Lexington* air groups) inflicted damage on enough ships (the Fourth Fleet appears to have been run on a shoestring) that the South Seas Force operations against Port Moresby were delayed considerably.

25. ComTaskForce 14 to CinCPac, "Report of Operations, 16 December–29 December 1941," 28 December 1941, NHC Operational Archives.

26. Lundstrom, *First Team*, 43.

27. "Notes on Interview with Admiral Aubrey W. Fitch, USN (Ret.) by Lieutenant Colonel [Robert D.] Heinl on 13 June 1947" in MCHC Archives. Heinl also reported that Fitch said "had he [Fitch] been able to establish any sort of effective local communication with Admiral Fletcher. . . . He and Fletcher could probably have worked out some way to disregard or 'misinterpret' the objectionable order." Fitch, Heinl reported, "wanted to go in, not only for the sake of relieving Wake, but because he felt convinced that a vigorous move-in to the atoll would result in hitting the Japanese when they could least afford to receive such a blow."

28. Neefus response to author's questionnaire; ltr, Col. Robert L. Dickey, USMC (Ret.), to author, 11 December 1981.

29. Lt. Donald A. Lovelace Diary, 23 December 1941.

CHAPTER NINE: "A Difficult Thing to Do"

Basic sources for the battle, from the defenders' perspective, are Barninger, "Defense of Wake Island"; Borth, "Report of Activities . . . at Wake Island"; Devereux, "Wake Island Report"; Cunningham, "History of Wake Island Defense," and *Wake Island Command*; Godbold, "Report of 'D' Battery Commander"; Greeley, "Informal Report"; Hamas, "Report on What Happened . . . Wake Island"; Keene, "Activities of Task Group 9.2"; Kessler, "Report on Wake Island Operations" and *To Wake and Beyond*, 36, 70–72; Kinney Diary, 23 December 1941; Kliewer, "Personal Diary"; Lewis, "Report on Action at Wake Island"; McAlister, "Report of 'L' Battery"; McKinstry, "Action during Period 7 December to 23 December 1941"; Platt, "Informal Report"; Poindexter,"Informal Report of Operations of the .30-Caliber MG Battery and the Mobile Reserve"; Putnam, "Report of VMF-211 on Wake Island," 12–13.

On Japanese operations: *Kōdōchōshos* for the *Hiryū* and *Sōryū*, 23 December 1941; *Kiyokawa Maru* Detailed Action Report for 23 December 1941, Japan War History Office; *Kiyokawa Maru* Battle Report (excerpt), No. 19-3, 1, WDC 160252, NHC Operational Archives Branch; Sixth Destroyer Squadron Detailed Action Report, 11–23 December 1941, Japanese Microfilm Reel JD-32; Eighteenth Cruiser Division Detailed Action Report, 11–23 December 1941, Japanese Microfilm Reel JD-18; "Translations of Captured Documents on Lessons Learned by the Japanese in the Attack on Wake Island," Joint Intelligence Center, Pacific Ocean Area Bulletin No. 1-43, "Japanese Land Forces, No. 5" [14 January 1943], 1, 3–11, in Monograph Comment File, *The Guadalcanal Campaign*, MCHC Archives; *Senshi Sōsho*, 38:215.

On the postwar recovery of Wake: CinCPacFlt/CinC Pacific Ocean Area, "Report of Surrender and Occupation of Japan," Serial 0395 of 11 February 1946, 186–87.

1. Joseph Conrad on "The Prestige, Privilege, and the Burden of Command," in Quotation File, NHC Ships' Histories Branch.

2. Doikawa had shot down two SBDs from the *Enterprise* near Ewa Mooring Mast Field on 7 December.

3. Fish's Bronze Star citation; also Poindexter interview.

4. ComSubScoFor WD, 22 December 1941, NHC Operational Archives.

5. Kessler, *To Wake and Beyond*, 36.

6. Okumiya and Horikoshi, *Zero!*, 122.

7. Heinl, "We're Headed for Wake," 37–38.

8. Kinkaid, "Four Years of War in the Pacific," 48, MSS in Kinkaid Papers, NHC Operational Archives Branch.

9. Ibid., 49–54.

10. Lt. (j.g.) James G. Daniels, III, "War Diary," 23 December 1941.

11. "War Record of Fighting Six."

12. Bronson Diary, 23 December 1941.

13. *Japan Times and Advertiser*, 24 December 1941, 1, and 26 December 1941, 2; also *New York Times*, 25 December 1941, 1 and 4.

14. *Japan Times and Advertiser*, 25 December 1941, 1.

15. "Kumesaka Nemeto Goes off to War," in United States Pacific Fleet and Pacific Ocean Areas, "Weekly Intelligence," 17, Vol. 1, No. 20, 24 November 1944, Box 143, World War II Japanese Records, NHC Operational Archives.

16. Ltr, Larkin to Rowell, 25 December 1941, Larkin Papers.

17. Ando Akiro, "Landing on Wake Island," in "Hawaii-Malaya Naval Operations," Allied Translator and Interpreter Section, South West Pacific Area, Enemy Publications, No. 6, 27 March 1943, 35.

18. Ibid., 35–36.

19. Kimmel testimony, *PHA*, 22:397ff.

20. Commander of the Prisoner Escort, Navy of the Great Japanese Empire, "Regulations for prisoners," n.d. [January 1942], in Cunningham Papers.

21. Captain Winfield S. Cunningham, U.S. Navy, Affidavit, n.d., 6, Cunningham Papers.

22. "Notes on the Defense of Wake Island," Encl A to ltr, CMC to ComInCh (n.d.), in Folder IL-2, MCHC Archives. Devereux did not mention this in his book, *The Story of Wake Island*. He claims that before Quartermaster Clerk Paul Chandler, who enjoyed diplomatic status at Shanghai, was repatriated back to the United States, Devereux took him aside and "gave him our casualty figures and a list of our dead and wounded and told him to inform Headquarters. I also told him to report orally how the Japanese had succeeded in their final attack—by landing at night and without naval gunfire support." That, Devereux reported in *The Story of Wake Island* (232–33) was "the only contribution I could make to our military intelligence."

23. U.S. Army, Chief of Staff, *Biennial Report of the Chief of Staff of the United States Army, July 1, 1941 to June 30, 1942, to the Secretary of War*, 5.

24. "Translations of Captured Documents," 1.

25. Potter, "Brief of Events at Wake Island."

26. Ibid.

27. Ibid.

28. Junghans, "Wake Island," 15.

29. Junghans, "Wake's POWs," 49–50.

30. Ibid., 50.

31. "Technical Report and Project History," A-503.

APPENDIX ONE: The Cunningham-Devereux Controversy

1. The exchange of correspondence concerning Simard's situation is in Simard ltr to RAdm. Claude C. Bloch, 7 November 1941, and in Bloch to Simard, 13 November 1941, in Box 3, Folder SM-SP, Bloch Papers.

2. Ltr, Devereux to Brig. Gen. W. E. Riley [Director, Division of Public Information], 26 February 1947, Wake Monograph Comment File, Folder 3, MCHC Archives.

3. Kinney, "The Last Days of Wake Island."

4. Lt. Col. Robert D. Heinl, Jr., "Report of Interview with Colonel Walter L. J. Bayler, USMC,"16 June 1947, in Folder 3, Wake Monograph Comment File, MCHC Archives.

5. Ltr, Teters to Cunningham, 27 July 1948, Appendix G to "Narrative of Captain W. S. Cunningham, U.S. Navy, relative to Events on Wake Island in December 1941, and Subsequent Related Events," Folder 6, ibid.

6. Ltr, Keene to Cunningham, 14 May 1948, Appendix F to "Narrative of Captain W. S. Cunningham, U.S. Navy, relative to Events on Wake Island in December 1941, and Subsequent Related Events," ibid.

7. [Robert D. Heinl, Jr.,] "Memorandum for the Record, Subj: Cunningham-Devereux controversy regarding Wake," 10 December 1948, ibid.

8. Ibid.

9. Cunningham, *Wake Island Command*, 103.

10. Heinl, "Memorandum for the Record."

11. Putnam, "Report of VMF-211 on Wake Island," 8.

12. Heinl, "Memorandum for the Record."

13. Ibid.

APPENDIX THREE: Wake Island's Wildcats

1. Unless otherwise specified, all information is derived from the individual Aircraft History Cards (filed by Bureau Number) held by the National Air and Space Museum, Washington, D.C.; from research notes compiled by David W. Lucabaugh; from the reconstructed diary of then Second Lieutenant John F. Kinney; and from material gathered by Major John Elliott, USMC (Ret.), through Elliott's interviews and correspondence with Brigadier General John F. Kinney, USMC (Ret.).

BIBLIOGRAPHY

DOCUMENTS

Key to any study of the defense of Wake Island in December 1941 are the documents (narratives by the senior commissioned and warrant officers and other related material) gathered in the course of the research for Robert D. Heinl, Jr.'s *Defense of Wake* (1946), as well as the Headquarters, Marine Corps, War Plans Division files, and the Historical Division's comment files on *The Defense of Wake* and John L. Zimmerman's *Guadalcanal Campaign* monographs. All of the foregoing are held by the Archives Branch of the Marine Corps Historical Center, located in Washington, D.C., in the Washington Navy Yard. Other important files in that repository are those held by the Reference Section (biographical files, principally on Marine Corps officers, and microfilm copies of muster rolls of units and squadrons), as well as those in the Oral History and Personal Papers collections.

The Operational Archives Branch of the Naval Historical Center (NHC), located across the street from the Marine Corps Historical Center, holds the World War II action reports (ship, unit, command, and individual personnel), war diaries for ships and commands, operations orders, command files, as well as officer biography files, strategic plans (formerly war plans), division files, as well as pertinent personal papers collections. In addition, it holds translated and untranslated Japanese materials (detailed action reports and war diaries).

The U.S. National Archives in Washington, D.C., holds the deck logs for the U.S. Navy ships referred to in the course of the narrative (Record Group 24), as well as the records of the Office of Naval Intelligence; the office of the Secretary of the Navy (Record Group 80); and the U.S. Army's Provost Marshal (Record Group 389). The National Archives's Pacific-Sierra Region facility at San Bruno, California, holds the records of the Fourteenth Naval District (Record Group 181).

Other key collections include the Library of Congress Manuscript Division, Washington, D.C., and the Boston University Library, whose special collections unit holds the papers of Rear Admiral Winfield S. Cunningham, USN (Ret.), and Brigadier General James P. S. Devereux, USMC (Ret.), two key figures in the battle for Wake.

J. Michael Wenger, Captain Chihaya Masataka, and Kageyama Kōichirō kindly enabled the author to obtain copies of important untranslated Japanese reports from the War History Office of the Japanese Self Defense Force. Mrs. Gordon W. Prange kindly allowed the author to copy items from her late husband's papers.

PARTICIPANTS

Major Robert O. Arthur, USMC (Ret.) (VMF-211).

Lieutenant Commander Richard H. Best, USN (Ret.) (Winfield S. Cunningham, and the voyage to Wake and back, November–December 1941).

Master Sergeant Walter A. Bowsher, USMC (Ret.) (Wake Detachment, First Defense Battalion).

Brigadier General Robert E. Galer, USMC (Ret.) (VMF-211).

Rear Admiral Wilmer E. Gallaher, USN (Ret.) (Voyage to Wake and back, November–December 1941).

Colonel Milo G. Haines, USMC (Ret.) (VMF-211).

Lieutenant Commander George H. Henshaw, USN (Ret.) (NAS Wake).

Clifford E. Hotchkiss (U.S. Army Communications Detachment, Wake Island).

Gunnery Sergeant Walter T. Kennedy, USMC (Ret.) (VMF-211).

Brigadier General John F. Kinney, USMC (Ret.) (VMF-211).

Brigadier General Victor H. Krulak, USMC (Ret.) (Lewis A. Hohn and Wesley M. Platt).

Colonel Arthur A. Poindexter, USMC (Ret.) (Wake Detachment, First Defense Battalion).

Sergeant Major Robert E. Winslow, USMC (Ret.) (Wake Detachment, First Defense Battalion).

PERSONAL PAPERS

Claude C. Bloch, Library of Congress Manuscript Division.

Winfield S. Cunningham, Boston University Library.

James P. S. Devereux, Boston University Library.

Henry T. Elrod, MCHC Personal Papers Collection.

Mrs. Marylee Fish, privately held.

William C. Halstead, privately held.

Thomas Holcomb, MCHC Personal Papers Collection.

Clifford E. Hotchkiss, privately held.

Thomas C. Kinkaid, NHC Operational Archives.

John F. Kinney, MCHC Personal Papers Collection.

Claude A. Larkin, MCHC Personal Papers Collection.

John L. McCrae, Library of Congress Manuscript Division.

Arthur A. Poindexter, privately held.

Paul A. Putnam, privately held.

Harold R. Stark, NHC Operational Archives.
Alexander A. Vandegrift, MCHC Personal Papers Collection.
Harry E. Yarnell, NHC Operational Archives.

PERSONAL DIARIES

Sergeant Robert E. Bourquin, Jr., USMC (VMF-211) (courtesy of Mrs. Marylee Fish).
Lieutenant Ward Bronson, (USS *Chicago*), NHC Operational Archives.
Lieutenant (j.g.) James G. Daniels, III, (VF-6) (courtesy of John B. Lundstrom).
Second Lieutenant John F. Kinney, USMC (VMF-211) (MCHC Personal Papers).
Lieutenant (j.g.) Norman J. Kleiss, USN (VS-6), privately held.
Lieutenant Donald A. Lovelace (VF-3) (courtesy of John B. Lundstrom).
Lieutenant (j.g.) Wilmer E. Rawie (VF-6) (courtesy of John B. Lundstrom).

UNPUBLISHED MANUSCRIPTS

Civil Aeronautics Board Docket Nos. 851 et al. Pan American Airways, Inc., "History of Transpacific Air Services to and through Hawaii." MCHC Reference Section.
Halsey, William F., Jr. "Life of Admiral W. F. Halsey." Virginia Historical Society, Richmond.
Hand, Charles L. "Old Timer: The War History of the U.S.S. *William Ward Burrows.*" USS *William Ward Burrows* (AP-6) Ship History File, NHC Ships' Histories Branch.
Heinl, Robert D., Jr. "Marine Coast Artillery: The Defense Battalions" (ca. 1940). MCHC Reference Section.
"History of the 407th Signal Company (Aviation)." U.S. Air Force History Research Collections, Maxwell Air Force Base, Alabama.
"History of the Marine Corps Air Station, Ewa, Oahu, T.H., 1941–1944." MCHC Reference Section.
Junghans, Earl A. "Wake Island, 1568–1946." NHC Library.
Kinkaid, Thomas C. "Four Years of War in the Pacific." NHC Operational Archives Branch.
Masterman, Howard W. "Chronicle of the American War of 1941." Naval Historical Foundation.
Pickett, Harry K., and Alfred R. Pefley. "The Defense of Wake, with Plans and Estimates for the Installation of the Defense Detachment, U.S. Marine Corps" (1938). MCHC Archives.
"The Story of the U.S.S. *William Ward Burrows* before the War." USS *William Ward Burrows* (AP-6) Ship History File, NHC Ships' Histories Branch.
"U.S. Army Detachment, Wake Island, North Pacific Ocean" [n.d. but probably prepared in February 1942]. Courtesy of Clifford E. Hotchkiss.

Urwin, Gregory J. W. "The Defenders of Wake Island: Their Two Wars, 1941–1945." Ph.D. dissertation, 1984.
"The War Record of Fighting [Squadron] Six." USS *Enterprise* (CV-6) Ship History File, NHC Ships' Histories Branch.

BOOKS

Amherst, Lord, and Basil Thomson, eds. *The Discovery of the Solomon Islands by Alvaro de Mendaña in 1568: Translated from the Original Manuscripts.* London: Hakluyt Society, 1901.
Arakaki, Leatrice R., and John R. Kuborn. *7 December 1941: The Air Force Story.* Hickam Air Force Base, Hawaii: Pacific Air Forces, Office of History, 1991.
Bayler, Walter L. J., as told to Cecil Carnes. *Last Man off Wake Island.* New York: Bobbs-Merrill, 1943.
Blair, Clay, Jr. *Silent Victory: The U.S. Submarine War Against Japan.* Philadelphia: J. B. Lippincott, 1975.
Bradford, James C., ed. *Crucible of Empire: The Spanish-American War and Its Aftermath.* Annapolis: Naval Institute Press, 1993.
Brereton, Lewis H. *The Brereton Diaries: The War in the Air in the Pacific, Middle East and Europe, 3 October 1941–8 May 1945.* New York: William Morrow, 1946.
Bueschel, Richard M. *Mitsubishi/Nakajima G3M1/2/3, Kusho L3Y1/2 In Japanese Naval Air Service.* Kent, Eng.: Osprey Publishing, 1972.
Bywater, Hector C. *Sea-Power in the Pacific: A Study of the American-Japanese Naval Problem.* Boston: Houghton Mifflin, 1921.
Cressman, Robert J., and J. Michael Wenger. *Steady Nerves and Stout Hearts: The U.S.S. Enterprise (CV-6) Air Group and Pearl Harbor, 7 December 1941.* Missoula, Mont.: Pictorial Histories Publishing Co., 1990.
Cunningham, W. Scott, with Lydel Sims. *Wake Island Command.* Boston: Little, Brown, 1961.
Darden, James B., III. *Guests of the Emperor: The Story of Dick Darden.* Clinton, N.C.: Greenhouse Press, 1990.
Devereux, James P. S. *The Story of Wake Island.* New York: J. B. Lippincott, 1947.
Dull, Paul. *A Battle History of the Imperial Japanese Navy (1941–1945).* Annapolis: Naval Institute Press, 1978.
Edmonds, Walter D. *They Fought with What They Had: The Story of the Army Air Forces in the Southwest Pacific, 1941–1942.* Boston: Little, Brown, 1951.
Francillon, Rene J. *Imperial Japanese Navy Bombers of World War Two.* Berkshire, Eng.: Hylton Lacy Publishers, 1969.
———. *The Mitsubishi G3M "Nell."* Surrey, Eng.: Profile Publications, 1967.
Gandt, Robert L. *China Clipper: The Age of the Great Flying Boats.* Annapolis: Naval Institute Press, 1991.

Goldstein, Donald M., and Katherine V. Dillon, eds. *The Pearl Harbor Papers: Inside the Japanese Plans.* Washington, D.C.: Brassey's (U.S.), 1993.

Hashimoto, Mochitsura. *Sunk: The Story of the Japanese Submarine Fleet, 1942–1945.* London: Cassell, 1954.

Hata, Ikuhiko, and Yasuho Izawa. *Japanese Naval Aces and Fighter Units in World War II.* Annapolis: Naval Institute Press, 1989.

Heinl, Robert D., Jr. *The Defense of Wake.* Washington, D.C.: U.S. Government Printing Office, 1946.

Holmes, Wilfred J. *Undersea Victory: The Influence of Submarine Operations on the War in the Pacific.* New York: Doubleday, 1966.

Hull, Cordell. *The Memoirs of Cordell Hull.* 2 vols. New York: Macmillan, 1948.

Iwaya, Fumio, *Chūkō.* Tokyo: Genshobo, 1976.

James, D. Clayton, *The Years of MacArthur,* Vol. 1, 1880–1941. Boston: Houghton Mifflin, 1970.

Japan, Self Defense Force, War History Office, *Senshi Sōsho* (War History Series). Vol. 10. *Hawai Sakusen.* Tokyo, 1970. Vol. 38. *Chubu Taiheiyo Homen Kaigun Sakusen.* Tokyo, 1976.

Jentschura, Hansgeorg, Dieter Jung, and Peter Mickel. *Warships of the Imperial Japanese Navy, 1869–1945.* Translated by Antony Preston and J. D. Brown. Annapolis: Naval Institute Press, 1977.

Kessler, Woodrow M. *To Wake and Beyond: Reminiscences.* Washington, D.C.: Headquarters Marine Corps, History and Museums Division, 1988.

Layton, Edwin T., with Roger Pineau and John Costello. *"And I Was There": Pearl Harbor and Midway—Breaking the Secrets.* New York: William Morrow, 1985.

Lundstrom, John B. *The First Team: Pacific Naval Air Combat from Pearl Harbor to Midway.* Annapolis: Naval Institute Press, 1984.

Miller, Edward S. *War Plan Orange: The U.S. Strategy to Defeat Japan, 1897–1945.* Annapolis: Naval Institute Press, 1991.

Mitchell, John H. *In Alis Vicimus: On Wings We Conquer, the 19th and 7th Bomb Groups of the United States Air Force in the Southwest Pacific in the First Year of World War Two.* Springfield, Mo.: G. E. M. Publishers, 1990.

Okumiya, Masatake, with Jiro Horikoshi and Martin Caiden. *Zero!* New York: E. P. Dutton, 1956.

Prange, Gordon W., et al. *At Dawn We Slept: The Untold Story of Pearl Harbor.* New York: McGraw-Hill, 1981.

A Report to Returned CPNAB [Contractors, Pacific Naval Air Bases] *Prisoner of War Heroes and Their Dependents.* Boise, Ida.: Pacific Island Employees Foundation, 1945.

Richardson, James O., as told to George C. Dyer. *On the Treadmill to Pearl Harbor: The Memoirs of Admiral James O. Richardson, USN (Retired).* Washington, D.C.: Naval History Division, 1973.

Schultz, Duane. *Wake Island: The Heroic, Gallant Fight.* New York: St. Martin's Press, 1978.
Schulz, Heinrich E., Paul K. Urban, and Andrew I. Lebed, eds. *Who Was Who in the USSR.* Metuchen, N.J.: Scarecrow Press, 1972.
Stillwell, Paul. *Battleship Arizona: An Illustrated History.* Annapolis: Naval Institute Press, 1991.
Terrett, Dulany. *The Signal Corps: The Emergency (to December 1941).* In *The United States Army in World War II.* Washington, D.C.: Department of the Army, 1956.
Thompson, George Raynor, et al. *The Signal Corps: The Test (December 1941 to July 1943).* In *The United States Army in World War II.* Washington D.C.: Department of the Army, 1957.
Toland, John. *But Not in Shame: The Six Months after Pearl Harbor.* New York: Random House, 1961.
Tsouras, Peter G., *Warrior's Words: A Quotation Book from Sesostris III to Schwarzkopf, 1871 B.C. to A.D. 1991.* London: Arms and Armour Press, 1992.
Ugaki, Matome. *Sensoroku* [War record]. Tokyo, 1952.
U.S. Army, Chief of Staff. *Biennial Report of the Chief of Staff of the United States Army, July 1, 1941 to June 30, 1942, to the Secretary of War.* Washington, D.C.: U.S. Government Printing Office, 1943.
U.S. Army, Far East Command, Military History Section. *Submarine Operations, December 1941–April 1942.* Japanese Monograph No. 102. Washington, D.C.: Office of the Chief of Military History, 1946.
———, ———, ———. *The Imperial Japanese Navy in World War II: A Graphic Presentation of the Japanese Naval Organization and List of Combatant and Non-Combatant Vessels Lost or Damaged in the War.* Japanese Monograph No. 116. Washington, D.C.: Office of the Chief of Military History, 1952.
U.S. Congress. *Hearings Before the Joint Committee on the Investigation of the Pearl Harbor Attack.* 39 parts. Washington, D.C.: U.S. Government Printing Office, 1946.
———, House of Representatives. *Hearings Before the Committee on Naval Affairs of the House of Representatives on Sundry Legislation Affecting the Naval Establishment, 1939.* Washington, D.C.: U.S. Government Printing Office, 1939.
———, ———. *Hearings Before the Committee on Naval Affairs of the House of Representatives on Sundry Legislation Affecting the Naval Establishment, 1940.* Washington, D.C.: U.S. Government Printing Office, 1941.
———, ———. *Report on Need of Additional Naval Bases to Defend the United States, Its Territories, and Possessions.* Washington, D.C.: U.S. Government Printing Office, 1939. [The Hepburn Board Report]
U.S. Navy. *Building the Navy's Bases in World War II.* Vol. 1 of *The History*

of the Bureau of Yards and Docks and the Civil Engineer Corps, 1940–1946. Washington, D.C.: U.S. Government Printing Office, 1947.

———. *Ship and Gunnery Drills, United States Navy.* Washington, D.C.: U.S. Government Printing Office, 1927.

U.S. Strategic Bombing Survey [Pacific] Naval Analysis Division. *Interrogations of Japanese Officials.* Vol. 2. Washington, D.C.: U.S. Government Printing Office, 1946.

Updegraph, Charles L., Jr. *U.S. Marine Corps Special Units of World War II.* Washington, D.C.: U.S. Government Printing Office, 1972.

Ward, R. Gerard, ed. *American Activities in the Central Pacific, 1790–1870: A History, Geography and Ethnography Pertaining to American Involvement and Americans in the Pacific Taken from Contemporary Newspapers, Etc.* Vol. 7. Ridgewood, N.J.: Gregg Press, 1969.

Whitney, Hans. *Guest of the Fallen Sun.* New York: Exposition Press, 1951.

Wilkes, Charles. *Narrative of the United States Exploring Expedition during the Years 1838, 1839, 1840, 1841, and 1842.* 5 vols. Philadelphia, 1849.

Woodbury, David O. *Builders for Battle: How the Pacific Naval Air Bases Were Constructed.* New York: E. P. Dutton, 1946.

ARTICLES

Barnes, G. M. "Antiaircraft Armament: The Guns and Fire Control for Air Raid Protection." *Army Ordnance* 20 (January–February 1940): 233–37.

Burroughs, John R. "The Siege of Wake Island: An Eyewitness Account." *American Heritage* 10 (June 1959): 65–76.

Dierdorff, Ross A. "Pioneer Party—Wake Island." U.S. Naval Institute *Proceedings* 69 (April 1943): 499–508.

Graybar, Lloyd J. "American Pacific Strategy after Pearl Harbor: The Relief of Wake Island." *Prologue* 12 (Fall 1980): 134–50.

Heinl, Robert D., Jr. "On the Mobility of Base Defense Artillery." *Marine Corps Gazette* 25 (September 1941): 23–24, 42–43.

———. "We're Headed for Wake." *Marine Corps Gazette* 30 (June 1946): 35–38.

Hirama, Yoichi. "Japanese Naval Preparations for World War II." *Naval War College Review* 44 (Spring 1991): 63–81.

Lacroix, Eric. "The Development of the 'A Class' Cruisers in the Imperial Japanese Navy," Pt. 1, "The Genesis of the 20 cm Gun 'Scout' Cruisers." *Warship International,* No. 4 (1977): 337–57.

Lengerer, Hans, Sumie Kobler-Edamatsu, and Tomoko Rehm-Takahara. "*Tone:* Modifications and War Service." *Warship* 44 (October 1987): 223–31.

McGill, Robert A. "Island Defense." *Marine Corps Gazette* 25 (March 1941): 16–18.

Mcpoil, William D. "The Development and Defense of Wake Island, 1934–1941." *Prologue* 23 (Winter 1991): 361–62.

Picking, Sherwood. "Wake Island." U.S. *Naval Institute Proceedings* 48 (December 1922): 2075–79.

Poindexter, Arthur A. "Our Last Hurrah on Wake Atoll." *American History Illustrated* 26 (January–February 1992): 64–67, 73–74.

Schlepper, Robert H., and Charles E. Anderson. "The Martin Clippers." *American Aviation Historical Society Journal* (Fall 1965): 172–83.

Seno, Sadao. "A Chess Game with No Checkmate: Admiral Inoue and the Pacific War." *Naval War College Review* 26 (1974): 26–39.

[Taussig, Edward D.] "Old Glory on Wake Island." U.S. Naval Institute *Proceedings* 61 (June 1935): 807–8.

Ullman, James R. "Wake: The Forlorn Island." *Holiday* 28 (November 1960): 149–51, 194–97.

von Lehmann, Hans G. "Japanese Landing Operations in World War II." In Merrill L. Bartlett, ed., *Assault from the Sea: Essays on the History of Amphibious Warfare*. Annapolis: Naval Institute Press, 1983.

Votaw, Homer C. "Wake Island." U.S. Naval Institute *Proceedings* 67 (January 1941): 52–55.

Wildenberg, Thomas, "Chester Nimitz and the Development of Fueling at Sea." *Naval War College Review* 46 (Autumn 1993): 52–62.

Withers, Thomas. "The Preparation of the Submarines Pacific for War." U.S. Naval Institute *Proceedings* 76 (April 1950): 387–93.

INDEX

(Italicized numbers indicate where a photo of the subject is found.)

ABOUT THE AUTHOR
ROBERT J. CRESSMAN graduated from the University of Maryland in 1972 with a bachelor's degree in history. He earned his master's degree at Maryland under Dr. Gordon W. Prange in 1978. He began his professional career as a historian in the Ships' Histories Branch of the Naval Historical Center (NHC) in May 1976 and contributed to volumes 7 and 8 of the *Dictionary of American Naval Fighting Ships*.

After a year and a half as a historian in the reference section of the Marine Corps Historical Center, Cressman returned to the NHC in May 1981. He was a major contributor to the revision of volume 1, part A of the *Dictionary of American Naval Fighting Ships*. He transferred to the Contemporary History Branch in June 1992, where he is currently involved in writing volume 3 of *The United States Navy and the Vietnam Conflict*.

A frequent contributor to *The Hook*, he also has had articles published in *Naval History* and the *Marine Corps Gazette*. In addition, he is the author of *That Gallant Ship: USS Yorktown (CV-5)* (1985); editor of and principal contributor to *A Glorious Page in Our History: The Battle of Midway, 4–6 June 1942* (1990); and coauthor, with J. Michael Wenger, of *Steady Nerves and Stout Hearts: The USS Enterprise (CV-6) Air Group and Pearl Harbor, 7 December 1941* (1990).

The NAVAL INSTITUTE PRESS is the book-publishing arm of the U.S. Naval Institute, a private, nonprofit society for sea service professionals and others who share an interest in naval and maritime affairs. Established in 1873 at the U.S. Naval Academy in Annapolis, Maryland, where its offices remain, today the Naval Institute has more than 100,000 members worldwide.

Members of the Naval Institute receive the influential monthly magazine *Proceedings* and discounts on fine nautical prints and on ship and aircraft photos. They also have access to the transcripts of the Institute's Oral History Program and get discounted admission to any of the Institute-sponsored seminars offered around the country.

The Naval Institute also publishes *Naval History* magazine. This colorful bimonthly is filled with entertaining and thought-provoking articles, first-person reminiscences, and dramatic art and photography. Members receive a discount on *Naval History* subscriptions.

The Naval Institute's book-publishing program, begun in 1898 with basic guides to naval practices, has broadened its scope in recent years to include books of more general interest. Now the Naval Institute Press publishes more than seventy titles each year, ranging from how-to books on boating and navigation to battle histories, biographies, ship and aircraft guides, and novels. Institute members receive discounts on the Press's nearly 400 books in print.

For a free catalog describing Naval Institute Press books currently available, and for further information about subscribing to *Naval History* magazine or about joining the U.S. Naval Institute, please write to:

Membership & Communications Department
U.S. Naval Institute
118 Maryland Avenue
Annapolis, Maryland 21402-5035
Or call, toll-free, (800) 233-USNI.